Clinical Behavior Therapy and Behavior Modification
Volume One

Clinical Behavior Therapy and Behavior Modification

Editor-in-Chief

Reid J. Daitzman, Independent Practice, Stamford, CT; and affiliated with Connecticut Center for Behavioral and Psychosomatic Medicine, New Haven, CT and the New England Center for Headache, Greenwich, CT

Editorial Consultants

Paula Bram Amar, Jefferson Medical College, Philadelphia, PA

L. Michael Ascher, Temple University, Philadelphia, PA

Alan S. Bellack, University of Pittsburgh, Pittsburgh, PA

H. J. Eysenck, University of London and Institute for Psychiatry, London, England

Cyril Franks, Rutgers University, New Brunswick, NJ

George Fuller, Biofeedback Institute of San Francisco, San Francisco, CA

Donald Levis, State University of New York at Binghamton, Binghamton, NY

Ronald J. Murphy, Independent Practice and Long Island Jewish-Hillside Medical Center, New Hyde Park, NY

Rosemary Nelson, University of North Carolina at Greensboro, Greensboro, NC

Robert J. Presbie, State University College, New Paltz, NY

Spencer Rathus, Northeastern University, Boston, MA

David Rimm, North Texas State University, Denton, TX

Gary Schwartz, Yale University, New Haven, CT

Martin Seligman, University of Pennyslvania, Philadelphia, PA

Richard Stern, University of London and Institute for Psychiatry, London, England

Richard Stuart, Weight Watchers International, Manhasset, NY

Susan R. Walen, Towson State University, Baltimore, MD

Robert Willoughby, University of Virginia, Charlottesville, VA

Ian E. Wickramasekera, Independent Practice, Peoria, IL

Aubrey J. Yates, University of Western Australia, New South Wales, Australia

Clinical Behavior Therapy and Behavior Modification

Volume One

Reid J. Daitzman

Editor-in-Chief

Garland STPM Press

New York and London

Copyright © 1980 by Garland Publishing, Inc.

All rights reserved. No part of this work covered by the copyright hereon may be reproduced or used in any form or by any means—graphic, electronic, or mechanical, including photocopying, recording, taping, or information storage and retrieval systems— without permission of the publisher.

15 14 13 12 11 10 9 8 7 6 5 4 3 2 1

Library of Congress Cataloging in Publication Data
    Main entry under title:
    Clinical behavior therapy and behavior modification, ed - by
        Bibliography: p.   Reid J. Daitzman.
        Includes index.
        1. Behavior therapy.   2. Behavior modification.
    I. Daitzman, Reid J.
    RC489.B4C58   616.8'914   79-14455
    ISBN 0-8240-7038-0

Published by Garland STPM Press
136 Madison Avenue, New York, New York 10016

Printed in the United States of America

*. . . that man's inhumanities to man
never be repeated and always remembered,
that science never be neutral,
that scientists apply knowledge with
dignity, compassion, and wisdom.*

Contents

Contributors

Thomas L. Boyd
University of South Carolina at Aiken
Aiken, South Carolina

Edward J. Callahan
West Virginia University
Morgantown, West Virginia

JoAnn Dahlkoetter
West Virginia University
Morgantown, West Virginia

Reid J. Daitzman
Independent Practice
Stamford, Connecticut and
affiliated with Connecticut Center for
Behavioral and Psychosomatic Medicine
New Haven, Connecticut and
the New England Center for Headache,
Greenwich, Connecticut

Mark S. Goldman
Wayne State University
Detroit, Michigan

Suzanne Bennett Johnson
University of Florida
Gainesville, Florida

Donald J. Levis
State University of New York at Binghamton
Binghamton, New York

R. L. Meredith
University of Alabama School of Medicine
Birmingham, Alabama

Jesse B. Milby
University of Alabama School of Medicine
Birmingham, Alabama

Kimberly Price
West Virginia University
Morgantown, West Virginia

Susan Walen
Towson State University
Towson, Maryland

Acknowledgments

This series has depended upon the support and encourgement of many individuals and organizations. I want to thank George Narita, Editor-in-Chief of Garland STPM Press, for his continued support, advice, gentle prodding, and enthusiasm for this series. His confidence in my ability to put the series together has continued to motivate me in its preparation. I also want to thank all my teachers (you know who you are) and clients for giving me the opportunity to listen, share, and learn. I especially want to thank Arnold H. Buss, presently at the University of Texas at Austin, William Groman of Virginia Commonwealth University, and Marvin Zuckerman at the University of Delaware for serving as mentors during the formative stages of my academic and professional development.

Introduction
Purpose of the Series

Reid J. Daitzman

This present volume, part of an ongoing series, is written for students and clinicians in all areas of mental health who have a serious interest in the efficient therapeutic application of behavior therapy and behavior modification. *Clinical Behavior Therapy and Behavior Modification* is for the psychiatrist, clinical psychologist, counselor, psychiatric social worker, occupational therapist, physical therapist, psychiatric nurse, and paraprofessional in these professions.

Empirically based assessment methods and standardized clinical prescriptions (*see* Goldstein and Stein, 1976) are a relatively recent development. *Clinical Behavior Therapy and Behavior Modification* assumes that interpersonal skills, empathy, rapport, placebo, timing, and transference are part of all therapies *in addition to empirically based prescriptive behavioral interventions based upon adequate diagnosis.* Regardless of therapeutic orientation, diagnosis is a prerequisite to effective and ethical intervention. The series uses the American Psychiatric Association Diagnostic and Statistical Manual of Mental Disorders DSM–II (1968) as a convenient and standardized conceptualization of mental disorders.

With these facts and background in mind, the purpose of the series is twofold:

1. If you are a clinician with limited experience in the chapter topic area, a study of the chapter will allow you to proceed with an empirically based strategy(ies) for intervention.
2. If you are a student or researcher reviewing crucial published (and unpublished) works in the chapter topic area, referencing the chapter will allow you to proceed with a well-designed project that is timely, relevant, and practical.

Outstanding researchers and clinicians were contacted and requested to submit chapters cross-referenced with the DSM–II. Each chapter has a common outline. In turn, an international editorial board reviewed each contribution for completeness, clarity, and quality.

Each chapter of the series is divided, more or less, into ten sections:

1. Introduction and scope of diagnostic category
2. Theoretical analysis, both behavioral and nonbehavioral
3. Assessment—projective, objective, behavioral
4. Proven treatment procedures based upon literature search
5. Prototype clinical prescription
6. Sample case report illustrating clinical prescription
7. Ethical and legal issues and need for special equipment/instrumentation
8. Suggestions for future clinical and experimental investigation(s)
9. One-thousand word summary
10. References and (optional) bibliography.

These ten sections outline the following six questions that the reader of a chapter should be able to answer:

1. What specific intervention(s) and strategies are the treatment(s) of choice for the specific disorder?
2. What is the empirical basis of these intervention strategies and *how well designed was the research?*
3. How are the intervention strategies best applied and what further education, supervision, and equipment is needed for best results?
4. How strong is the relationship between assessment(s) and treatment(s)? Is there discriminant and convergent validity of the various dependent assessment/intervention measures?
5. How can the optimal treatment methods be better standardized and what types of research can be designed in the near future to further refine the necessary and sufficient assessment/intervention variables?
6. What are the legal and ethical considerations and constraints to be considered before, during, and after implementation of the optimal treatment strategies?

There were some diagnostic categories that did not lend themselves to a precise 10-section outline. However, in every case the six questions could be answered after reading the chapter.

THE ROLE OF DIAGNOSIS AND THE
NEED FOR A STANDARDIZED TEXT

The *Clinical Behavior Therapy and Behavior Modification* series will include all of the current DSM-II diagnostic categories under the following major topic areas:

1. Mental Retardation (310–315)
2. Psychoses Associated with Organic Brain Syndromes (290–294)
3. Nonpsychotic Organic Brain Syndromes (309)
4. Neuroses (300)
5. Personality Disorders and Certain Other Nonpsychotic Mental Disorders (301–304)
6. Psychophysiological Disorders (305)
7. Special Symptoms (306)
8. Transient Situational Disturbances (307)
9. Behavior Disorders of Childhood and Adolescence (308)
10. Conditions Without Manifest Psychiatric Disorder and Nonspecific Conditions (316–318).

The decision to cross-reference *Clinical Behavior Therapy and Behavior Modification* with the 1968 DSM-II was based upon a number of practical considerations. Although the rationale and importance of diagnosis has been criticized (e.g., McLemore and Benjamin, 1979; Ward, Beck, Mendelson et al., 1962; Zigler and Phillips, 1961a, b), at the grass-roots level a primary and secondary diagnosis is required for record keeping, research, insurance carriers, workmen's compensation, legal consent and competency, and in private and university hospitals for budgeting and grant requests. Labeling and pigeonholing a client's covert and overt behaviors into confusing and unreliable diagnostic categories may be a necessary evil of the 1980s, especially with the formulation of a comprehensive National Health Insurance Plan now pending. In addition, many medical schools obviously continue to emphasize the medical model to their third-year clerkship psychiatric students and psychiatric residents.

Finally, and perhaps most important, the divergent professional disciplines of mental health care delivery suffer from an unavailability of an organized and unified standard text. Most professional textbooks advance a theoretical position and treatment is dependent upon the personality theories, developmental theories, psychopathology, and treatment parameters that are consistent with that model. Although the orientation of the present series is behavioral, other positions are represented to the extent that their literature and methods contribute to the prescriptive eclecticism advanced in this series. What is hoped for is the eventual development of a mental health reference similar to such medical volumes as the *Physician Desk Reference* (PDR) or *Merck Manual*. Since most physicians refer to the annual PDR when seeking information on a particular drug, it is hoped that mental health practitioners, when seeking information on the assessment, diagnosis, and treatment of mental disorders will consult this series.

An obvious criticism of cross-referencing this series with the DSM-II is that by the time the series appears it may be outdated by DSM-III. However, the DSM-III is not without its own problems and critics (*see* Schacht and Nathan, 1977).

> No longer will a clinician simply select the one or two categories into which the patient or client seems to fit best. Instead, it will be necessary to relate explicitly the primary diagnostic *axis,* based on presenting dysfunction, to other features also termed axes.
>
> The five axes that will be referenced in diagnosing an individual are (1) clinical psychiatric syndromes and other conditions, (2) personality disorders (adult) and specific developmental disorders (children and adolescents), (3) nonmental medical disorders, (4) severity of psychosocial stresses, and (5) highest level of adaptive functioning in the past year. (McLemore and Benjamin, 1979, p. 17)

The following includes an example of each axis as it might appear for a single patient (from Schacht and Nathan, 1977, p. 1019).

Axis I:	296.80 Atypical Depressive Disorder
Axis II:	301.81 Narcissistic Personality Disorder
Axis III:	Diabetes, Hypertension
Axis IV:	*Psychosocial stressors:*5, severe (business failure)
Axis V:	*Highest Adaptive Behavior past year:*3, good.

From a practical standpoint, many of the primary and sub-axes are easily cross-referenced with the DSM-II, with treatment following accordingly. However, a major improvement in the DSM-III over the DSM-II is in the operational criteria for diagnosis. For example, compare the two criteria for "Phobia":

300.2 Phobic Neurosis (DSM-II)

This condition is characterized by intense fear of an object or situation which the patient consciously recognizes as no real danger to him. His apprehension may be experienced as faintness, fatigue, palpitations, perspiration, nausea, tremor, and even panic. Phobias are generally

attributed to fears displaced to the phobic object or situation from some
other object of which the patient is unaware. A wide range of phobias
has been described. (DSM–II, p. 40)

300.24 Simple Phobia—All Should Be Present (DSM–III)

A. Avoidance of the irrationally feared object or situation. If there is
   any element of danger in these objects or situations, it is reacted to
   in a fashion out of proportion to reality.
B. The avoidance has a significant effect on the patient's life adjustment.
C. The patient has complete insight into the irrational nature of his
   fear.
D. The phobic symptoms do not coincide with an episode of Depressive Disorder, Obsessive Compulsive Disorder, or Schizophrenia,
   nor are they limited to a period of two months prior to, or two
   months after such an episode. (DSM–III Draft Version, 1968)

DSM–III operational criteria for phobia is clearer and less dependent on a theoretical orientation to mental health (e.g., psychodynamic). *I suggest that the readership of this series consult and cross-
reference the appropriate DSM-III operational criteria for the chapter
topics included in this series.*

The DSM–III also includes additional diagnostic categories not
clearly covered in DSM–II. For example, in the area of the sexual dys-
functions, male secondary impotence/erectile dysfunction is not included in DSM–II (although there will certainly be a chapter in this
area in the series). If, as a clinician, your own bias is that erectile dysfunction is a vascular disorder of deficits in myotonic vasocongestion,
then in DSM–II you would diagnose it as a psychophysiological
genito-urinary disorder (305.6). However, if you feel that erectile dysfunction is primarily dependent upon anxiety, then you may diagnose
it as anxiety neurosis (300.0). Or you may wish to bypass the problem
and classify it as a "Special Symptom Not Elsewhere Classified" (306.9).

The DSM–III contains a catchall diagnostic category that probably
includes primary and secondary erectile dysfunction, premature ejaculation, retarded ejaculation, primary and secondary orgasmic dysfunction, dyspareunia, and vaginismus. These disorders are classified as
"Psychosexual Disorders, Psychological Dysfunction." However, as
any sex therapist soon realizes, this category does not take into account
the problem of low sex drive or ejaculatory incompetence.

Sharpe, Kuriansky, and O'Connor (1976) propose a classification
of functional human sexual disorders. Their system is based upon objective behavior and reports of distress. Five categories of disorders are
proposed:

1. Disturbances of the physiological sexual response cycle
2. Disturbances of perceptual component of the sexual response cycle
3. Disturbances of subjective satisfaction in the sexual response cycle
4. Distress concerning sexual functioning associated with false beliefs or lack of sexual knowledge
5. Socio-sexual distress.

Within this nomenclature, the label of "low sex drive" would fall under category 2. Likewise, ejaculatory incompetence would also be classified under category 2. This category includes three components: (1) hypersexual feelings (e.g., "nymphomania"); (2) hyposexual feelings (e.g., low sex drive), and (3) anesthesia (e.g., ejaculatory incompetence). Only within such an original diagnostic system would these diagnoses be easily classifiable.

The basic point to be emphasized here is that the jury is still out concerning the classification of mental health problems, and that all diagnostic manuals will have critics and problems. In the meantime, this series will continue to cross-reference with the DSM-II and, where appropriate, with DSM-III. Perhaps future editions of clinicians and books will be reorganized under the DSM-IV that will be introduced in 20 years.

THE DESIGN QUALITY RATING (DQR)

Once a diagnosis is established, the resulting treatment(s) should be empirically based upon well-designed clinical and experimental research. Until the publication of this series, no one publication has systematically measured the design quality of the literature upon which the treatment was based. The contributors were asked to assign a design quality rating (Gurman and Kriskern, 1978) to each investigation in the chapter. Sometimes this proved to be extremely difficult. Not only were individual papers difficult to score, but entire diagnostic areas were hazy as to experimental design. Where the assignment of the DQR scores proved to be virtually impossible, it is assumed that the probable total score would be in the 0–10 range (poor).

The DQR involves the summation of 13 separate scores. In turn, those scores which have a value of "5," "3," "1," or "½" are totaled for the DQR. A 0–0 is poor; 10½–15 is fair; 15½–20 is good; and 20½–32 is very good. The 13 criteria and their individual scores follow.

1. *Controlled assignment to treatment conditions:* random assignment, matching of total groups or matching in pairs (5)
2. *Pre-post measurement of change* (5)

3. *No contamination of major independent variables,* e.g., therapists' experience levels, number of therapists per treatment condition, and relevant therapeutic competence, e.g., a psychoanalyst using behavior therapy for the first time offers a poor test of the power of a behavioral method (5)
4. *Appropriate statistical analysis* (5)
5. *Follow-up:* none (0), 1–3 months (½), 3–12 months (1), 13–18 months (3), more than 18 months (5)
6. *Treatments equally valued:* i.e., tremendous biases are often engendered for both therapist and patients when this criterion is not met (1)
7. *Treatment carried out as described or expected:* clear evidence (1), presumptive evidence (½)
8. *Multiple change indices* used (1)
9. *Multiple vantage points* used in assessing outcome (1)
10. *Data on other concurrent treatment:* evidence of no treatment, or of such treatment without documentation of amount or equivalence (½)
11. *Equal treatment length* in comparative studies (1)
12. *Outcome assessment allowing for both positive and negative change* (1)
13. *Therapist–investigator nonequivalence* (1).

Most behavior therapists would think that the DQR of "our" research would be higher than the DQR of "their" (nonbehavioral) research. In general, however, quality of experimental design had little to do with the theoretical orientation of the investigator or the fact that it was published in "better" journals.

PRESCRIPTIVE BEHAVIORAL ECLECTICISM

All therapies must be taken in the context of culture, subject and organismic variables, moderator variables, setting, and relationship variables. Modern behavior therapy has evolved a package of techniques that, when systematically applied by trained personnel, tend at least to produce equal results with other nonbehavioral interventions (*see* Dimond, Havens, and Jones, 1978; Sloane, Staples, Cristol, et al., 1975). The ultimate criteria for the choice of one method over another, one school over another, or one therapy over another often is based upon nonrational information (most recent book or workshop attended, favorite professor, orientation of supervisor, or personal philosophy (*see* Daitzman, Chapter 1, this volume). Whether there is an ultimate therapy based upon Truth is not as important as trying our best as individual therapists in applying what we know (as derived from the Truth of the Scientific Method) to the real problems of real people seeking our help.

To this extent, the readership of this series is assumed to be familiar with the *techniques* of implementation given the proper input (from this series and others) as to how best to apply behavioral prescriptive eclecticism (*see* Foa and Goldstein, in press). The social and natural sciences, desensitization, assertive training, psychopharmocology, biofeedback, thought stopping, sensate focus, family therapy, token economy, personality theory, psychopathology, psychophysiology, history and methodological design, developmental biopsychology, endocrinology, physical rehabilitation, and psychoanalysis are areas that every reader, independent of degree or orientation, should have a general knowledge of, both theoretically and clinically.

Volume I of *Clinical Behavior Therapy and Behavior Modification* has seven chapters, selected for their quality, comprehensiveness, and timeliness. Chapter 1, "Push-Button epistomology: The religious and philosophical foundations of the experimental analysis of behavior," explores the sociological and philosophical substructures and alternatives for the development of what is now termed behavior therapy. Subsequent chapters deal with seizure disorders, enuresis, drug abuse, alcoholism, obsessive-compulsive disorder, and depression. Subsequent volumes of the series will include seven to eight chapters of other diagnostic categories from DSM–II or DSM–III (where appropriate) published every 10–12 months.

REFERENCES

Committee on Nomenclature and Statistics of the American Psychiatric Association. *DSM–II diagnostic and statistical manual of mental disorders.* Washington, D.C.: American Psychiatric Association, 1968.

Dimond, R. E., Havens, R. A., and Jones, A. C. A conceptual framework for the practice of prescriptive eclecticism in psychotherapy. *American Psychologist,* 1978, *33,* 239–248.

Foa, E. and Goldstein, A. P. *Handbook of behavioral interventions.* New York: Academic Press, in press.

Garfield, S. and Bergin, A. (eds), *Handbook of psychotherapy and behavior change,* 2nd ed. New York: John Wiley, 1978.

Goldstein, A. P. and Stein, N. S. *Prescriptive psychotherapies.* New York: Pergamon Press, 1976.

Gurman, A. S. and Kriskern, D. P. Research on marital and family therapy: Progress, perspective and prospect. In S. Garfield and A. Bergin (eds), *Handbook of psychotherapy and behavior change,* 2nd ed. New York: John Wiley, 1978.

Kazdin, A. E. *History of behavior modification: Experimental foundations of contemporary research.* Baltimore: University Park Press, 1978.

McLemore, C. W. and Benjamin, L. S. Whatever happened to interpersonal diagnosis? A Psychosocial Alternative to DSM-III. *American Psychologist,* 1979, *34,* 17–34.

Schacht, T. and Nathan, P. E. But is it good for psychologists? Appraisal and status of DSM-III. *American Psychologist,* 1977, *32,* 1017–1024.

Sharpe, L., Kuriansky, J. B., and O'Connor, J. F. A preliminary classification of human functional sexual disorders. *Journal of Sex and Marital Therapy,* 1976, *2,* 106–114.

Sloane, R. B., Staples, F. R., Cristol, A. H., et al. *Psychotherapy versus behavior therapy.* Cambridge, Ma: Harvard University Press, 1975.

Task Force on Nomenclature and Statistics, American Psychiatric Association. *Diagnostic and statistical manual of mental disorders* (3rd ed.; draft version of January 15, 1978). Available from Task Force on Nomenclature and Statistics, American Psychiatric Association, 722 W. 168 Street, New York, New York 10032.

Ward, C. H., Beck, A. T., Mendelson, M., et al. The psychiatric nomenclature: Reasons for diagnostic disagreement. *Archives of General Psychiatry,* 1962, *7,* 198–205.

Zigler, E. and Phillips, L. Psychiatric diagnosis and symptomology. *Journal of Abnormal and Social Psychology,* 1961a, *63,* 69–75.

Zigler, E. and Phillips, L. Psychiatric diagnosis: A critique. *Journal of Abnormal and Social Psychology,* 1961b, *63,* 607–618.

1
Push-Button Epistemology

The Religious and Philosophical Foundations of an Experimental Analysis of Behavior

Reid J. Daitzman

The proliferation of successful "therapeutic" interventions ranging from prayer, pastoral counseling, psychoanalysis, encounter groups, and individual psychotherapy, to operant behavioral conditioning methods, necessitates a reexamination of the nature of man and his search for ultimate meaning. Conflicting images of man suggest that (1) the canons of logical positivism leave little room for religion to constitute anything more than humanistic ethics; (2) religious and scientific truths are different in kind and hence accessible to different modes of knowing and subject to different criteria of validity; (3) the social sciences cannot, in any ultimate sense, prove or disprove the existence of God or of a supernatural realm; (4) both natural and social scientists as persons will disagree about the adequacy of the deterministic assumption; (5) the failure of determinism to explain all of man's behavior has accounted for the rise in popularity of the phenomenological model; (6) both religion and phenomenology reject determinism; (7) there is a need for a system of ultimate meaning; however, no one image of man can supply all the values and norms which hold societies together and make existence meaningful; (8) a greater understanding of determinism will allow man to transcend freedom and exercise even greater control over his behavior.

Religion is perhaps the most ubiquitous of social institutions. Whatever other social institutions one is concerned with—the body politic, the economic order, the family—religion's influence on these institutions is always something to be considered. Recently, the influence of at least traditional religion on the other institutions of our society appears to be declining, and as these institutions generate their own value orientations the link with traditional religion has become increasingly tenuous and may eventually be broken. A case in point might be the relationship between religion and science. Spawned by what many agree was a religiously inspired ethic, science has gradually generated an internal and independent value system.

Religion as Scientific Ethics

In recent years, a lull has settled over the battle which once raged between science and religion (White, 1960). The militant and crusading spirit of an earlier era seems to be dissipated, and the public forums no longer ring with cries of "superstition" or "heresy." In these calmer days, a spate of apologetics suggests that a major preoccupation of many American theologians is to show either that there never was any basis for conflict between science or religion, or that old differences have been successfully accommodated (Monsma, 1962). Philosophers of science, however, seem less inclined to agree that any such rapprochement has taken place (see Russell, 1953, Reichenbach, 1963). Clearly, the canons of logical positivism leave little room for religion to constitute anything more than humanistic ethics (Feigl, 1953). Thus, the issue persists. Does the prevailing quiet represent an actual settlement of differences, or have religion and science merely become isolated from one another within a secularized social climate where attacks on either have lost their power to attract attention? For this reason it seems proper to raise the fundamental question once more: Is there a basic incompatibility between scientific and religious outlooks?

Science (now you see it) and Religion (now you don't)

The traditional argument that religion and science are incompatible perspectives is based on their contradictory evaluations of the authority of human reason. Religion, because of its ultimate commitment to a nonempirical system, must take the position that man's reason is subordinate to faith as a means to truth. From this view, reason is at best unreliable, and at worse, sinful pride (Maurer, 1925). Science, however, defines truth as that which may be demonstrated either logically or empirically, and thus opts for the supremacy of reason. A middle-of-the-road attempt to resolve this conflict has been to argue that religious and scientific truths are different in *kind*, and hence accessible to different modes of knowing and subject to different criteria of validity. But many modern philosophers have been loath to grant religion such a special dispensation from the canons of logic and evidence. Indeed, such separation of truth into truths has been branded as "anti-intellectualism" (White, 1962). Thus it appears that scientific scholars are as unwilling to admit religious modes of knowing as religionists are to submit their theology to scientific standards, and the basis for conflict remains. For instance, Herbert Feigl (1953) wrote in response to the question of whether science and religion were incompatible, that:

> If by religion one refers to an explanation of the universe and a derivation of moral norms from theological premises, then indeed there is a logical incompatibility with the results, methods, and general outlook of science. But, if religion means an attitude of sincere devotion to human values, such as justice, peace, relief from suffering, there is not only a conflict between religion and science but rather a need for mutual supplementation. (p. 16)

The claim advanced that men act as if religious and scientific perspectives are incompatible, is in contradiction to a prevailing body of contrary opinion. In the eyes of many, the war between religion and science that was waged so fiercely since the Enlightenment is now over. No side is the clear victor; both have had to compromise positions to the other, but neither side has been forced to capitulate entirely.

Reconciliation

The claimed accommodation of the two perspectives to each other is not viewed as complete. But there is a high degree of consensus that after the middle of this century a new era began. Science no longer claims, even implicitly, a capacity to deal with all that religion encompasses. There is a vital area in religious perspectives that science leaves untouched. In turn, religion is no longer adamant that all of its doctrines and dogma are immutable. There is a growing willingness to acknowledge that divine revelation is dynamic rather than static, and that science may be the source of new revelations of divine purpose (Chardin, 1959). Why do people deeply committed to a scientific perspective typically find it difficult to also entertain a religious perspective, and vice versa? The present paper addresses this question in the context of a more general examination of the interplay between science and religion.

In most, if not all, discussion about science and religion, science has meant the natural sciences, while religion has often meant the Christian religion, or at least religion which postulates a being imbued with divine power and purpose. In the present discussion this definition of religion is retained but the definition of science is expanded to include the social sciences. The themes that I wish to develop are: (1) The seeming rapprochement between the natural sciences and religion has tended to obscure a growing tension between religion and the social sciences, and (2) this tension explains, in part, the incompatibilities between religious and scientific perspectives.

Rules of the Game

Social scientists, when they include religion in their subject matter for study, do not conceive of their investigation of religion as a threat to religion, per se. Religion is characterized as being concerned with a different realm of being about which the social sciences have nothing to say. There are no grounds in the social sciences for establishing that there is or is not a supernatural world, a divine being, or a hereafter. These are questions which social scientific inquiry into religion must leave untouched. At most, what the social sciences can do is to assess how the religious institutions of societies and the religious behavior of individuals may be shaped and influenced by cultural, social, economic, and psychological factors and events. The knowledge thus gained supposedly leaves untouched the supernatural realm of being which religion postulates.

A central point in this argument is that the preceding assumption is not warranted. It is agreed by scientists that the social sciences cannot in any ultimate sense prove or disprove the existence of God or of a supernatural realm. However, no religion limits itself to the simple belief that God exists. Religious conceptions are always more particular than this and include a set of beliefs bearing on God's intentions for man, on man's responsibilities and accountability to God, and on God's capability to enter into human events. It is these more particular beliefs about God or the supernatural that the social sciences are capable of calling into question. The effect may not be to threaten religion's commitment to God's existence; however, I would assert that to conclude as well that the supernatural realm is left completely untouched is incorrect. The results of social science research, as will be shortly seen, are putting religion on the defensive about some of its traditional beliefs and the effect, in the long run, is likely to produce a process of accommodation parallel to that which religion experienced in its earlier confrontation with the natural sciences.

Forces in Nature

To set a suitable context for a more explicit discussion of the relationship between the social sciences and religion, it is necessary to consider briefly the more abiding controversy between the natural sciences and religion. The primary element in this controversy has been an essentially contradictory image of the forces operating in nature. Every theological system, Christian or otherwise, postulates a divine or supernatural force as operating in and upon nature. This force is responsible for creation and for establishing what appear to be the laws of nature. But it is also a force which is capable of contravening these laws through its own will—for example, the Biblical accounts of the burning bush, of the parting of the Red Sea, of Christ's walking on water and turning water into wine.

Scientists Are People

Science takes a different posture in its approach to nature. The basic assumptions which inform science are that every event in nature is determined by prior natural events, and that the character of this determinism can be discerned through scientific investigation. Individual scientists *as persons* will disagree about the adequacy of this deterministic assumption. *As scientists,* however, they are inextricably bound to it, both in the way that they formulate their hypotheses and the way that inquiry is pursued.

Scientists as persons may base a case for God as a causal agent on the existence of phenomena which they have been unable to explain from a naturalistic perspective. However, there is no way for them to account scientifically for divine intervention. They may choose to adopt a different perspective—a religious one, for example—to explain it. If they do so, however, they are no longer functioning as scientists. Confronted with inexplicability, the scientist as scientist has no recourse but to assume that his knowledge is incomplete and to look further for variables which will explain the phenomena in naturalistic terms (Giorgi, 1970; Schneider, 1946).

Faith

There is an element of faith in both religion and science; both are committed to a set of propositions which cannot be entirely proved or denied within our present capacities. But there is this important difference between the two commitments: Religious commitments are wholly based on faith, scientific ones only partially so. It is debatable, indeed highly unlikely, that the informing assumptions of science can ever be wholly warranted. However, unlike the assumptions of religion, they are and have been subject to partial proof. That is to say, there exists irrefutable scientific evidence that the naturalistic assumption is in part, at least, correct.

In the conflict between religion and science, science has had the best of it so far because its assumptions are subject to some degree of empirical proof. Theoretically, the balance could tip the other way if it were possible within the canons of science to warrant the existence of a supernatural agency. This is not possible, however. Science is in a position to understand only that part of reality which fits its naturalistic model. Phenomena which do not fit the model remain a residual category to which religion may refer as support for its assumptions. But science is not likely to be persuaded so long as the possibilities for natural explanation have not been exhausted.

Religious Phenomenology and Scientific Behaviorism

In contemporary psychology the debate of behaviorism (e.g., Craighead, Kazdin, and Mahoney, 1976) versus phenomenology (MacLeod, 1964) is a case in point. Many behaviorists refer to phenomenology as a "religion" since data is experiential.

In support of behaviorism
An adequate science of behavior must consider events taking place within the skin of the organism, not as psychological mediators of behavior, but as part of the behavior itself. It can deal with these events without assuming that they have any special nature or must be known in any special way . . . Public and private events have the same kinds of physical dimensions. (Skinner, 1964, p. 84)

Attack on behaviorism
It is quite unfortunate that we have permitted the world of psychological science to be narrowed to behavior observed, sounds emitted, marks scratched on paper, and the like. (Rogers, 1964, p. 118)

In support of phenomenology
I am . . . insisting that what, in the old, prescientific days, we used to call "consciousness" still can and should be studied. Whether or not this kind of study may be called a science depends on our definition of the term. To be a scientist, in my opinion, is to have boundless curiosity tempered by discipline. (MacLeod, 1964, p. 71)

Attack on phenomenology
Mentalistic or psychic explanations of human behavior almost certainly originated in primitive animism (p. 79). . . . I am a radical behaviorist simply in the sense I find no place in the formulation for anything which is mental. (Skinner, 1964, p. 106)

Viewed in these lights, the seeming rapprochement between religion and science is illusory. The grounds for conflict have not been settled;

without the innovation of a wholly new perspective which would resolve the determinacy issue, there is little prospect for a genuine rapprochement. At the same time it does not appear likely that the foreseeable future will find religion and science engaged in the same open conflicts of the past. In part, this is because of the accommodations which religion has already made in its positions. There is simply less of a concrete nature about which to argue. Moreover, on science's side, current doubts about the adequacy of its assumptions constitute, in effect, a compromise on its part with religion. Until such doubts are clarified, the principle issues which have divided religion and science are likely to be latent.

Religion as Humanistic Determinism

Religion is not likely to be in a position to relax during this period of quiescence in its relations with the natural sciences. While this conflict has abated for the time being, the grounds for a new controversy have arisen with the emergence and growth of the social sciences. The issue revolves once again around a conflicting set of basic assumptions, only now the assumptions concern not the order of nature but the nature of man.

The idea that man's behavior, like behavior in nature, might be not only naturally explicable but also wholly determined was not entirely alien to the historical controversy between religion and science. It is almost inevitable that the determinism issue as it arose with regard to nature would also be raised with regard to the image of man. However, the issue never became dominant. The natural sciences have only a limited interest in the study of man's behavior, and the natural science findings were not of a kind to make the determinism issue vis-à-vis man highly visable.

With the emergence of the social sciences, however, man becomes the focus of study—and with theory and methods borrowed very heavily from the natural sciences. The borrowing became so complete, in fact, that the social sciences adopted a position with respect to man which is virtually identical with natural science's position on nature. That is to say, the basic methodological assumption which has come to inform the social sciences is that man's behavior is determined in the same way that other natural phenomena are determined; that potentially every human act can be understood as a result of antecedent factors which operate to make the act inevitable (Immergluck, 1964).

Once again, it is important to recognize that this is the informing ideology of the social sciences and not the personal ideology of social scientists. As private persons, social scientists, by and large, are likely to reject the idea that man is wholly determined. Certainly, as they pursue their daily lives, many act, for the most part, as if this were not true. But, when they conduct scientific research, they have no alternative except to adopt the deterministic assumption. Hypotheses, whether simple or complex, are invariably stated in a deterministic mode—e.g., for y to occur, x must be antecedent. This is not to say that all work which is assigned the label social science research is undertaken in this perspective. It does not inform, for example, purely descriptive research where the aim is to describe systematically a personal or social situation. Nor does it inform that part of the research process commonly called conceptualization and index formation. To suggest that the populations of societies can be ordered into social classes, or to postulate the idea of an authoritarian personality, is to say nothing about the way social classes arise or the conditions under which authoritarian personalities occur. Finding answers to such questions may have motivated conceptualizations; however, the concepts themselves do not necessarily involve a deterministic posture. Nor is such a posture necessary to all examinations of the relation between variables. In the construction of an intelligence test, for example, the psychologist may discover that certain mental abilities are highly associated with one another without drawing any inference that one ability is the cause of another.

Determinism as Bastard Son

There is likely to be disagreement as to whether or not such work is scientific. I would not assert that descriptive research in the social sciences needs to be informed by a deterministic image of man. I am asserting, however, that whenever the goal of social science research is explanation, the model which the researcher adopts is a deterministic one. In fact, there is no alternative assumption which allows causal hypotheses to be stated, much less tested.

The basic impulse behind explanatory research in the social sciences is to test the deterministic assumption and to discover just how it operates. But, as in the natural sciences, the assumption has not been wholly validated. We can state the causes for only a small part of human behavior; and even the most carefully worked out models of certain limited aspects of behavior fail to account for all of the cases. There are always deviant cases which do not fit a given explanatory model.

The existence of such cases leaves the possibility that the deterministic assumption is not totally correct; that there is a range of behavior which cannot be accounted for within this assumption. Faced with such evidence, the social scientist may, as a person, agree that his perspective is an incomplete one. Functioning as a social scientist, however, he has no alternative but to search for factors overlooked in his research which in subsequent efforts might explain the deviant cases.

Man as Measure of All Things

This failure of determinism to explain all of man's behavior has accounted for a rise in popularity in the phenomenological model of man. Briefly, the model states:

> Man can be described meaningfully in terms of his consciousness; he is unpredictable; he is an information generator; he lives in a subjective world; he is arational; he is unique along side millions of other unique personalities; he can be described in relative terms; he must be studied in a holistic manner; he is potentiality; and more than we can ever know about him. (Hitt, 1969)

The phenomenological approach is surprisingly similar to the religious model of man which follows, with the most salient similarity being the rejection of determinism. Theological images of man differ, of course, in different religions and, over time, may differ within the same religion. In the midst of differences in detail, two central themes about the functioning of man are curiously combined in virtually all religions. The one idea sees man created by God and subject to God's will. The other accepts God as creator but conceives man as essentially in control of his own destiny. The idea that man is controlled by God seems, at first glance, in contradiction to the idea that man controls himself. However, the two ideas are so juxtaposed that they implement more than conflict with one another.

Determinism with a Capital "D"

The idea that God is in control is conveyed by such general themes as, "We are all created in God's image," "We are all children of God," or "We exist to reflect God's glory" (Jaeger, 1943). More explicitly, it is conveyed in Hinduism in the divine law of Karma, in Islam in the idea that man's position in life has been fated by Allah, in the Calvinistic conception of predestination, in Judaism in the Book of Life, and more generally in Christianity in the notion that whatever happens to us is God's will. What God determines, however, is never complete. In all religions man is left with considerable control of his own destiny. The law of Karma established the 'rules of the game' to be sure, but within these rules, man is left with considerable authority to decide his own fate, if not in his present incarnation, at least in his next. The fatalism of Islam asks man to resign himself to his station in life. At the same time, whatever his station, man is called upon to work for Allah's glory. Similarly, Calvinism conceives of man as having considerable freedom of action even though he comes to this life with his eternal fate predestined.

Both the belief that God possesses the power to intervene in human events and the belief that man is largely in control of his own destiny are crucial to religion. In combination, they form the basis for religious commitment. The one warrants commitment by establishing the ultimacy of divine authority; the other makes reasonable the reward and punishment system through which that authority is exercised. To assert God's power as absolute without a free-will image of man would leave man's fate entirely in God's hands. What man is and how he acts would be altogether God's will. Thus, there would be no ground for distinguishing good from evil or for asserting that good is preferable to evil. Because God would be in complete control, man's actions would be God's, not man's, responsibility.

Individual Freedom and Responsibility

The belief that man is possessed of extensive free will shifts the burden of responsibility and accountability to man. It makes meaningful both the establishment of standards of right and wrong and the universal religious injunction against sin. Together with the belief in God's ultimacy, it also gives meaning to religious systems of eternal rewards and punishments, and to the commitment which these systems generate. Only within a free-will image of man can a person be held accountable for his actions, and only if man is accountable can religion command his allegiance and commitment.

It is true that there is an element in some religions, including some versions of Christianity, that man's fate can not be influenced by his actions, i.e., by "works." This motif has never been a dominant one, at least not for any period of time. Invariably, to generate commitment, religions have had to include in their theologies some version of the idea that through his actions, man indeed contributes to his destiny.

What Is Man?

Religion and the social sciences could be expected to live comfortably together if only the issues to be decided were the existence of God and the question of whether or not man is possessed of free will. The phenomenological and behavioristic polarities within psychology are another moot issue. No social scientist would make the claim that we have the knowledge and understanding to resolve any of the preceding differences. Few, indeed, would claim that the answers can ever be known through human effort, and most perhaps would relegate the subjects as fit only for philosophical, not scientific, debate.

> It is apparent that we know very little about man. William James (1956) says: "Our science is a drop, our ignorance a sea." (p. 54) Erich Fromm (1956) believes that "Even if we knew a thousand times more of ourselves, we would never reach bottom." (Hitt, 1968, p. 31)

> What can we conclude? We must conclude that man is scientifically knowable—at least to a point. Yet there is no evidence to support the idea that man is—or ever will be—*completely* knowable. (Hitt, 1968, p. 657)

On both issues, then, the social sciences would neither confirm nor deny religion's claim, nor would they question religion's right to assert them.

Divine Force

The claims of religion are not simply that God and free will exist. Religion not only professes that God does exist, but that He is able to, and indeed does, intervene in human affairs. In turn, not only does free will exist, but it is held to be relatively unrestricted. Man enjoys wide latitude in his range of choices, for which he can be held responsible and accountable. It is with these claims and particularly their use as explanations for human behavior that the social scientist is likely to take exception. And it is because the social sciences (sometimes with the aid of other sciences) are increasingly capable of producing evidence to challenge these claims that the conflict between the social sciences and religion arises. The claims of the behavioristic model in psychology amply demonstrate the potential for friction between itself and religion:

> Man can be described meaningfully in terms of his behavior; he is predictable; he is an information transmitter; he lives in an objective world; he is rational; he has traits in common with other men; he may be described in absolute terms; his characteristics can be studied independently of one another; he is a reality; and he is knowable in scientific terms. (Hitt, 1968)

Thus, increasingly, human behavior which would be explained from a religious perspective as God's will or as a result of man making a conscious and reasonable choice to accept or reject God's will, is questioned by the results of social science research. Not only is the intervention of God rejected as a causal factor (in behaviorism *and* phenomenology), but the idea that man's freedom is as extensive as religion allows is rejected as well (*only* in behaviorism).

A Question of Semantics

There should be a clarification of the terms 'free will' and 'determinism.' Most simply put, a deterministic model regards human behavior as the invariant (though perhaps stated in probabilities) outcome of prior conditions. Free will doctrines assert that a knowledge of prior conditions does not facilitate predictions of subsequent behavior because at some moment in the shaping of an act men enjoy a moment of individual choice, a momentary liberation from all causation during which they may assert control over their future action independent of all prior conditions. As is apparent, the free-will doctrine is extremely difficult to express in any meaningful way because there is no appropriate language for describing or explaining the chaos of noncausality (Wilson, 1964).

Door One, Two, or Three

A major issue in all discussions of free will and determinism concerns the matter of choice, a term that has been misconstrued to distort the implications of a causal approach to the study of man. Wilson (1964) has used the word choice to mean a subjective state of assent, or a psychological process of formulating intentions and selecting a course of action, and by establishing the existence of such traits in human behavior he has sought to salvage a metaphysical commitment to notions of free will. But it is obvious to any serious social scientist that such states will, of necessity, play an important role in the formulation of deterministic propositions about human behavior. Surely, if psychology is to be taken seriously as a science, whatever its current state of unpreparedness, it should be presumed that these subjective states of the human psyche are themselves lawful, that is, subject to prediction on the basis of prior factors of both psychic and external origins. Thus, equating choice with subjective mental states in no way eludes the implications of determinism in social science.

The motive for this kind of attempt to salvage a theological concept of free will often seems to derive from a misunderstanding of the implications of deterministic thought for man's conception of himself as a dignified and self-aware creature. It seems that the notion of determinism, at first glance, constitutes an assault upon our sense of control over our own acts. This is largely because it seems to be assumed that to posit lawfulness in human behavior is to imply that men are the hapless creatures of great, blind forces; that human behavior, when viewed as determined, becomes puppet-like, and rationality and self-awareness are but mere illusions. This is an absurd reification of causality.

To say that particular features of human behavior are the probabilistic and even invariant outcomes of certain specifiable prior conditions in no way asserts that men will be unaware of any or all of these conditions, that acts thus caused are irrational, or that such acts occur contrary to human volition.

> This belief (that causes compel effects) seems largely operative in the dislike of determinism; but, as a matter of fact, it is . . . (incorrect). We may define "compulsion" as follows: "Any set of circumstances is said to compel A when A desires to do something which the circumstances prevent, or to abstain from something which the circumstances cause." . . . What I want to make clear at present is that compulsion is a very complex notion, involving thwarted desire. So long as a person does what he wishes to do, there is no compulsion, however much his wishes may be calculable by help of earlier events. And where desire does not come in, there can be no question of compulsion. (Russell, 1953)
>
> . . . We have in deliberation, a subjective sense of freedom, which is sometimes alleged against the view that volitions have causes. This sense of freedom, however, is only a sense that we can choose which we please of a number of alternatives: it does not show us that there is no causal connection between what we please to choose and our previous history. (Russell, 1953)

Who Man Is: Individual, Mean, or Mode

To the degree that human behavior is reasonable and conscious, surely deterministic approaches to explaining it are no threat to man's sense of identity. When behavior is irrational the reasons for which men think they are acting are not the actual ones producing their acts; determinism may imply an attack upon the human sense of freedom. But such an uncovering of hidden causes may also be seen as liberating the human spirit. Merely to unveil and admit that such unperceived forces are shaping one's life is to provide some opportunity to suspend their operation.

Lastly, the implications of a deterministic model of human behavior for man's sense of identity greatly depend on what one assumes the identity of man to be. If, in order to predict a man's behavior, it is necessary to include in the model all the salient details of his past experience, his conceptions of himself, his social situation, his physiological and psychological capacities and propensities, it may be that many would feel that the essence of this man's identity was built into the explanatory model. If this is the case, then such a model would seem virtually tautological to the man in question: Because the essential Me is built into the model, the prediction is no more than saying that I will do what I will do. Thus, the actual application of determinism should be limited to groups of men where the outcomes are of considerably greater interest and utility, and where the predictions are never likely to be invariants but rather probabilities which still leave room for men to be exceptions to any rule.

Relative to the natural sciences, the social sciences are in their infancy and there are still few assertions that they can make with authority concerning the ways in which man's behavior is determined. Nevertheless, enough work has been done to challenge seriously the assumptions that man is endowed with unlimited or even extensive free will (e.g., Skinner and Freud). Not only is there evidence to make and increasingly support this general point, but the social sciences have always been able to document their contention in concrete ways. In only a few cases has this involved the social sciences in direct confrontation with religion. Indirectly, however, religion is being profoundly affected by what the social sciences are learning about human behavior.

Religion as Ostrich

Religion is confronted directly with the results of social science research when these bear explicitly on religious phenomena. To some extent, the impact of such research is benign, or nearly so, because it is done in a descriptive mode. Religion, or more appropriately the church, is likely to feel itself informed by descriptive findings. On occasion, descriptive research may arouse apprehensions—as when it reveals gaps between what the church preaches and what its followers practice. It is unlikely, however, to threaten the church's more basic commitments, and specifically its commitments to view man as free and as responsible (Fitcher, 1954).

These commitments are challenged, nevertheless, by social science theory and research which purport to explain religious phenomena in social and psychological terms. At the theoretical level the challenge has existed, of course, for a considerable period of time. By the early part of the present century, Marx, Freud, Durkheim, and Weber, among others, had suggested that religion could be understood within naturalistic categories. In 1897, in fact, M. Guyau in his *The Non-Religion of the Future* was already postulating what society would be like when man came to recognize the illusory quality of his religious commitments.

These early writings were not, in their time, without effect. And since they were written, they have undoubtedly influenced many who have been exposed to them to question their own religious convictions. Marxist ideas, of course, have influenced the course of religion in entire societies.

Despite these signs of erosion, there is no evidence as yet that religion stands ready to capitulate to these conceptions. Certainly, in the West and particularly in America, there is little respect for Marxist ideas about religion. Freud's conception of religion as an illusion is not paid much heed—even by those committed to Freudian thoughts in other respects. However, the views of Durkheim and Weber are highly respected by professional sociologists (Personal communication. C. Thomas, 1970). Few religionists, however, are aware of these views and among those who are, there is little disposition to accept them as valid alternatives to their own religiously informed postures.

Accommodation or Osmosis

There are a number of signs which point to efforts on religion's part to accommodate traditional belief to the findings of social science research. Current efforts on the part of theologians to demythesize the scriptures, the intrusion of psychiatry into pastoral counseling, the increasing introduction of social science courses into the curricula of theological seminaries (Bugental, 1963), can all be interpreted as having been influenced, at least in part, by the new perspectives on man which the social sciences are providing.

How far these perspectives will eventually add to our understanding of man, and what will be their ultimate impact on religion as we have traditionally known it are questions about which it is possible only to speculate. It seems highly unlikely that the determinism hypothesis which informs science can ever be wholly confirmed. And, whatever the degree of confirmation, the effect is not likely to be the elimination of the religious component from human society. In the end, the existence of the universe, of nature, and of mankind will remain unexplained—man can only investigate the causal chain so far. Thus, there will always be a warrant for a supernatural realm and for God's existence.

For Sale: A System of Ultimate Meaning

The dilemma thus created is how the need for a system of ultimate meaning is to be satisfied. Science itself cannot fill the gap. It cannot supply the glue—the values and norms which hold societies together and make existence meaningful. Perhaps humanistic perspectives will come to supplant religious ones. Some, undoubtedly, would argue that the transition has already occurred for a large part of the world (Rogers, 1955).

Such a view, however, overlooks the capacity of institutions to survive and indeed, through threats to their survival, to be renewed and to enhance their authority and power. That religious institutions will change, there can be no doubt, and that they must find ways other than their traditional reliance on eternal reward and punishment systems to generate commitment seems also clear. That they will be weakened permanently by their confrontation with the social sciences is not, however, inevitable. Knowledge of how man's behavior is determined produces conflict within the social sciences themselves. Knowing how determinism operates may enable man to transcend freedom and indeed exercise greater control over his destiny.

> Such an experimental analysis of behavior shifts the determination of behavior from autonomous man to the environment—an environment responsible for the evolution of the species and for the repertoire acquired by each member. Early versions of environmentalism were inadequate because they could not explain how the environment worked, and much seemed to be left for autonomous man to do. But environmental contingencies now take over functions once attributed to autonomous man, and certain questions arise. Is man then "abolished"? Certainly not as a species or as an individual achiever. It is the autonomous inner man who is abolished, and that is a step forward. But does man not then become merely a victim or passive observer of what is happening to him? He is indeed controlled by his environment, but we must remember that it is an environment largely of his own making. The evolution of a culture is a gigantic exercise in self-control. It is often said that a scientific view of man leads to wounded vanity, a sense of hopelessness, and nostalgia. But no theory changes what it is a theory about; man remains what he has always been. And a new theory may change what can be done with its subject matter. A scientific view of man offers exciting possibilities. We have not yet seen what man can make of man. (Skinner, 1971, pp. 214–215)

> It is said that science will dehumanize people and turn them into numbers. That is false, tragically false. . . . Science is a very human form of knowledge. We are always at the brink of the known, we always

feel forward for what is to be hoped. Every judgement in science stands on the edge of error, and is personal. Science is a tribute to what we can know although we are fallible. . . . We have to close the distance between the push-button order and the human act. We have to touch people. (Bronowski, 1973, p. 374)

REFERENCES

Bartley, H. S. *The human organism as a person.* Philadelphia: Chilton Book Company, 1967.

Boulding, K. E. Dare we take the social sciences seriously? *American Psychologist,* 1967, *22*(11), 879–887.

Brett, A. *Brett's history of psychology.* Cambridge, MA: MIT Press, 1965.

Bronowski, J. *The ascent of man.* Boston: Litfle, Brown, 1973.

Bruner, J. S. The growth of mind. *American Psychologist,* 1965, *20*(12), 1007–1017.

Bugental, J. F. T. Humanistic Psychology: A new break-through. *American Psychologist,* 1963, *18*(11), 563–567.

Buhler, C. Humanistic Psychology as an educational program. *American Psychologist,* 1969, *24,* 736–742.

Chardin T. *Phenomenon of man.* New York: Harper and Row, 1959.

Craeger, J. A. Freedom-determinism controversies: Some why's and wherefore's. *American Psychologist,* 1967, *22*(3), 235–236.

Craighead, W. E., Kazdin, A. E., and Mahoney, M. J. *Behavior modification: Principles, issues, and applications.* Boston: Houghton Mifflin, 1976.

Esper, E. A. *A history of psychology.* Philadelphia: Saunders, 1964.

Feigl, H. Philosophical embarrassments of psychology. *American Psychologist,* 1959, *14*(3), 115–128.

Feigl, H., and Brodbeck, M. The scientific outlook: Naturalism and humanism. In *Readings in the philosophy of science.* New York: Appleton-Century Crofts, 1953.

Fichter, J. *Social relations in the urban parish.* Chicago: University of Chicago Press, 1954.

Frankel, C. *The case for modern man.* Boston: Beacon Press, 1967.

Fromm, E. *The art of loving.* New York: Harper and Row, 1956.

Fromm, E. *Psychoanalysis and religion.* New Haven: Yale University Press, 1967.

Giorgi, A. *Psychology as a human science: A phenomenologically based approach.* New York: Harper and Row, 1970.

Hall, E. W. *Philosophical systems.* Chicago: University of Chicago Press, 1960.

Hitt, W. D. Two models of man. *American Psychologist,* 1969, *24,* 651–658.

Hyman, R. *The nature of psychological inquiry.* New York: Prentice Hall, 1964.

Immergluck, L. Determinism freedom in contemporary psychology. *American Psychologist,* 1964, *19,* 270–281.

Jaeger, W. The Aquinas Lecture. In *Humanism and theology*. Milwaukee: Marquette University Press, 1943.

James, W. The individual and society. In *The philosophy of William James*. New York: Modern Library, 1925.

Kessel, F. S. The philosophy of science as proclaimed and science as practiced: Identity or dualism? *American Psychologist*, 1969, *24*, 999–1005.

Kingston, F. T. *French existentialism*. Toronto: University of Toronto Press, 1961.

Koch, S. Psychological science versus the science-humanism antimony: Intimations of a significant science of man. *American Psychologist*, 1961, *16*(10), 629–639.

Kockelman, J. J. *Phenomenology*. Garden City: Anchor Books, 1967.

Kohler, W. *The place of value in a world of facts*. New York: Liveright, 1938.

MacLeod, R. B. Phenomenology: A challenge to experimental psychology. In T. W. Wann (Ed.), *Behaviorism and phenomenology: Contrasting basis for modern psychology*. Chicago: University of Chicago Press, 1964.

Madden, E. H. *Philosophical problems of psychology*. New York: Odyssey Press, 1962.

May, R. *Psychology and the human dilemma*. New York: Van Nostrand, 1967.

Maurer, H. H. The problems of group consensus: Founding the Missouri Synod. *American Journal of Sociology*, 1925, *30*, 667.

Misiak, H. *The philosophical roots of scientific psychology*. New York: Fordham University Press, 1961.

Monsma, J. C. (Ed.). *Science and religion*. New York: Putman's Sons, 1962.

Nettler, G. Free will and cruelty. *American Psychologist*, 1961, *16*(8), 529.

Raab, E. *Religious conflict in America*. Garden City: Anchor Books, 1964.

Reichenback. H. *The rise of scientific philosophy*. Los Angeles: University of California Press, 1963.

Rogers, C. Persons or science? A philosophical question. *American Psychologist*, 1955, *10*(7), 267–278.

Rogers, C. Toward a science of the person. In T. W. Wann (Ed.), *Behaviorism and phenomenology: Contrasting basis for modern psychology*. Chicago: University of Chicago Press, 1964.

Russell, B. On the notion of cause, with applications to the free will problem. In *Readings in the philosophy of science*. New York: Appleton-Century-Crofts, 1953.

Skinner, B. F. *Science and human behavior*. New York: Free Press, 1953.

Skinner, B. F. Behaviorism at fifty. In T. W. Wann (Ed.), *Behaviorism and phenomenology: Contrasting basis for modern psychology*. Chicago: University of Chicago Press, 1964.

Skinner, B. F. *Beyond freedom and dignity*. New York: Knopf, 1971.

Swanson, G. E. *The birth of the gods*. Ann Arbor: University of Michigan Press, 1966.

White, A. D. *A history of the warfare of science with theology in Christendom*. New York: Dover, 1960.

White, M. Reflections on anti-intellectualism. *Daedalus,* 1962, *Summer,* 457–468.

Whiteley, C. H. Phenomenalism. In Edwards and Pap (Eds.), *A modern introduction to philosophy.* New York: Free Press, 1968.

Wilson, W. A brief resolution of the issue of free will versus determinism. *Journal for the Scientific Study of Religion,* 1964, *4,* 101.

Woleensberger, W. The free will controversy. *American Psychologist,* 1961, *16*(1), 36–37.

2
Obsessive-Compulsive Disorders

R. L. Meredith
Jesse B. Milby

Obsessive-compulsive behaviors may be viewed as a continuum from adaptive or mildly annoying characteristics to severely disabling behavioral, emotional, and cognitive patterns. On the positive end of the continuum an individual with obsessive-compulsive features may be described as industrious, hard working, conscientious, responsible, concerned, punctual, and so on. On the dysfunctional end, the individual may experience high levels of anxiety, guilt, and depression while being completely dominated by repetitious thoughts and intrusive behaviors which interfere with routine daily activities. A subjective loss of volition, associated with inability to control or modify unpleasant and intrusive cognitions and/or behaviors completes the clinical picture.

Carr (1974, p. 311) defined compulsive behaviors as "a recurrent or persistent thought, image, impulse or action that is accompanied by a sense of subjective compulsion and a desire to resist it." In assuming that both obsessive thoughts and compulsive behaviors were functionally similar responses, Carr suggested the generic term *compulsion* be employed to categorize intrusive behaviors in both modalities. He further suggested that cognitive and motor be used as qualifiers when more precision in description was necessary.

Some controversy exists about the appropriateness and use of the terms obsessive and compulsive. Wolpe (1958) challenged the appropriateness of the term *compulsive* in stating that the (primary) "feature of any example of obsessional behavior is not its inevitability but its intrusiveness." He pointed out that all behavior may be construed as compulsive from a deterministic model of human behavior, and therefore asserted that *obsessional behavior* may be the more appropriate term because it avoids a focus on the philosophical issues of determinism. The critical defining characteristic therefore becomes the subjective experience of intrusiveness.

Another conceptualization is based on the function of the symptom regarding its relationship to anxiety and discomfort. Thoughts, images, or behavior which *elicit or increase* anxiety or discomfort should be discriminated from those which decrease anxiety or discomfort. Foa and Tillmans (1978) have suggested that the former types of problems should be construed as obsessions, while the latter should be designated compulsions. Generally, thoughts and images, rather than behavior, tend to be anxiety-increasing, while overt behavior is predominant when anxiety-reduction is considered.

The differences suggested by these theorists highlight the primary defining characteristic of this disorder. Each theorist suggests loss of volition as a primary feature. Two other features interact to define the disorder: The behavioral and/or cognitive event must occur with sufficient frequency or intensity so that it is defined as intrusive. The event must also be subjectively defined as undesirable, unpleasant, or uncomfortable. Throughout this chapter, the term obsessive-compulsive disorder (OCD) will be used when both cognitive and behavioral events are present. Indeed, this appears to be the most common clinical presentation. Where a focus is on the cognitive event the term *obsessive behavior* will be employed. *Compulsive behavior* will be used to refer to a focus on a behavioral presentation, per se, with the salient feature being intrusiveness rather than inevitability.

THEORETICAL ANALYSIS

Nonbehavioral (Psychodynamic)

Two primary models, psychoanalytic and behavioral, have been advanced. The psychoanalytic model assumes obsessive-compulsive behaviors result from underlying dynamic processes. A primary function of such behaviors was thought to be the prevention of repressed material from expression in consciousness. This method of dealing with basic impulses and drives was thought to originate in the anal period of development. During this period the individual confronted environmental restrictions for the first time. The arena was the bathroom; the stage was the toilet. The "give and take of socialization" was an abrupt change from the rather immediate need gratification of the preceding oral period. The initial response of some children was to resist the demands of parents. Where such resistance led to parental punishment and guilt induction, the child was forced to deny pleasure-oriented behavior or risk parental rejection and hence loss of parental approval. Faced with this difficult situation some children developed the psychological defense mechanism of reaction formation, i.e., development of a posture of behavior completely opposite of that suggested by basic impulses and desires. The result was the development of excessive self-control and a demeanor of neatness and perfection which allowed the child to satisfy parental demands. In psychoanalytic terms, an excessively stringent superego developed. Parental injunctions were internalized and guided the child's subsequent behavior. Although originally acquired in the interaction with parents or parental figures, obsessive-compulsive behaviors were later utilized to control basic impulses and desires incongruent with parental expectancies. Although an interesting analysis, data have not been forthcoming to support these basic hypotheses (Carr, 1974).

Behavioral

Early behavioral formulations (Dollard and Miller, 1950) stressed the anxiety-reducing role of obsessive-compulsive behavior. Problematic obsessive thoughts or compulsive behaviors were viewed as exaggerations of previously employed anxiety-reducing behaviors, e.g., a hand-washing compulsion was etiologically associated with escape or avoidance of parental criticism or disapproval.

More recent behavioral theories (Rachman, Hodgson, and Marks, 1971) have retained an interest in the drive-reduction model for many obsessive-compulsive behaviors. Hodgson and Rachman (1972) provided empirical support for the anxiety-reduction model of compulsive behaviors. The results of this work with obsessive-compulsive individuals suggested: (a) touching an object perceived as contaminating increased subjective anxiety discomfort, (b) performing the compulsive ritual decreased subjective anxiety/discomfort, and (c) interruption of the washing ritual did not increase or decrease subjective anxiety/discomfort from the range associated with touching the contaminated object. These data provide support for the anxiety-reduction model with some patients, although Hodgson and Rachman caution generalization to other categories of OCD, namely obsessional checking and obsessional doubting, in which performance of the obsessional behavior may increase subjective anxiety/discomfort. This work has stimulated renewed interest in the anxiety-reduction model for conceptualizing some forms of OCD.

Wolpe (1958) was the first to hypothesize that not all obsessive-compulsive behavior was anxiety-reducing. He suggested that obsessive thoughts may be either anxiety-elevating or anxiety-reducing.

Anxiety-elevating obsessions were viewed as elicited cognitions which were part of the immediate anxiety response. Anxiety-reducing obsessions, however, were operant responses maintained by anxiety decrement, e.g., cognitive-problem solving. Wolpe, like most other early behaviorists, attributed obsessive-compulsive behavior to traumatic learning experiences. He also suggested that obsessive-compulsive behavior may become conditioned to interoceptive cues of anxiety through second-order conditioning, such that subsequently, anxiety elicited from any source could also elicit the obsessive-compulsive behavior.

Walton and Mather (1964) further modified the behavioral model in speculating that only in acute stages of the development of obsessive-compulsive behavior was the anxiety-reduction hypothesis valid. Secondary generalization was hypothesized to occur with time, so that in later stages of the disorder, initially unrelated stimuli elicited the behavior rather than the behavior being directly associated with a conditioned autonomic drive. Treatment implications seemed obvious: Acute cases should receive treatment designed to reduce the conditioned autonomic drive, while chronic cases would benefit from a focus on reducing the behavior, per se. Bandura (1969) criticized this model by suggesting that the issue was not a focus on a drive or a behavior, but whether responses should be extinguished to primary and/or generalized stimuli.

Rachman (1971), in discussing obsessional thinking, introduced an habituation model. He speculated that in a state of heightened arousal (associated with depression or elevated anxiety) sensitization of a thought occurred, particularly if the thought had "special significance." This sensitization led to a further increase in arousal or modification of mood which perpetuated the thought. He also suggested that social reinforcement contributed to response maintenance once the behavior occurred. The two necessary conditions for the development of obsessional thinking were a prevailing high state of arousal and the significance of the stimuli (obsession). Past history of censure or punishment for shameful thoughts, verbalizations, or behaviors was thought to result in a heightened stimulus valence for some thoughts.

Carr (1974) suggested a more cognitively oriented model. He hypothesized that individuals with obsessive-compulsive behaviors exhibit an abnormally high expectation of unfavorable consequences. This expectation and the estimation of the unpleasantness of the consequence should it occur (subjective cost) interacted to form "threat." Thus, because the individual with obsessive-compulsive behaviors assumes the probability that something undesirable will occur is high, even those situations with minor potential harmfulness generate relatively high threat. Obsessive-compulsive behaviors are threat-reducing because they lower the subjective probability of an unfavorable outcome. This model also addressed the content of obsessive concerns and behavior in suggesting that stimuli associated with a high subjective cost would likely comprise the content of obsessions. Thus, most compulsive behaviors and obsessive thoughts relate to health, sex, death, welfare of family or others, religion, work, and so on—these are significant concerns to most people.

ASSESSMENT

General Considerations

Five general assessment considerations demand specification prior to discussion of formal assessment instruments and procedures. OCD is suggested when the following considerations have been met:

1. *Absence of psychotic process or organic brain syndrome*
   The behavior of many individuals with OCD is frankly unusual and bizarre. These patients usually acknowledge the unusual nature of their behavior. They complain of a loss of volition and of the intrusiveness of their behavior and cognitions. Reality contact is good and no major signs of thought disorder or perceptual distortions are present. However, like those with organic brain syndrome, their behavior may be repetitive and stereotyped. There is frequently a certain rigidity to their behavioral disorder which mimics organic perseveration, but they do not evidence the major signs of organic brain syndrome (i.e., short-term memory impairment, intellectual deterioration, lability of affect, poor judgment, or impairment of orientation).

2. *Presence of anxiety and depression*
   Behavioral characteristics of anxiety and depression are frequent correlates of OCD. Anxiety is usually situation-specific with precise eliciting situations, events or cognitions, rather than being pervasive and seemingly unrelated to specific stimuli. Depressed mood most frequently accompanies the subjective loss of volition and the perception of helplessness which characterize this disorder. The inability to meet perfectionistic self-evaluative criteria is also a frequently observed component of the depressed mood of OCD.

3. *Presence of repetitive disturbing thoughts (obsessions)*
   These thoughts are characterized by their uncontrollable nature and often are characterized by the patient as nonsensical and illogical (e.g., "I know it makes no sense to think

this way, but I do it anyway"). These thoughts may be anxiety-reducing or anxiety-elevating.

4. *Presence of ritualistic and stereotyped behavior which the patient does not want to perform (compulsions)*
    These behaviors, like obsessive thoughts, are subjectively perceived as intrusive and uncontrollable. Anxiety-reduction usually accompanies the performance.

5. *Obsessive-compulsive behaviors constitute the patient's main complaint and/or are a major cause of dysfunction*
    The usual presentation of the patient involves a specific focus on the OCD even though additional problems are frequently revealed with careful assessment.

Assessment should start with examination of these five general assessment considerations. These considerations are usually easily resolved via clinical interview. In addition to clinical assessment via interview, three basic assessment approaches have been utilized. These include projective assessment, objective personality assessment, and behavioral assessment.

Each of these assessment approaches will be examined with respect to how well they accomplish the following assessment goals: (a) to determine the presence of OCD as discriminated from other types of disorder, and (b) to delineate the descriptive and quantitative aspects of OCD. Because behavioral assessment appears to be the most clinically useful, it will be reviewed in more detail than the other assessment approaches.

Projective Assessment

The Rorschach continues to be the most widely employed projective instrument (Klopfer and Taulbee, 1976). In spite of a more recent focus on actuarial assessment (Marks, Seeman, and Haller, 1974), and behavioral assessment (Hersen and Bellack, 1976; Cimminero, Calhoun, and Adams, 1977; Mash and Terdal, 1976), training in projective techniques, specifically the Rorschach, continues to be well represented in clinical psychology training programs (Ritzler and Del Gaudio, 1976).

Frequent utilization of an assessment instrument does not, however, serve as a justification for its perceived value. Without examining the extensive literature on reliability and validity of this instrument, a more focused examination of the use of the Rorschach with OCD will be presented. No attempt will be made to generalize from this specific focus to the value of the Rorschach or other projective techniques in assessment with other disorders.

The Rorschach has been used to discriminate between OCD and other psychiatric disorders. The research foundation, however, is relatively weak. The literature ranges from uncontrolled presentations of Rorschach protocols of individuals with OCD (Wagner, 1976) to theoretical discussions of constructs which presumably relate to OCD (Sherman, 1963; Stolorow, 1971), and to a relatively few comparisons between OCD and other psychiatric entities (Akhtar, Pershad, and Verma, 1975; Kates, 1950).

Kates (1950) provides the most pertinent comparison in examining the differences between individuals diagnosed as anxiety neurotics (AN) and individuals diagnosed as obsessive-compulsive (OC) neurotics. Twenty-five subjects were selected for each group by agreement of three clinical psychologists; all subjects were selected on the basis of presenting symptoms, independent of test results.

The groups were found to differ significantly on the following dimensions: (a) general maladjustment (AN > OC) determined by the Munroe Inspection Technique (1944), (b) mean number of responses (OC > AN), (c) rejection of cards (AN > OC), (e) frequency of exclusive form responses (AN > OC), (f) frequency of inanimate movement responses (OC > AN), (g) frequency of FC responses (OC > AN), and (h) total color (OC > AN). General conclusions drawn by Kates (1950) suggested that obsessive-compulsive individuals evidenced greater success in controlling anxiety via their symptoms, exhibited greater need to demonstrate adequacy, were characterized by more drive for completeness, showed more meticulousness and orderliness, demonstrated less fear of spontaneity, experienced more awareness of uncontrollable inner forces, and were more emotionally responsive to others.

Akhtar, Pershad, and Verma (1975) examined the protocols of 34 obsessional neurotics in India. They evidenced none of the differences observed by Kates (1950) when compared with nonobsessional neurotics. Cultural differences may have obscured the pattern he found.

At this point, there is little experimental data to support the utility of using the Rorschach to discriminate between OCD and other neuroses, much less between OCD and other categories of psychiatric disorder. Whereas most research has focused on quantitative aspects of test responses, most clinicians employ behavioral observations and examine the pattern of test responses and the relationship of one test response to another. This paucity of research data does not then necessarily mean that the Rorschach has no value in assessment with OCD. In fact, clinicians using the Rorschach frequently do appear to be able to make meaningful discriminations.

The typical clinical picture on the Rorschach which reflects obsessive-compulsive features includes a number of behavioral observations, in addition to specific types of Rorschach responses. The obsessive-compulsive individual frequently approaches the test with care and precision. Responses are made with much forethought and deliberation. Response content tends to be conventional and relatively innocuous. Verbal behavior is frequently intellectualized with many qualifying remarks.

Specific Rorschach responses seen with obsessive-compulsive individuals include a higher than normal number of responses, moderate to high F+%, high number of popular responses, and a high latency and total time. Although the obsessive-compulsive individual may show high organizational ability and, hence, high Z, a relatively high number of rare details would also be observed. Reflecting an active inner experience, a high number of movement responses also would be observed. A lack of emotional responsiveness would be seen in a relatively low total C. High use of shading would be observed, depending on the success of the neurotic behavior in reducing anxiety.

Although this pattern would be typical, more recent data (Hersen and Greaves, 1971) have suggested that subtle changes in situational variables associated with test administration may have profound effects upon the resulting protocol. Thus, patterns deviating from the preceding would not necessarily be useful in concluding that obsessive-compulsive features were not a component of the clinical picture. The probability of an error in assessment using the Rorschach thus appears to be highest with false negatives rather than false positives. Although the Rorschach may be useful to skilled clinicians in discriminating OCD from other forms of psychopathology, it does not appear more useful than more objective forms of assessment.

The Rorschach also does not appear to have much value in addressing the second assessment goal, i.e., assessment of the descriptive and quantitative aspects of obsessive-compulsive neurosis. As this instrument was not designed from a model of personality that examines situational variables, it can hardly be expected to accomplish assessment goals which are situational in nature.

Objective Assessment

Objective assessment is used to accomplish both assessment goals. Usually associated with clinical interview, objective tests are used to detect the presence of an OCD. Since the goal of this first level of assessment is to determine if there is an OCD as opposed to other disorders, objective tests typically used are relatively wide-band instruments designed to discriminate multiple forms of psychopathology.

The most commonly utilized objective tests have been the Eysenck Personality Inventory (EPI) and the Minnesota Multiphasic Personality Inventory (MMPI).

The Eysenck Personality Inventory (EPI) was developed to measure two primary aspects of personality found in a number of factor analytic studies. The factors are: extroversion-introversion and neuroticism-stability. The scale also contains MMPI lie-scale items to assess test-taking attitude. This instrument seems useful especially for discriminating neurotics from less disturbed and normal groups. However, EPI scores indicating neuroticism provide only a gross discrimination between the presence versus absence of psychopathological characteristics of the neurotic type. Scores indicating introversion versus extroversion seem less useful. The utility of the EPI thus appears limited as a general assessment screening tool because once individuals with high neuroticism scores are discovered, further discriminations among these individuals need to be made to discern the small percentage who may evidence obsessive-compulsive behavior.

The MMPI, with nine clinical scales and three validity scales plus numerous derived scales of varying utility, offers the clinician a more comprehensive instrument for discriminating among various types of psychopathology. The MMPI score patterns indicating OCD are relatively high elevations on scale 7, Psychasthenia, associated with elevation on scale 2, Depression. Strongest indications of OCD include profiles with high point codes of 72' or 27' where both scales are higher than a T score of 70. High point codes 7'2 or 2'7 also strongly imply the presence of OCD. Where dysfunction is extensive, elevations on scale 8, Schizophrenia and the F scale also appear. High point codes above, but including scale 8 in any position, are common. Milder forms of OCD and obsessive-compulsive personality types are more likely to have the 2–7 or 7–2 scale configurations below a T score of 70, and without associated elevation on F and scale 8.

Of the two wide-band objective tests, the MMPI clearly seems the most useful. One of the major reasons the EPI is found in so much of the research on OCD is because of the extensive research being done by the British in the area of assessment and treatment of OCD. The EPI is one of the most popular objective tests used in Great Britain, and thus subjects in studies conducted by the British are likely to have been exposed to this test.

The MMPI seems most useful because it discriminates OCD from several other similar forms of psychopathology which need to be ruled out before intervention can begin, i.e., psychotic process and other forms of neurosis. It provides some initial assessment of several complicating factors which need to be taken into account in designing treatment plans. Specifically, it provides an objective index to the presence and extent of anxiety and depression. It also may provide some indication of the presence of irrational beliefs about obsessive-compulsive symptoms which are related to the selection of intervention strategies and prognosis (Foa and Goldstein, 1978). Indication of unusual beliefs are often indicated in elevations of scale 6, scale 8, and review of the critical items.

At least two objective tests show some promise for accomplishing the second goal of assessment, to delineate descriptive and quantitative aspects of OCD. These instruments appear useful once the disorder has been discriminated from other forms of psychopathology.

The Leyton Obsessive Compulsive Scale (LOCS) (Cooper, 1970) is a measure of obsessive-compulsive phenomena which yields four scores: trait, symptom, resistance, and interference. Its four scores appear highly intercorrelated but show little to moderate correlation with other measures of obsessive-compulsive phenomena. Rachman, Marks, and Hodgson (1973) found the four scores to have a negative or low correlation with a fear thermometer rating (range: -0.18 to $.04$), low to moderate correlation with a semantic differential (range: $.27$ to $.49$), low correlation with performance on a behavioral test (range: $.04$ to $.19$), and moderate correlations with self-reported obsessive anxiety (range: $.22$ to $.52$). In a more recent investigation (1975), these authors reported somewhat higher correlations between the Leyton and various measures: clinical ratings of severity by the patient and by independent raters (range: $.61$ to $.81$), fear thermometer ratings ($.47$), avoidance tests ($.52$), and semantic differential ratings (range: $.53-.73$). Further experimentation with this instrument is required before its clinical utility can be objectively evaluated.

The Maudsley Obsessive-Compulsive (MOC) Inventory (Hodgson and Rachman, 1977) is a 30-question inventory focused upon various obsessive-compulsive behaviors. Each question is answered either true or false. It is designed to assess the existence and extent of different obsessive-compulsive complaints. In the original development of the Inventory, a principal components' analysis with oblique rotation was performed on inventories of 100 obsessive-compulsives. A 4-component solution was identified which accounted for 43 percent of the variance, partitioned as follows into four major types of obsessive-compulsive behavior: checking, 17 percent; cleaning, 11 percent; slowness, 8 percent; and doubting, 6 percent. Test-retest reliability was assessed by administering the Inventory to 50 night-school students one month apart. Of 1500 response pairs available, agreement was obtained on 1341, yielding a Kendall's $\tau = 0.8$. Validity was assessed on two of the subscales via correlation with pre- and post-treatment retrospective ratings, and yielded gamma coefficients of 0.7 for the cleaning and checking subscales. The investigators also assessed validity by correlating the "total obsessionality" score with the Leyton Symptom Score and found a correlation of 0.6.

If one defines the presence of a symptom as a score of 2 standard deviations above the mean for the nonobsessional neurotic comparison group, 48 percent of the obsessional sample complained of cleaning/contamination problems, 53 percent had checking problems, 52 percent had slowness, and 60 percent doubting.

Although this research did not purport to cover all obsessional problems, only those associated with observable rituals, this short questionnaire may be useful to clinicians as well as researchers. The neurotic but nonobsessional groups' mean scores and standard deviations, and the nonneurotic night-school students' mean scores and standard deviations may serve to derive clinical scores of obsessive-compulsive symptomology. The Inventory thus could be useful in the focused stage of assessment to formulate treatment strategies. It also could be used as an ongoing assessment and outcome measure. Available reliability and validity data necessary to use the instrument are found in Hodgson and Rachman (1977).

The two objective tests which appear to have the most clinical utility are thus the MMPI and the MOC. The MMPI facilitates a discrimination between OCD and other general types of psychopathology while also providing a quantitative index to anxiety and depression, two associated disorders which frequently complete the clinical picture of the obsessive-compulsive patient. The MOC provides a more precise exploration of specific obsessive-compulsive behavioral patterns.

Behavioral Assessment

Purpose of Behavioral Assessment. Behavioral assessment has four general objectives. The first is to provide a detailed, objective definition of the behavioral problems. This initial step includes specification of behaviors and examination of antecedent and consequent variables. The second is to devise behavioral objectives and to detail an intervention program. The third is to develop an ongoing objective evaluation of treatment. Ongoing evaluation follows from the definition of treatment objectives and implies that relative attainment or nonattainment of such objectives is included in the evaluation. The fourth often goes unacknowledged but is inherent in a comprehensive and detailed assessment process (Ciminero, Calhoun, and Adams, 1977; Mash and Terdal, 1976). The fourth objective involves increasing motivation for change via specification of problems, communication of understanding, and increasing expectancy of change. This goal is realized as the assessment proceeds and the patient learns to articulate his/her problems in behavioral terms and perceives that a detailed understanding of presenting problems is possible. This understanding is facilitated as the assessor is increasingly able to predict the patient's behavioral, cognitive, and affective reactions to various situations and events. Every attempt is made to totally involve the patient as an active participant in the assessment process. This involvement allows the patient to perceive himself/herself as actively and competently meeting assessment goals. Expectation for change tends to increase as the patient experiences success in confronting the demands of the assessment process, and as the patient experiences positive products of his/her collaboration with the assessor. This fourth objective of assessment is critical in treatment of OCD because the treatment procedures require a great expenditure of the patient's time and energy. The treatment of choice also frequently requires the patient to perform treatment tasks which are extremely difficult and uncomfortable, requiring high levels of motivation to complete.

Behavioral Assessment Techniques.   The primary tool of behavioral assessment is the focused clinical interview. This interview usually involves very careful and detailed questions about the patient's behavior, thoughts, images, sensations, and so on. Good examples of behavioral analysis via interview can be found in Wolpe (1973; 1976). Typically, the interview process extends over several appointment hours. The interview should include the history of the patient regarding: development, relationships with immediate and extended family, educational and vocational history, sexual development and history, and moral-religious development. A useful questionnaire to facilitate collection of personal history data is provided in Lazarus (1971). Within this historical context detailed questioning is done in order to define current problem(s) and to discover their antecedent and consequent controlling variables. Several techniques are often used to gather information during the assessment process. The Subjective Units of Discomfort Scale (SUDS) of patient-reported levels of anxiety scaled from 0 (absolute calm) to 100 (absolute panic) is useful in eliciting precise levels of anxiety to various antecedent and consequent events (Wolpe, 1958). Analysis of anxiety levels via the SUDS can then be used to construct hierarchies for flooding and to assess progress of treatment over time.

Logs in which the patient records incidents of target behaviors, along with their antecedent external and internal events and consequent events, can often be a valuable aid in behavioral analysis. Likewise, the charting and/or graphing of symptomatic behaviors can be useful. Charts can then be used as an ongoing assessment of treatment progress and to provide systematic feedback.

Although not often used in treatment without research objectives, behavioral avoidance tests can be an adjunct to the clinical behavioral assessment process. Hence specific behavioral tasks involving the discomforting condition or contaminating material are devised, with the patient asked to perform the tasks unless he feels more than mildly uncomfortable. The tasks are usually graded from lowest to highest SUDS levels. Assessment on behavioral tests includes whether or not the patient can perform the behaviors, ratings of anxiety by therapist and patient, latency of response measures, and can also involve physiological assessment (Epstein, 1976). Pretreatment testing then allows subsequent tests to assess progress in treatment. Initial testing also helps put verbal report data into a context of observable behavior which is usually sensitive to intervention gains.

Lazarus' (1976) multimodal strategy for assessment and treatment across a broad range of functioning can be a helpful way to organize behavioral assessment data for OCD. Assessment of the various dimensions of an individual's functioning, provides a good guideline for the assessment process which helps prevent the myopic focus a behavioral assessment can yield when multiple dimensions of a patient's functioning are not attended to.

Figure 1 is useful in developing a comprehensive assessment. It incorporates the various objectives and techniques of behavioral assessment reviewed previously.

Critical Discriminations for Behavioral Assessment. Behavioral analysis of OCD must discriminate among the various types of obsessive-compulsive behavior patterns. Because these patterns may respond differentially to specific interventions, it is important to discriminate among them so that the treatment plan is appropriate, i.e., is known to be the most effective with the particular pattern identified in the behavioral assessment.

Several distinct behavior patterns are observed clinically: washing, checking, slowing, cognitive compulsions, doubting and idiosyncratic compulsions like compulsive eating and gambling. Of the six, washing seems to be the most common, followed by checking and cognitive compulsions. Doubting and primary obsessive slowness have only recently been identified as discriminable and primary types of OCD. Idiosyncratic compulsive behaviors like compulsive eating and gam-

figure 1

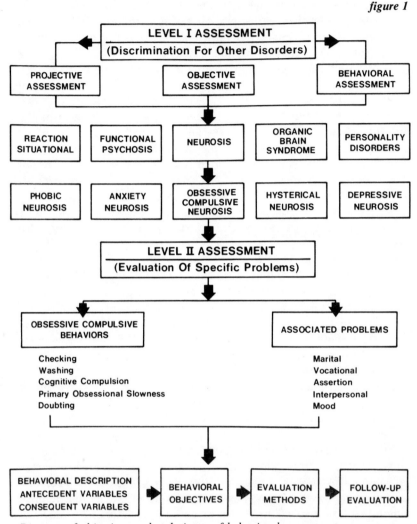

Diagram of objectives and techniques of behavioral assessment.

bling are probably more prevalent than washing, but they are not often identified as obsessive-compulsive phenomena. Obviously there is overlap with certain forms of addictive behavior and what DSM-II refers to as special symptoms, e.g., feeding disturbances, and so on. Idiosyncratic "compulsive behaviors" are included here under obsessive-compulsive phenomena because many of these behavior patterns seem to be functionally indistinguishable from other forms of obsessive-compulsive phenomena as revealed by a thorough behavioral analysis.

Where such behavior patterns are discovered to be functionally similar to the other obsessive-compulsive patterns, the most effective treatment may prove to be that derived from treatment of other types of OCD. Given this caveat, the other five types will receive primary focus.

Compulsive Washing

Washing stems from the subjective feeling of contamination and discomfort occurring with exposure to certain objects or thoughts, i.e., obsessions. The compulsive behavior usually consists of stereotyped patterns of excessive washing of body parts and/or other objects. Washing most frequently serves an anxiety-reducing function by allegedly removing the specific contaminant.

Compulsive Checking

Checking involves repetitious, stereotyped behaviors performed by the patient which *functionally serve to avoid* presumed aversive consequences the patient usually perceives as "catastrophic." Many times, though not always, checking is associated with anxiety-provoking thoughts or images. Some checking is rationally related to the obsessions. For example, preoccupation with having her home burglarized, and being attacked, was associated, in one patient, with checking all door and window locks and making the children's room appear as if the children were not there.

Slowing

Rachman (1974) has identified what he believes to be a primary form of OCD that is not a secondary consequence of other symptoms like washing and checking. It remains to be seen whether other clinicians will be able to verify his findings that primary obsessive slowness is a reliably discriminable clinical obsessive-compulsive entity like washing and checking. However, his findings are noteworthy and appropriate for review here.

The primary complaint of these patients is that simple tasks of living absorb a great amount of their time. For example, they spend hours getting ready for the day with normal morning activities of washing, brushing hair and teeth, shaving and dressing consuming most of the morning. They are "fanatically meticulous," each task being completed in a certain "correct" manner and all components of the task done in a prescribed order which does not vary from day to day. These activities are carried out with normal speed, i.e., they did not involve psychomotor retardation as is sometimes seen in profoundly depressed patients. Obsessive slowness seems to be a general dysfunction affecting most aspects of the patient's life.

Cognitive Compulsions

Some patients have cognitive rituals which occur in the presence of anxiety or discomfort-arousing external or internal stimuli such as thoughts, images, or feelings. For example, ritualized prayers may be repeated certain numbers of times at bedtime or when feeling anxious or guilty. Other common cognitive rituals involve repeating certain sequences of numbers, words, or phrases. Behavioral analysis reveals that these compulsions do not differ functionally from those involving motoric behavior. Both serve to reduce anxiety and discomfort. It often occurs that such cognitive compulsions accompany other obsessive-compulsive phenomena, so a treatment plan for them must often be articulated with other treatment strategies.

Doubting and Other Anxiety-Elevating Obsessions

Doubting is the label Hodgson and Rachman (1977) use to describe a kind of obsessional problem often seen in clinical practice associated with other obsessive-compulsive patterns. Sixty percent of their obsessive-compulsive sample obtained high scores on the "doubting" component of the Maudsley Obsessive-Compulsive Inventory. These persons are rarely sure they have performed a behavior properly, and thus often have serious doubts about the simplest of daily activities. Like obsessive slowness, the reliability of obsessive doubting as a discriminable clinical entity remains to be demonstrated and confirmed by independent researchers.

Other anxiety-elevating obsessions also need to be discriminated. The function of the obsession in raising or reducing anxiety is important for treatment planning, and therefore must be carefully analyzed during the behavioral assessment.

Behavioral Assessment: An Ongoing Process During Treatment

To accomplish the third goal of behavioral assessment, devising ongoing objective evaluation of treatment, the assessment process must be conceptualized as an ongoing process. When assessment is conducted in this manner, the therapist has regular objective data by which to evaluate the effectiveness of his interventions. Such data may be in the form of objectively defined behavioral events which are at least potentially verifiable. In this case the patient would typically report the frequency of specific overt behaviors or cognitions. Ongoing evaluation using these data would be based on the relative attainment versus nonattainment of these behaviorally defined tasks or events. Daily charts of targeted symptomatic behaviors either overt or covert, provide a good source of treatment evaluation data. Another form of data is the reported SUDS level of the patient at the beginning and end of each therapy session. Some therapists also record this every 10 or 15 minutes during therapy when they are doing flooding. These data provide an excellent ongoing evaluation of the efficacy of flooding for treating the emotional component of OCD. For a good example of this kind of evaluation and the results obtained in flooding treatment, see Foa and Chambless (1978). Periodic administrations of the Leyton or MOC Inventories may prove to be an effective tool for ongoing evaluation.

The development and use throughout therapy of an individually designed Shapiro Personal Questionnaire (Shapiro, 1961) provides an excellent method of idiographic assessment of specific behaviors or cognitions. This system involves the development of a symptom statement (e.g., I wash my hands more than 25 times per day), an improvement statement (e.g., I wash my hands less than 10 times a day), and a recovery statement (e.g., I wash my hands no more than 5 times per day). Each statement is paired with the other two alternatives and presented on 3" x 5" index cards. At periodic intervals during therapy and follow-up the patient is asked to sort through the various cards (3 cards per problem) and select in a forced choice manner the statement which best describes his condition. These responses are quantifiable, and provide a relatively reliable, though subjective, index to treatment efficacy. This technique appears to be particularly useful in tracking obsessive behavior which is usually extremely idiosyncratic. It should be used cautiously in the absence of more observable indices of change.

Although this section has focused primarily on behavioral assessment of specific problems associated with OCD, it would be an error to limit initial assessment only to these. In keeping with a comprehensive assessment approach, it would generally be useful to explore other major areas of functioning to include social behavior such as assertion (Alberti and Emmons, 1970; Eisler, 1976), cognitive behavior (Meichenbaum, 1977), social competence and problem-solving behavior (Goldfried and D'Zurilla, 1969), interpersonal anxiety (Watson and Friend, 1976), phobic behavior (Hersen, 1973), and marital adjustment (Weiss and Margolin, 1977). Where specific problems are identified in these modalities, assessment should continue throughout treatment and follow-up. Little is presently known about the effect of behavioral treatments of OCD on these or other problems. Careful ongoing evaluation will allow the therapist to modify treatment goals as problems emerge or decrease in other areas of the patient's adjustment. Comprehensive treatment may demand intervention for additional problems which are not ameliorated with specific intervention focused on the OCD, per se.

The ongoing process of behavioral assessment to evaluate treatment effectiveness serves different functions. It gives constant feedback on treatment efficacy. If treatment is not effective, it becomes apparent immediately. Therapist and patient can then do more assessment and problem-solving to revise the treatment plan accordingly. Thus, the ongoing assessment helps therapist and patient use their time and energy efficiently. Frequently, data from other modalities of ongoing assessment will give clues as to how to revise the treatment plan. An often unacknowledged function of ongoing assessment is its motivational effect. Goal attainment can be a highly reinforcing phenomena. Graphic displays of the reduction of symptomatic behavior and/or the increase of adaptive behaviors can be an important source of client motivation to work in the therapeutic process.

KNOWN TREATMENT PROCEDURES

Three main treatment approaches have been reported: psychodynamically oriented psychotherapy, psychosurgery, and behaviorally oriented treatment. Psychodynamically oriented psychotherapy and psychosurgery will be briefly reviewed prior to a more thorough examination of behavioral treatment procedures.

Psychodynamically Oriented Psychotherapy

Treatments derived from the psychodynamic model have been relatively unsuccessful. Yates (1970) reviewed 11 studies which employed psychodynamically oriented psychotherapy either alone or in conjunction with medical treatments. Percent cured or much improved ranged from 25–70 percent, with most studies reporting a rate of approximately 50 percent. Generally these studies were poorly controlled retrospective investigations which relied heavily on patient report of improvement. Although these studies are characterized by little experimental rigor, they cast considerable doubt on the utility of psychodynamic formulations to produce efficacious treatments for OCD.

Psychosurgery

Psychosurgery, specifically the leucotomy procedure, has until recently not enjoyed success rates any different from traditional psychosocial intervention strategies. Yates (1970) reviewed the literature on leucotomy treatment for obsessive-compulsives and found "percent cured" or "much improved" to range from 51–62. A recent, large outcome study employing a stereotoxic leucotomy procedure has shown more promising results (Mitchell-Heggs, Kelly, and Richardson, 1976). These investigators report 24 of 27 obsessional patients treated were clinically improved and 18 were either symptom-free or much improved. Though this was strictly a clinical outcome study with no control or comparison treatment groups, multiple modes of assessment were employed and findings were consistent across modes. It is noteworthy that all of these patients were intractable to other forms of treatment. Surgery was considered only as a last resort following various psychotherapeutic interventions; in some cases previous therapy was behavioral in nature. Thus it is possible that high success rates were achieved despite a selection bias operating to load the population with the most severe and intractable cases.

Behavioral Treatments

Numerous behavioral techniques have been employed to treat obsessive-compulsive patterns of adjustment. In contrast to other treatment procedures, behavioral treatments appear promising.

Systematic Desensitization. Systematic desensitization (Wolpe, 1958) is a procedure whereby anxiety-eliciting situations are presented to the patient in graded order from least to most anxiety-arousing. The presentation may be in vivo or in imagination. During presentation of these graded situations an anxiety-inhibiting competing state is developed in the patient. For treatment of OCD, the anxiety-inhibiting state is usually induced using some form of progressive relaxation (Jacobson, 1938), and the graded anxiety arousal situations are usually presented in imagination.

Table 1 presents a summary of five studies which employed systematic desensitization. In four of five (Wickramasekera, 1970 [7]; Gentry, 1973 [8.5]; McGlynn and Linder, 1971 [12]; Tanner, 1971 [13]) single case reports, this intervention technique was reportedly effective in reducing both obsessions and compulsive behavior. In the remaining report, two cases of long-standing obsessional behavior did not re-

Table 1. Review of studies using systematic desensitization in treatment of obsessive/compulsive behavior

Treatment Modality	Type of Investigation	DQR	Targets	Follow-up/Efficacy
Walton and Mather (1964)	Single-subject	6.0	Obsessions: S_1: Obsessional sexual thoughts S_2: Claustrophobia and concern with being buried alive (Both S_1 and S_2 were long-standing cases)	At termination significant decrease in anxiety but not obsession
Wickramasekera (1970)	Single-subject	7.0	Obsessive sexual thoughts and urges to check on wife's fidelity	Obsessions controlled at 6-month follow-up
Gentry (1970)	Single-subject	8.5	Obsessional fear of breast cancer with associated checking ritual	Obsessions controlled at one-year follow-up
McGlynn and Linder (1971)	Single-subject	12.0	Compulsive hand-washing in presence of wooden matches	Compulsive behavior controlled at one-year follow-up
Tanner (1971)	Single-subject	13.0	Multiple compulsive behaviors (doubting manias and checking behavior)	Compulsions controlled at 10-month follow-up

spond to systematic desensitization (Walton and Mather, 1964 [6]). Walton and Mather suggested these results support their theoretical speculations in that obsessions of a long-standing nature may no longer be primarily associated with the conditioned autonomic drive, but instead to other stimuli. In the Tanner study (1971), and in the McGlynn and Linder study (1971), systematic desensitization was effective with onset of the problem dating four years and ten years, respectively. These results certainly challenge the acute versus chronic stage notions of Walton and Mather. These results also suggest that systematic desensitization may be useful with some obsessive-compulsive patients. Systematic desensitization has not received much research attention with OCD, probably largely due to the Walton and Mather hypothesis. More rigorous research is indicated, especially in treatment of specific types of OCD.

Modeling.   Research on the use of modeling in the treatment of OCD includes two distinct types of techniques. The technique which has received the most attention is participant modeling. This involves the use of a hierarchy of stimuli which elicit distress (e.g., fear of contamination). Starting at the lowest hierarchy item (least anxiety), the therapist demonstrates exposure. The patient then confronts the stimulus situation until able to complete the sequence without assistance. Subsequent to observation and successful confrontation at the lowest anxiety situation, the next highest item on the hierarchy is approached and this pattern continues until the hierarchy is completed. Following each session, the patient is encouraged not to perform the compulsive behavior (e.g., washing, checking, and so on). The second technique, passive modeling, involves the observation of the therapist confronting the various stimuli in a graduated fashion and involves response prevention instruction, but it does not involve direct exposure of the patient to the various stimuli.

The research on these techniques has been conducted exclusively by Rachman and his associates in a series of investigations (Rachman, Hodgson, and Marzillier, 1970 [9.5]; Rachman, Hodgson, and Marks, 1971 [21.5]; Hodgson, Rachman, and Marks, 1972 [15.5]; Rachman, Marks, and Hodgson, 1973 [15.5]; Roper, Rachman, and Marks, 1975 [22.5]). The studies are reviewed in Table 2. These studies are summarized with two-year follow-up in Marks, Hodgson, and Rachman (1975).

The first report (Rachman et al., 1970) in this series involved a case study of successful participant modeling treatment of a patient with a relatively severe washing ritual. Follow-up evaluation at six months supported treatment efficacy.

Table 2. Review of studies using modeling or variations thereof in treatment of obsessive/compulsive behavior

Treatment Modality	Type of Investigation	DQR	Targets	Follow-up/Efficacy
Modeling (included response prevention) Rachman et al. (1970)	Single-subject	9.5	Obsession of contamination with washing rituals	Significant improvement at 6-month follow-up
Modeling (included response prevention) Rachman et al. (1971)	Repeated measures design with five subjects (relaxation control versus modeling)	21.5	Obsessional and compulsive behavior	4 of 5 much improved at six months' follow-up
Modeling plus flooding (included response prevention) Hodgson et al. (1972)	Repeated measures design with five subjects (relaxation control versus modeling plus flooding)	15.5	Obsessional and compulsive behavior	4 of 5 much improved at six-month follow-up
Modeling plus flooding (included response prevention) Rachman et al. (1973)	Repeated measures design with five subjects (relaxation control versus modeling plus flooding)	15.5	Obsessional and compulsive behavior	3 of 5 much improved; 1 improved at 6-month follow-up
Modeling (passive and participant) Roper et al. (1975)	Repeated measures design with three treatment conditions (passive modeling, participant modeling and placebo relaxation control)	22.5	Obsessional and compulsive behavior	4 of 10 much improved; 4 improved and 2 unchanged at 6-month follow-up

The second report (Rachman et al., 1971) involved a comparison of flooding with participant modeling. Flooding differed from modeling in two primary respects: it did not involve an observational component and it used a rapid exposure (i.e., therapy started at the high anxiety end of hierarchy) to the stimulus situations rather than graduated exposure used in modeling. Both techniques involved direct exposure to anxiety-eliciting situations and both involved response prevention instructions. Each patient was randomly assigned to the two treatment conditions. Prior to either flooding or modeling, each group received a control treatment, progressive relaxation. Order effects were not controlled. Results suggested modeling and flooding were superior to controls. Modeling significantly differed from controls on independent assessor and patient ratings. Flooding differed from the relaxation control condition on these same types of measures and also on a behavioral avoidance measure. Only one difference emerged between the modeling and flooding treatments, with the modeling group rating themselves as significantly less anxious after treatment. At six months' follow-up (Hodgson et al., 1972), four individuals who received modeling were rated as much improved, leaving one individual who received modeling treatment and three individuals who received flooding as evidencing no improvement.

The third report (Hodgson et al., 1972) in this series involved the assignment of five additional obsessive-compulsive patients to a treatment package combining flooding and participant modeling. This package included an observational component, rapid and direct exposure to the anxiety-eliciting stimulus, and response prevention instructions. As in the second report, each of the five patients was exposed to the relaxation control treatment. A number of comparisons were made utilizing the subjects reported in the second report. The combined treatment was found to be more effective than participant modeling at termination of therapy on patient ratings and two subscales of the Leyton Inventory. The combined treatment was more effective than flooding on patient ratings, the avoidance test, the interference subtest of the Leyton Inventory, and on an independent assessor rating of depression. All patients (N = 15) utilized in this and the second report, were combined to form a modeling and/or flooding group. This group was compared to the relaxation control condition, and significantly greater therapeutic changes were observed on patient and independent assessor ratings, two subscales of the Leyton Inventory, the behavioral avoidance test, and four attitude dimensions. At the end of six-month follow-up, four of five patients who received modeling and flooding were rated much improved. Only one patient was rated as not improved.

The fourth report (Rachman, et al., 1973) in this series involved a second examination of the flooding plus modeling treatment with five obsessive-compulsive patients. Analysis did not find a difference among flooding, modeling, and modeling plus flooding; the results reported in the previous study suggesting a superiority of the combined package were not supported. Significantly greater therapeutic changes were observed when the combined treatment (N = 5) was compared with the relaxation control condition (N = 15). These differences were found on patient and independent assessor ratings, the Leyton Inventory, and the avoidance test. At six months' follow-up three patients were rated much improved and one patient each was rated improved and not improved. At six months' follow-up, combining the results of the previous report, seven of ten patients who had received modeling plus flooding were rated as much improved.

In the last study in this series, Roper et al., 1975, compared participant modeling with passive modeling (observation but no direct exposure to anxiety-eliciting stimuli). Patients randomly received passive modeling followed by participant modeling (N = 5) or modeled relaxation followed by participant modeling (N = 5). Passive modeling was found to differ significantly from the relaxation control on patient ratings, the avoidance test, and the interference subtest of the Leyton Inventory. Presentation of results was not clear and hence interpretation is rendered difficult. The authors assert, however, that participant modeling again produced therapeutic change and that these changes exceeded those due to passive modeling. At six months' follow-up, looking at all ten subjects, four were rated much improved, four were rated improved, and two were rated unchanged.

To summarize this series of reports, 20 patients received flooding, modeling, or modeling plus flooding. Ten additional patients received passive plus participant modeling (N = 5) or relaxation modeled plus participant modeling (N = 5). For the original 20 patients, improvement rates at two years' follow-up were: 14 much improved, 1 improved and 5 unchanged. The one improved patient subsequently received further treatment, and at three years' follow-up was symptom-free. Only one patient showed spontaneous improvement not related to any specific intervention. It is noteworthy that three successfully treated cases required booster sessions during the period of follow-up.

A number of tentative conclusions can be drawn from this series of studies: (a) passive modeling, participant modeling, flooding plus modeling, and flooding appear more effective than progressive relaxation, although order effects have not been controlled; (b) participant modeling may be more effective than passive modeling; (c) although no major differences have been found between modeling and flooding, if differences are isolated the effects of the observation condition and the speed of exposure condition would need to be separated out, as these two variables differentiate modeling and flooding; (d) the combination of modeling and flooding does not result in more efficacious treatment than either alone; (e) the addition of modeling to flooding does not increase therapeutic efficacy; and (f) there do not appear to be major differences between graduated and rapid exposure to anxiety-eliciting stimuli.

Several issues demand attention. It certainly appears that exposure to anxiety-eliciting stimuli is a necessary component to successful treatment. The role of response prevention, however, is not fully understood. Due to the small number of available subjects, questions about order effects and placebo factors have not been specifically addressed. A need exists for greater experimental rigor, and due to the small number of available subjects, more use of controlled experimental case methodology (Hersen and Barlow, 1976) to identify salient treatment variables.

Flooding. Flooding has been increasingly employed as a treatment for OCD since the early 1970s. Though there are several variations in how the procedure is applied, typically the patient is exposed, either in vivo or in imagination, to high anxiety arousing stimuli. The exposure is continuous and prolonged until there is a reported diminution of anxiety to a relatively comfortable level. Provision for prolonged exposure requires abandoning the typical 50–60 minute therapy hour for therapy sessions of 2 hours or longer.

Table 3 presents seven studies (Rachman et al., 1971 [21.5]; Hodgson, Rachman, and Marks, 1972 [15.5]; Rachman, Marks, and Hodgson, 1973 [15.5]; Boulougouris and Bassiakos, 1973 [9.5]; Rainey, 1972 [8.5]; Hersen, 1968 [1.5]; Foa and Goldstein, 1978 [1.5]), in which flooding was employed. In each study the effects of flooding alone are contaminated with response prevention (subjects were encouraged not to perform compulsive behaviors or were supervised to prevent such behavior). In two studies (Hodgson et al., 1972; Rachman et al., 1973), modeling and flooding are contaminated.

In addition to the series of studies done at the Maudsely in London (reviewed in the modeling section), one other major outcome study with flooding has been reported. Foa and Goldstein (1978) treated 21 obsessive-compulsives with the combination of in vivo exposure plus response prevention. Multiple types of assessment, including independent assessor measures, showed two-thirds of the patients asymptomatic after treatment and follow-up of three months to three years.

Table 3. Review of studies using flooding or variations thereof in treatment of obsessive/compulsive behavior

Treatment Modality	Type of Investigation	DQR	Targets	Follow-up/Efficacy
Flooding (included response prevention) Rachman et al. (1971)	Repeated measures design with 5 subjects (relaxation control versus modeling)	21.5	Obsessional and compulsive behavior	2 of 5 much improved at 6-month follow-up
Flooding plus modeling (included response prevention) Hodgson et al. (1972)	Repeated measures design with 5 subjects (relaxation control versus flooding plus modeling)	15.5	Obsessional and compulsive behavior	4 of 5 much improved at 6-month follow-up
Flooding plus modeling (included response prevention) Rachman et al. (1973)	Repeated measures design (flooding plus modeling, N = 5, versus relaxation control)	15.5	Obsessional and compulsive behavior	3 of 5 much improved; 1 improved at 6-month follow-up
Flooding (included response prevention) Boulougouris and Bassiakos (1973)	Single-subject	9.5	S_1: Compulsive washing S_2: Compulsive washing S_3: Ritual behavior	With each case, compulsions controlled at termination of therapy
Flooding (included response prevention) Rainey (1972)	Single-subject	8.5	Obsessional thought of contamination with washing ritual	Obsessions and compulsive behaviors controlled at 18-month follow-up
Flooding (included response prevention) Hersen (1968)	Single-subject	1.5	Ritual behavior and school avoidance	Controlled at 6-month follow-up
Flooding (included response prevention) Foa and Goldstein (1978)	Repeated measures within subject design (N = 21)	1.5	Obsessional and compulsive behavior	Two-thirds asymptomatic at 3-month to 3-year follow-up

Examination of published studies using direct exposure (flooding, flooding plus modeling, and participant modeling) plus response prevention resulted in 42 of 56 cases being rated improved or much improved with lengthy follow-up intervals. This is a successful treatment rate of 75 percent which compares favorably with nonbehaviorally oriented psychotherapy (Grimshaw, 1965). Flooding and modeling outcome data were combined because they tend to share many treatment components.

Although there are some potentially important theoretical issues involved in differences between flooding and participant modeling (e.g., role if any, of vicarious extinction in treatment efficacy) clinical differences between flooding and participant modeling are perhaps more apparent than real. Differences may be due as much to reified conceptualization of them as "treatments" as based on *actual* procedural differences. *Both* procedures often involve modeling and both involve exposure to contaminating materials. Participant modeling may only critically differ from flooding in the length of time the model exposes himself to the stimuli before the patient is exposed. The central point here is that most therapists, while doing flooding in vivo, pickup, handle, spread, open, apply, and so on, the contamination stimuli to the patient (Foa and Goldstein, 1978). In doing this the therapist *models* exposure before the patient is exposed. Thus, both "flooding" and "modeling" involve essentially the same components. For clinical purposes such fine line distinctions between these treatments may be irrelevant. Learning theorists might chose to deal with these fine theoretical differences, while clinicians might focus on discovering the impact of response prevention on the efficacy of "exposure" treatment.

Response Prevention. Response prevention is just what the term implies: prohibiting the compulsive response. However, in practice the compulsive response is rarely actually prevented. Rather, in most studies patients are *encouraged* to not perform compulsive rituals. When treatment is conducted in an inpatient setting, staff can observe to determine if the patient is not performing ritual behavior. In outpatient settings, more supervision may be necessary to produce ritual response prevention. Foa and her colleagues (Foa and Goldstein, 1978) involve a family member in more formal supervision and observation during response prevention when the patient stays at home.

Response prevention has been examined separately in three studies (Meyer, 1966 [5.5]; Mills, Agras, Barlow, and Mills, 1973 [15]; Rachman, DeSilva, and Roper 1976 [18]). Table 4 presents these results. In the Meyer study (1966), two cases were moderately improved at two-year follow-up. In a series of single-case experiments, Mills et al. (1973)

Table 4. *Review of studies using response prevention to treat obsessive/compulsive behaviors*

Treatment Modality	Type of Investigation	DQR	Targets	Follow-up/Efficacy
Meyer (1966)	Single-subject (discussion of two cases)	5.5	Compulsive behavior	Moderate improvement in 2 cases at 2-year follow-up
Mills et al. (1973)	Single-subject (replication across five cases)	15.0	4Ss: Compulsive hand-washing 1S: Night-time ritual behavior	Compulsive behavior controlled in 4 of 5 patients at termination

demonstrated that the effectiveness of response prevention could not be attributed to placebo factors, instructions alone, or to exposure alone. They further noted that effectiveness of response prevention did not demand the arousal of high levels of anxiety.

Rachman, DeSilva, and Roper (1976) demonstrated the efficacy of response prevention in reducing anxiety/discomfort and the strength of compulsive urges during a three-hour response prevention period. It is interesting to note that the greatest reduction in both discomfort and compulsive urges occurred within one hour and there was little sign of displaced ritual activity.

Aversive Procedures.   Table 5 presents seven studies (Yen, 1971 [8]; Kraft, 1970 [1.5]; Seager, 1970 [1.5]; Bass, 1973 [9.5]; Kenny, Solyom, and Solyom, 1973 [8.0]; O'Brien and Raynes, 1973 [13.5]; Kenny et al., 1978 [21.5] which have employed an aversive paradigm in reducing such behaviors as compulsive checking behavior, shoplifting, gambling, compulsive talking, and an obsession of self-injury. Aversive stimuli have included faradic stimulation, scheduling of inconvenient activities contingent on response performance, audio-tape replay of one's own description of obsessional ideation, flick of a rubber band on the wrist, and so on. Although these data are only suggestive, each of the six case studies suggest some clinical utility associated with the various punishment techniques.

Only one minimally well-controlled study (Kenny et al., 1978) of the impact of punishment on obsessive behavior was reported. This study examined the relative efficacy of faradic disruption and a waiting list control condition. The six patients receiving faradic disruption were asked to reproduce obsessive ideation or imagery. A painful electric shock was then administered until they signalled termination of the obsession. Following treatment, four patients considered themselves greatly improved and one moderately improved. Five of six patients receiving faradic disruption improved while no patient in the control condition reported improvement. This study suggests this technique's potential for reducing obsessional behavior; however, adequate controls were not present to attribute treatment effects exclusively to faradic disruption.

Review of these studies on punishment of obsessive-compulsive behaviors leaves many questions unanswered. Foremost is whether changes observed with relatively uncontrolled single case investigations and the Kenny et al., (1978) investigation can be accounted for by variables other than punishment. If this question is addressed experimentally and answered negatively, further research should address the patient and procedural variables which impact on the efficacy of

Table 5. *Review of studies using aversive procedures to treat obsessive/compulsive behaviors*

Treatment Modality	Type of Investigation	DQR	Targets	Follow-up/Efficacy
Punishment (scheduling inconvenient activities contingent on response) and extinction Yen (1971)	Single-subject	8.0	Compulsive checking behavior	Compulsive behavior controlled at 12-week follow-up
Punishment (elastic band) Bass (1973)	Single-subject	9.5	Obsessions	Improvement with specific obsession
Punishment (send check to store for amount of stolen article) and extinction Kraft (1970)	Single-subject	1.5	Compulsive shoplifting	No shoplifting at 1-year follow-up
Aversion therapy Seager (1970)	Single-subject (14 cases presented)	1.5	Compulsive gambling	5 of 14 not gambling at 1-year follow-up
Faradic disruption Kenny et al. (1973)	Single-subject (5 cases presented)	8.0	Obsessional-compulsive behavior	3 of 5 greatly improved; 1 substantial improvement at average of 4.8-month follow-up
Punishment (listening to own voice) and extinction O'Brien and Raynes (1973)	Single-subject (2 cases presented)	13.5	S₁: Obsessions of self-injury S₂: Compulsive talking	Both controlled at 18-month and 20-month follow-up
Faradic disruption Kenny et al. (1978)	Repeated measures design with 10 subjects (Faradic disruption versus waiting list control)	21.5	Obsessive-compulsive behavior	5 of 6 moderately or greatly improved at termination; data inconclusive at follow-up

punishment procedures for reducing obsessive-compulsive features. A number of related questions arise with examination of a procedurely similar technique, thought-stopping.

Thought-stopping. Seven studies (Stern, 1970 [1.0]; Yamagami, 1971 [7.0]; Kumar and Wilkinson, 1971 [9.0]; Campbell, 1973 [11.5]; Stern, Lipsedge, and Marks, 1973 [19.5]; Hachman and McLean, 1975 [21.0]; Emmelkamp and Kwee, 1977 [20.5]) have reported the use of thought-stopping with obsessional thinking. The thought-stopping technique is originally attributed to Bain (1928), but seems to have been introduced to behavior therapists by Taylor in a personal communication to Wolpe (1973). It involves scheduling the presentation of an aversive event contingent on the appearance of the undesired obsessional behavior. While relaxed with eyes closed, the individual is instructed to self-verbalize his obsessional thought and signal its occurrence. This signal is immediately followed by administration of an aversive stimulus. The typical procedure involves the therapist shouting "stop" and/or introducing a loud noise. After repeated trials the subject is instructed to self-present the aversive stimulus (shouting stop) and subsequently present the aversive stimulus subvocally (thinking stop), contingent on the occurrence of the maladaptive thought. Variations of this technique have included using high intensity noises (e.g., buzzer) or electric shock as the aversive stimulus. The imagination of a reinforcing scene following successful interruption of the obsession has also been employed as a variant to the typical procedure.

An examination of outcome studies utilizing this technique with obsessional behavior reveals most investigations have been poorly controlled single case studies. Although these case studies generally support the clinical efficacy of thought-stopping, adequate controls were not present to unequivocally attribute treatment effects to the use of this technique. Three rudimentary but better controlled investigations raised questions about the clinical efficacy of thought stopping.

Stern et al. (1973) employed a crossover design with 11 subjects who alternately received thought-stopping for obsessional thoughts or thought-stopping for neutral thoughts. There was no convincing evidence that thought-stopping was more effective than the control treatment. Alternating the control condition with thought-stopping resulted in four subjects rated as markedly improved and three subjects rated as slightly improved at termination of therapy (see Table 6).

Emmelkamp and Gwan Kwee (1977) likewise found no substantial difference in effectiveness when thought-stopping was alternated with prolonged exposure of obsessive thoughts. Prolonged exposure involved therapist presentation of obsessive ideation and associated

Table 6. *Review of studies using thought-stopping in the treatment of obsessive/compulsive behavior*

Treatment Modality	Type of Investigation	DQR	Targets	Follow-up/Efficacy
Stern (1970)	Single-subject	1.0	Doubting manias	Obsessions controlled at termination of treatment
Yamagami (1972)	Single-subject	7.0	Obsessive counting, color naming, etc.	Obsessions controlled at 7-month follow-up
Kumar and Wilkinson (1971)	Single-subject (4 case presentations)	9.0	S_1: Obsessions of heart attacks, public places, nocturnal enuresis S_2: Obsessions of cancer and disease S_3: Obsessions of cancer and other illnesses S_4: Death	With each case, obsessions controlled at 12-month follow-up
Cambell (1973)	Single-subject	11.5	Obsessions about deceased sister	Obsessions controlled at 3-year follow-up

Table 6. *(Continued)*

Treatment Modality	Type of Investigation	DQR	Targets	Follow-up/Efficacy
Stern et al. (1973)	Crossover design with all subjects (N = 11) receiving thought-stopping with obsessions and with control thoughts	19.5	Multiple obsessions	At termination of treatment, 4 markedly improved; 3 slight improvement; 4 no change (thought-stopping not more effective than control condition)
Emmelkamp and Gwan Kee (1977)	Single-subject (5 cases)	20.5	Obsessional behaviors	2 much improved; 1 moderate improvement; 1 unsuccessful at termination
Hackman and McLean (1974)	Crossover design (all subjects received other flooding followed by thought-stopping or vice versa) (N = 10)	21.0	Obsessive-compulsive behavior	No differences between treatment (no individual data reported)

antecedents via imagery, with the request that the client not avoid imagining the scenes in imagery. Although neither treatment appeared superior, the combination of treatments resulted in at least moderate improvement in three of five subjects.

Hackmann and McLean (1975) employed a crossover design in which ten obsessive-compulsive patients received a randomly determined sequence of either thought-stopping then flooding, or vice versa. No data were presented which suggested a marked superiority of either treatment. No firm conclusions could be derived from this study, as the two principle treatments were confounded with other treatment components.

Although clinicians have attributed therapeutic changes to the use of the thought-stopping technique, no data currently exist which demonstrate its superiority over placebo factors or nonspecific therapeutic factors. Furthermore, no research has examined the various components of this procedure to isolate variables which might contribute to its therapeutic usefulness. At least three variables demand further investigation. These include examination of the impact of interruption of obsessions by nonaversive techniques, the role of aversive stimuli, and the impact of repeated exposure to the obsessional ideation.

Additional Techniques.   A number of additional techniques have been reported, including several single case studies which have employed multiple behavioral techniques (Melamed and Siegel, 1975 [9.0]; Hallam, 1974 [9.5]; Mather, 1970 [0.5]), and several which have combined behavioral techniques with more traditional approaches (Gullick and Blanchard, 1973 [8.0]; Lambley, 1974 [1.0]; Hersen, 1970 [1.5]). Stern and Marks (1973) [4.5] reported a case study in which intractable (not responsive to response prevention or flooding) obsessive-compulsive behaviors were successfully treated using marital contracting. Follow-up at one year suggested that treatment efficacy was maintained in spite of increasing social stress.

Meyer (1973) [1.5] treated two patients with delay therapy. Prior to performance of the compulsive behavior, the subject was instructed to call the therapist and contract for a specified time that he/she could resist the behavior. During the phone calls the therapist was supportive and reinforced any previously successful delays. The subject was also instructed to call a second time at completion of the contract, if the impulse still existed, to discuss initiation of a new delay contract. Delays were gradually increased. A case of obsessional thinking about hospitalization, and a compulsive eater were effectively treated with improvement maintained at follow-up intervals of two years and seven months, respectively.

Weiner (1967) [1.5] successfully treated a ritual behavior with a response substitution technique whereby the positive aspects of the ritual were accomplished by the performance of less disruptive behavior. Improvement was maintained at seven-month follow-up.

In an interesting and significant single-case study, Daitzman (1978) [8.5] successfully treated a severe OCD using behavioral techniques within a reattribution model. Behavioral techniques included thought-stopping, thought-stopping plus EMG feedback, thought-stopping with bogus EMG feedback, and various relaxation procedures. Thought-stopping involved a punishment condition (i.e., flick of rubber band on wrist) and a substitution technique, introducing another thought following interruption of obsessional thinking. By providing false EMG feedback contingent on the use of the thought-stopping procedure, the patient reduced the frequency of obsessive thoughts and EMG responding to levels comparable to the bogus feedback. Data suggested the patient acquired a more internally oriented locus of control which facilitated a belief that he could control his obsessive-compulsive behaviors. This change in cognitive set seemed to be a critical treatment variable, one which has not received sufficient attention with behavioral treatments of OCD.

Rabavilas, Boulougouris, and Stefanis (1977) [9.0] employed a technique which involved negative practice with four compulsive checkers. These authors suggested that completion of a ritual may acquire reinforcing properties and be construed as a safety signal (Gray, 1971), i.e., an arbitrary number of checks have been bestowed with reinforcement value because it seems to successfully avoid undesired consequences of not checking. Although reinforcement from this model may be associated with checking per se, the safety signal, a subjectively defined number of checks, is also a potent reinforcer which tends to maintain the compulsive behaviors. The safety signal derives its reinforcement value via repeated pairings with successful avoidance. From this model, performance of the compulsive behavior beyond the safety signal would cease to be reinforcing, and hence would provide a series of nonreinforced trials.

The patients in this study were requested to perform the checking behavior at least 50 times once the ritual was initiated. Interestingly, none of the patients consistently performed the technique but all evidenced substantial decreases in the frequency of the compulsive behavior. The patients reported that they lost interest in checking, and hence there was no purpose in performing the negative practice technique. The instructions associated with the technique were characterized by a paradoxical flavor (Frankl, 1960), i.e., perform the ritual as often as you want but make sure that once you initiate the checking continue at least 50 trials. To not perform the techniques once the ritual behavior was initiated would constitute a clear violation of the therapy contract. To perform the behavior repeatedly was likely perceived as annoying and/or uncomfortable. One resolution of this dilemma for the patient was to not initiate the checking; this behavior successfully avoided a violation of the therapeutic contract while also avoiding the discomfort of performing the additional checking.

These results on the outcome of behavior therapy with obsessive-compulsives may be summarized as follows: (a) an empirical data base is rapidly accumulating to support the use of behavioral techniques with OCD; (b) the package of flooding plus response prevention appears to be the most effective technique to date for treatment of compulsive behaviors (e.g., washing and checking); (c) less data is available concerning the treatment of obsessional behavior (e.g., cognitive compulsions and doubting) and, in fact, very little attention has been directed to examining the role of cognitive variables in the assessment or treatment of OCD; (d) a large variety of techniques, even some control procedures, have been effective with some cases of OCD.

CLINICAL PRESCRIPTION

Although several different behavioral approaches have shown effectiveness in treating OCD, it is clear that flooding or exposure with response prevention has been applied most extensively and studied most thoroughly. This research, including cross-cultural replication, has consistently shown the efficacy of this treatment package. Therefore, flooding plus response prevention should presently be considered the treatment of choice with compulsive behaviors (e.g., washing and checking). The relative contribution of response prevention to this package remains an open question, awaiting answers from future research.

Given that flooding plus response prevention seems the treatment of choice for compulsive disorders, an examination of how this package is applied clinically will follow. The treatment of an OCD can be divided into four components: (1) identification of OCD, (2) behavioral analysis, (3) intervention, (4) follow-up or follow-up plus treatment for other concurrent problems. Each component shall be discussed in detail.

Identification of Obsessive-Compulsive Disorder

The first step in treatment involves broad-band assessment to discriminate OCD from other forms of psychopathology. Typically some battery of objective or objective plus projective tests are used to accomplish this, along with a clinical interview. The reader should refer to the section on assessment for details of which tests are more valuable for accomplishing certain assessment goals. The goal of the identification phase is to discriminate the OCD from other types of psychopathology. When this goal is accomplished, the clinician can proceed with confidence to the next stages of treatment with the working assumption that he is treating an OCD and not something else.

Behavioral Analysis

During this stage the clinician focuses on the idiosyncrasies of the disorder. He determines what are the components of the disorder. He discovers if the individual has rituals and exactly what the rituals are, i.e., washing, checking, and so on, and what other avoidance behaviors the individual exhibits. He also examines the cognitive behavior of the client to determine the presence or absence of obsessional behavior. Likewise, he should question the patient about behaviors which are consistent with Rachman's (1974) formulation of primary obsessive slowness. He usually teaches the Subjective Units of Discomfort Scale (SUDS) (Wolpe, 1958) to help the patient precisely communicate the intensity of his feelings. Using a 0 to 100 rating scale, a hierarchy of situations, events, or thoughts is constructed that produces least (0) to most (100) discomfort, and which would elicit anxiety or avoidance. At this point it would be determined if discomfort decreases or increases and by how much with performance of the obsessive or compulsive behavior. Included in this determination of stimuli which elicit the obsessive-compulsive behavior is an examination of possible internal states, like depression or anger, which may elicit this behavior. Another aspect of the analysis is determining what consequences other than anxiety reduction may perpetuate the behavior, particularly interpersonal reactions. Interpersonal reactions are significant as obsessive-compulsive-like behaviors have been observed in which the main reinforcement is interpersonal control rather than anxiety reduction. The behavioral analysis should discover, in addition, any other problems which may be contributing to, be a result of, or are independent of the OCD but nonetheless require interventions. Especially with severe OCD, it is unusual not to discover other problems. Common associated problems are: disturbed interpersonal relationships, especially marriage and family relationships, subassertive behavior, mood disturbances (anger and depression), preoccupation with unusual thoughts or ideas, sexual dysfunction, vocational dysfunction or dissatisfaction, and phobias independent of the OCD.

The goal of the behavioral analysis is fourfold (see section on behavioral assessment). As the analysis proceeds and detailed information from which the treatment program and evaluation procedures can be derived are collected, the fourth goal of behavioral assessment looms more important. The fourth goal is more subtle and sometimes overlooked. It is to stimulate or increase motivation for treatment. This motivation increases as the patient realizes the clinician listens and understands, and after the behavioral analysis, can predict with great accuracy how the patient's problems relate to behavior in various situations. As this detailed understanding develops, the patient's trust level in the therapist increases and his expectation of change also increases. Creating an optimum level of motivation is extremely important because of the difficult and uncomfortable tasks required of the patient in the exposure and response prevention phases of intervention.

The behavioral analysis usually takes 5–10 hours and is often scheduled in 2-hour sessions. Toward the end of this period the patient's commitment to treatment must be ascertained. This must be done after the major specific components of the flooding and response prevention treatment package have been identified and shared with the patient. Thus, the patient *must* be fully informed of the essential details of treatment and the rationale for it. Only after the patient has this information can he/she consent to a treatment package which requires the experience of discomfort and the expenditure of a great deal of effort and energy. If the patient agrees to participate in the recommended treatment, then the therapist, with the patient's cooperation, must assess whether the patient is capable of participating in treatment while an outpatient or whether hospitalization is necessary. The critical issue here is whether the patient can manage exposing himself to antecedent stimuli (e.g., contaminants) at home each day while voluntarily inhibiting avoidance and ritualistic behavior (response prevention). If the patient reports a low likelihood of accomplishing these assignments without assistance, or only with the support available to him at home, hospitalization is probably necessary.

Intervention

Intervention may assume several different forms depending on the results of the behavioral analysis. With most compulsive behaviors (e.g., washing and checking), flooding and response prevention will be the most appropriate treatment. Exposure treatment and response prevention for compulsive behaviors will be reviewed prior to an examination of treatment considerations for other obsessive-compulsive phenomena (e.g., cognitive compulsions, doubting, and other anxiety-eliciting cognitions and primary obsessive slowness).

Exposure Treatment. The exposure and response prevention phases usually occur concurrently, but here are divided to accomplish clarity of presentation. The exposure must be scheduled in sessions of at least two hours. Research has shown that prolonged exposure is needed to accomplish reductions in anxiety. Brief flooding, even if it is repeated, may be not only less effective, but can increase anxiety and discomfort.

Starting with items or situations on the low end of the hierarchy of SUDS (range 30–40), the patient is repeatedly exposed to the eliciting stimuli. For example, if the patient is a washer and various types of dirt make up the hierarchy, the 40 SUDS item (e.g., vacuum cleaner dirt) would be spread by the therapist on the patient's hands, face, and any other parts of his body shown by analysis to be important. This would be done every 10–15 minutes for the 2-hour session. After each exposure or at several times during the session the patient's SUDS levels are recorded. If the session is scheduled to end but the therapist finds SUDS levels to be extremely high, 70 or above, the therapist must be prepared to give repeated exposures until reduction to a SUDS range of 30–40 is accomplished. Usually, however, 2-hour flooding sessions provide ample time for anxiety levels to first increase and then return to more adaptive levels.

Homework assignments of more exposure for three to four additional hours are made each day. Response prevention homework is initiated on the first day of exposure treatment.

The first 15 minutes or so of the session each day is thereafter spent on review of progress in homework, assessment of any new avoidance behavior the patient discovers or heretofore has thought too inconsequential to mention, and providing continuous support, encouragement, and reinforcement for progress made.

When SUDS levels for each newly introduced hierarchy item are reduced to a SUDS range of 20–30 or below, the next higher item is used in exposure sessions and homework until even the highest item produces near zero SUDS. That point typically requires at least one and one-half to two weeks of daily sessions to accomplish. Of course, the most severe disorders may require more time but the need for more than two weeks of two-hour sessions is rare (Foa, 1978). When this response to exposure treatment occurs, assuming response prevention has been concurrently applied, the patient is ready to enter follow-up or to be provided treatment for other problems on a less intensive basis. Patients who have required hospitalization are usually discharged at this point.

Response Prevention.   This part of the treatment package is usually conducted along with exposure. It consists of having the patient not utilize any of his rituals or other avoidance behaviors. Descriptively, it sounds simple to do but in practice it is often very difficult for the patient to accomplish. For example, if the patient is a compulsive washer, he will be asked to *refrain from all bathing and washing for one week.* After one week he will be allowed one ten-minute shower or bath *without any rituals,* and he will be asked to not wash or bathe for another four days. On subsequent days, normal washing and bathing *without rituals* is introduced with supervision of washing initially used to insure compliance to the treatment regimen. Supervision is phased out as progress is identified.

Home treatment may require the assistance of other family members or individuals who spend a substantial amount of time with the patient. These individuals require a detailed explanation of the problem, the treatment rationale, and a specific guide for their interactions with the patient. If treatment is conducted in a hospital, staff must be so informed and be able to give structured supervision for response prevention. Supervision is required initially for the "homework assignments" involved in the response prevention treatment phase.

The treatment of choice for compulsive checking and compulsive washing is essentially the same. However, flooding in imagination may have to be used with compulsive checkers. Many checkers perform their rituals in order to avoid future "disasters," punishment, guilt, and so on, which cannot be used with in vivo flooding. Flooding in imagination, however, lends itself nicely to constructing situations where behavior results in the feared disastrous consequences.

Foa and Tillmans (1978) point out that, for checkers more than for washers, compulsion to ritualize may be weaker where they do not feel responsible for safety from the disasters, i.e., they tend to attribute positive changes to a safe environment rather than to their own behavior. Thus, if treated in the hospital, they may feel that the hospital staff is responsible for the positive changes they experience. In such cases, it is critical that treatment be conducted or extended to an outpatient basis with the patient living at his home. Checkers also can avoid disasters by assigning responsibility for a safe environment to their parents, spouses, or even the therapist. Such circumstances must be guarded against because they will interfere with treatment. The principle here is to have the patient assume responsibility *without* urges to ritualize and without ritualizing.

Other Treatment Procedures.   A number of additional treatment considerations demand attention. Typically, where compulsive rituals are observed obsessional behavior is also present. In many cases, treatment of the compulsive disorder results in corresponding changes in the obsessional patterns. With some patients, however, obsessional behavior does not change and hence a need may exist to develop a treatment program to modify obsessive ideation. This need also exists when the patient presents with an obsessive disorder in the absence of ritualized compulsive behavior. As noted earlier obsessions may be anxiety-decreasing or anxiety-increasing. Different interventions are suggested based on this dichotomy.

Treatment for anxiety-decreasing obsessions or cognitive compulsions (see assessment section) generally follows the same plan as that employed with washing and checking. It involves exposure, i.e., flooding, with stimuli which elicit the compulsions and response prevention. Where eliciting stimuli are covert, flooding in imagery is the recommended treatment. Because targeted behaviors are cognitive, therapist modeling of more appropriate self-statements followed by the patient's imitation of these cognitive responses is useful. Homework assignments usually involve the practice of more appropriate self-statements in the presence of covert or overt eliciting stimuli. Although no data on efficacy presently exist, it appears clinically that homework assignments involving overt verbal behavior in the presence of a family member, or someone who can supervise, is helpful for those patients who have difficulty completing assignments which involve monitored cognitive events.

Treatment for anxiety-elevating obsessions is less well developed and, in fact, is characterized by little research. Included within this category is obsessive-doubting and other repetitive cognitions which elicit anxiety. At this point there is no treatment of choice to deal specifically with this type of problem. The treatments reported in the literature include prolonged exposure (negative practice), thought-stopping, faradic disruption, and various procedures that fit best within an aversive therapy model. Research has not identified the components of these treatments which account for their efficacy. Little research is available employing anxiety-reducing techniques such as systematic desensitization. No research was isolated which employed the more cognitively oriented behavioral approaches. There is a definite need for further clinical research in this area.

A final treatment consideration involves intervention with primary obsessive slowness (Rachman, 1974). Rachman and his colleagues have tried several behavioral therapy treatment strategies with such patients, including flooding, modeling, and a combination of prompting, shaping, and pacing. They suggest that the most useful treatment may be the latter combination. After providing instructions and after modeling, the therapist prompts quicker behavior while the patient carries out a task. Shaping instructions and feedback are used to encourage a faster pace and discourage errors or persistent slowness. External pacing by timing devices is used. Once progress is made the patient is shown how to monitor and encouraged to monitor his own performance so supervision may be faded out. It seemed that many of these patients were socially isolated and remained so after this combination treatment, suggesting that some social skills and assertive behavior training may also be beneficial.

Although primary obsessive slowness remains to be verified by other clinicians and clinical researchers as a reliable obsessive-compulsive entity, readers should be aware that such an entity has been identified and is awaiting independent confirmation. It appears that Rachman's combination of prompting, shaping, and pacing was relatively effective for such patients and should serve at least as a starting point in devising a treatment plan for similar patients.

Follow-up or Follow-up Plus Treatment

If little additional treatment needs to be accomplished—usually the exception—a schedule of less and less frequent follow-up appointments can be made. A schedule used and found effective at Temple University Behavior Therapy Unit is to schedule follow-up appointments: two weeks, four weeks, two months, four months, six months, one year, and two years post-therapy. During these follow-up appointments checks are made for the reappearance of any ritual or avoidance behavior and if found, treatment is designed and initiated immediately. Assessment of other areas of functioning is also made. Any dysfunction so noted is dealt with by either providing treatment or referral.

If the patient has contracted for treatment to deal with additional problems related to his/her OCD, the follow-up period is structured to provide this additional intervention. Typically, follow-up treatment sessions would be less frequent than the daily two-hour sessions used during exposure and response prevention.

CASE REPORT

The patient was a 15-year-old male of above average intelligence enrolled in a suburban Catholic high school and working part-time as a busboy. He presented with excessive handwashing and showering rituals related to a fear of contamination from feces, body fluids, and related materials. Washing required an average of 30 minutes of hand-washing and 65 minutes of showering per day. In addition, the patient was obsessed about punishment from God and prayed ritualistically to allay these fears. The cognitive compulsion of praying ceased spontaneously during the pretreatment interview period.

Washing rituals had begun two years prior to treatment. No precipitating events were recalled, although his uncle was described as having washed excessively due to a preoccupation with germs, especially related to venereal disease. The uncle had warned the patient to avoid various situations for fear of contamination.

At the time of treatment the patient's fears and rituals had begun to interfere with scholastic performance, but not his functioning at work. Sexual development, family relationships, and peer relationships appeared relatively normal. No previous psychiatric treatment had been attempted.

The behavioral assessment was completed in three and a half 2-hour sessions. In addition to detailed interviewing, assessment included a patient's daily log of the number, type, duration, and time at which ritual behavior occurred and the antecedent and consequent events associated with the rituals. It included the administration of several rating scales including the EPI, MMPI, MOC, and the WAIS vocabulary subscale. Also included was a behavioral avoidance test employing the most feared sources of contamination, human feces and urine.

The assessment revealed that ritualized washing occurred when the patient was exposed to contamination from feces, body fluids, and other related items. A SUDS analysis of various types of contamination revealed the following hierarchy of contamination:

Source	SUDS
human feces, other	100
animal feces	95
own feces	90
human urine, other	85
own urine	80
pubic hair, other	75
pubic hair, own	60
bird droppings	55
semen	50
washing machine water	45

rain sewer water	40
shoe sole bottom	35
vomit	30
belly button lint	25
bathroom doorknob	20
dirty floor	15
fingernail dirt	10

During assessment, details of the treatment plan involving two weeks of exposure followed by two weeks of response prevention were agreed upon. In addition the patient signed a consent form to participate in a clinical study which also spelled out the major aspects of the treatment program.

Flooding treatment began using a moderate SUDS level contaminant, washing machine water (SUDS = 45). After initial review of progress and problems, the 2-hour session was divided into 15-minute exposure segments. Every 15 minutes washing machine water was spread on the patient's hands and face. He was permitted to wash immediately after exposure but he chose not to. His SUDS levels were recorded every 10 minutes throughout the session. Between exposures, discussion of progress and problems would often continue. However, some effort was made to direct conversation to topics which were not anxiety-arousing and which could serve as counterconditioning agents. When the patient showed clear diminution of SUDS levels during flooding, semen was added to the washing machine water; when SUDS levels diminished to this, urine and bird droppings were added. Lastly, human feces were used. Homework exposure involved the same procedure and schedule of spreading contamination materials on his face and hands every 15 minutes for 4 consecutive hours. Between exposures he was encouraged to engage in his normal routine. Homework also involved self-monitoring and recording of washing activities and any avoidance behavior. Flooding sessions were scheduled five days per week for two weeks. Homework continued seven days per week except exposure homework was eliminated the last weekend while self-monitoring continued. Because this patient was treated as part of a research protocol, response prevention was administered in a second 2-week period. Aside from supervised response prevention (i.e., no bathing or washing for a week at a time), this plan of treatment was essentially the same as the first two weeks. During the last five days, therapist supervised showers and handwashing were introduced. Showering was limited to 10 minutes and handwashing to 30 seconds, both without rituals. Therapist supervision was gradually phased out over the last three days of treatment.

Two weekly follow-up sessions were scheduled to monitor progress, detect any rituals or other avoidance behavior, and work on a conflict situation between the patient and his mother. Additional follow-up sessions were scheduled at one, two, and three-month intervals.

Hand-washing and showering ritual behavior is illustrated in Figure 2. At the start of flooding treatment hand-washing averaged 30 minutes and showering 65 minutes per day. As can be seen in the graph, ritualized behavior tended to increase during flooding, an understandable and predictable result when one recalls the patient was exposed to contamination for as long as six hours per day. After flooding, but before the combination of flooding plus response prevention was introduced, ritual behavior significantly reduced to below baseline levels although it was still above what was considered normal limits. With the introduction of flooding plus response prevention, ritual behavior dropped to zero, remaining there until supervised normal washing and showering was introduced during the second week of treatment.

Following flooding plus response prevention and up to three months' follow-up, there was no ritualized behavior. Levels on the graph represent the normal amount of time to wash hands (2–3 minutes per day) and to bathe or shower (8–10 minutes per day).

Behavioral exposure test data are illustrated in Figure 3. In this test the patient was asked to touch contamination materials, a combination of human feces and urine, using a glove and then starting with eight paper towels, progressing with fewer paper towels until he touched materials with his bare hand. With each progression his SUDS levels for anxiety, contamination, and urge to wash were assessed. The first exposure test was given before treatment began. He did not touch the contamination materials with his bare hand but completed the rest of the progression, showing higher SUDS levels through the progression. Test 2 was conducted after flooding but before the combination treatment was given. As can be seen in Figure 3, SUDS levels were significantly reduced but still above zero. In both tests 2 and 3 he did touch contamination materials with his bare hand. In test 3 SUDS are near zero except for when he touched materials using one towel and with his bare hand. These are interpreted as normal level reactions.

Aside from changes on the MOC reflecting decreased obsessive and compulsive symptoms, other paper and pencil assessment instruments showed no significant changes during or after treatment.

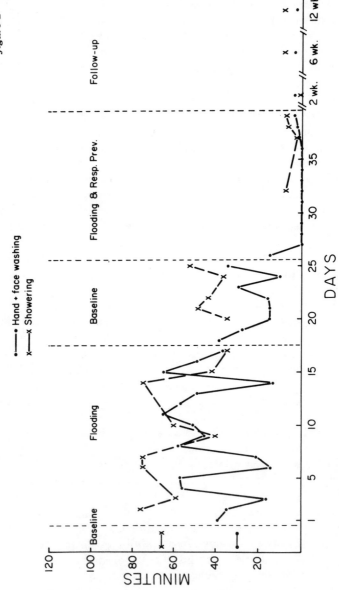

Flooding treatment of hand-washing and showering ritual behavior.

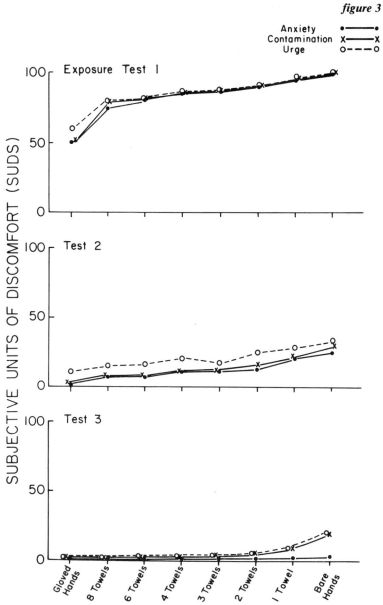

figure 3

Behavioral exposure test data: assessment of SUDS levels for anxiety, contamination, and urge to wash.

ETHICAL AND LEGAL ISSUES

Perhaps the most important ethical issue in treating obsessive-compulsive patients with the flooding/response prevention package is obtaining informed consent to undergo treatment. Any failure to inform patients as completely as possible regarding the circumstances and details of treatment is not only questionable on ethical grounds, but also likely to elicit resistance from the patient. Such resistance and any lack of cooperation in treatment consequent to it, is likely to interfere with treatment and perhaps negatively influence treatment efficacy. Since flooding and response prevention are often difficult for the patient and involve unpleasant and discomforting activities, the patient should know the details (e.g., what, how, when, and how often) concerning such treatment. For example, the washer who only knows the principle of response prevention but not the details is likely to resist strongly, and may even terminate treatment if he doesn't know in advance that response prevention involves no washing or bathing for up to one week!

The experienced clinician should discuss details of treatment with the patient repeatedly, not only to provide him with information but to allow some of the anticipatory emotional responses to treatment to diminish. The patient's record should document a detailed discussion of the treatment process as well as a discussion of the difficult, unpleasant and discomforting aspects of treatment. The record can then serve as an informal documentation of informed consent if any legal or ethical questions are subsequently raised regarding treatment.

If the patient is participating in a clinical research project, the above precautions are necessary but not sufficient. In addition, the patient's record should contain a document indicating that the research project in which the patient is participating has been reviewed and approved by a formal Human Use Committee. This of course requires that the investigator submit his research protocol to a Human Use Committee and make any changes they require in order to obtain formal approval. The investigator must include in the patient's record the formal document of informed consent to participate in the clinical research project. This document should be signed and dated by the patient, by the investigator, and by a witness.

Whenever a patient's family or individuals other than hospital or clinic staff participate as a therapeutic cohort in the treatment program, the issue of confidentiality arises. For example, the treatment plan may involve a family member or someone else who assists the patient in homework assignments and recording of behaviors. Clearly, the best procedure from an ethical and legal standpoint would involve obtaining a signed informed consent summary by which the patient formally agrees to have another person involved in his/her treatment program, and thus be privy to confidential information. A less formal arrangement would involve eliciting the patient's consent to invite the therapeutic assistant to a treatment session(s). A discussion of the assistant's role and the issues of confidentiality could then be built into the therapy program. With patient approval, following this type of discussion, the assistant could subsequently be involved in treatment. The involvement of an assistant in a treatment session(s) and the verbal consent of the patient to allow this should be recorded in the patient's record.

The most questionable procedure which may violate the patient's confidentiality, would involve the therapist contacting or enlisting the assistance of another person without the patient's verbal permission. Contacting another person to enlist his support and/or involvement in the treatment program without permission of the patient, clearly violates the patient's right to confidentiality. Such a procedure is unethical and violates professional ethical guidelines, certain federal laws, as well as some state laws regarding confidentiality.

Because clinical research over the last decade has amassed a convincingly great amount of support for the use of certain techniques (e.g., flooding and response prevention with compulsive behaviors), the ethicality of withholding the treatment-of-choice must be addressed. Clearly, if the individual therapist has the skills and facilities to offer the treatment-of-choice for an OCD and he knowingly provides another form of treatment, or does not administer the treatment-of-choice, he is on questionable ethical ground. Some behavior therapists feel strongly that flooding plus response prevention is the treatment-of-choice for most forms of compulsive disorders, and that failure to provide this treatment package is unethical (Foa, 1978). If the therapist is unskilled with the treatment-of-choice he has a dilemma. If he uses techniques which he feels he is skilled at using and which have been effective with other similar clients, he may confront an ethical problem in that the treatment-of-choice has not been administered. However, if, despite his feeling that he can successfully treat the obsessive-compulsive patient with a treatment other than the treatment-of-choice, he is sensitive to the ethical issue of withholding treatment and therefore refers the patient elsewhere, he loses a patient he feels he can provide useful services to. As more research data confirms the superiority of one treatment or treatment package, this type of dilemma is likely to occur. Obviously, a therapist who is not skilled in the treatment-of-choice and feels uncertain about his ability to help the obsessive-compulsive patient, should refer him to someone he feels can help the patient. To treat rather than to refer a patient when one does not have the competencies to help the obsessive-compulsive patient is unethical. Ethical issues become less clear when someone competent to provide the treatment-of-choice is not reasonably available as a referral source. It would seem the therapist who is unskilled in providing the treatment-of-choice only operates within professional ethical constraints when: (1) he feels he has some skills to help the patient; (2) no one competent in providing the treatment-of-choice is reasonably available to accept referrals; and (3) he has discussed with the patient the preceding *and* after so being informed, the patient nonetheless agrees to enter a treatment contract with the therapist.

SUGGESTIONS FOR CLINICAL AND EXPERIMENTAL RESEARCH

Behavioral research concerned with the assessment and treatment of OCD has progressed in a relatively systematic fashion, primarily due to the efforts of Rachman, Marks, and their British colleagues. Less attention has been devoted to systematic investigation by researchers in this country; however, Foa (Foa and Goldstein, 1978) has recently initiated an impressive and well-formulated research-oriented program which promises to advance current knowledge.

Although a good empirical foundation is being established, many questions remain unanswered. Research related to both assessment and treatment is needed.

Assessment-oriented research could advance the field by focusing on three basic areas. First, the newly developed Leyton Obsessive-Compulsive Inventory and the Maudsley Obsessive-Compulsive Inventory require closer scrutiny. Behaviorally oriented clinicians have been remiss in failing to subject measurement instruments to the same quality of scrutiny required of treatment techniques. The reliability, validity, and utility of these measures could be further evaluated using traditional psychometric methods with cross-cultural replication. Both the Leyton and the Maudsley show promise as research instruments and may have value as diagnostic instruments, as well as outcome measures. But they should be used cautiously in the absence of documentation that classical psychometric criteria have been attained.

A second area of assessment-oriented research should focus on examining more closely the various behavioral patterns which define the OCD, e.g., washing, checking, slowing, and so on. No empirical data is available concerning the ability of clinicians to reliably discriminate such behavioral patterns. There is also no empirical data to suggest that such discriminations will be useful. It is reasonable to hypothesize that these patterns may require different interventions and may be characterized by differential prognosis. The development of operational definitions for these patterns would greatly aid research in this area.

If these various behavioral patterns can be reliably discriminated, descriptive data could be generated. Specifically, it would be potentially useful to examine the frequency of presentation of the various response patterns with individuals classified as OCD. These data would make it possible to identify response clusters which occur with relatively high frequency.

Two types of response clusters are observed with OCDs. In addition to the presentation of two or more obsessive-compulsive responses, the clinician also frequently observes a number of associated clinical problems, e.g., difficulties with assertion, poor social skills, mood disorders, and so on. The discernment of specific problems within these two types of response clusters is a potentially important assessment issue, as the presence or absence of various problems may be of prognostic importance. For example, individuals with more than one obsessive-compulsive response pattern might be less likely to respond favorably to treatment than less complicated cases. Likewise, an individual who presents with one obsessive-compulsive response pattern but who exhibits marked social skills deficits may also be a difficult treatment case. A multivariate model is suggested to isolate prognostic variables which warrant consideration during assessment.

A third assessment consideration addresses the generalization of treatment issue. Multiple outcome measures are required to accurately assess the impact of treatment. Specifically, it is important to identify measurement instruments or techniques to sensitively measure various obsessive-compulsive responses and to utilize instruments to accurately assess changes in associated problems. Assessment should therefore be sensitive to generalization of treatment which may occur across obsessive-compulsive responses, e.g., what impact does flooding for compulsive washing have on frequency of cognitive compulsions? It should also be sensitive to generalization of treatment from specific obsessive-compulsive responses to other associated problems, e.g., what impact does flooding for compulsive washing have on mood? Where possible, it makes sense clinically to treat the discrete disorder and to monitor the impact of a given treatment focus on remaining problems. To assume, however, that treatment is completed once obsessive-compulsive features have been modified may be a critical treatment error.

Treatment-oriented research with OCD has not been extremely rigorous or thorough. Most reports are of uncontrolled single case investigations. A sizeable number of investigations have employed crossover designs to deal with the problem of a small number of available subjects. Very few studies have employed appropriate waiting-list control groups, or even attention-only control groups, in spite of some evidence that the spontaneous improvement rate may be as high as 50 percent (Grimshaw, 1965).

In addition to improving research methodology, several areas warrant attention. One significant issue is the need for examination of differential treatment effects. Little information is available concerning which treatment packages are most effective with which specific obsessive-compulsive behavioral patterns. This level of research is the logical next step following the isolation of a number of treatments which appear useful in treating patients with heterogeneous obsessive-compulsive response patterns. Component research to examine what variables account for treatment efficacy in complex treatment packages like flooding and response prevention would help in developing maximally efficient and cost effective treatment.

While a limited amount of differential treatment data is available, there are also several problems for which no treatments have emerged as being particularly promising. Not much is known about how to modify doubting and other anxiety-elevating obsessions. No well-controlled study has demonstrated the efficacy of thought-stopping or the various aversive procedures, and yet clinically both types of techniques have been associated with improvement in uncontrolled single case studies. At least three treatment variables deserve attention: response interruption with nonaversive procedures, use of response-contingent aversive procedures, and the impact of repeated exposure of anxiety-elevating thoughts.

Little research has been devoted to the treatment of primary obsessional slowness, as this response pattern has only recently been identified. The treatment package suggested by Rachman (1974) appears sound, but additional techniques may also prove beneficial.

A number of additional treatment techniques have been employed with various types of OCD in single case studies. These techniques should be subjected to the next level of research to employ control groups, multiple measures, and extensive follow-up evaluation. This is not to suggest that small N research cannot continue to be useful, but rather that single case studies should be more carefully designed and incorporate more sophisticated single subject research methodology (Hersen and Barlow, 1976).

An additional research area which warrants attention is the impact of more cognitively oriented behavioral approaches in the treatment of OCDs. Several single case investigations (Daitzman, 1978; Rabavilas et al., 1977) suggested that cognitive variables may be of substantial importance in treatment of OCD. Although cognitively oriented thera-pies have been used effectively with many other clinical problems, no research documents their use with OCD. Many "thinking disturbances" which characterize other neurotic disorders are also frequent correlates of obsessive-compulsive behavior. In addition to Ellis' (1962) dire needs for approval and strivings for perfection, many obsessive-compulsive individuals also present with primarily extrinsic self-evalu-ation criteria (Lazarus, 1977), and with a number of thinking problems identified by Beck (1976), e.g., overgeneralization, catastrophic think-ing, dichotomous reasoning, and so on. It remains an open question whether a treatment focus on these specific cognitive patterns would generalize to specific obsessive-compulsive response patterns. If gener-alization was demonstrated, comparisons with more traditional be-havioral techniques would be indicated.

As with other areas of behavior therapy, a broad-spectrum ap-proach which addresses multiple response modalities is a tempting treatment model. There is no data at present to suggest that a multi-modal model is more efficient or more effective as a therapy approach for OCD. Research addressing this issue would certainly be a major contribution to the literature.

SUMMARY

In this chapter obsessive-compulsive neurosis is reviewed. Nonbe-havioral and behavioral theories of the etiology and treatment of OCD are reviewed with a focus on behavioral theories. Particular attention is paid to the drive reduction theory of OCD symptom-atology; however, it is pointed out that some obsessive-compulsive behaviors do not fit within this model.

General objectives for assessment of OCD are introduced and three approaches to assessment are reviewed: projective, objective, and behavioral. Major instruments and procedures employed in each type of assessment are covered. Included is an evaluation of how well each type of assessment meets its objectives. Briefly, projective assessment techniques are not judged to be particularly useful at any stage of assessment. When useful they appear to make a contribution in early phases of assessment where OCD must be discriminated from other forms of psychopathology. The MMPI seems to be the most useful of the objective instruments for making this type of discrimination. Two experimental assessment instruments that focused on types of OCD symptomatology were viewed as having potential for providing detailed information about specific behavioral problems, which is necessary for effective clinical behavior therapy. Recommendations for integrating objective and behavioral assessment approaches into a comprehensive assessment package for OCD are made.

A typology for OCD is presented based on objective and behavioral assessment which has been validated in recent research. Six behavioral patterns of OCD are delineated with the caveat that the identity of all the types has not been validated by observations of other clinicians. The six are: washing, checking, slowing, cognitive compulsions, doubting, and idiosyncratic compulsions, like eating and gambling. Implications for differences in treatment approaches are derived from enumeration of the taxonomy.

A relatively broad survey of known treatment procedures based upon a literature search is presented. Included are reviews of the following forms of treatment: psychodynamically oriented psychotherapy, psychosurgery, and a variety of behavioral techniques including systematic desensitization, modeling, flooding, response prevention, aversion therapy, thought-stopping, and several novel behavioral approaches. It is concluded that the treatment of choice for most forms of compulsive behavior is some combination of in vivo or imaginary flooding plus response prevention. In flooding the patient is continuously exposed for up to several hours, to specific anxiety-evoking stimuli. For example, with in vivo flooding for a washer, contamination materials would be placed on his hands, face, clothing, and so on, and continuously replaced if he washed or removed them. Response prevention involves contracting with the patient to not perform any of his ritual or other avoidance behavior while being continuously exposed to sources of contamination. It is emphasized that most obsessive-compulsive neurotics present with additional problems other than obsessive-compulsive behaviors. These problems require assessment and treatment to prevent a myopic and ineffective therapy approach.

A clinical prescription reviewing the most useful treatment techniques is presented. Clinicians familiar with behavioral therapy principles and procedures should be able to utilize this clinical prescription as a guide to effective interventions. A case study where flooding and response prevention were utilized is provided to give a detailed clinical example of assessment, treatment application, and follow-up.

Ethical and legal issues related to treating OCD and the use of empirically validated treatments are discussed. Alternatives for ethically dealing with confidentiality, informed consent, and other issues are reviewed with an effort to examine real-life contexts and decision ramifications.

Suggestions and recommendations for clinical and basic research are made. It is suggested that reliability and validity research is especially needed for the newly developed objective tests with clinical potential. Reliability and validity studies of the Leyton Obsessive-Compulsive Inventory and the Maudsley Obsessive-Compulsive Inventory are in need of crosscultural replication. Extensive work on interassessor reliability and convergent validity is needed to anchor the behavioral assessment process to empirical foundations. Thus far, behavioral assessment has been demonstrated to have face validity and clinical utility. However, the application of classic psychometric criteria for reliability and validity have rarely been invoked and when they have, many behavior assessment instruments have been found wanting. It is expected that clinical utility of many assessment instruments will improve when investigations begin to attend to these classic psychometric criteria, and utilize tested methods for assessing and improving psychometric instruments.

Both basic and applied clinical research are needed to examine differential treatment effects. Specific attention is needed to discern which treatments are most useful with what obsessive-compulsive response patterns. Component research is also necessary to identify those variables which account for therapy efficacy in complex treatment packages, such as flooding with response prevention. Several innovative treatment approaches for OCD have been reviewed, some of which appeared to be quite effective. In most cases however, case study methodology was employed. There is much room for the next level of research to employ control groups, multiple measures and extensive follow-up, and so on, in order to critically evaluate some of these promising approaches.

An extensive bibliography is included with the most significant and representative articles. Major articles are designated with an asterisk to provide the reader with an overview of the literature on OCD.

REFERENCES

Articles with asterisks are considered the most significant and representative of the topic.

Akhtar, S., Pershad, D., and Verma, S. K. A Rorschach study of obsessional neurosis. *Indian Journal of Clinical Psychology,* 1975, *2,* 139–143.

Alberti, R. E., and Emmons, M. L. *Your perfect right: A guide to assertive behavior.* San Louis Obispo, CA.: Impact Press, 1970.

Bain, J. A. *Thought control in everyday life.* New York: Funk and Wagnalls, 1928.

Bandura, A. *Principles of behavior modification.* New York: Holt, Rinehart and Winston, 1969.

Bass, B. A. An unusual behavioral technique for treating obsessive ruminations. *Psychotherapy: Theory, Research and Practice*, 1973, *10*, 191–192.

Beck, A. T. *Cognitive therapy and the emotional disorders*. New York: International Universities Press, 1976.

Boulougouris, J. C., and Bassiakos, L. Prolonged flooding in cases of obsessive-compulsive neurosis. *Behavior Research and Therapy*, 1973, *11*, 227–231.

Campbell, L. M. A variation of thought-stopping in a twelve-year-old boy: A case report. *Journal of Behavior Therapy and Experimental Psychiatry*, 1973, *4*, 69–70.

Carr, A. T. Compulsive neurosis: A review of the literature. *Psychological Bulletin*, 1974, *81*(5), 311–318.

Ciminero, A. R., Calhoun, K. S., and Adams, H. E. (Eds.), *Handbook of behavioral assessment*. New York: Wiley, 1977.

Cooper, J. The Leyton obsessional inventory. *Psychological Medicine*, 1970, *1*, 48–64.

Cooper, J., and Kelleher, M. The Leyton obsessional inventory: A principle component analysis of normal subjects. *Psychological Medicine*, 1973, *3*, 204–208.

Daitzman, R. J. Overcoming learned helplessness: Reattribution therapy in the treatment of obsessive-compulsive neurosis. Unpublished manuscript, 1978. Stamford, Conn.

Dollard, J., and Miller, N. E. *Personality and psychotherapy: An analysis in terms of learning, thinking and culture*. New York: McGraw-Hill, 1950.

Eisler, R. M. The behavioral assessment of social skills. In M. Hersen and A. S. Bellack (Eds.), *Behavioral assessment: A practical handbook*. New York: Pergamon Press, 1976.

Ellis, A. *Reason and emotion in psychotherapy*. New York: Lyle Stewart, 1962.

Emmelkamp, P., and Kwee Gwan, K. Obsessional ruminations: A comparison between thought stopping and prolonged exposure in imagination. *Behavior Research and Therapy*, 1977, *15*, 441–444.

Epstein, L. H. Psychophysiological measurement and assessment. In M. Hersen and A. S. Bellack (Eds.), *Behavioral assessment: A practical handbook*. New York: Pergamon Press, 1976.

Foa, E. Personal communication. March, 1978.

*Foa, E., and Chambless, D. L. Habituation of subjective anxiety during flooding in imagery. *Behavioral Research and Therapy*, 1978, in press.

*Foa, E., and Goldstein, A. Continuous exposure and complete response prevention in the treatment of obsessive-compulsive neurosis. *Behavior Therapy*, 1978, in press.

Foa, E., and Steketee, G. Emergent fears during treatment of three obsessive-compulsives: Symptom substitution or deconditioning. *Journal of Behavior Therapy and Experimental Psychiatry*, 1977, *8*, 353–358.

Foa, E., and Tillmans, A. The treatment of obsessive-compulsive neurosis. In

E. Foa and A. Goldstein (Eds.), *The Handbook of behavioral interventions.* New York: Wiley Interscience, 1978.

Frankl, V. E. Paradoxical intention. *American Journal of Psychotherapy,* 1960, *14,* 520–535.

Gentry, W. D. In vivo desensitization of an obsessive cancer fear. *Behavior Research and Therapy,* 1973, *11,* 227–231.

Goldfried, M. R., and D'Zurilla, T. J. A behavioral-analytic model for assessing competence. In C. D. Spielberger (Ed.), *Current topics in clincial and community psychology.* New York: Academic Press, 1969.

Gray, J. *The psychology of fear and stress.* London: World University Library, 1971.

Grimshaw, L. The outcome of obsessional disorder III: A follow-up study of 100 cases. *British Journal of Psychiatry,* 1965, 1051–1056.

Gullick, E. L., and Blanchard, E. B. The use of psychotherapy and behavior therapy in the treatment of an obsessional disorder: An experimental case study. *The Journal of Nervous and Mental Disease,* 1973, *156,* 427–431.

Hackman, A., and McLean, C. A comparison of flooding and thought-stopping in the treatment of obsessional neurosis. *Behavior Research and Therapy,* 1975, *13,* 263–269.

Hallam, R. S. Extinction of ruminations: A case study. *Behavior Therapy,* 1974, *5,* 565–568.

Hersen, M. Treatment of a compulsive and phobic disorder through a total behavior therapy program: A case study. *Psychotherapy: Theory, Research, and Practice,* 1968, *5,* 220–225.

Hersen, M. The use of behavior modification techniques within a traditional psychotherapeutic context. *American Journal of Psychotherapy,* 1970, *25,* 308–313.

Hersen, M. The self-assessment of fear. *Behavior Therapy,* 1973, *4,* 241–257.

Hersen, M., and Barlow, D. H. *Single case experimental designs.* New York: Pergamon Press, 1976.

Hersen, M. and Bellack, A. (Eds.), *Behavior-assessment: A practical handbook.* New York: Pergamon Press, 1976.

Hersen, M., and Greaves, S. T. Rorschach productivity as related to verbal reinforcement. *Journal of Personality Assessment,* 1971, *35,* 436–444.

*Hodgson, R. J., and Rachman, S. The effects of contamination and washing in obsessional patients. *Behavior Research and Therapy,* 1972, *10,* 111–117.

*Hodgson, R. J., and Rachman, S. Obsessive-compulsive complaints. *Behavior Research and Therapy,* 1977, *15,* 389–395.

Hodgson, R., Rachman, S., and Marks, I. M. The treatment of chronic obsessive-compulsive neurosis: Follow-up and further findings. *Behavior Research and Therapy,* 1972, *10,* 181–189.

Jacobson, E. *Progressive relaxation.* Chicago: University of Chicago Press, 1938.

Kates, S. L. Objective Rorschach response patterns differentiating anxiety reactions from obsessive-compulsive reaction. *Journal of Consulting Psychology,* 1950, *14,* 226–229.

Kenny, F. T., Mowbray, R. M., and Lalani, S. Faradic disruption of obsessive ideation in the treatment of obsessive neurosis. *Behavior Therapy,* 1978, *9,* 209–221.

*Kenny, F. T., Solyom, L., and Solyom, C. Faradic disruption of obsessive ideation in the treatment of obsessive neurosis. *Behavior Therapy,* 1973, *4,* 448–457.

Klopfer, W. G., and Taulbee, E. S. Projective tests. In M. R. Rosenzweig and L. W. Porter (Eds.), *Annual review of psychology.* Palo Alto, CA.: Annual Reviews, 1976.

Kraft, T. Treatment of compulsive shoplifting by altering social contingencies. *Behavior Research and Therapy,* 1970, *8,* 393–394.

Kumar, K., and Wilkinson, J.C.M. Thought-stopping: A useful treatment in phobias of "internal stimuli." *British Journal of Psychiatry,* 1971, *119,* 305–307.

Lambley, P. Differential effects of psychotherapy and behavioral techniques in a case of acute obsessive-compulsive disorder. *British Journal of Psychiatry,* 1974, *125,* 181–183.

Lazarus, A. A. *Behavior therapy and beyond.* New York: McGraw-Hill, 1971.

Lazarus, A. A. *Multimodal behavior therapy.* New York: Springer, 1976.

Lazarus, A. A. Toward an egoless state of being. In A. Ellis and R. Griege (Eds.), *Handbook of rational-emotive therapy.* New York: Springer, 1977.

*Marks, I. M., Hodgson, R., and Rachman, S. Treatment of chronic obsessive-compulsive neurosis by in vivo exposure: A two-year follow-up and issues in treatment. *British Journal of Psychiatry,* 1975, *127,* 349–364.

Marks, P. A., Seeman, W., and Haller, D. *The actuarial use of the MMPI with adolescents and adults.* Baltimore, MD.: William and Wilkins, 1974.

Mash, E. J., and Terdal, L. G. *Behavior therapy assessment: Diagnosis, design and evaluation.* New York: Springer, 1976.

Mather, M. D. The treatment of an obsessive-compulsive patient by discrimination learning and reinforcement of decision making. *Behavior Research and Therapy,* 1970, *8,* 315–318.

McGlynn, F. D., and Linder, L. H. The clinical application of analogue desensitization: A case study. *Behavior Therapy,* 1971, *2,* 385–388.

Meichenbaum, D. *Cognitive-behavior modification: An integrative approach.* New York: Plenum, 1977.

Melamed, B. G., and Siegel, L. J. Self-directed in vivo treatment of an obsessive-compulsive checking ritual. *Journal of Behavior Therapy and Experimental Psychiatry,* 1975, *6,* 31–35.

Meyer, R. G. Delay therapy: Two case reports. *Behavior Therapy,* 1973, *4,* 709–711.

Meyer, V. Modification of expectations in cases with obsessional rituals. *Behavior Research and Therapy,* 1966, *4,* 273–280.

Mills, H. L., Agras, W. S., Barlow, D. H., and Mills, J. R. Compulsive rituals treated by response prevention: An experimental analysis. *Archives of General Psychiatry,* 1973, *28,* 524–529.

Mitchell-Heggs, N., Kelley, D., and Richardson, A. Stereotactic limbic leucotomy. A follow-up at 16 months. *British Journal of Psychiatry*, 1976, *128*, 226–240.

Munroe, R. The inspection technique: A method of rapid evaluation of the Rorschach protocol. *Rorschach Research Exchange*, 1944, *18*, 46–70.

O'Brien, J. S., and Raynes, A. E. Treatment of compulsive verbal behavior with response contingent punishment and relaxation. *Journal of Behavior Therapy and Experimental Psychiatry*, 1973, *4*, 347–352.

Rabivilas, A. D., Boulougouris, J. C., and Stefanis, C. Compulsive checking diminished when over-checking instructions were disobeyed. *Journal of Behavior Therapy and Experimental Psychiatry*, 1977, *8*, 111–112.

*Rachman, S. Obsessional ruminations. *Behavior Research and Therapy*, 1971, *9*, 229–235.

*Rachman, S. Primary obsessional slowness. *Behavior Research and Therapy*, 1974, *12*, 9–18.

Rachman, S., De Silva, P., and Roper, G. The spontaneous decay of compulsive urges. *Behavior Research and Therapy*, 1976, *14*, 445–453.

Rachman, S., Hodgson, R., and Marks, I. The treatment of chronic obsessive-compulsive neurosis. *Behavior Research and Therapy*, 1971, *9*, 237–247.

Rachman, S., Hodgson, R., and Marzillier, J. Treatment of an obsessional-compulsive disorder by modeling. *Behavior Research and Therapy*, 1970, *8*, 385–392.

Rachman, S., Marks, I. M., and Hodgson, R. The treatment of obsessive-compulsive neurotics by modeling and flooding in vivo. *Behavior Research and Therapy*, 1973, *II*, 463–471.

Rainey, C. A. An obsessive-compulsive neurosis treated by flooding in vivo. *Behavior Therapy and Experimental Psychiatry*, 1972, *3*, 117–121.

Ritzler, B. A., and Del Guadio, A. C. A survey of Rorschach teaching in APA approved programs. *Journal of Personality Assessment*, 1976, *40*, 451–453.

*Roper, G., Rachman, S., and Marks, I. Passive and participant modeling in exposure treatment of obsessive-compulsive neurotics. *Behavior Research and Therapy*, 1975, *13*, 271–279.

Seager, C. P. Treatment of compulsive gamblers by electrical aversion. *British Journal of Psychiatry*, 1970, *117*, 545–553.

Shapiro, M. B. A method of measuring psychological changes specific to the individual psychiatric patient. *British Journal of Medical Psychology*, 1961, *34*, 151–155.

Sherman, M. H. The diagnostic significance of constriction-dilation on the Rorschach. In M. H. Sherman (Ed.), *A Rorschach reader*. New York: International University Press, 1963.

Stern, R. Treatment of a case of obsessional neurosis using thought-stopping techniques. *British Journal of Psychiatry*, 1970, *117*, 441–442.

Stern, R. S., Lipsedge, M. S., and Marks, I. M. Obsessive ruminations: A controlled trail of thought-stopping techniques. *Behavior Research and Therapy*, 1973, *11*, 659–662.

Stern, R. S., and Marks, I. M. Contract therapy in obsessive-compulsive neurosis with marital discord. *British Journal of Psychiatry,* 1973, *123,* 681–684.

Stolorow, R. D. Causality-interpretation and obsessive versus hysterical functioning. *Journal of Personality Assessment,* 1971, *2,* 273–279.

Tanner, B. A. A case report on the use of relaxation and systematic desensitization to control multiple compulsive behaviors. *Journal of Behavior Therapy and Experimental Psychiatry,* 1971, *2,* 273–279.

Wagner, E. E. The facade compulsive: A diagnostic formulation derived from projective testing. *Journal of Personality Assessment,* 1976, *40,* 352–362.

Walton, D., and Mather, M. D. The application of learning principles to the treatment of obsessive compulsive states in the acute and chronic phases of illness. In H. J. Eysenck (Ed.), *Experiments in behavior therapy.* Oxford: Pergamon Press, 1964.

Watson, D., and Friend, R. Measurement of social-evaluative anxiety. In E. J. Mash and L. G. Terdal, *Behavior therapy assessment: Diagnosis, design and evaluation.* New York: Springer, 1976.

Weiner, I. B. Behavior therapy in obsessive compulsive neurosis: Treatment of an adolescent boy. *Psychotherapy: Theory, Research, and Practice,* 1967, *4,* 27–29.

Weiss, R. L., and Margolin, G. Assessment of marital conflict and accord. In A. R. Ciminero, K. S. Calhoun, and H. E. Adams (Eds.), *Handbook of behavior assessment.* New York: Wiley Interscience, 1977.

Wickram, I. Desensitization, re-sensitization and desensitization again: A preliminary study. *Journal of Behavior Therapy and Experimental Psychiatry,* 1970, *1,* 257–262.

Wolpe, J. *Psychotherapy by reciprocal inhibition.* Stanford, CA.: Stanford University Press, 1958.

Wolpe, J. *The practice of behavior therapy.* New York: Pergamon Press, 1973.

Wolpe, J. *Theme and variations: A behavior therapy casebook.* New York: Pergamon Press, 1976.

Wolpe, J., and Lang, P. J. A fear survey schedule for use in behavior therapy. *Behavior Research and Therapy,* 1964, *2,* 27–30.

Yamagami, T. The treatment of an obsession by thought-stopping. *Journal of Behavior Therapy and Experimental Psychiatry,* 1971, *2,* 133–135.

Yates, A. J. *Behavior therapy.* New York: Wiley, 1970.

Yen, S. Operant therapy for excessive checking. *Canadian Journal of Behavioral Science,* 1971, *3*(2), 194–197.

3
Enuresis

Suzanne Bennett Johnson

Micturition is a complex process. In the normal human adult it involves the ability (1) to inhibit contractions of the bladder wall until the bladder is full, (2) to recognize the perception of full bladder distention as a need to void, (3) to postpone micturition until a socially acceptable micturition site can be located and a micturition posture adopted, and (4) to initiate micturition in the appropriate setting when the bladder is full or only partially full. During the first 6 months of a child's life, none of these abilities have yet developed. The child's bladder reacts to distention by immediate evacuation and consequently, micturition is very frequent. Over the next two years, there is a gradual but progressive increase in bladder capacity with a concomitant decrease in frequency of urination. During this time, contractions of the detrusor muscle in the bladder wall are unconsciously inhibited, presumably by one or more controlling centers in the subcortical levels of the brain. When the child is 18 to 30 months, he becomes able to convey to his mother that he is about to micturate (i.e., he has developed the perception of bladder distention) and begins to consciously inhibit urination for increasing periods of time. He learns to go to the toilet, remove his pants, and then initiate micturition (Yates, 1975). Finally, he learns to go to the toilet and initiate urination even when his bladder is not full. This latter skill, however, does not normally develop until the child is 5 or 6 years of age (Campbell, 1970).

Although there is a good deal of variability, children are usually reliably continent during the day by 2 years and develop nocturnal continence by 3 years. Some children, however, are not dry after the age of 3 and are described as *enuretic* if there is no organic pathology to account for their continual wetting (Campbell, 1970). Most of these children are bedwetters (nocturnal enuretics), although a few wet during the day as well (diurnal enuretics). Primary enuretics are those children who have never been consistently dry, while secondary enuresis is used to refer to those children who revert to wetting after a substantial period of urinary control. Primary enuresis is generally more common than secondary (Forsythe and Redmond, 1974; Forsythe, Merrett, and Redmond, 1972a; Shaffer, Costello, and Hill, 1968).

Although there have been a good number of studies reporting incidence or prevalence data on enuresis, their findings are often not directly comparable. (See De Jonge, 1973, and Yates, 1970, for reviews.) Investigators use different criteria in defining enuresis, focus on different populations, and use different data collection procedures. Nevertheless, some consistent findings do emerge. Enuresis, for example, clearly diminishes with age. While prevalence rates do vary, rates of 15–20 percent for 4- and 5-year olds, 5 percent for 10-year olds, and 1–2 percent for 15-year olds are not considered unreasonably high (Campbell, 1970; Enfield, 1976; Kolvin, 1975; Young, 1969). Nocturnal enuresis is much more common than diurnal wetting. Nevertheless, as many as 10–28 percent of bedwetters have day-wetting problems as well (Campbell, 1970; De Jonge, 1973; Forsythe and Redmond, 1974; Maguire, 1970). Other factors consistently related to the prevalence of enuresis are the sex of the child, socioeconomic class, and family history. Nocturnal enuretics are more often males; diurnal enuretics are more often females (De Jonge, 1973; Forsythe and Redmond, 1974; Maguire, 1970). Lower socioeconomic status is associated with higher rates of enuresis (Blomfield and Douglas, 1956; Miller, 1973), and a family history of enuresis is more common in enuretic than nonenuretic children (MacKeith, Meadow, and Turner, 1973; Miller, 1973; Young, 1969).

Spontaneous remission rates are more difficult to assess. Lovibond (1964) calculated annual spontaneous cure rates of 16–19 percent for children over five; a similar estimate of 13.5 percent has been offered by De Jonge (1973) in his more recent review. In a long-term follow-up of over 1,100 enuretic children, Forsythe and Redmond (1974) reported rates of 14–16 percent. Although there is not a great deal of information on this issue, the available data is remarkably consistent.

It is probably worth reiterating that enuresis is defined by a set of symptoms (involuntary micturition) that must occur in the context of two exclusionary principles: age and organic pathology. The same behaviors (e.g., wetting one's clothes or bed) are only considered symptomatic of true enuresis if they occur in a child over 3 years with normal urogenital and neurological physiology. If the child is under 4 or has clear organic pathology, wetting would be considered "normal" or "expected." Nevertheless, because the definition includes exclusionary criteria, there is some disagreement as to what those criteria should be. Some suggest the age criteria is either too arbitrary or should be set at 5 years instead of 3 (e.g., Forsythe and Redmond, 1974; Kolvin, 1975). Others argue that organic pathology is too often overlooked and should not play an exclusionary role in the very definition of the disorder (e.g., Mahoney and Laferte, 1973). Still, the vast majority of investigators have continued to adhere to the criteria outlined above.

THEORETICAL ANALYSIS

A variety of intrapsychic, behavioral, and biological explanations of enuresis have been discussed. Most models focus on central aspects of urinary control (e.g., poorly developed cortical inhibition; failure to appreciate bladder sensations), but some argue that small bladder capacity or bladder hypersensitivity may be at fault.

Psychodynamic or Intrapsychic Formulations

Intrapsychic explanations view enuresis as the symptom of a more important, usually deep-seated, emotional disturbance. The exact nature of the disturbance varies from writer to writer. Freud (1916) described enuresis as a substitute for masturbation. Sperling (1965) emphasized enuresis as an indication of a disturbed mother-child relationship which can lead to psychosexual problems (e.g., impotence, frigidity) in adulthood. In addition to the sexual pleasure and exhibitionism the child may derive from his wetting, it is also a means of expressing hostility toward his mother who sleeps with the father and not with the child. Other theorists have described enuresis as an expression of deep-seated anxiety, a wish to return to babyhood, a fear of the opposite sex, an inferiority complex, and feelings of jealousy (Campbell, 1937; Cohen, 1975; Mowrer and Mowrer, 1938; Stockwell and Smith, 1940). The various intrapsychic theories can probably best be categorized as focusing on repressed feelings of (1) sexuality, (2) anxiety or fear, (3) hostility toward the parent, or (4) desires to return to or maintain an infantile relationship with the mother. Since enuresis is viewed as a symptom of an underlying psychological disorder, no single intrapsychic disturbance would necessarily account for all cases of enuresis. Further, an enuretic child could potentially suffer from several different kinds of repressed feelings at the same time (e.g., sexual desires and feelings of hostility toward the mother).

Exactly how deep-seated psychological problems cause the child to wet is left unclear, although presumably they interfere with higher-order inhibitory mechanisms.

Behavioral or Learning Theory Formulations

Behavioral theories emphasize urinary continence as a learned response. As such, discriminative cues must be learned both at a physiological and situational level. The child must learn to discriminate a full bladder as the physiological cue that he needs to void. He must also learn what are the environmental cues (e.g., toilet) for micturition to occur. And finally, he must learn to postpone a desire to void until he can get himself to a bathroom where he engages in very specific pre-micturition behaviors (e.g., removing pants and sitting on the toilet if the child is a girl, unzipping pants and standing in front of the toilet if the child is a boy). Both classical conditioning and instrumental learning are assumed to be involved, although authors differ as to which plays the greater role (Lovibond, 1964; Mowrer and Mowrer, 1938; Yates, 1975). In this model, enuresis is considered to be a failure in learning the necessary skills. Inappropriate reward or punishment contingencies have been applied and/or internal and environmental cues have not become discriminative stimuli for the various behaviors necessary to stay dry.

Learning theories of enuresis clearly focus on the presumed lack of higher cortical control. Either the child has not learned to appreciate full bladder cues as a signal he has to void, or he has not learned to inhibit the micturition response, or he has not learned to urinate in a socially acceptable place and manner.

Biological or Medical Formulations

It is clear that diurnal or nocturnal wetting can be caused by illness or organic pathology (e.g., uropathological obstructions or lesions, diabetes, spina bifida). Children with such disorders are not considered "true" enuretics and account for less than five percent of all youngsters presenting with wetting problems (Campbell, 1970; Cohen, 1975; Forsythe and Redmond, 1974; Kendall and Karafin, 1973). Some investigators claim that organic pathology is overlooked in children with poor bladder control and that it accounts for the symptoms of as many as 95 percent of these cases (Arnold and Ginsburg, 1973; Mahoney, 1971). However, this is currently a minority view and has been criticized as leading to inappropriate and potentially dangerous urethral instrumentation or surgical intervention (Kendall and Karafin, 1973; Scott, 1973).

Clearly, the possibility that organic pathology is responsible for a child's wetting should not be overlooked. However, the focus of this chapter is the "true" enuretic—the child with inadequate control who does not suffer from organic pathology. A number of physiological models have been proposed to account for this problem including profoundness of sleep or poor arousal mechanisms, small bladder capacities and/or bladder spasms (Gerrard and Zaleski, 1969). The more general notion of maturational or developmental delay has also been proposed, suggesting that some sort of neurophysiological immaturity is at fault (Barbour, Borland, Boyd et al., 1963).

Some biological theories, like the intrapsychic and learning theories, focus primarily on cortical aspects of bladder control. Others focus more on peripheral aspects of the micturition process (e.g., bladder capacity or spasms) or on deficits in subcortical inhibitory or arousal mechanisms.

Comments

While the various attempts at explaining enuresis can be classified as intrapsychic, learning, or biological in nature, no one theory may be necessarily "right" to the exclusion of all others. Different children may be enuretic for different reasons, or a single child may be enuretic in response to an interaction of physiological and/or psychological factors. If a child is physiologically immature, he may have greater difficulty learning the appropriate controlling responses. His failure in this regard may lead to increased anxiety with further detrimental effects on learning. Or, a child who experiences a great deal of punitive behavior from his mother may have heightened anxiety, and consequently, greater difficulty in learning the necessary skills for complete bladder control. Obviously, there are numerous possible interactional hypotheses one could put forward to explain any individual child's enuresis.

The adequacy of the various theories is open to question. Relevant data will be presented in both the assessment and treatment sections of this chapter.

ASSESSMENT

To a large extent, intrapsychic and biological theories have guided assessment efforts in enuresis. As such, a good number of studies have focused on personality characteristics of the child or physiological measures. Some family history and social class variables have been studied and behavioral checklists have been occasionally used. However, attempts at direct observation of the enuretic child have been rare.

Personality Assessment

Efforts to assess the child's personality stem primarily from intrapsychic formulations that enuretics suffer from an underlying emotional disorder. Although a number of studies have assessed personality characteristics associated with enuresis, only those using control groups and/or standardized personality measures will be discussed here. Studies focusing on behavioral characteristics of the enuretic child (e.g., temper tantrums, nail biting, crying) will be discussed under behavioral assessment.

One of the earliest controlled studies (Anderson, 1930) reporting a high incidence of emotional disturbance among enuretics, described these children as infantile, overly sensitive, timid, but sometimes aggressive. However, Anderson's (1930) controls differed considerably from his enuretics on a number of important variables (e.g., age, sex, race, IQ). And as Halgren (1957b) pointed out, the differences between enuretics and controls was statistically significant only for the "infantile" characteristic. Cust (1952) carried out a better study in which enuretics were selected from a general school population and compared to matched controls. By mothers' reports, 45 percent of the enuretic children suffered emotional problems as compared to 15 percent of controls. Similar data were reported by Halgren (1957b) for children with diurnal or diurnal and nocturnal enuresis; no differences were found for children who wet only at night. Both of these studies asked parents for a global rating of the "emotional" or "nervous" problems of their children.

When asking a parent to rate his own child's emotional development, there is a risk that the enuretic child's parent will see him as more emotionally disturbed solely because of his enuresis. Given the often reported view that enuresis is a sign of an underlying psychological disorder, it would not be surprising if more generally negative parental attitudes toward a child might develop. In fact, Lovibond (1964) found most mothers do believe enuresis is caused by "nerves" or emotional disturbance. To circumvent such potentially negative halo effects, some studies have asked adults other than the child's parents (e.g., teachers, health-care workers, psychologists) to rate the child's emotional adjustment. Staff "personality" ratings were obtained by Stein and Susser (1965) on enuretic and nonenuretic delinquent boys. In this study, enuretic boys were rated as more submissive, lacking dominance and leadership, and disinterested in sex. Oppel, Harper, and Rider (1968) used a psychologist to rate each child on a variety of personality characteristics. Primary enuretics were described as significantly more sensitive, withdrawn, likely to suppress feelings, and less ambitious. Halgren (1957a) also reported a greater incidence of stubborn, introverted, regressive, and immature behavior in enuretic children than in their nonenuretic siblings. Interview data from enuretic naval recruits were rated as more indicative of psychiatric disturbance than the same data obtained from controls (Pierce, Lipcon, McLary, and Noble,

1956). Only Halgren (1957b) and Lickorish (1964) reported no differences in emotional adjustment between enuretics and nonenuretic comparison groups.

Although an independent examiner may help reduce negative halo effects, only the Oppel et al. (1968) study specifically used a blind examiner. Consequently, almost all of the studies cited above are susceptible to the bias of the examiner involved. Further, large population differences exist from study to study. Halgren (1957a) and Lickorish (1964) focused on children from inpatient or outpatient psychiatric services. Stein and Susser (1965) used delinquents. Pierce et al. (1956) focused on adults. Over half of Oppel et al.'s (1968) children were clearly underweight at birth. Only Halgren (1957b) obtained subjects from a general school population.

Not all investigators have sought data on enuretic emotional development solely from parents or other adults. Some have chosen to examine the child's responses both to objective and projective tests. A variety of measures have been used including the Draw-A-Person Test, the Draw-Your-Family Test, the Self-Image Questionnaire, the Blacky Test, the Rorschach, the Family Relations Test, the Neurotic Inventory, and Cattel's Child Personality Questionnaire. In no study have differences between enuretics and controls been found (Baker, 1969; DeLuca, 1968a, 1968b; Kahane, 1955; Kolvin, Taunch, Currah et al., 1972; Lovibond, 1964; Sacks, DeLeon, and Blackman, 1974; Smith, Mark, and Blerk, 1973). Only Scallon and Herron (1969) report differences between their lower socioeconomic enuretic boys and matched controls using the Children's Embedded Figures Test (CEFT). Although the CEFT is a test of perceptual style and not personality, they nevertheless conclude that the enuretic boy "has poorly developed controls and defenses which result in passive, helpless, and confused responding" (p. 412).

As is perhaps obvious from the previous discussion, most investigators have chosen to assess the enuretic child's personality by assessing the child directly or by obtaining information from significant others. Another approach has been to look at the prevalence of enuresis among "deviant" groups in comparison to prevalence in the "normal" population. Levine (1943), for example, reported that while 1.2 percent of naval recruits were bedwetters, 24 percent of those discharged for psychiatric reasons were enuretics. Michaels and Goodman (1939) reported that 43.8 percent of patients in a state mental hospital for "psychiatric behavior problems" had had enuresis in comparison to 24.7 percent of nonhospitalized normals. The difference between the two populations was even greater if one considered only those persons with enuresis after the age of 10. Such data is often cited as support for the intrapsychic position that enuresis is only the symptom of a more important psychiatric disturbance. Both of these studies, however, focused on disordered adults. In children, the data is equivocal. Rutter, Tizard, and Whitmore (1970) found more enuresis among psychiatrically disturbed youngsters (24–30 percent) than among normals (4–7 percent), a finding contradicting early work reported by Tapia, Jekel, and Domke (1960).

Overall, the personality data on enuretics must be viewed as inconclusive. Parental report or independent examiners who are aware of the child's enuresis are typically employed, making any data obtained highly susceptible to bias. The enuretics studied are often from populations with a higher known incidence of deviance than the normal population (e.g., outpatient psychiatric clinics, schools for delinquents). The personality measures used are either global in nature and consequently highly susceptible to bias (Kent, O'Leary, Diament, and Dietz, 1974; Shuller and McNamara, 1976), or are of questionable reliability and validity. Finally, since the data are only correlational in nature, it seems premature to conclude that emotional disturbance causes enuresis. Even if enuretics were more deviant than normals (which has not been conclusively demonstrated), such deviance could be the result rather than the cause of enuresis.

Behavioral Assessment

Behavioral Checklists.   Most of behavioral assessment has been in the form of behavioral checklists filled out by the child's parent or teacher. Although such data have been collected with primarily intrapsychic theories in mind, it is discussed here since its focus is behavior rather than the personality characteristics of the child.

In an early study by Michaels and Goodman (1934), the parents of a large group of campers were interviewed. The presence or absence of a number of child behaviors considered to be "neurotic manifestations" were checked (e.g., nail biting, thumb sucking, tantrums, speech impediments). If a child had one of these behaviors he was slightly more likely to be or have been enuretic. However, some two-thirds of the children with such "neurotic manifestations" were not enuretic. Similar behaviors were noted by Halgren (1957a) for enuretic children seen in psychiatric clinics and also for their siblings. Tics, headaches, nail biting, finger sucking, and temper tantrums were more common among the enuretics, but well over half of the nonenuretic siblings had at least one of these behavioral characteristics. Werry and Cohrssen (1965) also studied enuretics from an outpatient clinic and used nonenuretic siblings as controls. As a group, the enuretics had significantly more problem behaviors scored on a behavioral checklist. Nevertheless, over half of these children did not obtain a deviant score and were considered mentally healthy. When enuretics are selected from a general school population rather than a psychiatric clinic, the data is equivocal. Douglas (1973) and Wolkind (1976) found greater behavioral disturbance among enuretics, while Halgren (1957b) and Lovibond (1964) did not.

Rutter and his colleagues (Rutter et al., 1970; Rutter, Yule, and Graham, 1973) also focused on the general population but used both teacher ratings and parental reports. At all ages studied, parents of enuretics rated their children as more deviant on a behavioral checklist than did parents of nonenuretics. Nevertheless, some two-thirds of the enuretics received ratings within normal limits. To help control potential halo effects, the children's teachers were also asked to fill out a behavioral questionnaire. Most of the teachers did not know a particular child was enuretic. Only the female enuretics were consistently rated as more deviant than their female nonenuretic controls. Again, the great majority of these enuretic girls were not scored as deviant. Baker (1969) and Tapia et al. (1960) also used teacher ratings on a behavioral checklist. In both studies no differences between enuretics and matched controls were found.

Much of the work using behavioral checklists suffers from the same criticisms as the research focusing on personality variables: possible parent, examiner, or population biases, and the use of checklists of unknown reliability and validity. To their credit, Lovibond (1964), Werry and Cohrssen (1965), Rutter et al. (1973), and Baker (1969), all used checklists with at least some published data as to their adequacy as measurement instruments. Given the available data, however, no conclusive statements can be made. Perhaps most interesting is the repeated finding that the majority of enuretics do not suffer from a significant behavioral disorder. Even those studies cited as evidence for psychological disturbance among enuretics (Michaels and Goodman, 1934; Halgren, 1957a; Werry and Cohrssen, 1965) report high rates of specific problem behaviors among nonenuretics and/or a high percentage of enuretic children without serious behavioral deviations. Whatever relationship behavioral problems have to enuresis, it is certainly not a highly predictive one.

Toilet Training. If faulty learning is involved in enuresis, an assessment of toilet-training practices might offer some support for such a position. Data on such practices, however, is entirely retrospective. Most investigators report no differences between enuretics and controls as to what age toilet training was initiated or the general procedures used (Cust, 1952; Dimson, 1959; Klackenberg, 1955; Lovibond, 1964; Stein et al., 1965; Umphress, Murphy, Nickols, and Hammar, 1970). However, some reports suggest that enuretic children were more uncooperative during training (Cust, 1952; Dimson, 1959) and that mothers of enuretics experienced more frustration and anger during training (Umphress et al., 1970). Given the retrospective nature of this data, it is difficult to assess its validity. It is possible that some children are difficult to train, leading to frustration and impatience in the mother with ultimate incomplete learning in the child. Or, initial impatience of the mother in handling the child may lead to uncooperative behavior on the child's part and again, incomplete learning. Still another possibility is that a parent will remember interactions with her child during toilet training as particularly difficult solely because of the negative halo effects the child's current enuresis may create. Until better prospective data is collected on this issue, the role of toilet-training practices in enuresis will remain unclear.

Developmental Level.   A number of studies have assessed IQ, neuropsychological, and other developmental characteristics of the enuretic child, primarily as an outgrowth of the developmental lag hypothesis. Most investigators agree that enuretic children are of normal intelligence (Bindelglas, Dee, and Enos, 1968; Boyd, 1960; Halgren, 1959; Murphy, Nickols, and Hammar, 1970). Although an uncontrolled study by Campbell, Weissman, and Lupp (1970) reported evidence of a lag in sensorimotor development, this finding was not supported by either the controlled work of Werry and Cohrssen (1965) or that of Murphy et al. (1970). Speech defects or delays have been reported by several investigators (Douglas, 1973; Halgren, 1957a; Michaels and Goodman, 1934) and are sometimes seen as evidence of maturational delay. Other writers list them as examples of "nervous behavior." In any event, their incidence is low and the studies addressing this issue are not consistent in their findings (Macfarlane, Allen, and Honzik, 1954). In fact, Murphy et al. (1970) found no evidence for developmental differences in childhood or adolescence between their enuretics and matched controls. If maturational differences exist they do not seem to be readily apparent from behavioral tests of intelligence or development.

Recording of Enuretic Behavior.   The labeling of a child as enuretic is almost always based on parent report. Similarly, any treatment program's effectiveness is based on parent or child records of wetting behavior. Although such behavior is relatively easily defined and measured, rarely have any efforts been made to assess the reliability or validity of these reports. Taylor and Turner (1975) found that a mother's report of the frequency of her child's wetting correlated r = .85 with subsequent baseline recordings. In contrast, Shaffer et al. (1968) found that most records collected during pre-treatment indicated that the child wet substantially less than his mother had indicated upon initial interview. It is difficult to know whether mothers' initial reports were inaccurate or whether recording had a reactive effect on wetting behavior. Possible reactive effects of self-recording have been noted by Maxwell and Seldrup (1971). Other investigators have commented on the difficulty of obtaining any consistent records from parents or children involved in treatment (Freyman, 1963; Turner and Taylor, 1974).

Family Assessment

One of the most consistent findings in the literature is the high rate of enuresis in parents, sibs, and close relatives of the enuretic child. In Halgren's (1957a) study, 32 percent of fathers and 20 percent of mothers of enuretics were themselves enuretic in childhood. Both figures are higher than the expected risk in the general population and are in keeping with earlier data reported by Frary (1935). Bakwin (1973) reported that if both parents were enuretic, 77 percent of their off-spring would also have wetting problems. Of course, such data could be explained from either a nature or nurture point of view.

A second consistent finding is the higher prevalence of enuresis among lower socioeconomic classes (Douglas, 1973; Halgren, 1957a, 1957b; Oppel et al., 1968; Stein, Susser, and Wilson, 1965; Umphress et al., 1970). Perhaps more informative are those studies that have assessed specific family characteristics. In particular, disruptive, deviant families are more often associated with enuresis. Stein et al. (1965), for example, reported that when the child is 5, the family's level of aspiration was the most significant family factor related to enuresis (i.e., non-aspirant families had a greater incidence of enuresis). At 10, however, family deviance was most often associated with persistent wetting. Cust (1952) and Umphress et al. (1970) also reported more home problems in families of enuretics than in matched controls. Mother-child separation seems to be a particularly important variable (Halgren, 1957a; Stein and Susser, 1965). Perhaps the best study of this type was carried out by Douglas (1973) who collected data at regular intervals on all children born in Great Britain in March of 1946 when these children were from 4 to 15 years of age. Some 36 percent of children 6 years or older who had lost their mother through death during their first 6 years of life were enuretic. This figure compares to 28 percent of children whose parents were separated or divorced, and 16 percent of children from unbroken families. If a child was separated from his mother for a month or more prior to age 6 and was temporarily placed in an unfamiliar environment with an unfamiliar caretaker, the incidence of enuresis after age 5 jumped to 45 percent. Hospital admissions were also related to enuresis. Children admitted three or more times during their first 5 years of life had incidence rates two to three times as high as children never admitted. Cust (1952) also reported a higher incidence of illness between the ages of 2 and 3 in children who subsequently became enuretic.

While the epidemiological approach has been the most common method of assessing enuretics' family patterns, some studies have focused more closely on the personality characteristics and child-rearing practices of the enuretic child's parent(s). Umphress et al. (1970) reported that enuretics seen in an adolescent clinic often had rejecting, punitive parents who used inconsistent discipline and encouraged acting-out behavior. These characteristics were relatively uncommon in parents of nonenuretic, nonclinic adolescent controls. Oppel et al. (1968) had social workers rate maternal attitudes and behavior during a home interview. A higher percentage of primary enuretics were found among children whose mothers negatively evaluated the child, had poor social contacts, and poor marital adjustment. A number of other maternal characteristics (e.g., use of fear to control the child, rejection of the child, maternal anxiety) were related to primary enuresis in females only. Wolkind (1976) found mothers of 4-year-old preschool enuretics to have more somatic complaints and to describe themselves as more tired than mothers of nonenuretic 4-year olds. Finally, Stehbens (1970) examined MMPI scores from mothers of enuretics in comparison to controls. These women proved significantly higher on only one scale, Paranoia, which the author suggests may be solely a chance finding.

A rare, prospective study was reported by Nilsson, Almgren, Kohler, and Kohler (1973). One hundred sixty-five women in Sweden were interviewed by psychiatrists on three occasions: in the middle of their pregnancy, 1 or 2 days after the baby was born, and 6 months later. On each occasion the psychiatrist rated the woman's emotional adjustment and she filled out several personality questionnaires. Four years later, 71 of these women had their children independently evaluated for the presence or absence of enuresis. Mothers of enuretic children were younger (a finding also reported by Douglas, 1973), had a shorter interval between pregnancies, more often were not married when pregnant, and more often gave birth to a child of their non-preferred sex. They had a low degree of perceived similarity with their mothers, had earlier and more frequent sexual contacts, and often came from strict and moralistic homes. They were seen as more disturbed immediately after the child's birth and had more neurotic symptoms 6 months later. They more often worked outside the home and frequently perceived their children as having more behavior problems, as attention seeking, and as overly dependent.

There are, of course, a number of methodological problems that exist throughout this literature. The reliability of judgments is never assessed. Decisions as to parental personality characteristics are made by examiners aware of the enuretic or nonenuretic status of the parent's child. Parents who are willing to admit their child is enuretic may also be more willing to admit their own fears and frustrations. Despite these methodological flaws, the consistency of the available data does argue rather strongly for early environmental stress as a factor in enuresis. The stress may involve the loss of the mother through illness (either the child's or the mother's), divorce, or economic necessity (e.g., working during hours one would normally interact with the child). Or, the mother may be stressed even prior to the child's birth, with the child's birth only adding to her difficulties. Exactly how these factors lead to poor bladder control is not clear. Under such conditions, a poor mother-child relationship may develop which could lead to the kind of intrapsychic formulations discussed earlier. Or, environmental or personal stresses may prevent the mother from engaging in the patient, consistent training required to teach a child bladder control. The child may also become anxious and insecure living in a rather chaotic household, making it difficult for him to learn from even reasonably adequate training techniques. In addition, it should be pointed out that while stresses within the family may be associated with enuresis, such factors do not explain the disorder in its entirety. Many children from unbroken homes develop enuresis and many children experiencing relatively severe disruptions in their homelife still manage to develop bladder control prior to age 4.

Physiological Assessment

Physiological assessment of enuretics has focused primarily on brainwave activity, bladder capacity, and the timing and magnitude of bladder contractions.

Electroencephalographic (EEG) Recordings. Monitoring enuretics' brainwave activity has occurred in response to one of several theories involving: (1) the role of depth of sleep and arousal in enuresis; (2) the possible relationship of enuresis to epilepsy or convulsive disorders; and (3) enuresis as a consequence of cortical immaturity.

Parents often report that their enuretic children are unusually difficult to arouse (Arnold, 1968; Boyd, 1960; Braithwaite, 1955; Geppert, 1953; Noack, 1964). Boyd (1960), however, woke enuretic children and matched controls by calling their names and, if they did not respond, by shaking them gently. No evidence was found suggesting enuretics were more difficult to arouse. Since this study was conducted in a hospital setting, it is possible that the enuretic children were sleeping less deeply in this unfamiliar environment than at home. Nevertheless, other investigators using EEG recording have not found any consistent differences in sleep patterns between enuretics and controls (Graham, 1973; Weinmann, 1968). Pierce (1963) reported that enuretics had less rapid-eye-movement (REM) than nonenuretics and, as a consequence, had fewer dreams. In fact, Pierce (1963) went so far as to suggest that the enuretic episode may be a dream substitute. Such speculations, however, were made in the absence of EEG data from nonenuretic controls.

One of the few replicated findings on this literature is the absence of wetting episodes during dreaming or REM sleep (Broughton, 1968; Ritvo, Ornitz, Gottlieb et al., 1969; Pierce, 1963; Schiff, 1965). However, there is not a great deal of agreement as to when during the various stages of sleep enuretic behavior typically happens. Initially, children's wetting was thought to occur during deep sleep (Ditman and Blinn, 1955; Schiff, 1965). More recently, though, several studies have reported that children's wetting occurs in both light and deep sleep (Broughton, 1968; Ritvo et al., 1969; Weinmann, 1968). Of interest are the behavioral and heart rate changes (e.g., gross body movement, tachycardia) that have been recorded just prior to micturition (Broughton, 1968; Pierce, Whitman, Maas, and Gray, 1961; Evans, 1971). EEG changes often occur as well (Diperri and Laura, 1968; Pierce et al., 1961; Ritvo et al., 1969). It is unclear, however, why these behavioral and physiological changes do not culminate in full awakening as they do in the normal child. Although the data currently available disconfirm any direct association of enuresis with dreaming, they do not explain what role sleep or arousal patterns have in enuresis. No single sleep phase seems characteristic of enuresis. The fact that pre-micturition behavioral and EEG changes do not lead to full wakening and/or further inhibition of the micturition reflex could be explained by any number of hypotheses (e.g., arousal defects in the reticular activating system of the brain, suppression of arousal mechanisms by the cortex in response to intrapsychic conflicts, faulty learning in which full bladder cues are not an adequate conditioned stimulus to lead to full arousal).

While most investigators using EEG recordings have focused on the sleep patterns of enuretics, others have seen enuresis as a kind of convulsive disorder (Campbell and Young, 1966; Fermaglich, 1969; Szab'o and Popoviciu, 1969), or as a sign of immaturity (Barbour et al., 1963; Boyd, 1960; Gunnarson and Melin, 1951; Ovary and Zsadanyi, 1967). Although all of these studies have reported a relatively high incidence of "abnormal" EEG records among enuretics, none have used nonenuretic controls. Furthermore, scoring of the EEG records is not typically done by someone ignorant of the child's enuresis. In fact, a rare controlled EEG study (Murphy et al., 1970) reported no difference between enuretic and normal adolescents. Even if enuretics do have more "abnormal" EEG recordings, the role of such activity in enuresis remains unclear. In their excellent review, Salmon, Taylor, and Lee (1973) point out that many persons with atypical EEGs do not have epilepsy. Simply because an enuretic child has an abnormal EEG is not evidence enough that he suffers from a clinical or subclinical convulsive disorder. Similarly, the maturational lag hypothesis cannot be adequately assessed until prospective controlled studies are carried out. At this point in time there is just too little known as to what EEG changes occur through normal development, and what is the functional significance of an unusual recording in childhood.

Bladder Capacity. In 1950, Hallman reported that enuretics had a smaller functional bladder capacity than normals. Since that time a number of investigators (Arnold, 1966; Doleys, Ciminero, Tollison et al., 1977; Linderholm, 1966; Muellner, 1960) have replicated this finding and discussed what causal role bladder capacity may play in enuresis.

Maximum functional bladder capacity (MBC) is usually measured by one of two methods. The child may be given an oral waterload of 30 ml/kg body weight (maximum volume of 500 ml) and told to refrain from voiding until he feels discomfort. When the child voids, his urine output is measured. Usually the larger of two voided specimens is taken as the MBC. The second method is to have the child's parents measure and record every time the child micturates at home for up to one week. The largest volume of urine passed at any one time is taken as the MBC (Zaleski, Gerrard, and Schokier, 1973).

Carefully controlled studies by Starfield (1967) and Starfield and Mellits (1968) demonstrated quite conclusively that enuretics do have smaller bladder capacities than nonenuretics. This leads to more frequent micturation even during their waking hours. Troup and Hodgson (1971) measured enuretics' urine volumes when they wet at night. They found day and nighttime volumes to be equivalent, and both were less than nonenuretic controls. They also report that the child's "true" bladder capacity measured under mild anesthesia was not different between the groups. A recent study by Zaleski et al. (1973) replicated Starfield's findings, but also noted that enuretics with daytime urgency or wetting have even smaller MBCs than enuretics with nighttime symptoms only. There is some evidence that primary enuretics have smaller MBCs than secondary enuretics (Starfield, 1967). Also of interest is the increase in MBC that has been found with treatment cures (Esperanca and Gerrard, 1969; Starfield and Mellits, 1968; Zaleski et al., 1973).

Often associated with small bladder capacity are uninhibited bladder contractions at low urine volumes (Arnold, 1966; Johnstone, Ardran, and Ramsden, 1977; Linderholm, 1966; Pompeius, 1971; Torrens and Collins, 1975; Whiteside and Arnold, 1975). There is some evidence to suggest that such contractions occur more often in enuretics with both day and night symptoms rather than night wetting only (Whiteside and Arnold, 1975).

Although research on uninhibited bladder contractions is not as well controlled as that on MBC, it does offer some support for the notion that enuretic children have not developed the inhibiting mechanisms that naturally occur in most children. At birth, the infant has an "automatic" bladder leading to very frequent micturition. Over time, his bladder capacity increases and actually doubles between the ages of 2 and 4 (Muellner, 1960). The fact that enuretics have not developed the same bladder capacity as normals has led some investigators to point to maturational delay in central nervous system inhibitory centers (Linderholm, 1966; Troup and Hodgson, 1971). Muellner (1960) suggests that the enuretic child has not yet mastered the "voluntary mechanism" by which urination is inhibited or initiated. In his view, it is this voluntary control that leads the child to increase his bladder capacity so substantially between the ages of 2 and 4. Arnold (1966) postulates a more psychosomatic explanation, suggesting that some children are born with a greater tendency toward uninhibited bladder contractions which are then exacerbated by psychological factors. Starfield (1972) suggests that it is excessive bladder contractions in combination with slow-wave sleep patterns that lead to nighttime wetting.

While the data on MBC is compelling, we do not yet know the exact role small MBC plays in enuresis. On the average, enuretics have smaller MBC than nonenuretics but there is overlap between groups (i.e., not all enuretics have small MBC and some nonenuretics do). Further, even if the enuretic child must urinate more often, why does he not awake in response to his more frequent urgency? Although a larger MBC may help a child sleep through the night without ever needing to use the toilet, normal children and adults are able to awake and go to the bathroom if need be. Simply pointing to "maturational lag" seems too vague an explanation of the available data. Finally, it is probably worth noting that small MBC could very well be the result rather than the cause of enuresis.

Comments

In reading the assessment literature on enuresis, one is struck not only by its extensiveness but by its strict adherence to particular theoretical models of the disorder. Those with a psychoanalytic bent have spent a great deal of effort looking for psychopathology in the enuretic child or his parents. Those who adhere to medical formulations have stayed narrowly focused on physical aspects of the problem. Epidemiologists have made some rather interesting observations, and behaviorists have had little to do with assessment at all! No position has been able to adequately explain enuresis, yet there remains a distinct lack of integration between the various data domains. Similarly, assessment is almost never related to treatment, but this issue will be discussed in more detail later in this chapter.

Currently, the assessment literature seems to be mired down by each group's narrow adherence to its own particular model. Some enuretics have emotional or behavioral problems, some come from chaotic households, some have disturbed parents, some have parents and siblings who are or were enuretic, some have small bladder capacities, some have abnormal EEGs. None of these characteristics describe all or even most enuretics and certainly, causal interpretations are premature. What then should be done? First, it is clear that enuretics are a heterogeneous group and it is probably best to abandon all hope of explaining the disorder in its entirety by one particular theoretical model. Second, it may be of some use to distinguish between what causes the disorder in a child of 4 and what is currently maintaining the problem in a 10-year-old youngster or in an adult. Early causal hypotheses can best be answered by prospective studies which assess physical, behavioral, emotional, and parent-child relationships of children prior to the age of 4 or 5. This type of approach might very well identify a set of characteristics that make a particular child "high risk" for the development of enuresis. For those children who are already enuretic, a careful assessment of the child's current physical, social, and emotional functioning seems more appropriate than a retrospective analysis of what might have "caused" this problem when he was in preschool. In this regard, too little attention seems to be paid to what factors may be maintaining the child's wetting behavior in his current environment. Some children may receive a lot of attention for their problem, others may not. Depending on the current factors involved, different treatment approaches might be suggested. In any event, it is time that an enuretic child is assessed from a multidimensional perspective. Most of us would agree that human behavior is multidetermined; enuretic behavior seems to be no exception.

TREATMENT

In most ways, the treatment of enuresis has not been guided by the assessment literature. Two forms of therapy seem to prevail—the use of medication and the use of various learning techniques. Psychotherapy has not been studied extensively despite the strong influence of the intrapsychic model within the assessment literature. As we shall see, the learning or behavioral model has been very powerful with regard to the treatment of enuresis. The use of medication (tricyclic drugs in particular) seems to be an "accidental" discovery rather than a product of a specific theoretical approach. Nevertheless, theory has been used extensively to explain the effectiveness of these drugs, post-hoc.

Advice and Suggestion

Probably the most common sense approach to enuresis is simply waking the child during the night and having him use the toilet. Such a procedure has been used in four controlled studies with only minimal success. McConaghy (1969) had parents wake their child at random intervals one to three times a night. Only one child (11 percent of the sample) responded to this approach, and great difficulty was noted in getting parents to continue for the full 10-week treatment interval. Even less success was found using a similar approach by Turner, Young, and Rachman (1970). Baker (1969) reports a significant drop in frequency using this procedure over waiting-list controls. Nevertheless, only two of these children (14 percent) actually became dry. Creer and Davis (1975) also report improvement using this method, although no child became completely dry during 6 weeks of treatment. One child (11 percent) had been dry for 1 month at follow-up.

Another approach has been to advise the parents not to punish the child for his wetting and that he will eventually "grow out" of the problem. Typically, the child is seen on a regular basis and is asked to keep track of his dry nights. He also is given the strong suggestion that he will definitely improve. Dische (1971) has found this approach to be successful in about a third of her cases. White (1968) also reports good success, giving a placebo along with strong suggestion and self-recording of dry nights. Novick (1966) found this procedure was particularly effective with secondary enuretics, but relapse often occurred. Although all of these authors view their efforts as merely "supportive," the reactive effects of self-recording and effects of social reinforcement by the "supportive" person seeing the child are no doubt involved.

Psychotherapy

Despite the commonly held view that enuresis is the symptom of an underlying emotional disorder, only two controlled studies using psychotherapy have been carried out. Werry and Cohrssen (1965) used brief psychotherapy (6–8 sessions) over a 3-month period. Only two children (10 percent) were cured which was not significantly better than no treatment at all. Similar results were found by DeLeon and Mandell (1966) who used a slightly longer (12 sessions) treatment interval. Of course, it is possible that a longer course of psychotherapy would prove more effective. Nigam, Tandon, Lal, and Thacore (1973) reported cure rates of 40 percent for children given psychotherapy plus a placebo. However, since no placebo controls were used, it is impossible to tell how much of this success was due to psychotherapy and how much to the suggestion effects of the placebo.

Medication

Imipramine and other tricyclic antidepressant drugs have been used extensively with enuretics. Their use was first suggested by a psychologist, Hugh Esson, who noted difficulty in urination by many depressed patients treated with imipramine (MacLean, 1960). A variety of other types of drugs have been tried, but only the tricyclics have shown any consistent effectiveness. (See Blackwell and Currah, 1973, for a review.)

Fortunately, there have been quite a number of reasonably well-controlled studies comparing one of the tricyclics to a placebo. Those achieving design quality ratings of good or very good (Curman et al., in press) are presented in Tables 1, 2, and 3. The tables have been arranged by subject grouping. Table 1 lists those studies using noninstitutionalized children. Table 2 focuses on the research done with enuretic children who have been institutionalized for any number of reasons (e.g., neglect, emotional disturbance, mental retardation). And Table 3 cites those studies using adult populations (both institutionalized and noninstitutionalized).

Table 1. *Studies comparing tricyclic antidepressants to placebos in noninstitutionalized children*

Authors	Drug	Type of Subject	Number of Subjects	Percent Cured on Drug	Percent Cured off Drug at Follow-up	Drug Significantly Better than Placebo?
Agarwala and Heycock (1968)	Imipramine	outpatients	29	7	21	yes
Bindeglas et al. (1968)	Imipramine	volunteers	63	20	38	yes
Forsythe and Merrett (1969)	Imipramine; Nortriptyline	outpatients	247	1	2	yes
Forsythe et al. (1972a)	Trimipramine	outpatients	186	0	3	no
Forsythe et al. (1972b)	Amitriptyine	outpatients	241	2	1	yes
Friday and Feldman (1966)	Imipramine	outpatients	51	?	no follow-up	yes
Kardash et al. (1968)	Imipramine	outpatients	45	47	30	yes
Kolvin et al. (1972)	Imipramine	volunteers	94	?	?	yes
Lake (1968)	Nortriptyline	outpatients	54	?	no follow-up	yes
Laybourne et al. (1968)	Imipramine	outpatients	24	?	no follow-up	yes
Liederman et al. (1969)	Desipramine	outpatients	53	23	no follow-up	at 1 mo.—yes at 2 mos.—no

Table 1.   *(Continued)*

Authors	Drug	Type of Subject	Number of Subjects	Percent Cured on Drug	Percent Cured off Drug at Follow-up	Drug Significantly Better than Placebo?
Manhas and Sharma (1967)	Imipramine	outpatients & inpatients	72	?	no follow-up	yes
Martin (1971)	Imipramine	outpatients	57	11	22	yes
Maxwell and Seldrup (1971)	Imipramine	outpatients	125	?	no follow-up	yes
Miller et al. (1968)	Imipramine	volunteers	56	?	?	yes
Petersen et al. (1974)	Imipramine; Imipramine-N-oxide	outpatients	38	?	no follow-up	yes
Poussaint and Ditman (1965)	Imipramine	outpatients	47	24	24	yes
Poussaint et al. (1966)	Amitriptyline	outpatients	50	18	10	yes
Shaffer et al. (1968)	Imipramine	outpatients	59	36	9	yes
Werry et al. (1977)	Imipramine	outpatients	20	?	no follow-up	yes
Werry et al. (1975)	Imipramine	volunteers	21	?	no follow-up	yes

?=data unavailable

101

Table 2. *Studies comparing tricyclic antidepressants to placebos in institutionalized children*

Authors	Drug(s)	Type of Subject	Number of Subjects	Percent Cured on Drug	Percent Cured off Drug at Follow-up	Drug(s) Significantly Better than Placebo?
Abrams (1963)	Imipramine	Psychologically disturbed	13	?	no follow-up	no
Alderton (1970)	Imipramine	Character disorder or schizophrenic	9	0	0	yes
Alderton (1967)	Imipramine	Character disorder or borderline schizophrenic	12	?	?	yes
Drew (1966)	Imipramine	Youngsters living in children's homes	28	?	0	yes
Kelly (1974)	Amitriptyline	Mentally retarded children and adults	22	?	no follow-up	no
Harrison and Albino (1970)	Imipramine	Youngsters living in orphanages	62	?	?	yes

Table 2. (Continued)

Authors	Drug(s)	Type of Subject	Number of Subjects	Percent Cured on Drug	Percent Cured off Drug at Follow-up	Drug(s) Significantly Better than Placebo?
Mariuz and Walters (1963)	Imipramine	Psychologically disturbed	23	13	?	yes
Smith and Gonzalez (1967)	Nortriptyline	Mentally retarded	34	?	?	yes
Thomsen et al. (1967)	Imipramine	Psychologically disturbed	19	?	?	yes
Treffert (1964)	Imipramine	Psychologically disturbed	9	?	?	no
Valentine and Maxwell (1968)	Imipramine	Mentally retarded	16	0	no follow-up	no
Waitzell et al. (1969)	Imipramine	Psychologically disturbed	2	0	no follow-up	?

? = data not available

Of course, a drug could be significantly more effective than a placebo by simply reducing the frequency of wetting, but "cure" almost no one. Consequently, also presented on each table is the percent of subjects cured while on the drug, and the percent remaining cured once the drug is withdrawn. The meaning of the term cure varies somewhat from study to study, but is used here to connote a period of complete dryness. Nevertheless, the amount of time that the child must be completely dry to be considered cured varies across studies (e.g., from 2 weeks to 2 months). The percentages presented in Tables 1–3 reflect the idiosyncratic time requirements made by each author. However, for a child to be counted as cured he had to be completely dry for whatever time period the authors chose. Often, only group data was presented so it was impossible to ascertain whether any child could be classified as cured. In such instances, a question mark has been placed in the appropriate place on the table.

As is apparent from Table 1, most of the research done has been with outpatient children. The consistent effectiveness of imipramine or one of the other tricyclics across studies is immediately obvious. Still, the percent of children cured varies from a low of 0 percent to a high of 47 percent, and is often not stated at all. Even less information is available after the drug is withdrawn, but relapse is not uncommon.

When tricyclics have been used with institutionalized children (see Table 2), the results are generally positive but clearly not as consistently powerful as those found with outpatients. Individual subject data is rarely presented, so percent cured is impossible to assess. However, it was this author's impression from reading these studies that cures were extremely rare. Furthermore, relapse to pre-drug levels of wetting occurred once the drug was withdrawn in *every* study reporting follow-up data.

In adults (see Table 3), tricyclics have been consistently ineffective. Only one study reported positive results of any kind, and these varied considerably across patient populations. Although drug-placebo differences were sometimes statistically significant, they were almost always small and of questionable practical value.

It is clear that tricyclics do have an impact on enuresis in reasonably normal, noninstitutionalized children. A milder effect seems to also occur with institutionalized youngsters. The data simply do not support the use of tricyclics with adults. Even their use with children is problematic in view of their low cure rates, high relapse rates, and possible side effects.

The relapse problem has been addressed by several authors who argue that gradual withdrawal will lead to better maintenance of treatment effects (Kardash, Hillman, and Werry, 1968; Martin, 1971;

Table 3. *Studies comparing tricyclic antidepressants to placebos in adults*

Authors	Drug	Type of Subject	Number of Subjects	Percent Cured on Drug	Percent Cured off Drug at Follow-up	Drug Significantly Better than Placebo?
Blackman et al. (1964)	Imipramine	Army recruits	35	?	no follow-up	no
Dorison and Blackman (1962)	Imipramine	Army recruits	30	?	no follow-up	no
Drew (1967)	Imipramine; Amitriptyline	mentally retarded	47	?	?	no
Fisher et al. (1963)	Imipramine	mentally retarded	34	?	no follow-up	no
Hicks and Barnes (1964)	Imipramine	Navy recruits	100	16	no follow-up	no
Milner and Hills (1968)	Imipramine; Nortriptyline; Desipramine	psychiatric inpatients	212	?	no follow-up	variable effects depending on population
Robson (1969)	Imipramine	geriatric	17	0	no follow-up	no

? = data available

Poussaint, Ditman, and Greenfield, 1966). However, of the two studies that experimentally manipulated this variable, one found no difference between gradual and abrupt withdrawal (Shaffer et al., 1968). The other found better maintenance with gradual withdrawal but did not analyze the results statistically (General Practitioner Research Group Report No. 139, 1969). Obviously, more research is needed on this issue.

Side effects have been reported by many authors and include dryness of mouth, dizziness, drowsiness, irritability, difficulty concentrating, appetite and sleep disturbances (Blackwell and Currah, 1973). More serious side effects are sometimes reported (e.g., an epileptic fit reported by Fisher, Murray, Walley, and Kiloh, 1963; cardiac effects and postural hypertension reported by Koehl and Wenzel, 1971), but are considered very rare. An excellent double-blind, placebo-controlled, and crossover study by Werry, Dowrick, Lampen, and Vamos (1975) assessed physiological, behavioral, and cognitive effects of imipramine in enuretic children. In addition to a significant decrease in wetting that was associated with the administration of imipramine, a number of other effects were found. These included increases in heart rate and diastolic blood pressure along with slight weight loss. Children were described by their parents as more cooperative and less disruptive than during the placebo control phase. Global clinical ratings by psychiatrists were more positive for these children as well. The behavioral "side effects" seemed quite positive, although this may be a direct result of the decrease in wetting rather than a result of the drug per se. In any event, the general consensus seems to be that tricyclics are safe if they are not taken for prolonged periods of time and are given under adequate medical supervision (Ayd, 1965; Blackwell and Currah, 1973). Like any other drug, they should be kept out of the reach of small children. Between 1962 and 1969, 31 children died of imipramine poisoning (Parkin and Fraser, 1972).

The mechanism by which tricyclics affect enuresis is not completely understood. However, three theoretical explanations have been proposed: (1) enuresis is a symptom of an underlying depression which is lifted through medication; (2) enuretics are deep sleepers and tricyclics affect these children's arousal mechanisms; and (3) enuretics have small bladder capacities which are increased by tricyclic medication due to the drug's relaxing effect on the detrusor muscle.

The evidence that enuresis is a symptom of an underlying depression is unconvincing. There is a good deal of argument as to whether enuresis is the symptom of *any* underlying psychological disorder; there is even less data to suggest that a specific disorder—depression—is involved (see preceding section on personality assessment). The study cited previously by Werry et al. (1975) does suggest that imipramine may have some positive psychotropic effects, although such changes may be simply in response to a decrease in wetting. Given the available data, it remains doubtful that drug-related improvement in bladder control is the indirect result of positive drug-induced psychotropic effects. Furthermore, the fact that tricyclics are used as antidepressants with adults is an insufficient reason to presume that depression is the causal mechanism underlying enuresis in children.

The arousal explanation is also open to question. There is no experimental data that tricyclics make enuretics easier to arouse. Several studies have reported that imipramine decreases REM sleep (Kales, Kales, Jacobson et al., 1977; Kales, Scharf, Tan et al., 1970; Ritvo et al., 1969). However, enuresis is known *not* to occur during this particular sleep stage (see previous section on physiological assessment). One sleep study of enuretics treated with imipramine reported no relationship between decreases in wetting and changes in sleep patterns (Kales and Kales, 1970).

Several studies have demonstrated increases in the bladder capacity of enuretics with the use of anticholinergic drugs (Johnstone, 1972; Thompson and Lauvetz, 1976). Since tricyclics have anticholinergic properties, their effectiveness with enuretics may be through this mechanism. Hagglund and Parkkulainen (1965) offer some support for this notion. An increase in bladder capacity was found in their enuretic children treated with imipramine as compared to untreated controls; similar results have been reported by Esperanca and Gerrard (1969). Although this particular theory is the most compelling of the three, it too suffers from discrepancies in the available literature. For example, other anticholinergic drugs have not been particularly successful in treating enuretics (see Blackwell and Currah, 1973, for a review). And, a recent study by Johnstone (1972) found that initial changes in bladder capacity in response to an anticholinergic drug— probanthine—did not predict ultimate success or failure during a three-month drug trial.

In sum, tricyclic drugs have been more effective than placebos in treating childhood enuresis. Nevertheless, the exact mechanism producing these effects is unknown. Tricyclics often decrease the frequency of wetting episodes. However, they rarely lead to complete bladder control. No well-controlled study reports cure rates of even 50 percent and most report rates considerably lower. Relapse remains a significant problem with many children returning to prior rates of wetting once the drug is withdrawn. It is clear that tricyclics are primarily effective with outpatient children, although some effect has been found with institutionalized children as well. There has been little or no success with adult enuretics. It is not clear what underlies these population differences; perhaps different causal mechanisms are involved.

Conditioning

In 1938, Mowrer and Mowrer introduced a device which they believed would enhance a child's learning of nocturnal urinary control. In their view, enuretics suffer from faulty learning and can be cured by presenting the discriminative cues and contingencies necessary for learning in a more precise and consistent manner. To this end they developed a device which has been popularly referred to as the "bell and pad," the "urine alarm," or the "bed-buzzer." Although a number of modifications have been made since its original development and several different devices are now currently available (see Dische, 1973), the basic mechanism has remained the same. The child sleeps on a pad or pads which are connected to a buzzer. When the child wets, his urine completes an electrical circuit and the alarm sounds. The most common type of detector consists of two wire mesh or aluminum foil pads kept separate by a layer of cloth. Each pad remains connected to the alarm. But, the circuit is only completed if the child urinates, wetting the separation cloth and thereby "connecting" the two pads (see Fig. 1).

figure 1

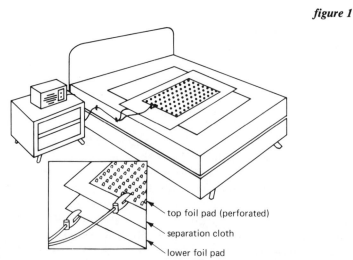

top foil pad (perforated)

separation cloth

lower foil pad

Urine alarm properly positioned on a bed. (Adapted from instructions for use of the "Wee Alert" distributed by Sears, Roebuck & Company).

A very similar device was developed as early as 1904 by a German pediatrician, Pfaundler. His purpose was to alert the nursing staff caring for a hospitalized child when that child had wet the bed and needed changing. He was somewhat surprised to note that the device, which was designed for convenience, seemed to have some therapeutic effect as well (Mowrer and Mowrer, 1938).

Mowrer and Mowrer (1938) explained the learning mechanism by which Pfaundler's device and their own urine alarm "cured" enuresis as classical conditioning. The bell and pad's alarm served as an unconditioned stimulus (US) producing waking, the unconditioned response (UR). Through repeated trials, feelings of bladder distention which occurred prior to the alarm, became a conditioned stimulus (CS) leading to arousal. When learning was complete, bladder distention (CS) would lead to waking *prior to* urination and the subsequent onset of the alarm. The child would then use the toilet instead of wetting the bed.

This formulation, however, is not entirely adequate. Responses to conditioned stimuli, for example, rapidly drop out if the CS is not repeatedly paired with the US. In other words, once the child is waking to his own bladder cues (CS), the alarm (US) no longer sounds and CS–US pairing is eliminated. This, in turn, should lead to extinction of the arousal response to the CS (bladder distention) and a return to wetting. Other theories involving instrumental learning (e.g., models of active or passive avoidance; models of social learning) have been proposed as more parsimonious explanations of the mechanism involved (Azrin, Sneed, and Foxx, 1974; Lovibond, 1964; Turner et al., 1970).

Although the urine alarm was developed in the 1930s, it was not used extensively until the 1960s. Since it treated the child's "symptoms," it was not held in very high regard by those who had a more psychoanalytic view of the disorder (O'Leary and Wilson, 1975).

Most of the initial research using this device was uncontrolled. These studies are presented in Table 4. (See also earlier reviews by Jones, 1960; Lovibond, 1964; Lovibond and Coote, 1970; Turner, 1973; and Doleys, 1977). For comparison purposes, the percent of the total sample who dropped out prematurely is presented, as well as the percent of those remaining in treatment who were initially cured. The percent of the total sample (including dropouts) initially cured is also presented, as well as relapse rates, length of follow-up, type of patient, and whether use of the device was supervised. All of the studies cited used a urine alarm in the usual fashion except Kennedy and Sloop (1968) and Lovibond (1964). Some of Kennedy and Sloop's (1968) subjects were given medication in addition to the alarm; no effect of

Table 4. Uncontrolled studies using the urine alarm

Authors	Type of Patient	Number of Patients	Supervision	Percent Dropout	Percent Initially Cured Who Completed Treatment	Percent of Total Sample Initially Cured	Relapse: Percent of Initially Cured	Length of Follow-up (months)
Baller and Schalock (1956)	outpatient children; 3 adults	55	?	0	98	98	47	24–35
Behrle et al. (1956)	Outpatient children	20	yes	10	100	90	33	18–39
Davidson and Douglas (1950)	Children living in an orphanage; 2 adult outpatients	20	?	0	75	75	27	4–9
Deacon (1939)	Mentally retarded institutionalized children	7	yes	14	83	71	60	?
Dische (1971)	Outpatient children	84	yes	10	92	81	30	6–48

Table 4. (Continued)

Authors	Type of Patient	Number of Patients	Supervision	Percent Dropout	Percent Initially Cured Who Completed Treatment	Percent of Total Sample Initially Cured	Relapse: Percent of Initially Cured	Length of Follow-up (months)
Forsythe and Redmond (1970)	Out-patient children	200	?	12	75	66	19	12–36
Freyman (1959)	Out-patient children	15	yes	13	77	73	50	1–13
Freyman (1963)	Out-patient children	71	yes	28	94	68	56	10
Geppert (1953)	Out-patient children	42	yes	?	90	90	13	?
Gillison and Skinner (1958)	Out-patient children	100	yes	4	94	90	14	?
Kennedy and Sloop (1968)	Out-patient children; institutionalized retarded children	10	?	0	100	100	30	13
		10	yes	0	40	40	?	No follow-up

? = data not available

111

Table 4. *(Continued)*

Authors	Type of Patient	Number of Patients	Supervision	Percent Dropout	Percent Initially Cured Who Completed Treatment	Percent of Total Sample Initially Cured	Relapse: Percent of Initially Cured	Length of Follow-up (months)
Lovibond (1964)	Volunteers—children	152	yes	0	98	98	40	46
Martin and Kubly (1955)	Consumers	220	no	?	?	?	?	?
McKendry et al. (1964)	Outpatient children	204	?	40	59	·35	15	1–12
Mowrer and Mowrer (1938)	Residents of a children's center	30	?	0	100	100	?	?
Novick (1966)	Outpatient children	36	no	0	89	89	?	8–12
Okasha and Hassan (1966)	Outpatient children; one adult	32	?	0	75	75	13	9

Table 4. (Continued)

Authors	Type of Patient	Number of Patients	Supervision	Percent Dropout	Percent Initially Cured Who Completed Treatment	Percent of Total Sample Initially Cured	Relapse: Percent of Initially Cured	Length of Follow-up (months)
Owens and Fischer (1966)	Out-patient children	21	?	0	67	67	43	?
Schwartz et al. (1972)	Out-patient children	26	yes	?	93	?	23	?
Sieger (1952)	Out-patient children	106	?	0	100	100	17	3–144
Turner and Taylor (1974)	Out-patient adults	10	yes	0	90	90	56	3–22
Young (1955)	Out-patient children	105	yes	35	100	65	13	12
Wikes (1958)	Out-patient children	108	?	14	54	46	18	6–24

?=data not available

113

medication was found. Lovibond's (1964) data is the sum of a number of studies using the device with either continuous (buzzer sounds every time the child wets) or intermittent (buzzer sounds only on some occasions when the child wets) reinforcement; both procedures were found to be effective. Occasionally, investigators reported giving medication to individual children who were unusually difficult to arouse (e.g., Okasha and Hassan, 1966). Also of note is the Gillison and Skinner (1958) study which reports a relapse rate of only 14 percent. This figure is probably excessively low, as the authors assumed that any relapsed patients would recontact their clinic. They made no concerted effort to systematically follow their patients subsequent to treatment.

Overall, these studies indicate a reasonably good rate of success with those patients remaining in treatment. The lowest rate, 40 percent, was with institutionalized retarded children (Kennedy and Sloop, 1968). More than half of the studies report initial cures of over 80 percent. Three studies worked with adults (Baller and Schalock, 1956; Davidson and Douglas, 1950; Turner and Taylor, 1974) and note reasonably good success, although such patients still seem more difficult to treat than children. A case study of an adult male successfully employing the urine alarm has also been published by Shader (1968). Relapse remains a problem with rates as high as 60 percent (Deacon, 1939, working with institutionalized mentally retarded children). However, most studies report relapse rates of about 33 percent or less. Moreover, many of these children become permanently dry if retreated (Behrle, Elkin, and Laybourne, 1956; Forsythe and Redmond, 1970; Geppert, 1953; Sieger, 1952).

The dropout rate varies considerably from study to study, from a low of 0 percent to a high of 40 percent. Given the considerable effort and patience required to appropriately use the device, some drop out would be expected. Authors using small, selected populations may have less difficulty with this problem. However, studies dealing with larger masses of patients seen through outpatient hospital or community clinics are undoubtedly faced with numerous examples of missed appointments, failure to follow instructions, and even sabotage on the part of the child (Forsythe and Redmond, 1970; Freyman, 1963; McKendry, Williams, and Matheson, 1964). Almost half of the studies do not give enough procedural detail to assess whether close supervision of the use of the device was carried out. It is unclear what role this variable may have on either dropout rates or rates of initial cure.

While the results presented in Table 4 compare favorably to the studies using drugs (see Tables 1–3) and to spontaneous remission rates of 14–19 percent (De Jonge, 1973; Forsythe and Redmond, 1974;

Lovibond, 1964), the lack of appropriate controls detract considerably from their overall scientific value. Fortunately, there are a number of controlled investigations using the urine alarm. These are presented in Table 5. Data similar to that presented in Table 4 is listed, including the percent of those treated who were initially cured, as well as the percent initially cured who subsequently relapsed. Also listed are the comparison or control groups in each study and its design quality rating using Curman et al.'s (in press) scoring system. All of the studies involved children identified either through advertisement or outpatient clinics. The exception is the Sloop and Kennedy (1973) study which focused on institutionalized mentally retarded youngsters.

As might be expected, the overall "cure" rates in these controlled investigations are somewhat lower and the relapse rates are somewhat higher than those reported in the uncontrolled studies discussed earlier (see Table 4). Nevertheless, the urine alarm is consistently more effective than controls. Only Peterson, Wright, and Hanlon (1969) and Turner et al. (1970) report no statistically significant effects in favor of the alarm. Both of these studies used very short treatment periods (e.g., 3–4 weeks) which may not represent a fair test of the alarm's effectiveness. In fact, in the Turner et al. (1970) study, subjects continued using the urine alarm after the first month when the treatment-control comparisons were made. Over 80 percent of these children were ultimately cured and most of these cures occurred after the first month.

Most of these studies cite initial cure rates of over 60 percent. The Sloop and Kennedy (1973) and the Werry and Cohrssen (1965) studies are exceptions in this regard. As was mentioned previously, Sloop and Kennedy (1973) used institutionalized retarded children which may explain their poor findings. Werry and Cohrssen (1965), however, used outpatient normals so their unusually low cure rate (30 percent) is probably not the result of population differences. Perhaps the lack of close supervision of their urine-alarm users may have been involved. Peterson et al. (1969) also did not closely supervise their subjects and reported no treatment effects. However, the Peterson et al. (1969) findings are as likely due to their very short (3 weeks) treatment interval. Also of interest is the extremely high relapse rate (80 percent) reported by DeLeon and Mandell (1966). It is not immediately apparent what may be responsible for this discrepant result. The authors do use a stringent criterion for determining relapse (i.e., even a single incident of wetting within 6 months was considered a relapse). As the authors point out, it is difficult to know what criterion to employ since no studies have reported how many normal children have wetting "accidents" over the course of 6 months to a year.

Table 5. Controlled studies using the urine alarm

Authors	Number of Subjects	Supervision	Percent of Those Treated Initially Cured	Relapse: Percent of Initially Cured	Length of Follow-up (months)	Comparison Groups	Urine Alarm Significantly Better?	Design Quality Rating
Baker (1969)	30	yes	79	20	6	nightly waking; no treatment	yes	good
Collins (1973)	60	yes	61	48	3–9	delayed alarm; no treatment	yes	good
DeLeon and Mandell (1966)	87	?	79	80	1–7	psychotherapy; no treatment	yes	fair
Finley et al. (1973)	30	yes	85	29	3	delayed waking	yes	good
Forrester et al. (1964)	37	yes	63 at follow-up	?	6	amphetamine	yes	good
Jehu et al. (1977)	32	yes	95	28	7–18	no treatment	yes	very good
Kahane (1955)	59	?	100	62	1–7	no treatment	?	poor
McConaghy (1969)	60	?	70	15	12	random waking; medication	yes	fair

Table 5. *(Continued)*

Authors	Number of Subjects	Supervision	Percent of Those Treated Initially Cured	Relapse: Percent of Initially Cured	Length of Follow-up (months)	Comparison Groups	Urine Alarm Significantly Better?	Design Quality Rating
Peterson et al. (1969)	28	no	?	?	no follow-up	delayed alarm; no treatment	no	good
Sloop and Kennedy (1973)	42	yes	52	36	7–11	nightly waking	yes	very good
Thorne (1973)	20	?	?	?	1	no treatment	yes	poor
Turner et al. (1970)	62	yes	81	52	36	random waking; placebo	no	good
Werry and Cohrssen (1965)	70	no	30	?	no follow-up	psychotherapy; no treatment	yes	fair
Wright and Craig (1974)	23	?	?	?	1	medication; placebo	yes	good

?=data unavailable

117

In summary, the findings of both uncontrolled and controlled research strongly suggest that most children will benefit from the urine alarm. The work with adults is too minimal to be conclusive but seems to be more favorable than no treatment at all or the use of medication. Relapse remains a problem, with as many as half of the children treated and initially cured, having reoccurrences of wetting episodes at some later point in time.

A number of investigators have assessed factors presumably related to a child's success or failure with the urine alarm. The most predominant reason for failure seems to be poor parental cooperation (Forsythe and Redmond, 1970; Freyman, 1963; Geppert, 1953; Taylor and Turner, 1975; Turner et al., 1970; Wikes, 1958; Young, 1965). Usually, parents simply stop using the device and quit coming to the clinic. Sometimes they remain in treatment but use the alarm inconsistently. Collins (1973) divided his subjects into those who had been treated consistently and those who had used the urine alarm inconsistently. Nearly half of his enuretics had been given inconsistent treatment and only one-third of these children became dry. In contrast, 84 percent of the enuretics who appropriately used the alarm were cured. Strikingly similar findings have been reported by Forrester, Stein, and Susser (1964). An interesting study by Morgan and Young (1975) found parental intolerance of their child's enuresis to be significantly associated with premature treatment withdrawal. It is not clear to what extent close supervision or involvement by the therapist with the family would ameliorate some of these problems. There seems to be a great deal of variability across studies as to how much therapist supervision and contact is involved. Sometimes the investigator simply gives the device to the parents with instructions to return it when the child is dry (Werry and Cohrssen, 1965). Baker (1969) reported no differences between treatment groups receiving differing amounts of supervision. However, his sample size was small and both comparison groups received some continual contact over the course of treatment. Other factors related to treatment failure include poor cooperation by the enuretic child, fear of the alarm, and failure to wake in response to its sounding (Forsythe and Redmond, 1970; Freyman, 1963; Philpott, 1970; Taylor and Turner, 1975; Turner et al., 1970; Young, 1965). A recent study (Finley and Wansley, 1977) found a louder alarm was more successful with "slow responders," possibly because it aroused them more readily. Young and Morgan (1972a) reported that long periods spent waiting for treatment were associated with nonattendance when treatment was offered. However, whether a child is a primary or secondary enuretic does not seem to be related to treatment success or failure (Collins, 1973; Freyman, 1963; Sacks and DeLeon, 1973;

Young and Morgan, 1973a, 1973b). In two studies, personality characteristics of the enuretic child's mother were related to treatment outcome (James and Foreman, 1973; Young and Morgan, 1973b). Although interesting, studies of this kind await further investigation and replication.

The problem of relapse has been addressed in several ways. One approach has been to use intermittent instead of continuous reinforcement, since intermittent schedules typically produce slower rates of extinction. A number of investigators have reported that intermittent reinforcement is as effective (although sometimes slightly slower) in producing initial cures but seems to lead to lower rates of relapse (Finley, Besserman, Bennett et al., 1973; Finley, Wansley, and Blenkarn, 1977; Lovibond, 1964; Taylor and Turner, 1975; Turner et al., 1970; Finley and Wansley, 1976). However, differences in relapse rates between intermittent and continuous schedules were statistically significant only in the Finley et al. (1973) study.

Another approach has been labeled "overlearning" and involves administering extra fluid to the child when an initial criterion of dryness is achieved. The bell and pad continues to be used until the child meets criterion (e.g., 14 consecutive dry nights) under this new condition of extra fluids just prior to retiring. This procedure was originally suggested by Mowrer and Mowrer in 1938, but no controlled investigations were done until recently. Young and Morgan (1972b, 1972c) report significantly lower relapse rates than the usual continuous reinforcement procedures. Taylor and Turner (1975) also reported better results with overlearning than either continuous or intermittent reinforcement. However, the differences were not statistically significant. Young and Morgan (1972c) did note that some children (9 percent of their sample) relapsed so badly when initially introduced to the overlearning procedure that it had to be withdrawn. Similar problems have been reported by Davidson and Douglass (1950). Perhaps gradually increasing fluid intake before retiring would be a more successful approach.

Central nervous system stimulants have sometimes been used in conjunction with the urine alarm. Presumably, they enhance the child's arousal so that he may condition more quickly. There is some evidence to suggest that medication does accelerate learning (Philpott, 1970; Young and Turner, 1965), although Kennedy and Sloop (1968) did not find this to be the case. In any event, relapse rates are unusually high among children treated with both medication and the urine alarm (Turner, 1966) so whatever initial gains might be made are lost at follow-up.

Before leaving this particular treatment literature, some comments as to side effects are in order. "Buzzer ulcers" have occurred when the child wets but does not get out of bed, remaining in contact with the electrical current passing through the wet pads (Borrie and Fenton, 1966; Greaves, 1969a, 1969b; Neal and Coote, 1969; White, 1968). This problem is very rare (Stewart, 1975) but points out the importance of using good batteries and making sure the child is aroused in response to the alarm. Some devices employ both a light and a buzzer. It is important that the child not be permitted to turn off the buzzer while leaving the light circuit intact (Greaves, 1969b). From a psychoanalytic point of view, symptom substitution might be expected since the urine alarm does not deal with the underlying emotional disorder presumably causing the child's enuresis. Most studies, however, note no evidence of symptom substitution (Behrle et al., 1956; Dische, 1971; Freyman, 1963; Gillison and Skinner, 1958; Sacks et al., 1974; Young, 1965; Werry and Cohrssen, 1965). In fact, several investigators report general improvement in other areas after the child became dry (Baker, 1969; Baller and Schalock, 1956; Collins, 1973; Dische, 1971; Geppert, 1953; Lovibond, 1964). Owens and Fischer (1966) described two cases in which new behavior problems developed subsequent to treatment. However, they considered these children to be doubtful examples of symptom substitution. Novick (1966) remarked on the substantial deterioration of behavior in a number of treated enuretics he followed for 8 months to 1 year. Since no controlled comparisons were made, it is difficult to attribute these changes solely to the elimination of the children's wetting behavior.

Overall, the urine alarm seems to be a relatively successful approach to the treatment of enuresis. This is particularly true if the device is used in a consistent and safe manner and overlearning or intermittent schedules are used to reduce the chance of relapse. Should relapse occur, most children seem to respond to a second course of treatment.

Operant Approaches

From an operant point of view, the enuretic child must be rewarded for urinary control and appropriate toileting behavior and/or punished for inappropriate wetting behavior. Although a variety of operant procedures have been used in a number of case studies (e.g., Bach and Moylan, 1975; McDonagh, 1971; Ross, 1974; Tough, Hawkins, Mc-Arthur, and Ravenswaay, 1971), the most common approaches are Retention Control Training (RCT) attributed to Kimmel and Kimmel

(1970) and Dry-Bed Training (DBT) developed by Azrin, Sneed, and Foxx (1973).

In RCT, the child is rewarded for holding his urine for longer and longer periods of time. The desired behavior is the expansion of bladder capacity so that the child may sleep through the night without needing to urinate. The training procedure is carried out during the day by having the child inform his parent or trainer when he has to micturate. Initially he is asked to hold his urine for 5 additional minutes. For this he is rewarded and then permitted to use the toilet. Gradually he is asked to hold his urine up to 45 minutes after he has indicated a need to void. As his bladder capacity increases, his enuresis should be eliminated. Although this procedure is attributed to Kimmel and Kimmel (1970), it was suggested earlier by Muellner (1960) and Starfield and Mellits (1968). Starfield and Mellits (1968) reported 19 percent of their children were cured and 66 percent improved. They also reported that increases in bladder capacity were associated with improvement, although this was not true for every child. In Kimmel and Kimmel's (1970) initial report, three children were all cured using RCT and no relapses occurred within 12 months. In a subsequent larger study (Paschalis, Kimmel, and Kimmel, 1972), 48 percent of the children were cured although one child required added involvement by the therapist. None relapsed within a three-month follow-up. Good success has been reported in several individual cases (Miller, 1973; Stedman, 1972) but three controlled studies have not found RCT to be particularly effective (Doleys et al., 1977; Harris and Purohit, 1977; Rocklin and Tilker, 1973). Although children often increase their bladder capacity with RCT, a subsequent improvement in enuresis does not always or even typically occur.

DBT is a fairly complicated procedure initially developed and used with institutionalized retarded adults (Azrin et al., 1973). Later, it was modified slightly and applied to normal children (Azrin et al., 1974; Bollard and Woodroffe, 1977; Doleys et al., 1977). It involves one night of intensive training in which the child is encouraged to drink large amounts of fluid before retiring. He is then given "Positive Practice" in which he lies in his room with the light off for about one minute, gets up and goes to the bathroom and tries to urinate. After 20 practice trials of this kind, he is permitted to go to bed but has to sleep on a urine alarm. That evening, he is aroused every hour by the trainer and sent to the bathroom. At the bathroom door, the trainer asks the child if he can hold his urine for another hour. If the child says yes, he is returned to bed. If he says no, he is asked to inhibit urination for a few minutes and then is permitted to micturate. He is praised for holding his urine and having a dry bed. Should the child accidently wet, the alarm sounds, and the child is sent to the bathroom to finish urinating. He is then given "Cleanliness Training" which involves changing the bed sheets and his pajamas, wiping off the mattress and disposing the wet sheets in the appropriate place. He is then given another 20 trials of Positive Practice before being allowed to go back to sleep. On the evening following an accident the child must perform another 20 Positive Practice trials before going to bed. After this initial intensive training, the child continues to sleep on the urine alarm but is not repeatedly aroused except when his parents go to bed. However, should an accident occur he must carry out Cleanliness Training and Positive Practice. All dry nights are socially reinforced. After a number of consecutive dry nights the urine alarm is removed. In the initial study (Azrin et al., 1973), all 12 of the retarded subjects reached criterion of 7 consecutive dry nights. One resident relapsed within 3 months (relapse was defined as wetting twice within 1 week). With normals, Azrin et al. (1974) also report 100 percent initial cures, although 29 percent had to be re-treated. Similar data have been reported by Bollard and Woodroffe (1977). However, results of a study published by Doleys et al. (1977) are not as favorable. Only 38 percent of their subjects became dry within 6 weeks of treatment and one-third of these children relapsed. The length of treatment does not seem to be a factor here since the initial cures reported by Azrin et al. (1974) and Bollard and Woodroffe (1977) occurred within 6 weeks. In the Azrin et al. (1974) study, DBT was found to be more effective than the urine alarm and in the Doleys et al. (1977) study, it was more successful than RCT.

A great deal is involved in DBT including punishment through Positive Practice and Cleanliness Training, social reinforcement for a dry bed, training in inhibiting urination, the use of the urine alarm, and intensive initial involvement with an outside "trainer." It is not yet clear which variables are crucial to treatment success. Bollard and Woodroffe (1977) reported that parents could be successfully trained to carry out the entire procedure, thereby eliminating the necessity of an outside trainer entering the home for the child's initial intensive training session. They also report, however, that using the procedure without the urine alarm reduced its effectiveness considerably. No child in this condition was cured even after 13 weeks of treatment. In contrast, recent studies by Azrin and his colleagues (Azrin, Hontos, and Besalel-Azrin, 1979; Azrin and Thienes, 1978) describe excellent success with DBT procedures even when the urine alarm component was eliminated.

Operant approaches do seem to have something to offer to the treatment of enuresis but research in this area is in its infancy. DBT looks somewhat more promising than RCT. However, DBT seems to incorporate aspects of RCT in that it encourages and rewards the child for holding his urine. It would be of interest to assess what role this particular aspect of DBT has in its overall success.

Comments

While the literature on the treatment of enuresis is extensive, reasonably well controlled, and sometimes creative, it seems to be lacking in several respects. Primarily, assessment is rarely associated with treatment. Children are given one particular treatment or another with no consideration for the specific characteristics of the child. Treatment effectiveness is almost always measured solely by parental report with no data as to the reliability or validity of these records. Further, frequency of wetting is typically the only dependent variable of interest. Other relevant measures of the child's behavioral, social, or physiological functioning are rarely assessed before, during, or after treatment. Some studies have used multiple measures (e.g., Baker, 1969; Doleys et al., 1977; Werry et al., 1975) but they are all too rare. Multiple measures would help us understand not only what the broader effects of a treatment program are, but also what child characteristics seem to lead to what kind of improvement with what kind of treatment.

In a similar vein, further consideration needs to be given to the effects of family and parent characteristics on treatment. Certainly, in the conditioning and operant approaches the parent plays a very large role in the ultimate outcome of a program. Even drug treatment, which is much less demanding on the parent, necessitates proper administration of the drug. Very little is known about what kinds of parental characteristics enhance what kind of treatment or what kinds of factors can encourage parental cooperation. Perhaps certain types of parent-child interactions enhance or discourage treatment effectiveness and/ or relapse.

Finally, overall treatment effectiveness tells us little about what are the specific mechanisms involved. Different treatment programs may have children attend to bladder cues, increase their bladder capacity, increase their motivation, increase or decrease their anxiety or change parent-child interactions, all to a greater or lesser degree. While some or all of these factors may be important for successful treatment of most enuretics, some may be particularly important for an individual child. Again, the importance of integrating assessment and treatment seems obvious.

CLINICAL PRESCRIPTION

If a child presents with the problem of enuresis, he should first be sent to a pediatrician to be sure there is no organic involvement. Although organic pathology is rare, it should not be automatically discounted. Further, some of these children do suffer from urinary tract infections which should be treated and cleared (Stansfeld, 1973).

Once the child has received a clean bill of health, assessment for treatment can begin. Some data on the frequency and duration of the problem should be obtained, as well as the child and parents' attitude toward the problem. Is the child motivated to change? To what extent is the parent willing to help the child in this regard? It is probably wise to have the child begin recording his wet and dry nights during the assessment phase. This will give the therapist some notion as to how motivated the child is, as well as getting data on the child's current wetting patterns. If the child is very young, his mother may have to help him with the recording. Of course, sometimes simply recording the behavior and reporting to the therapist cures the problem and no further efforts will be necessary.

If this is not the case, the therapist must proceed in information gathering in order to develop a treatment plan. What are the child's deficits? What are his strengths? Does he wet only at night or does he have daytime frequency, urgency or wetting as well? Does he ever wake to use the toilet? Does he wake while wetting the bed? How easy is he to arouse? What secondary gains (if any) are there for his problem? Does he take responsibility for changing the bed linen and/or washing it? Does he sleep with a sibling and if so, what is the sibling's response to his bedwetting? What kinds of negative consequences is he experiencing? Do friends and relatives know about his problem? Has he been prevented from attending camp or staying overnight with a friend because of it? If so, are these activities important to the child?

A similar assessment needs to be carried out with the child's mother and/or father. How have they handled the problem in the past? Are there certain activities that are very difficult for them to carry out vis-à-vis their child (e.g., rewarding or punishing him for his wetting)? How much support and instruction would they need to carry out a particular program? Is there disagreement between the child's parents as to how his wetting should be handled?

Other characteristics of the child and his living situation should be considered. Is enuresis his only problem? Is the family reasonably stable? Are parent-child interactions generally positive or negative? Are the demands of the treatment regimen going to be "too much" for those involved?

After getting a reasonably good understanding of the extent and nature of the child's problem(s) and what resources within himself and his family are available, the therapist may proceed with a treatment plan. The demands of treatment and the extent of the therapist's involvement should be geared to the particular strengths and deficits of the youngster and his family. However, both the child and his parents should be involved as much as possible. In some cases, a behavior other than enuresis may be treated first in order to teach the parents and child the importance of consistency and cooperation. A treatment approach that has previously failed should probably not be used unless the reasons for failure are obvious and the family is enthusiastic about trying the approach again. If several approaches (e.g., urine alarm and Dry-Bed Training) seem equally appropriate, their demands and expected length of treatment should be discussed with the family and a decision jointly reached. Otherwise, the therapist should strongly suggest the approach he considers most likely to succeed. Techniques may be combined to best fit an individual child's problem. For example, a child who wets at night and has a small bladder capacity as well, might benefit from both reinforced practice at holding his urine during the day and using the urine alarm at night. As much as possible, expected problems should be discussed and planned for in advance (e.g., a child who is difficult to arouse may need his parents to assist in waking him if he does not automatically respond to the alarm).

In general, drugs are not recommended since other approaches seem to have a greater likelihood of success. However, in some cases, the family may be so marginal or so discouraged with behavioral treatment techniques that a drug trial might be indicated. Still, if a family is very marginal they may be unable to give the medication appropriately.

Once treatment is effective, the therapist should gradually withdraw his or her involvement. However, termination should not occur before plans are made and carried out to discourage any relapse. Nevertheless, should relapse occur, the child and parent should know how they should approach it.

CASE REPORT

This is the case of a 7-year-old female primary enuretic described by Samaan (1972). This child, Marva, was always nocturnally enuretic, wetting as often as three times a night. Occasionally she had diurnal wetting problems as well. She had additional difficulties relating with peers and adults, and was frequently inattentive and disruptive at school.

At the age of five, she began to see a psychoanalytic psychiatrist who urged Marva's parents to give her plenty of love and attention. This continued for nearly 2 years with no signs of improvement. During the second year of treatment Marva was place on medication with no change in her wetting.

Marva's parents decided to terminate psychoanalytic therapy and entered behavior therapy. First, the urine alarm was used but with little success. Apparently, Marva did not wake readily to the alarm and a trial on a stimulant did not alleviate the problem. After approximately 5 weeks of no significant improvement, an operant program was designed. Marva was aroused by her parents no more than 1 hour after she first went to bed. She was guided to the bathroom and rewarded with a piece of chocolate when she started urinating. She was then sent back to bed but aroused three more times during the night and rewarded each time for urinating in the the toilet. This program was continued over a number of successive evenings with less prompting used each night to get Marva up and to the bathroom. After 10 dry nights, Marva's parents aroused her only if she did not get up spontaneously about an hour after retiring. Intermittent waking by the parents continued to occur but less frequently, as Marva began getting up more and more often on her own. During this interval, chocolate was left for Marva on the water-tank so she could continue to be rewarded when waking spontaneously. A great deal of social reinforcement was also used each morning after she had a dry night. The candy was gradually withdrawn with no return to nocturnal wetting. The program was completely successful; the child was still dry some two years later. During that time she wet only once. She also was reported to be functioning much better interpersonally both at school and at home. It is interesting to note that a number of elements of Marva's successful treatment program are similar to aspects of the Dry-Bed Training approach subsequently developed by Azrin et al. (1973).

ETHICAL AND LEGAL ISSUES

The ethical and legal issues in treating a child with enuresis are no different than treating a child with any behavior problem. The therapist must always act in the best interest of the child. He should not make demands on the child that the child is incapable of meeting. He should not encourage or support parent-child interactions that are essentially punitive or degrading for the child. Some of the behavioral treatment techniques do use punishment and potentially could be inappropriately used by excessively punitive or abusing parents. Similarly, drugs should not be given to a child if his parents cannot be trusted to administer them appropriately. Enuresis is generally a self-limited problem; eventually, most children will "out grow" it. In most cases, treatment will help the child lead a more comfortable, happier life. However, a therapist should never become so myopic that he treats a child's enuresis without a broader perspective as to the child's total welfare.

SUGGESTIONS FOR CLINICAL AND EXPERIMENTAL RESEARCH

The research literature on enuresis is quite extensive and sometimes well conducted with attention paid to long-term follow-up. Nevertheless, many questions remain unanswered. Future research must consider both the defects and assets of past attempts to answer these questions. Those paradigms that offer the most promise should be kept, but new approaches to old questions should also be considered. Where appropriate, new questions should be asked and hopefully answered as well.

Much effort has been spent in the past on attempts to identify the causes of enuresis. While a number of variables have been associated with the disorder, no causal interpretations can be made. It is probably time to drop correlational or retrospective approaches to this disorder and to begin prospective analyses. Given the available data, we have a number of good guesses as to what factors might predict or lead to enuresis. These include family history factors, personality or behavioral characteristics of the child, attitudes and coping styles of the child's parents, parent-child interactions, toilet-training practices, small bladder capacity, sleep or arousal or EEG patterns, developmental level. By observing these characteristics in 2- and 3-year olds who are subsequently followed, we may have a better idea of what factors precede or predict enuresis, and which develop concurrent with or subsequent to the disorder. Prediction, of course, does not imply causation. Still, it is a viable next step toward the search for causal variables. And, prediction itself has some real merit since possible prevention of the disorder can then be considered.

A great deal of effort has also been expended on questions relating to the treatment of enuresis. However, in the past, treatment research has generally been carried out with little attention to assessment and with a focus on a single outcome—decreased wetting. We need to broaden our perspective and use multidimensional assessment prior to, during, and subsequent to treatment. Particular assessment characteristics of a child or adult need to be matched with particular treatment strategies. The effects of treatment need to be measured from a broader perspective than a simple number of wet or dry nights. In choosing our multiple measures, we can and should be guided by our current knowledge of what assessment variables seem potentially relevant. Nevertheless, the use of multiple measures is not enough. In the past, too little concern has been given to the adequacy of our measurement techniques. Our measures must be reliable and valid if they are ever to have any ultimate value.

In past attempts to answer questions as to what treatment(s) work best, new questions have developed. Most are not surprising, but remain important areas for future research. Questions regarding relapse—who relapses and how best to treat or prevent relapse—are probably most obvious. Also of interest are questions concerning the mechanisms or variables crucial to a specific treatment's success. What factors are involved in keeping a child, parent, or adult in treatment and consistently following the treatment program also need to be addressed. And finally, through further data gathering, theorizing, and serendipity, new and potentially more successful treatment programs or approaches may be devised.

SUMMARY

Enuresis is defined as diurnal or nocturnal wetting after the age of three when there is no organic pathology to account for the absence of complete bladder control. The prevalance of the disorder diminishes with age. Some 15–20 percent of 5-year olds are enuretic as compared to 1–2 percent of 15-year olds. Annual spontaneous remission rates are estimated at 15–20 percent.

Several theories have been proposed to account for the disorder. Psychodynamic formulations describe enuresis as the symptom of an underlying emotional disturbance. Behavioral theorists emphasize bladder control as a learned response and enuresis as an example of incomplete or faulty learning. Medical explanations focus on profound sleep, poor arousal mechanisms, small bladder capacities, or the general notion of maturational delay.

Efforts at assessing enuresis have been guided primarily by psychodynamic and medical models of the disorder. A substantial number of studies have attempted to demonstrate that enuretics have greater psychological or behavioral problems than nonenuretics. Despite an extensive literature, methodological problems involving rater bias, population selection, and inadequate assessment instruments prohibit any conclusive statements. Further, it is probable that not all or even most enuretics are psychologically or behaviorally disturbed. There is no data to support the notion that psychological problems cause enuresis since the reverse interpretation (i.e., enuresis causes psychological problems) is equally likely. To date, there is no evidence that toilet-training practices are different for enuretic and nonenuretic children, and there is little support for the notion of developmental delay.

Some interesting epidemiological data strongly suggest that a family history of enuresis is indicative of subsequent enuresis in any offspring. Further, disruptive, deviant families are associated with the disorder. In particular, mother-child separation when the child is under 6 is predictive of subsequent problems with bladder control. There is some preliminary but prospective data to suggest that certain types of mothers more often have enuretic children. Nevertheless, it is clear that family factors do not explain the disorder in its entirety.

Physiological assessment has focused primarily on (1) the role of sleep and arousal in enuresis, (2) the possible relationship of enuresis to epilepsy or convulsive disorders, and (3) the role of small bladder capacity in the development of the disorder. Enuresis seems to occur in all sleep stages *except* dreaming. However, there appears to be no pattern of sleep peculiar to enuretics. Physiological and cortical changes often occur prior to micturition but do not lead to full awakening as occurs in the normal child. Many enuretics have abnormal electroencephalographic recordings. However, the significance of this finding is unclear. The most compelling physiological data available is the high frequency of small bladder capacities among enuretics. Still, not all enuretics have small bladder capacities, some nonenuretics do, and causal interpretations are premature. Further, simply pointing to "maturational lag" as the explanation of any or all of these findings seems insufficient.

In general, the treatment of enuresis has not been guided by the assessment literature. Two approaches have prevailed—the use of medication and the use of various learning techniques. Advice and suggestion have only minimal effects. There is no current controlled data supporting the use of psychotherapy.

Tricyclic antidepressants have been used extensively. Most childhood enuretics are helped by these drugs but substantially less than half are cured. Medication seems to work best for outpatient children and seems to be almost totally ineffective with adults. Relapse once the drug is withdrawn is a serious problem even with outpatient children. And, a variety of side effects while on medication have been reported. It is not clear what mechanisms underlie the effectiveness of tricyclics. The most likely explanation involves the drugs' anticholinergic effects which substantially increase bladder capacity. This explanation, however, is not seen as entirely adequate.

Behavioral approaches to treatment have employed principles of both classical conditioning and instrumental learning. The urine alarm, first developed by Mowrer and Mowrer in the 1930s has been extensively employed with reasonably good success. Approximately 70 percent of children using this device will become cured although as many as half of these cures will relapse. Several techniques (e.g., overlearning and intermittent reinforcement) have been successfully used to decrease the probability of relapse. In addition, many children when re-treated become dry. Care should be taken to use the device appropriately so that "buzzer ulcers" do not occur.

Other behavioral approaches have included training children to hold their urine for longer periods of time in order to increase their bladder capacity (Retention Control Training) and a complex operant procedure involving both positive reinforcement and punishment (Dry-Bed Training). Both of these treatment approaches are relatively recent developments and have not been as extensively studied as the urine alarm. Dry-Bed Training seems to be particularly promising.

A number of future research directions are suggested. These include: (1) a prospective analysis of enuresis, (2) the use of multidimensional assessment approaches, (3) a greater concern for the adequacy of measurement techniques, (4) an integration of assessment with treatment, (5) the study of factors related to maintaining an enuretic in treatment, (6) the study of factors related to the consistent implementation of a treatment approach, (7) the study of factors related to relapse, and (8) the study of what are the mechanisms crucial to a particular treatment's success.

REFERENCES

Abrams, A. Imipramine in enuresis. *American Journal of Psychiatry*, 1963, *120*, 177–178.

Agarwala S. and Heycock, J. A controlled trial of imipramine ('Tofranil') in the treatment of childhood enuresis. *British Journal of Clinical Practice*, 1968, *22*(7), 296–298.

Alderton, H. Imipramine in childhood nocturnal enuresis: Relationship of time of administration to effect. *Canadian Psychiatric Association Journal*, 1967, *12*(2), 197–203.

Alderton, H. Imipramine in childhood enuresis: Further studies on the relationship of time of administration to effect. *Canadian Medical Association Journal*, 1970, *102*, 1179–1180.

Anderson, F. The psychiatric aspects of enuresis. *American Journal of Diseases of Children*, 1930, *40*, 591–618 and 818–850.

Arnold, J. Cystometry and enuresis. *Journal of Urology,* 1966, *96,* 194–202.

Arnold, S. Consequences of childhood urethral disease. *Postgraduate Medicine,* 1968, *43,* 191.

Arnold, S. and Ginsburg, A. Enuresis: Incidence and pertinence of genitourinary disease in healthy enuretic children. *Urology,* 1973, *2,* 437.

Ayd, F., Jr. Amitriptyline: Reappraisal after six years experience. *Diseases of the Nervous System,* 1965, *26*(11), 719–727.

Azrin, N., Hontos, P., and Besalel-Azrin, V. Elimination of enuresis without a conditioning apparatus: An extension by office instruction of the child and parents. *Behavior Therapy,* 1979, *10,* 14–19.

Azrin, N., Sneed, T., and Foxx, R. Dry bed: A rapid method of eliminating bedwetting (enuresis) of the retarded. *Behaviour Research and Therapy,* 1973, *11*(4), 427–434.

Azrin, N., Sneed, T., and Foxx, R. Dry-bed training: Rapid elimination of childhood enuresis. *Behaviour Research and Therapy,* 1974, *12*(3), 147–156.

Azrin, N. and Thienes, P. Rapid elimination of enuresis by intensive learning without a conditioning apparatus. *Behavior Therapy,* 1978, *9,* 342–354.

Bach, R. and Moylan, J. Parents administer behavior therapy for inappropriate urination and encopresis: A case study. *Journal of Behavior Therapy and Experimental Psychiatry,* 1975, *6*(3), 239–241.

Baker, B. Symptom treatment and symptom substitution in enuresis. *Journal of Abnormal Psychology,* 1969, *74*(1), 42–49.

Bakwin, H. The genetics of enuresis. In I. Kolvin, R. MacKeith, and S. Meadow (Eds.), *Bladder control and enuresis, clinics in developmental medicine,* 1973, nos. 48/49.

Baller, W. and Schalock, H. Conditioned response treatment of enuresis. *Exceptional Children,* 1956, *22,* 233–236 and 247–248.

Barbour, R., Borland, E., Boyd, M., et al. Enuresis as a disorder of development. *British Medical Journal,* 1963, *2,* 787–790.

Behrle, F., Elkin, M., and Laybourne, P. Evaluation of a conditioning device in the treatment of nocturnal enuresis. *Pediatrics,* 1956, *17,* 849–854.

Bindelglas, P., Dee, G., and Enos, F. Medical and psychosocial factors in enuretic children treated with imipramine hydrochloride. *American Journal of Psychiatry,* 1968, *124,* 1107–1112.

Blackman, S., Benton, A., and Cove, L. The effect of imipramine on enuresis. *American Journal of Psychiatry,* 1964, *120,* 1194–1195.

Blackwell, B. and Currah, J. The psychopharmacology of nocturnal enuresis. In I. Kolvin, R. MacKeith, and S. Meadow (Eds.), *Bladder control and enuresis, clinics in developmental medicine,* 1973, nos. 48/49.

Blomfield, J. and Douglas, J. Bedwetting: Prevalence among children aged 4–7 years. *Lancet,* 1956, *1,* 850–852.

Bollard, R. and Woodroffe, P. The effect of parent-administered dry-bed training on nocturnal enuresis in children. *Behaviour Research and Therapy,* 1977, *15*(2), 159–165.

Borrie, P. and Fenton, J. Buzzer ulcers. *British Medical Journal,* 1966, *5506,* 151–152.

Boyd, M. The depth of sleep in enuretic school children and in non-enuretic controls. *Journal of Psychosomatic Research,* 1960, *4,* 274–281.

Braithwaite, J. Some problems associated with enuresis. *Proceedings of the Royal Society of Medicine,* 1955, *49,* 33–38.

Broughton, R. Sleep disorder: Disorder of arousal? *Science,* 1968, *159,* 1070–1077.

Campbell, E., Jr. and Young, J., Jr. Enuresis and its relationship to electroencephalographic disturbances. *Journal of Urology,* 1966, *96,* 947.

Campbell, M. Enuresis. *Archives of Pediatrics,* 1937, *54,* 187.

Campbell, M. Neuromuscular uropathy. In M. Campbell and H. Harrison (Eds.), *Urology.* Philadelphia: Saunders, 1970.

Campbell, W., III, Weissman, M., and Lupp, J. Bender Gestalt test and the urodynamics of enuresis. *Journal of Urology,* 1970, *104,* 934–939.

Cohen, M. Symposium on behavioral pediatrics. Enuresis. *Pediatric Clinic of North America,* 1975, *22*(3), 545–560.

Collins, R. Importance of the bladder-cue buzzer contingency in the conditioning treatment for enuresis. *Journal of Abnormal Psychology,* 1973, *82,* 299–308.

Creer, T. and Davis, M. Using a staggered-wakening procedure with enuretic children in an institutional setting. *Journal of Behavior Therapy and Experimental Psychiatry,* 1975, *6,* 23–25.

Cust, G. The epidemiology of nocturnal enuresis. *Lancet,* 1952, *2,* 1167–1170.

Davidson, J. and Douglass, E. Nocturnal enuresis: A special approach to treatment. *British Medical Journal,* 1950, *1,* 1345–1347.

Deacon, J. The conditioned habit treatment of nocturnal enuresis. *American Journal of Mental Deficiency,* 1939, *44,* 133–138.

De Jonge, G. Epidemiology of enuresis: A survey of the literature. In I. Kolvin, R. MacKeith, and S. Meadow (Eds.), *Bladder control and enuresis, clinics in developmental medicine,* 1973, nos. 48/49.

DeLeon, G. and Mandell, W. A comparison of conditioning and psychotherapy in the treatment of functional enuresis. *Journal of Clinical Psychology,* 1966, *22*(3), 326–330.

DeLeon, G. and Sacks, S. Conditioning functional enuresis: A 4-year follow-up. *Journal of Consulting and Clinical Psychology,* 1972, *39,* 299–300.

DeLuca, J. Psychosexual conflict in adolescent enuretics. *Journal of Psychology,* 1968a, *68*(1), 145–149.

DeLuca, J. A Rorschach study of adolescent enuretics. *Journal of Clinical Psychology,* 1968b, *24*(2), 231–232.

Dimson, S. Toilet training and enuresis. *British Medical Journal,* 1959, *2,* 666–670.

DiPerri, R. and Laura, A. Effects of the micturition reflex on cerebral electrical activity of sleep in enuretic and normal subjects. *Electroencephalographic & Clinical Neurophysiology,* 1968, *25*(5), 516.

Dische, S. Management of enuresis. *British Medical Journal,* 1971, *2*(752), 33–36.

Dische, S. Treatment of enuresis with an enuresis alarm. In I. Kolvin, R. MacKeith, and S. Meadow, eds., *Bladder control and enuresis. Clinics in developmental medicine,* 1973, nos. 48/49.

Ditman, K. and Blinn, K. Sleep levels in enuresis. *American Journal of Psychiatry,* 1955, *111,* 913–920.

Doleys, D. Behavioral treatment for nocturnal enuresis in children: A review of the recent literature. *Psychological Bulletin,* 1977, *84*(1), 30–54.

Doleys, D., Ciminero, A., Tollison, J., et al. Dry-Bed Training and retention control training: A comparison. *Behavior Therapy,* 1977, *8*(4), 541–548.

Douglas, J. Early disturbing events and later enuresis. In I. Kolvin, R. Mac-Keith, and S. Meadow (Eds.), *Bladder control and enuresis, clinics in developmental medicine,* 1973, nos. 48/49.

Dorison, E. and Blackman, S. Imipramine in the treatment of adult enuretic. *American Journal of Psychiatry,* 1962, *119,* 474.

Drew, L. Control of enuresis by imipramine. *Medical Journal of Australia,* 1966, *2*(26), 1225–1227.

Drew, L. Drug control of incontinence in adult mental defectives. *Medical Journal of Australia,* 1967, *2*(5), 206–207.

Enfield, C. Enuresis. *Medical Journal of Australia,* 1976, *2*(24), 908–910.

Esperanca, M. and Gerrard, J. Nocturnal enuresis: Comparison of the effect of imipramine and dietary restriction on bladder capacity. *Canadian Medical Association Journal,* 1969, *101*(12), 65–68.

Evans, J. Sleep of enuretics. *British Medical Journal,* 1971, *3,* 110.

Fermaglich, J. Electroencephalographic study of enuretics. *American Journal of Diseases of Childhood,* 1969, *118*(3), 473–478.

Finley, W., Besserman, R., Bennett, L., et al. The effect of continuous, intermittent, and "placebo" reinforcement on the effectiveness of the conditioning treatment for enuresis nocturna. *Behaviour Research and Therapy,* 1973, *11,* 289–297.

Finley, W. and Wansley, R. Use of intermittent reinforcement in a clinical-research program for the treatment of enuresis nocturna. *Journal of Pediatric Psychology,* 1976, *4,* 24–27.

Finley, W. and Wansley, R. Auditory intensity as a variable in the conditioning treatment of enuresis nocturna. *Behaviour Research and Therapy,* 1977, *15*(2), 181–185.

Finley, W., Wansley, R., and Blenkarn, M. Conditioning treatment of enuresis using a 70% intermittent reinforcement schedule. *Behaviour Research and Therapy,* 1977, *15,* 419–427.

Fisher, G., Murray, F., Walley, M., and Kiloh, L. A controlled trial of imipramine in the treatment of nocturnal enuresis in mentally subnormal patients. *American Journal of Mental Deficiency,* 1963, *67,* 536–538.

Forrester, R., Stein, Z., and Susser, M. A trial of conditioning therapy in nocturnal enuresis. *Developmental Medicine and Child Neurology,* 1964, *6,* 158–166.

Forsythe, W. and Merrett, J. A controlled trial of imipramine ('Tofranil') and nortriptyline ('Allegron') in the treatment of enuresis. *British Journal of Clinical Practice,* 1969, *23*(5), 210–215.

Forsythe, W., Merrett, J., and Redmond, A. A controlled clinical trial of trimipramine and placebo in the treatment of enuresis. *British Journal of Clinical Practice,* 1972a, *26*(3), 119–121.

Forsythe, W., Merrett, J., and Redmond, A. Enuresis and psychoactive drugs. *British Journal of Clinical Practice,* 1972b, *26*(3), 116–118.

Forsythe, W. and Redmond, A. Enuresis and the electric alarm: Study of 200 cases. *British Medical Journal,* 1970, *1,* 211–213.

Forsythe, W. and Redmond, A. Enuresis and spontaneous cure rate: Study of 1129 enuretics. *Archives of Diseases in Childhood,* 1974, *49*(4), 259–263.

Frary, L. Enuresis, a genetic study. *American Journal of Diseases of Children,* 1935, *49,* 557.

Freeman, E. The treatment of enuresis: An overview. *International Journal of Pediatric Medicine,* 1975, *6*(3), 403–412.

Freud, S. *Three contributions to the theory of sex.* New York: Nervous and Mental Disease Publishing Co., 1916.

Freyman, R. Experience with an enuresis bell-apparatus. *Medical Officer,* 1959, *101,* 248–250.

Freyman, R. Follow-up study of enuresis treated with a bell apparatus. *Journal of Child Psychology and Psychiatry,* 1963, *4,* 199–206.

Friday, G. and Feldman, E. Treatment of enuretic children with imipramine (Tofranil®). *Clinical Pediatrics,* 1966, *5*(3), 175–176.

General Practitioner Research Group Report No. 139. Imipramine in enuresis. *Practitioner,* 1969, *202*(213), 94–97.

Geppert, T. Management of nocturnal enuresis by conditional response. *Journal of the American Medical Association,* 1953, *152,* 381–383.

Gerrard, J. and Zaleski, A. Nocturnal enuresis. *Pakistan Medical Review,* 1969, *4,* 77.

Gillison, T. and Skinner, J. Treatment of nocturnal enuresis by the electric alarm. *British Medical Journal,* 1958, *2,* 1268–1272.

Graham, P. Depth of sleep and enuresis: A critical review. In I. Kolvin, R. MacKeith, and S. Meadow (Eds.), *Bladder control and enuresis, clinics in developmental medicine,* 1973, nos. 48/49.

Greaves, M. Hazards of enuresis alarm. *Archives of Diseases in Childhood,* 1969a, *44,* 285–286.

Greaves, M. Scarring due to enuresis blankets. *British Journal of Dermatology,* June, 1969b, *81*(6), 440–442.

Gunnarson, S. and Melin, K. The electroencephalogram in enuresis. *Acta Paediatrica,* 1951, *40,* 496–501.

Hagglund, T. and Parkkulainen, K. Enuretic children treated with imipramine. *Annales Paediatrial Fenniae,* 1965, *11,* 53–59.

Halgren, B. Enuresis—A clinical and genetic study. *Acta Psychiatrica et Neurologica Scandinavica,* 1957a, 114 (Supplement).

Halgren, B. Enuresis II. A study with reference to certain physical, mental, and social factors possibly associated with enuresis. *Acta Psychiatrica et Neurologica Scandinavica,* 1957b, *31,* 405–436.

Halgren, B. Nocturnal enuresis: Etiologic aspects. *Acta Paediatrica*, 1959, *48*(66), 118 (Supplement).

Hallman, N. On the ability of enuretic children to hold urine. *Acta Paediatrica*, 1950, *39*, 87–93.

Harris, L. and Purohit, A. Bladder training and enuresis: A controlled trial. *Behaviour Research and Therapy*, 1977, *15*, 485–490.

Harrison, J. and Albino, V. An investigation into the effects of imipramine hydrochloride on the incidence of enuresis in institutionalized children. *South African Medical Journal*, 1970, *44*, 253–255.

Hicks, W. and Barnes, E. A double-blind study of the effect of imipramine on enuresis in 100 naval recruits. *American Journal of Psychiatry*, 1964, *120*, 812–814.

James, L. and Foreman, M. A-B status of behavior therapy technicians as related to success of Mowrer's conditioning treatment for enuresis. *Journal of Consulting and Clinical Psychology*, 1973, *41*, 224–229.

Jehu, D., Morgan, R., Turner, R., and Jones, A. A controlled trial of the treatment of nocturnal enuresis in residential homes for children. *Behaviour Research Therapy*, 1977, *15*(1), 1–16.

Johnstone, J. Cystometry and evaluation of anticholinergic drugs in enuretic children. *Journal of Pediatric Surgery*, 1972, *7*(1), 18–20.

Johnstone, J., Ardan, G., and Ramsden, P. A preliminary assessment of bladder distension in the treatment of enuretic children. *British Journal of Urology*, 1977, *49*, 43–49.

Jones, H. The behavioral treatment of enuresis nocturna. In H. J. Eysenck (Ed.), *Behavior therapy and the neuroses*. Oxford, England: Pergamon Press, 1960.

Kahane, M. An experimental investigation of a conditioning treatment and a preliminary study of the psychoanalytic theory of the etiology of enuresis. *American Psychologist*, 1955, *10*, 369–370.

Kales, A. and Kales, J. Evaluation, diagnosis, and treatment of clinical conditions related to sleep. *Journal of the American Medical Association*, 1970, *213*, 2229–2235.

Kales, A., Kales, J., Jacobson, A. et al. Effects of imipramine on enuretic frequency and sleep stages. *Pediatrics*, 1977, *60*(4), 431–436.

Kales, A., Scharf, M., Tan, T., et al. Sleep laboratory and clinical studies of the effects of Tofranil, Valium, and Placebo on sleep stages and enuresis. *Psychophysiology*, 1970, *7*, 348.

Kardash, S., Hillman, E., and Werry, J. Efficacy of imipramine in childhood enuresis: A double-blind control study with placebo. *Canadian Medical Association Journal*, 1968, *99*(6), 263–266.

Kelly, M. Trial of sustained release amitriptyline on enuresis. *Journal of the Irish Medical Association*, 1974, *67*(12), 343–344.

Kendall, A. and Karafin, L. Editorial: Enuresis. *Journal of Urology*, 1973, *109*(137).

Kennedy, W. and Sloop, W. Methedrine as an adjunct to conditioning treatment of nocturnal enuresis in normal and institutionalized retarded subjects. *Psychological Reports*, 1968, *22*, 997–1000.

Kent, R., O'Leary, K., Diament, C., and Dietz, A. Expectation bias in observational evaluation of therapeutic change. *Journal of Consulting and Clinical Psychology*, 1974, *42*(6), 774–780.

Kimmel, H. and Kimmel, E. An instrumental conditioning method for the treatment of enuresis. *Journal of Behavior Therapy and Experimental Psychiatry*, 1970, *1*, 121–123.

Klackenberg, G. Primary enuresis: When is a child dry at night? *Acta Paediatrica*, 1955, *44*, 513–518.

Koehl, G. and Wenzel, J. Severe postural hypotension due to imipramine therapy. *Pediatrics*, 1971, *47*(1), 132–134.

Kolvin, I. Enuresis in childhood. *Practitioner*, 1975, *214*(1279), 33–45.

Kolvin, I., Taunch, J., Currah, J., et al. Enuresis: A descriptive analysis and controlled trial. *Developmental Medicine and Child Neurology*, 1972, *14*, 715–726.

Lake, B. Controlled trial of nortriptyline in childhood enuresis. *Medical Journal of Australia*, 1968, *2*, 582–585.

Laybourne, P., Jr., Roach, N., Ebbesson, B., and Edwards, S. Double-blind study of the use of imipramine (Tofranil®) in enuresis. *Psychosomatics*, 1968, *9*(5), 282–285.

Levine, A. Enuresis in the Navy. *American Journal of Psychiatry*, 1943, *100*, 320–325.

Lickorish, J. One hundred enuretics. *Journal of Psychosomatic Research*, 1964, *7*, 263–267.

Liederman, P., Wasserman, D., and Liederman, V. Desipramine in the treatment of enuresis. *Journal of Urology*, 1969, *101*(3), 314–316.

Linderholm, B. The cystometric findings in enuresis. *Journal of Urology*, 1966, *96*, 718–722.

Lovibond, S. *Conditioning and enuresis.* New York: Macmillan, 1964.

Lovibond, S. and Coote, M. Enuresis. In C. Costello (Ed.), *Symptoms of psychopathology: A handbook.* New York: Wiley, 1970.

McConaghy, N. A controlled trial of imipramine, amphetamine, pad-and-bell conditioning and random wakening in the treatment of nocturnal enuresis. *Medical Journal of Australia*, 1969, *2*, 237–239.

McDonagh, M. Is operant conditioning effective in reducing enuresis and encopresis in children? *Perspectives on Psychiatric Care*, 1971, *9*(1), 17–23.

Macfarlane, J., Allen, L., and Honzik, M. *A developmental study of the behavior problems of normal children between 21 months and 14 years.* Berkeley: University of California Press, 1954.

MacKeith, R., Meadow, R., and Turner, R. How children become dry. In I. Kolvin, R. MacKeith, and S. Meadow (Eds.), *Bladder control and enuresis, clinics in developmental medicine*, 1973, nos. 48/49.

McKendry, J., Williams., and Matheson, D. Enuresis: A three-year study of value of a waking apparatus. *Canadian Medical Association Journal*, 1964, *90*, 513.

MacLean, R. Imipramine hydrochloride (tofranil®) and enuresis. *American Journal of Psychiatry*, 1960, *117*, 551.

Maguire, J. Treatment of enuresis in a public health clinic. *Public Health,* 1970, *84*(3), 145–149.

Mahony, D. Studies of enuresis: I. Incidence of obstructive lesions and pathophysiology of enuresis. *Journal of Urology,* 1971, *106*(6), 951–958.

Mahoney, D. and Laferte, R. Enuresis: A plea for objectivity and sensitivity. *Journal of Urology,* 1973, *109*(4), 531–532.

Manhas, R. and Sharma, J. Tofranil (imipramine) in childhood enuresis: A controlled trial of tofranil (imipramine) in treatment of 72 cases of childhood enuresis in Kashmir. *Indian Practitioner,* 1967, *20,* 663–669.

Mariuz, M. and Walters, C. Enuresis in non-psychotic boys treated with imipramine. *American Journal of Psychiatry,* 1963, *120,* 597–599.

Marshall, S., Marshall, H., and Lyon, R. Enuresis: An analysis of various therapeutic approaches. *Pediatrics,* 1973, *52,* 813–817.

Martin, B. and Kubly, D. Results of enuresis by a conditioned response method. *Journal of Consulting Psychology,* 1955, *19*(1), 71–73.

Martin, G. Imipramine pamoate in the treatment of childhood enuresis: A double-blind study. *American Journal of Diseases of Childhood,* 1971, *122*(1), 42–47.

Maxwell, C. and Seldrup, J. General practitioners' forum. Imipramine in the treatment of childhood enuresis. *Practitioner,* 1971, *207*(242), 809–814.

Meadow, R. Childhood enuresis. *British Medical Journal,* 1970, *4,* 787–789.

Michaels, J. and Goodman, S. Incidence and intercorrelations of enuresis and other neuropathic traits in so-called normal children. *American Journal of Orthopsychiatry,* 1934, *4,* 79–106.

Michaels, J. and Goodman, S. The incidence of enuresis and age of association in one thousand neuropsychiatric patients: With a discussion of the relationship between enuresis and delinquency. *American Journal of Orthopsychiatry,* 1939, *9,* 59–71.

Miller, P. An experimental analysis of retention control training in the treatment of nocturnal enuresis in two institutionalized adolescents. *Behavior Therapy* 1973, *4,* 288–294.

Miller, P., Champelli, J., and Dinello, F. Imipramine in the treatment of enuretic schoolchildren: A double-blind study. *American Journal of Diseases of Childhood,* 1968, *115*(1), 17–20.

Milner, G. and Hills, N. A double-blind assessment of antidepressants in the treatment of 212 enuretic patients. *Medical Journal of Australia,* 1968, *1*(22), 943–947.

Morgan, R. and Young, G. Parental attitudes and the conditioning treatment of childhood enuresis. *Behaviour Research Therapy,* 1975, *13*(2–3), 197–199.

Mowrer, O. and Mowrer, W. Enuresis: A method for its study and treatment. *American Journal of Orthopsychiatry,* 1938, *8,* 436–459.

Muellner, S. Development of urinary control in children. *Journal of the American Medical Association,* 1960, *172,* 1256–1261.

Murphy, S., Nickols, J., and Hammer, S. Neurological evaluation of adolescent enuretics. *Pediatrics,* 1970, *45*(2), 269–273.

Neal, B. and Coote, M. Hazards of enuresis alarm. *Archives of Diseases in Childhood* 1969, *44*, 651.

Nigam, P., Tandon, V., Lal, N., and Thacore, V. Enuresis—its background and management. *Indian Journal of Pediatrics,* 1973, *40*(304), 180–187.

Nilsson, A., Almgren, P., Kohler, E., and Kohler, L. Enuresis: The importance of maternal attitudes and personality. A prospective study of pregnant women and a follow-up of their children. *Acta Psychiatrica Scandinavia,* 1973, *49*(2), 114–130.

Noack, C. Enuresis nocturna: A long-term study of 44 children treated with imipramine hydrochloride ('tofranil') and other drugs. *Medical Journal of Australia,* 1964, *1*, 191–192.

Novick, J. Symptomatic treatment of acquired and persistent enuresis. *Journal of Abnormal Psychology,* 1966, *77*, 363–368.

Okasha, A. and Hassan, A. Positive conditioning in nocturnal enuresis. *Journal of the Egyptian Medical Association,* 1966, *49*(9), 601–610.

O'Leary, K. and Wilson, G. *Behavior therapy: Application and outcome.* Englewood Cliffs, N.J.: Prentice-Hall, 1975.

Oppel, W., Harper, P., and Rider, R. Social, psychological, and neurological factors associated with nocturnal enuresis. *Pediatrics,* 1968, *42*(4), 627–641.

Ovary, F. and Zsadanyi, O. Nocturnal enuresis: Electroencephalographic and cystometric examinations. *Acta Medica Academiae Scientiarum Hungaricae,* 1967, *23*(2), 153–168.

Owens, J. and Fischer, I. Conditioning in enuresis—its efficacy and the factors involved. *Journal of Irish Medical Association,* 1966, *59*(351), 81–82.

Parkin, J. and Fraser, M. Poisoning as a complication of enuresis. *Developmental Medicine and Child Neurology,* 1972, *14*, '727–'730.

Paschalis, A., Kimmel, H., and Kimmel, E. Further study of diurnal instrumental conditioning in the treatment of enuresis nocturna. *Journal of Behavior Therapy and Experimental Psychiatry,* 1972, *3*, 253–256.

Petersen, K., Andersen, O., and Hansen, T. Mode of action and relative value of imipramine and similar drugs in the treatment of nocturnal enuresis. *European Journal of Pharmacology,* 1974, *7*(3), 187–194.

Peterson, R., Wright, R., and Hanlon, C. The effects of extending the CS-UCS interval on the effectiveness of the conditioning treatment for nocturnal enuresis. *Behaviour Research and Therapy,* 1969, *7*, 351–357.

Philpott, M. The treatment of enuresis: Further clinical experience with imipramine. *British Journal of Clinical Practice,* 1970, *24*(8), 327–329.

Pierce, C. Dream studies in enuresis research. *Canadian Psychiatric Association Journal,* 1963, *8*, 415.

Pierce, C., Lipcon, H., McLary, J., and Noble, H. Enuresis: Psychiatric interview studies. *U.S. Armed Forces Medical Journal,* 1956, *7*, 1265–1280.

Pierce, C., Whitman, R., Maas, J., and Gray, M. Enuresis and dreaming: Experimental studies. *Archives of General Psychiatry,* 1961, *4*, 166–170.

Pompeius, R. Cystometry in paediatric enuresis. *Scandinavian Journal of Urology and Nephiology,* 1971, *5*, 227–228.

Poussaint, A. and Ditman, K. A controlled study of imipramine ('tofranil') in the treatment of childhood enuresis. *Journal of Pediatrics,* 1965, *67,* 283.

Poussaint, A., Ditman, K., and Greenfield, R. Amitriptyline in childhood enuresis. *Clinical Pharmacology Therapy,* 1966, *7*(1), 21–25.

Ritvo, E., Ornitz, E., Gottlieb, F. et al. Arousal and non-arousal types of enuresis. *American Journal of Psychiatry,* 1969, *126,* 77–84.

Robson, P. Nocturnal urinary incontinence in elderly psychiatric patients: A controlled trial of imipramine. *British Journal of Geriatric Practice,* 1969, 27–30.

Rocklin, N. and Tilker, H. Instrumental conditioning of nocturnal enuresis: A reappraisal of some previous findings. Proceedings of the 81st Annual Convention of the *American Psychological Association,* (1973), *8,* 915–916.

Ross, J. Behavioral treatment of enuresis: Case study. *Psychological Report,* 1974, *35*(1), 286.

Rutter, M., Tizard, J., and Whitmore, K. *Education, health and behavior: A psychological study and medical study of childhood development.* London, England: Longman Group Limited, 1970.

Rutter, M., Yule, W., and Graham, P. Enuresis and behavioral deviance: Some epidemiological considerations. In I. Kolvin, R. MacKeith, and S. Meadow (Eds.), *Bladder control and enuresis, clinics in developmental medicine,* 1973, nos. 48/49.

Sacks, S. and DeLeon, G. Conditioning two types of enuretics. *Behaviour Research and Therapy,* 1973, *11*(4), 653–654.

Sacks, S., DeLeon, G., and Blackman, S. Psychological changes associated with conditioning functional enuresis. *Journal of Clinical Psychology,* 1974, *30*(3), 271–276.

Salmon, M., Taylor, D., and Lee, D. On the EEG in enuresis. In I. Kolvin, R. MacKeith, and S. Meadow (Eds.), *Bladder control and enuresis, clinics in developmental medicine,* 1973, nos. 48/49.

Samaan, M. The control of nocturnal enuresis by operant conditioning. *Journal of Behavior Therapy and Experimental Psychiatry,* 1972, *3,* 103–105.

Scallon, R. and Herron, W. Field articulation of enuretic boys and their mothers. *Perception and Motor Skills,* 1969, *28*(2), 407–413.

Schiff, S. The EEG, eye movements and dreaming in enuresis. *Journal Nervous Mental Disorders,* 1965, *140,* 397–404.

Schwartz, M., Colligan, R., and O'Connell, E. Behavior modification of nocturnal enuresis: A treatment and research program at the Mayo Clinic. *Professional Psychology,* 1972, *3,* 169–172.

Scott, J. A surgeon's view of enuresis. In I. Kolvin, R. MacKeith, and S. Meadow (Eds.), *Behavioral control and enuresis, clinics in developmental medicine,* 1973, nos. 48/49.

Shader, R. Behavioral treatment of enuresis. *Diseases of the Nervous System,* 1968, *29*(5), 334–335.

Shaffer, D., Costello, A., and Hill, I. Control of enuresis with imipramine. *Archives of Diseases in Childhood,* 1968, *43,* 665–671.

Shuller, D. and McNamara, J. Expectancy factors in behavioral observation. *Behavior Therapy*, 1976, *7*, 519–527.

Sieger, H. Treatment of essential nocturnal enuresis. *Journal of Pediatrics*, 1952, *40*, 738–749.

Sloop, E. and Kennedy, W. Institutionalized retarded nocturnal enuretics treated by a conditioning technique. *American Journal of Mental Deficiency*, 1973, *77*, 717–721.

Smith, A., Mark, H., and Blerk, P. The wet-bed syndrome. *South African Medical Journal*, 1973, *47*(40), 1916–1918.

Smith, E. and Gonzalez, E. Nortriptyline hydrochloride in the treatment of enuresis in mentally retarded boys. *American Journal of Mental Deficiency*, 1967, *71*, 825–827.

Sperling, M. Dynamic considerations and treatment of enuresis. *Journal of the American Academy of Child Psychiatry*, 1965, *4*, 19–31.

Stansfeld, J. Enuresis and urinary tract infection. In I. Kolvin, R. MacKeith, and S. Meadow (Eds.), *Bladder control and enuresis, clinics in developmental medicine*, 1973, nos. 48/49.

Starfield, B. Functional bladder capacity in enuretic and non-enuretic children. *Journal of Pediatrics*, 1967, *70*(5), 777–781.

Starfield, B. Enuresis: Its pathogenesis and management. *Clinical Pediatrics*, 1972, *11*, 343–349.

Starfield, B., and Mellits, E. Increase in functional bladder capacity and improvements in enuresis. *Journal of Pediatrics*, 1968, *72*, 483–487.

Stedman, J. An extension of the Kimmel treatment method for enuresis to an adolescent: A case report. *Journal of Behavior Therapy and Experimental Psychiatry*, 1972, *3*, 307–309.

Stehbens, J. Comparison of MMPI scores of mothers of enuretic and control children. *Journal of Clinical Psychology*, 1970, *26*(4), 496.

Stein, Z., and Susser, M. Socio-medical study of enuresis among delinquent boys. *British Journal of Preventative Social Medicine*, 1965, *19*, 174–181.

Stein, Z., Susser, M., and Wilson, A. Families of enuretic children. Part I: Family type and age. Part II: Family culture, structure, and organisation. *Developmental Medicine and Child Neurology*, 1965, *7*, 658–676.

Stewart, M. Treatment of bedwetting. *Journal of the American Medical Association*, 1975, *232*, 281–283.

Stockwell, L. and Smith, C. Enuresis: A study of causes, types and therapeutic results. *American Journal of Diseases of Childhood*, 1940, *59*, 1013.

Szab'o, L. and Popoviciu, L. Clinical EEG and polygraphic investigations of sleep in children with simple enuresis or associated with other nonconvulsive nocturnal episodic manifestations. *Electroencephalography and Clinical Neurophysiology*, 1969, *27*(6), 635–636.

Tapia, F., Jekel, J., and Domke, H. Enuresis: An emotional symptom? *Journal of Nervous and Mental Disease*, 1960, *130*, 61–66.

Taylor, P. and Turner, R. A clinical trial of continuous, intermittent, and overlearning "bell and pad" treatments for nocturnal enuresis. *Behaviour Research and Therapy*, 1975, *13*, 281–293.

Thompson, I. and Lauvetz, R. Oxybutynin in bladder spasm, neurogenic bladder, and enuresis. *Urology,* 1976, *8*(5), 452–454.

Thomsen, W., Reid, W., and Hebeler, J. Effect of Tofranil on enuretic boys. *Diseases of the Nervous System,* 1967, *28*(3), 167–169.

Thorne, E. Instrumented counterconditioning of enuresis with minimal therapist intervention. *Proceedings, 81st Annual Convention, American Psychological Association,* 1973, 541–542.

Torrens, M. and Collins, C. The urodynamic assessment of adult enuresis. *British Journal of Urology,* 1975, *47*(4), 433–440.

Tough, J., Hawkins, R., McArthur, M., and Ravenswaay, S. Modification of enuretic behavior by punishment: A new use for an old device. *Behavior Therapy,* 1971, *2,* 567–574.

Treffert, D. An evaluation of imipramine in enuresis. *American Journal of Psychiatry,* 1964, *121,* 178–179.

Troup, C. and Hodgson, N. Nocturnal functional bladder capacity in enuretic children. *Wisconsin Medical Journal,* 1971, *70*(7), 171–173.

Turner, R. CNS stimulant drugs and conditioning treatment of nocturnal enuresis: A long-term follow-up study. *Behaviour Research and Therapy,* 1966, *4*(3), 225–228.

Turner, R. Conditioning treatment of nocturnal enuresis: Present status. In I. Kolvin, R. MacKeith, and S. Meadow (Eds.), *Bladder control and enuresis, clinics in developmental medicine,* 1973, nos. 48/49.

Turner, R. and Taylor, P. Conditioning treatment of nocturnal enuresis in adults: Preliminary findings. *Behaviour Research and Therapy,* 1974, *12*(1), 41–52.

Turner, R., Young, G., and Rachman, S. Treatment of nocturnal enuresis by conditioning techniques. *Behaviour Research and Therapy,* 1970, *8,* 367–381.

Umphress, A., Murphy, S., Nickols, J., and Hammar, S. Adolescent enuresis. *Archives of General Psychiatry,* 1970, *22,* 237–244.

Valentine, A. and Maxwell, C. Enuresis in severely subnormal children—a clinical trial of imipramine. *Journal of Mental Subnormality,* 1968, *14,* 84–90.

Waitzell, I., Gallagher, E., and Marshall, R. Control of enuresis in disturbed adolescent boys. *Journal of the National Medical Association,* 1969, *61*(6), 474–475.

Weinmann, H. Telemetric recording of sleep rhythms in enuretic children. *Electroencephalography & Clinical Neurophysiology,* 1968, *24*(4), 391.

Werry, J., Aman, M., Dowrick, P., and Lampen, E. Imipramine and chlordiazepoxide in enuresis. *Psychopharmacology Bulletin,* 1977, *13*(2), 38–39.

Werry, J., and Cohrssen, J. Enuresis: An etiologic and therapeutic study. *Journal of Pediatrics,* 1965, *67,* 423–431.

Werry, J., Dowrick, P., Lampen, E., and Vamos, M. Imipramine in enuresis—psychological and physiological effects. *Journal of Child Psychology and Psychiatry,* 1975, *16*(4), 289–299.

White, M. A thousand consecutive cases of enuresis: Results of treatment. *Medical Officer,* 1968, *120,* 151–155.

Whiteside, C., and Arnold, E. Persistent primary enuresis: A urodynamic assessment. *British Medical Journal,* 1975, *1*(5954), 364–367.

Wikes, I. Treatment of persistent enuresis with the electric buzzer. *Archives of Diseases in Childhood,* 1958, *33,* 160–164.

Wolkind, S. Bed wetting and emotional disorders: An interactional model. *Child: Care Health and Development,* 1976, *2*(2), 77–81.

Wright, L. and Craig, S. A comparative study of amphetamine, ephedrine-atropine mixture, placebo, and behavioral conditioning in the treatment of nocturnal enuresis. *Journal of Oklahoma State Medical Association,* 1974, *67*(10), 430–433.

Yates, A. *Behavior therapy.* New York: Wiley, 1970.

Yates, A. *Theory and practice in behavior therapy.* New York: Wiley, 1975.

Young, G. Conditioning treatment of enuresis. *Developmental Medicine and Child Neurology,* 1965, *7,* 557–662.

Young, G. The problem of enuresis. *British Journal of Hospital Medicine,* 1969, *2,* 628–632.

Young, G. and Morgan, R. Analysis of factors associated with the extinction of a conditioned response. *Behaviour Research and Therapy,* 1973a, *11*(2), 219–222.

Young, G. and Morgan, R. Rapidity of response to the treatment of enuresis. *Developmental Medicine and Child Neurology,* 1973b, *15,* 488–496.

Young, G. and Morgan, R. Non-attending enuretic children. *Community Medicine,* 1972a, *127,* 158–159.

Young, G. and Morgan, R. Overlearning in the conditioning of enuresis: A long-term follow-up. *Behaviour Research and Therapy,* 1972b, *10,* 419–420.

Young, G. and Morgan, R. Overlearning in the conditioning treatment of enuresis. *Behaviour Research and Therapy,* 1972c, *10,* 147–151.

Young, G. and Turner, R. CNS stimulant drugs and conditioning of nocturnal enuresis. *Behaviour Research and Therapy,* 1965, *3,* 93–101.

Zaleski, A., Gerrard, J., and Schokier, M. Nocturnal enuresis: The importance of a small bladder capacity. In I. Kolvin, R. MacKeith, and S. Meadow (Eds.), *Bladder control and enuresis, clinics in developmental medicine,* 1973, nos. 48/49.

4
Seizure
Disorders

Susan Walen

A seizure may be defined as an altered state of consciousness, measurable by abnormal bursts of electrical activity in the brain (Baird, 1972; Puletti, 1969). To the observer, the seizure appears as an involuntary shift in muscular movement, either an abrupt increase or sudden cessation of motion.

Recurrent seizures may result from a wide variety of organic conditions including lesions, trauma, perinatal injuries, infections, and metabolic disorders (Katz and Zlutnik, 1974). Most commonly, seizures are labeled as *idiopathic,* a term which simply means of unknown cause. *Epilepsy* is a general label for such recurrent idiopathic seizures.

Epilepsy is usually classified into four types: grand mal, petit mal, Jacksonian, and psychomotor. The *grand mal seizure,* perhaps the most frightening to an observer, typically consists of four phases. Initially the patient experiences an aura of premonitory sensations such as a feeling of dizziness or ringing in the ears. Within moments the tonic phase begins; the muscles of the body become suddenly rigid and the patient may stop breathing. After approximately a minute the clonic phase begins, during which the muscles spastically contract and relax. These violent convulsions may be accompanied by loss of sphincter control and the appearance of foamy saliva at the mouth. Finally, the patient passes into the fourth or coma phase. Recovery from unconsciousness is gradual and the patient may remain confused and fatigued for hours after the attack.

Petit mal attacks, by contrast, are much milder, and often go unnoticed by the patient and those around him. They present neither an aura nor a convulsion. Typically, the patient simply stops what he is doing; his eyes roll up, his head nods, and he experiences loss of consciousness for a few seconds.

Jacksonian seizures tend to be localized to a particular area of the body, such as a twitch in the fingers, although the effect may spread and become more generalized. For example, the muscular spasm may spread from the hand to the arm, the shoulder, the trunk, and sometimes to the whole body. The attack may, therefore, resemble a grand mal seizure.

Psychomotor epilepsy consists of loss of consciousness, but during the seizure the patient performs an organized set of behaviors. The acts may be simple repetitive movements of a limb, or complex and unusual activities. Rarely, violent or antisocial behaviors may occur during the attack, but the patient will not be able to recall seizure events.

Convulsive disorders affect 1–2 percent of the population (Cautela and Flannery, 1973), with a somewhat greater incidence among men than women (Bagley, 1971). Ninety percent of seizure disorders begin before age 20 (Livingston, 1972). Since convulsions are much more common among children than adults, it has been suggested that as the brain matures its resistance to seizures seems to increase (Robb, 1969).

Although there is no evidence which definitely proves the role of hereditary factors in epilepsy (Livingston, 1972), many authorities feel that there may be transmission of a "convulsive predisposition" which may be expressed under physiologic or emotional stress (Bagley, 1971). In the typical family history of an epileptic, an average of one parent and at least half of the patient's relatives show evidence of brain dysrhythmia, although they might not display full-blown seizures (Mostofsky, 1972).

THEORETICAL ANALYSIS

Nonbehavioral

The two major nonbehavioral approaches to seizure disorders are (a) psychodynamic, and (b) medical. In the former category, the seizure is viewed as an involuntary release of psychic energy reflecting underlying conflicts or anxieties. Presumably, by resolving these conflicts at a conscious level, seizure control can be obtained. There is little evidence in the literature to support such a contention, however, and in the few reported cases of psychoanalytic treatment, therapy was quite prolonged, treatment interventions are confounded with one another and with maturation. More parsimonious interpretations of behavior change are available (e.g., Gottschalk, 1953).

The three most prominent medical treatments of seizure disorder are (1) drugs, (2) diet, and (3) surgery. *Anticonvulsant medications* are widely used, often with fairly rapid remission of symptoms. Patients with high blood levels of anticonvulsants display a number of negative side effects, however, including psychomotor slowing, reduced intellectual function, and occasionally pathologic personality changes

(Reynolds and Travers, 1974). Although success rates as high as 70–80 percent have been reported (Schmidt and Wilder, 1968), one study found that 25 percent of the treated children did not respond at all, and another 25 percent responded only partially (Carter and Gold, 1968). Some recent research on animal models of epilepsy has suggested that the amino acid taurine may offer possibilities for treatment in some forms of convulsive disorders, although the validity of the animal model is still in question (Gaito, 1976).

Ketogenic diets have also been used for seizure control. In a hospital setting, all food is withheld from the patient until urinanalysis reveals the presence of ketone bodies. The patient is then placed on a high fat, low carbohydrate diet, the weight of the fat content being four times the combined weight of carbohydrate and protein. Such a procedure is recommended only when drug management fails or produces unsatisfactory side effects. The limitations of the procedure, however, include the fact that it is most effective in children between the ages of 2–5, but is rarely successful with patients over 8 years of age (Livingston, 1972). Since it is difficult to adhere to such a diet, it cannot be used with children who have strong food preferences, or whose parents are unlikely or unable to cooperate with the dietary demands (Baird, 1972).

When a focal injury to the brain is thought to be the cause of the epilepsy, *surgery* may be considered as a last option (Bagley, 1971). It is never the treatment of choice unless the seizures are a symptom of a tumor, abcess, or hematoma (Livingston, 1972). Surgical treatment consists of removal of the neurons responsible for the abnormal electrical discharge; thus, the problem must be localized and in an accessible and expendable area of the cortex. Although the best therapeutic results are obtained in patients with psychomotor epilepsy who have resection of their temporal lobe, complete success is seldom found. At best, the usual result is a reduction in the frequency and severity of attacks.

Behavioral

Although it is well established that normal as well as pathologic neural activity can be conditioned (Efron, 1957), it is also clear that seizures are typically not simply conditioned reflexes. Forster (1966) administered repeated pairings of a sensory stimulus (CS) with electrically induced seizures (UCS) to animals with an intact nervous system. Although both behavioral and electroencephologic (EEG) changes occurred, no true seizures were conditioned.

Nevertheless, neurologists have long acknowledged the relationship between convulsive behavior and environmental stimuli (Mostofsky, 1972). Some attacks are quite reliably predicted, and there are
epileptic patients who find that they have some control over their
seizures (Katz and Zlutnik, 1974). However, it is only within the past
ten years that behavioral analysis and treatment interventions for the
control of seizures have been attempted. The present chapter discusses
a variety of treatment approaches to seizure control and the behavioral
principles underlying them. Briefly, these treatments focus upon one
(or a combination) of the following: (a) antecedent stimuli, (b) the
seizure behavior itself, (c) consequences of the seizure, and (d) cognitions of the patient, especially as these become antecedents themselves. Thus, behavioral interventions in seizure disorders join the
ranks of techniques used with other diseases in the emerging specialty
of behavioral medicine.

ASSESSMENT

Two major diagnostic problems confront the clinician: Does the
patient indeed have a seizure disorder, and if so, what data are needed
to develop a treatment plan? The first problem may occur if the patient
has not come from a referring physician and, as is often the case, the
presenting problems do not fit neatly into descriptive seizure categories. As Small (1973) states: "Epileptic phenomena shade imper-
ceptibly from frank convulsions toward normal behavior, and as the
normal end of the continuum is approached, the certainty of diagnosis
diminishes markedly."

Although some clinicians utilize pencil and paper tests to determine the presence of cerebral dysfunction (e.g., widely disparate scores
on verbal and motor performance in IQ tests, or projective measures
such as the Bender Gestalt drawings), three other important procedures may help to establish the diagnosis of epilepsy: (a) electroencephalogram recordings, (b) response to medication, and (c) behavioral observation by the patient or by others.

In some cases of unclear diagnosis, referral to a neurologist or
epileptologist may clarify the clinical picture; abnormal EEG activity
or paroxysmal spikes in the EEG tracing may provide useful information. Unfortunately, however, EEG studies may not always provide
a clear answer to the question of whether the patient's problem is one
of "genuine" epilepsy. Mostofsky and Balaschak (1977) report that "a
definable percentage of the 'normal' population has been found to have
EEG abnormalities and does not suffer from seizure disorders (i.e.,

does not require any medical attention for seizure problems), whereas a number of patients present frank clinical seizure disorders without accompanying EEG aberrations. It is not at all uncommon to hear reports of an improved clinical picture while the EEG seems to deteriorate, or of the converse. In short, the dictum to treat the patient, not the EEG pointedly reminds one that the EEG must be evaluated as one of the many measures in the total perspective of the patient's symptomatic profile."

The diagnosis of epilepsy may also be revealed by the patient's response to anticonvulsant medications which may be prescribed. It is also useful to ask the patient what drugs he has taken (prescribed or illegally obtained). Barbiturates and some amphetamines have an anticonvulsant effect, and the patient may have been self-medicating in an attempt to control his symptoms. Once again, however, response to medication may not be a clear diagnostic indicator, since not all anticonvulsants work equally well in all types of seizure disorders or in all cases of the same type of seizure disorder (Small, 1973). Often, significant adjustments of both dose and type of medication are needed to achieve an effective combination for the individual patient.

Ultimately, interview and direct observation techniques may be the therapist's best diagnostic ally. In obtaining a behavioral description of the seizure, the therapist will want to ascertain the following:

> form of the behavioral disturbance
> time of onset of the seizure
> duration of the seizure
> setting and immediate antecedents to the seizure
> number of seizures per unit of time
> triggering events to the seizure
> aura: presence or absence and its form
> cognitions preceding the seizure
> immediate environmental consequences to the seizure
> cognitive consequences to the seizure
> patient's ability to control the seizure
> patient's subjective reaction to his seizure.

It will be important for the therapist to determine the validity and reliability of the patient's self-report of seizures, as well as reports by observers of the patient's behavior, particularly when the patient is a child and the primary source of information is the parents' report. In this case, the subjective reactions of the parents to the seizure may be critical pieces of information.

BEHAVIORAL TREATMENT PROCEDURES

Control of Seizure Antecedents

Antecedent control of seizures may be an appropriate focus for treatment when triggering stimuli or stimulus complexes can be identified. Three broad categories of seizure antecedents include (a) sensory-evoked seizures, (b) stress-evoked seizures, and (c) self-induced seizures. In some cases the triggering stimuli are easily identified by the patient or his family, but others require good detective work on the part of the therapist. In any case, it is recommended that detailed logs of the seizure episode be kept, indicating such information as time of day, situation, mood of the patient, pre-seizure behaviors, and the immediate consequences to the seizure. A detailed log sheet for use by hospital personnel was developed by Daitzman (personal communication) and is included, in modified form, in Figure 1.

Sensory-evoked (reflex) seizures account for at least 5 percent of all seizure cases (Daube, 1965). In its most common form, the sensory event that triggers the seizure is a visual stimulus, such as a flashing light, a striking visual pattern, or even repeated closing of the eyelid. In some cases seizures are induced by auditory stimuli such as sudden loud noises. Some rarer types include seizures triggered by listening to music, by reading, by hearing certain voices, or even by touching specific parts of the patient's body (Forster, 1966).

When the triggering sensory stimulus cannot reliably be avoided, the behavioral technique of *fading* has been successfully employed to increase stimulus tolerance (Adams, 1976). Simply, the offending stimulus is presented in a manner which will not elicit seizures; gradually the intensity and/or duration of the stimulus is increased as long as seizures do not occur.

An example of the use of fading was reported by Forster (1969) working with a patient whose seizures were triggered by a flashing light. While the patient's cortical activity was monitored by an EEG fed into an online computer, a flashing light was presented to the patient in a very brightly lit room. Since the ambient light was so high, the light flashes were not easily detected and were thereby rendered ineffective. As long as the EEG indicated no sign of imminent seizure, the ambient light was gradually faded while the flashing light, by contrast, became more visible. If seizure activity occurred, the ambient light was increased two logarithmic steps for the next few trials, and then fading was begun again. Essentially the same procedure has been successfully used with auditory stimuli. Thus, if a patient's seizures are initiated by sudden, loud noises, these stimuli are embedded in loud background noise which is gradually faded out as seizures fail to appear (Forster, 1967). Similarly, fading can be done in the reverse direction. The epileptogenic stimulus can be presented at a very low intensity or for very brief durations, and can gradually be faded in along the relevant stimulus dimension. In a related technique, the trigger stimulus is presented to the patient immediately after a seizure has occurred, when the EEG reveals that the cerebral cortex is in a seizure-refractory period (Forster, 1969). The duration of the stimulus is then gradually extended.

Although clinical benefit has been obtained from such procedures, they may be complex and expensive to implement. Additionally, improvements may be temporary unless the therapist can devise a way for the patient to practice the technique in his normal environment (Baird, 1972; Fabisch and Darbyshire, 1965). Care must be taken in the presentation of the stimuli to avoid resensitizing the patient, although such resensitizations have been found to be reversible (Adams, 1976).

For some patients the triggering stimuli for seizures may be feelings of stress or anxiety. For example, in one study convulsions were elicited in known epileptics by "insight" feedback which these patients found difficult to accept emotionally (Miller, 1969). Procedures which have been found useful for the control of *anxiety-elicited seizures* are relaxation training and systematic desensitization.

Relaxation may be induced in a variety of ways (e.g., with drugs, autogenic training, or biofeedback), but most commonly the patient is taught some variant of Jacobson's relaxation exercises (Jacobson, 1938). He is trained to concentrate on various muscle groups and to discriminate their tense or relaxed state. This training may also directly produce an interruption of worrisome or anxious thoughts, and thereby may be viewed as having two components: skeletal muscle release and cognitive shifts of attention (Walen, Hauserman, and Lavin, 1977). It has been reported that lack of sleep is an important stress factor in patients with stress convulsions (Friis and Lund, 1974). Since relaxation training has been well demonstrated to be useful in the control of sleep difficulties, it is a recommended first step in working with stress-induced seizures.

The technique of *systematic desensitization* can be built upon a foundation of relaxation training. Thus, once the patient can enter a relaxed state, he can be imaginally presented with a hierarchy of situations which he normally finds to be stressful to him. Parrino (1971), for example, described the application of systematic desensitization in which hierarchies were constructed on themes of meeting an authority figure, being the focus of attention in a group, and so forth. Relaxation and systematic desensitization provide the patient with an alternate response and, since they focus attention on internal states, may allow the patient to recognize premonitory signs of seizure activity and thereby abort some attacks (Katz and Zlutnik, 1974).

A special application of antecedent control of seizures is provided

figure 1

Patient's Name_____ Date_____ Time of seizure_____

Was aura present?_____ Describe:

Was seizure REPORTED or OBSERVED? (circle one)

If OBSERVED, by whom? (circle all that apply)

    ward personnel

    other patients (list)

    other (list)

If REPORTED, to whom? (circle all that apply)

    ward personnel

    other patients (list)

    other (list)

Describe the seizure:

Where on ward did seizure occur? (circle all that apply)

    seated in chair

    standing

    watching TV

    playing games

    eating

Report of seizure

in cases in which the *patient voluntarily induces convulsions.* Most commonly, such seizures are of the petit mal type and are usually self-induced by flashing light or hyperventilation. Statistically, these seizures are most common among females with low-seizure thresholds and of below-average intelligence (Katz and Zlutnik, 1974). In such cases it appears that the convulsion may serve a number of functions: as an escape from tension, as a manipulative social device, or most directly as a source of self-pleasure (Bagley, 1971). Thus, the behavior may be maintained by the positive reinforcement which presumably occurs in brief periods of clouding of the consciousness, or by negative *figure 1* *(Continued)*

playing guitar

asleep

other (describe):

IMMEDIATELY AFTER SEIZURE what happened?
(circle all that apply)

patient upset but OK

patient unconcerned, but observers upset

patient made to lie down or go to room

patient's physician called

patient acts as if nothing happened; if seizure not reported
by observer entire incident would have gone unnoticed

patient approached by nurse

nurse approached by patient

patient confused and uncommunicative

other (describe):

AFTER ABOUT 30 MINUTES: (circle all that apply)

patient left alone

patient engaged in new activity

patient discusses seizure with nurse

other patients ask about seizure

other: (describe)

reinforcement. For example, Fabisch and Darbyshire (1965) reported a case in which a shopgirl regularly induced seizures to escape from dealing with difficult customers. The need for a careful behavioral analysis, therefore, can be appreciated.

Self-induced seizures have most commonly been treated by *punishment* or *aversion techniques* (Katz and Zlutnik, 1974). An example of unprogrammed punishment for self-induction was reported by Fabisch and Darbyshire (1965) whose young client induced seizures by hyperventilation, at an increasing frequency. One day, however, the child experienced three convulsive episodes which led to vomiting and prolonged stupor; these aversive consequences produced a six-month period of abstention from hyperventilation and seizures.

Programmed punishment was used by Wright (1973) with a 5-year-old retarded boy whose baseline rate of convulsions was measured in hundreds of seizures each hour. The child induced seizures by waving his hands in front of his eyes or by rapid blinking. Hand-waving was totally suppressed by five punishment sessions using shock to the child's leg; a subsequent course of shock sessions significantly reduced the blinking. At a 7-month follow-up, seizure remission remained at only 90 percent of the baseline rate.

Punishment was also used by Scholander (1972) in an interesting case of an epileptic boy whose attacks were accompanied by painful twists of his head. Although the epilepsy responded somewhat favorably to medication, the boy had developed the habit of gripping and holding his neck with his hands, thereby precluding many normal activities. The patient was provided with portable shock equipment which automatically delivered a wrist shock whenever his hand got close to his neck. At the end of a six-month follow-up, not only was there significant improvement in the patient's general social behavior, but also complete elimination of epileptic symptoms.

Control of Seizure Activity

In some cases of seizure the patient may be able to identify internal premonitory symptoms as an aura to the seizure itself. When this is possible, *biofeedback* may be clinically useful in helping the patient to control the attack (Johnson and Meyer, 1974). Using auditory or visual feedback of their EEG recordings, patients may be trained to control their slow rhythm (alpha) cortical activity, or even to suppress their EEG seizure activity. Alpha waves reflect rhythmic activity in the cortex within a range of 8–13 Hz; the behavioral concomitant is a state of relaxed wakefulness, often subjectively described by the patient as a tranquil floating feeling. Several recent reports on alpha control have shown significant reductions in patients' seizure rates.

Brown (1977), for example, cites the biofeedback work of Poirier, who has taught seizure patients either to produce specific EEG patterns such as alpha or theta waves at will, or to suppress seizure waves. Although often immediate results have been demonstrated with individual patients, Poirier has not yet conducted systematic studies of these clinical effects.

Johnson and Meyer (1974) reported the case of an 18-year-old girl with a 10-year history of grand mal seizures. Under medication her seizure frequency averaged three per month. The treatment regimen included three stages: (1) two weeks of relaxation training, (2) seven half-hour sessions of EEG biofeedback to supplement the relaxation training and accustom the patient to the use of equipment, and (3) 36 sessions of EEG training spaced over a one-year period. The patient was also instructed to practice using these "relaxation" skills whenever she felt a seizure aura. The results of treatment were a 46 percent reduction in seizure frequency which was maintained over a 3-month follow-up. Although she remained unable to suppress a seizure once it started, the patient found that she could occasionally prevent one after experiencing the premonitory signs by relaxing and, as she put it, "going into an alpha state."

Kuhlman (1975, cited in Brown, 1977) used a reversal design to study the effect of alpha feedback. He met with five patients, two or three times a week, for two months, during which time only random EEG feedback was provided. The actual training then began, with biofeedback being given for cortical activity in the 9–14 Hz range. Three of the five patients responded with an *average* seizure reduction of 60 percent. A subsequent reversal to random biofeedback did not, however, lead to seizure increases. Kuhlman found significant increases in the amount of alpha activity seen in these patients which he interpreted to mean that EEG biofeedback "facilitated normal resting EEG pattern development." In other words, training may enable the epileptic patient to function at a lower level of arousal (Brown, 1977).

Sterman and his colleagues have reported work with feedback of slightly higher frequency waves (12–16 Hz) which they term Sensori-Motor Rhythm (SMR). In their early work with cats, the SMR activity was found to be associated with relaxation and absence of movement. Further, cats trained to increase this EEG rhythm became resistant to drug-induced seizures. It was found that similar patterns could, with difficulty, be detected in man, and with feedback, the frequency of these waveforms could be increased (Brown, 1977).

In a systematic study conducted by Sterman, MacDonald, and Stone (1974), epileptic and nonepileptic subjects were given many sessions of SMR biofeedback. Both groups showed significant EEG modification and an increase in the number of trains of 12–16 Hz activity. Most importantly, the frequency of major motor seizures was reduced for all epileptic subjects, most dramatically for the youngest, a 7-year-old boy. Although significant EEG changes were not seen before two to three months of continuous training, with extended practice the effectiveness was maintained.

In evaluating the overall effectiveness of biofeedback in the control of epilepsy, a number of points should be kept in mind. First, as Brown (1977) points out, the EEG is but a "faint mirror" of very complex events occurring within the brain, a far distance from the electrodes on the scalp. We are as yet very unsure of the significance of the components of recorded brain wave activity or even of recurrent patterns of activity. Second, many failures to replicate positive findings have been reported, which may be attributable to differences in patient selection, length of training, or instrumentation which, perhaps understating the case, "requires considerable electronic sophistication (Brown, 1977)". Third, the specific cortical activity under training is critical; Sterman et al. (1974) found, for example, that biofeedback for lower frequency rates (6–9 Hz) worsened seizure frequency. Finally, although some patients do seem to be able to learn to abort attacks, once a seizure begins, control is often not possible. The research indicates that if biofeedback facilities are available, it may hold promise for help in the control of epilepsy. An important aspect of this new procedure may be the changed feeling of the patient that he has personal, internal control of his problem.

If the seizure is viewed as the end product of a longer chain of events, the identification of an aura may make it feasible to *interrupt the chain* at various points. Zlutnick, Mayville, and Moffat (1975) described five cases in which the seizure chain was broken by positively reinforcing incompatible behaviors and interrupting pre-seizure rituals. One of their cases was that of a 17-year-old female diagnosed as mentally retarded, with major motor epilepsy. Before each major motor seizure the following chain of behaviors was reliably observed: the patient's body became tense and rigid, she clenched her fists and raised her arms at a 90-degree angle from her body, and her head snapped back while a grimace appeared on her face. In the treatment procedure, as soon as the patient was observed to be raising her hands, an attendant placed them back at her side or in her lap if she was seated. Then, after a five-second delay, she was praised and given a piece of candy for having her arms lowered. Immediately after treatment began, the patient's seizure rate dropped from a baseline level of 16 per day to near zero; when the contingencies were experimentally reversed, seizure frequency rose again, but was easily reversible when treatment was reintroduced. The near-zero rate of seizures was maintained at the nine-month follow-up.

The interruption and Differential Reinforcement of Other behavior (DRO) procedures were found to be particularly useful when the seizure included gross motor movements, and when the seizure was reliably predictable from clear-cut pre-seizure behaviors. An advantage of these techniques is that they can be conducted by nonprofessionals, such as family members, and in the patient's normal environment.

The development of *competing responses* to inhibit seizures has also been reported by Forster, Paulsen, and Baughman (1969) who treated a case of reading epilepsy. Whenever the patient read for over a minute, he would experience a seizure. He was then instructed to tap his knee whenever he encountered certain letters of the alphabet. While engaging in this competing activity he was able to read for increasingly longer periods of time. Eventually, this competing response was faded from tapping with the full hand to tapping with one finger, and ultimately to merely moving the upper part of a finger. All seizure activity and EEG dysrhythmic patterns were eliminated.

Occasionally one may find a patient whose seizure activity can be arrested by an *external sensory event* such as a strong odor. The function of such an inhibiting stimulus may then be transferred to a less obvious stimulus via classical conditioning. In a famous case reported by Efron (1957), odor of jasmine was found to be effective in aborting a patient's seizure, and was then paired with the sight of a silver bracelet. The patient stared at the bracelet while inhaling from the vial of scent every 15 minutes (with 7 hours off for sleep) for a period of 8 days. During the succeeding 2 weeks, she practiced twice a day in the presence of different people and in different surroundings. After 8 days, when the patient looked at her bracelet, she experienced an olfactory hallucination. During the second week, she was able to abort a seizure by staring at the bracelet. Eventually, higher order control was established; by merely thinking about the bracelet she was able to control her attacks in a variety of social situations.

Control of Seizure Consequences

In some cases an examination of the typical environmental consequences to a convulsive episode may provide the key to control (Carter and Gold, 1968). It is not unusual to find that others in the patient's home environment have subtly shaped and maintained the seizures. Since the convulsive behaviors may obviously be distressing to family members, they usually respond immediately with solicitous caring. The importance of *social attention* to the understanding of a particular case may be discovered by taking seizure frequency counts when the patient knows he is being observed, and when he is alone or thinks he is alone. The influence of *modeling* from the behavior of others may also commonly be seen in such cases.

G. Gardner (1973), for example, described a case of an 8-year-old girl whose fits were characterized by an abnormal EEG pattern and flutterings of her eyelids. These symptoms were essentially identical to those of her older brother, and the patient was obviously jealous of her parents' attention to him. The therapist observed that the child could keep her eyes open when watching TV, but not when she thought others were watching her. Treatment in this case involved relaxation training, hypnosis, and perhaps most importantly, *positive reinforcement for nonseizure behavior.* The child was praised for keeping her eyes open during training sessions with the therapist, and her parents were instructed to extinguish lid flutters and pay attention to non-blinking, general alertness, and responsiveness.

In a similar case, J. Gardner (1967) treated a 10-year-old girl whose seizure-like behavior was often coupled with tantrums and other somatic complaints. No clear organic etiology was found, but history-taking revealed hints of possible unintentional modeling and shaping of these behaviors by the parents. With guidance from the therapist, the parents devised a plan of extinction for the undesired behaviors and positive reinforcement (attention) for appropriate behaviors such as playing with her siblings, helping mother, drawing, and so on. The parents reported a rapid reduction in undesired behaviors; in a planned reversal, seizure behavior reoccurred within 24 hours, but a return to contingency management rapidly eliminated the problem again.

Social support for "sick" behaviors may not only occur in home environments, but in school, work, and institutional settings as well. Although the practical problems of supervision of contingencies in a complex environment are more difficult, consequent control of seizures is often possible in institutional settings. Iwata and Lorentzson (1976) treated a 41-year-old institutionalized retarded male who displayed frequent "seizure-like" behavior. Treatment was implemented in three ways: (a) the patient's daily activity schedule was greatly increased, (b) he was praised and offered a root beer every 20 minutes that he was seizure-free, and (c) if a seizure occurred, he was placed in a curtained-off cubicle for a time-out period. The use of an A-B-A-B experimental reversal design supported the effectiveness of these procedures, and as seizure control was reestablished, the contingencies were gradually faded out to approximate the care given to other patients on the ward.

A striking case with a clear course of response to treatment in a medical hospital was reported by Fowler, Niranjan, Lehmann, and Tindall (1971). The patient was a 58-year-old woman whose spells of severe vertigo had increased to the point that she had remained flat in bed for 13 months preceding treatment. She was given total support by her husband, family, and friends. As the authors describe it, "she essentially held court in her bedroom and entirely escaped demands for housekeeping or strenuous activity."

Treatment was conducted in a hospital, and consisted of shaping with positive reinforcement across various behaviors: increasing tolerance of the tilt of her bed, tilting of her reclining wheelchair, standing and then turning in parallel bars, and so on. Reinforcement consisted of attention and praise from the medical staff, her family, husband, and friends, who were instructed in the procedures. In addition, the staff used rest from her exercises as a reward, as well as graphic displays of the patient's progress which were posted by her bed. "Sick" behavior or complaints of dizziness resulted in minimal staff attention; visitors were escorted from her room, and if she was eating, her tray was removed. At the end of 55 days, the patient was discharged from the hospital able to walk 1200 feet with the aid of a cane; one year later she was able to walk independently and perform her cooking and housekeeping chores.

Control of Seizure Fears

The patient with a convulsive disorder may not only suffer physical distress, but also social stigmatization and practical problems such as job discrimination and denial of a driver's license. A vicious cycle may thus be perpetuated in which the seizure itself produces stress, thereby increasing the probability of further seizures or other behavior problems. Pinto (1972), for example, described a case of agoraphobia consequent to epilepsy. The patient was a 31-year-old male whose fears of being witnessed during an epileptic attack had generalized so that he was unable to leave his house without his wife, and had been unemployed for over a year. Treatment consisted of presenting ten imaginal *flooding* scenes on tape to the patient; in each scene the patient was described as entering a feared situation and developing a full-blown seizure attack. Each scene was repeated until it ceased to evoke anxiety, following which the patient immediately practiced actually entering the feared situation he had mastered in fantasy. Treatment was completed during a 3-week period and resulted, at a 16-week follow-up, in a general reduction of anxiety and a cessation of seizures.

Ince (1976) described the case of a 12-year-old boy who had several grand mal and petit mal seizures each day. The child developed increasing fear of the seizures and of the social stigma he felt was attached to them; in addition, he expressed great anxiety about a new experimental medicine he was soon to take. Therapy focused on the removal of these anxieties by *relaxation* and *systematic desensitization*. The hierarchies that were used included: (a) having seizures in school, (b) having seizures on a baseball field, (c) being ridiculed by other children, and (d) receiving the new experimental medication. By the fifth therapy session the child reported that he was no longer "nervous" about any of the hierarchy items. At this point the focus of therapy shifted to the seizure itself. The therapist taught the child cue-controlled relaxation; as soon as he was in a relaxed state, the boy repeated the word "relax" ten times, slowly. He was also instructed to say the word repeatedly as soon as he sensed a pre-seizure aura. Eventually, complete elimination of both grand and petit mal seizures was achieved.

Occasionally, even when a patient responds favorably to pharmacologic control of his seizures, his fear of having another seizure may remain. Anthony and Edelstein (1975) treated a woman whose seizures had been completely controlled by medicine for two years, yet she continued to suffer terrible anxiety about the possibility that a seizure would occur. Her obsessive ruminations about seizures resulted in severe anxiety attacks which occurred at the rate of five to six times per week. The technique of *thought-stopping* was taught to the patient, phasing from therapist interruption of overt thoughts about having a seizure in a public place, to patient covert interruption of covert thoughts (Rimm and Masters, 1974). By the third week of practice, the anxiety attacks had disappeared; the patient reported the procedures had enabled her to identify and then eliminate the thoughts which served as cues for the escalating ruminations. No further anxiety attacks were reported at a six-month follow-up.

Rational-emotive Therapy (RET) may also be a useful therapeutic component; whether or not the patient can achieve some control over his seizures, he can always learn to control his overemotional reactions to them. RET therapists teach the client that he has the ability to control emotions such as fear and panic, and urges the client to give up the irrational belief that he *must* have approval and acceptance from others at all times. The client is taught to actively examine and refute his irrational beliefs. As one part of this active therapy, the patient may be required to close his eyes and to conjure up the image of the "dreadful" seizure event, allowing himself to experience the reaction of "awfulness." On a signal from the therapist, the patient is instructed to reduce his emotion from "awful" to "merely annoying," a feat which he is assured he can perform. The therapist can thus point out to the patient that he does, indeed, have control of his own emotional states, and that while one may not be able to alter an aversive event (such as having a seizure in a public place), one can certainly alter the degree of awfulness attached to the aversive event (Ellis, 1973).

CLINICAL PRESCRIPTION

The first order of business in working with a patient with seizures is to obtain as much neurologic and medical information as possible about the case. Before initiating behavioral treatments, the clinician must be sure to have carefully ruled out the possibility of a tumor, abcess, or hematoma as being the direct cause of the problem, since in those instances surgery might be a necessary intervention. It will also be important to determine what medical or pharmacologic treatments have been or are currently being used with the patient, as these may interact with or possibly impede progress. A heavily sedated patient, or a family that reacts fearfully to a seizure episode by calling in the physician or by increasing the dosage of medications, may require preliminary attention.

In order to determine the appropriate focus of treatment, the clinician will next want to obtain as much information about the seizure episodes as possible. The patient, his family, and the nursing staff may help to fit together the pieces of this diagnostic puzzle. In accord with the outline of this chapter, the major areas to include in this investigation will involve discovering the antecedents to the seizure, exploring the nature of the seizure itself, determining the consequences to the seizure, and discussing the patient's fears relating to his problem. Obviously, the need for detailed information in these areas is essential. Particular attention should be paid to any previously attempted treatments (both successes and failures), and to any stimuli which either exacerbate or seem to help control the seizures. These details may be useful clues to treatment prescription.

The presence of clear-cut external antecedents to seizures may suggest that the focus of treatment begin here. Thus, seizures reliably induced by sensory events may require an adaptation of a fading procedure. Seizures elicited by stress may respond to systematic desensitization to the external triggers. Seizures that are predominantly self-induced may most efficiently be relieved by suppressing the antecedent operants with the application of punishment.

When seizures are accompanied by the internal antecedents of a relatively prolonged aura, and when access to biofeedback technology is available, EEG training may be of direct help. If the history has revealed the presence of an externally inhibiting stimulus, seizure control may be accomplished by establishing a program to generalize the effectiveness of this suppressor. For seizures that have reliable motor preliminaries and are easily discriminable to others in the patient's environment, a trial of simple interruption of the seizure behavior chain and reinforcement for incompatible behaviors may be attempted. When seizures reliably occur during specific activities of the patient, a course of shaping in competing behaviors can be designed.

It can thus be appreciated that the ability of the therapist to zero in on the key or keys to a treatment focus clearly will depend on obtaining adequate history and observation data on the patient. No matter what focus is selected, however, the therapist can be sure that the patient and the significant others in his daily environment are reacting emotionally to the distressing seizure symptoms. Fear, embarrassment, anxiety, guilt, and other unpleasant reactions are components of the seizure case that cannot afford to be overlooked. Emotional distress may motivate the patient's family to unwittingly reinforce sick behavior and, more subtly yet directly, may function to produce a vicious cycle for the patient himself, since emotional stress may lower the seizure threshold. It will usually be appropriate, therefore, to program a broad-spectrum intervention plan which focuses not only on the seizure activity itself, but on the internal and external cognitive/emotional vectors with which it interacts. Thus, the focus is not merely on a symptom, but on the total patient as well as the family (see Table 1).

CASE REPORT

From among the many case reports in the literature, the following example by J. Parrino (1971) was chosen to illustrate a specific treatment strategy. The case of Mr. S is particularly interesting because, although this patient's physical symptoms were flamboyant and had received a recognized medical diagnosis, simple behavioral observation began to reveal a pattern of emotional antecedents to the attacks. A more careful behavior analysis enabled the therapist to delimit some specific trigger stimuli to which the patient could be desensitized.[1]

Mr. S was a 36-year-old male, a well-known personality in his community. He began having serious difficulties in April, 1969, when he experienced his first grand mal seizure. He had been diagnosed at a reputable medical center as having Jakob Creutzfeldt Syndrome, a progressive neurological disorder characterized by dementia and violent episodes of bizarre muscular movements. The diagnosis was based on the following factors: (1) complaints of failure of recent memory, (2) several grand mal seizures, (3) right-sided twitches and transient loss of balance, and (4) an EEG which showed diffuse abnormality with questionable temperoparietal spikes. A pneumoencephalogram, lumbar puncture, and biopsy of nerve and muscle revealed no abnormality. All other medical and neurological findings were normal.

Following this, the patient resided in two other general hospitals before his admission to the present psychiatric institution in September, 1969. He was seen as a serious management problem who required constant supervision for his own safety. His sudden uncontrollable movements often left him unable to balance himself. He had been placed on anticonvulsant medication during his first hospitalization which had been continued except for small changes in dosage. There were, however, no significant changes in the patient's condition or seizure activity.

Table 1. Summary of treatment interventions

Locus of Intervention	Treatment	Most Appropriate Seizure Type
Control of Seizure Antecedents	fading	sensory-evoked seizures
	relaxation & systematic desensitization	anxiety-elicited seizures
	punishment & aversive conditioning	self-induced seizures
Control of Seizure Activity	EEG biofeedback	seizures with clear sensory aura
	interrupting the behavior chain & DRO	seizures with clear motoric preliminary
	establishing competing response	seizures occurring during specific activities
	external inhibition	seizures affected by strong external stimuli
Control of Seizure Consequences	positive reinforcement and shaping	plentiful social attention for seizures and/ or presence of model for sick behavior
Control of Seizure Fear	flooding; relaxation & systematic desensitization; thought-stopping; RET	fear of seizure → stress → increased probability of seizures or other behavior problems

Several months after his admission to our hospital, Mr. S's general mood, attention span, and physical appearance improved. The change in his behavior led the staff to question the accuracy of the neurological diagnosis. For the first time, he was well-oriented enough to be placed on the general token system on the unit. Extensive behavioral observations were initiated, which provided further evidence of emotional triggers to the episodes of bizarre muscular movements.

At this time, Mr. S began to participate in a work adjustment program run by the vocational rehabilitation counselor. There was further improvement during the next four months of hospitalization, but the seizures continued at very high frequency. The staff felt that behavior therapy might help reduce them and also accelerate the improvement in his general condition. They referred him for behavior therapy on June 4, 1970.

Mr. S was informed of the impending change in therapy, and was asked to count his seizures for 13 days before it began. Staff members were asked to observe the seizures in order to check the reliability of his seizure count. During these 13 days, the seizures ranged from a low point of 22 to a high point of 95 on June 16, 1970, the day before therapy began (see Fig. 2). The average rate for this period was 58 per day. The variability in seizure activity during this period seemed to be related to Mr. S's activity: the seizures would diminish at work and increase upon his return to the unit. Also, seizure activity would decrease during visits on weekends to close friends and relatives. In general, Mr. S's level of anxiety was a good positive predictor of daily rate of seizure activity.

Treatment

From the behavioral observations of the staff and the reports provided by the patient, it appeared that Mr. S's seizures were triggered by particular anxiety-provoking stimuli in the ward and at work. The following are some of the anxiety-provoking situations which triggered seizures:

1. Socializing with fellow patients in the unit, particularly when Mr. S was the focus of attention.
2. Meeting someone in authority, friend, or stranger (e.g., the director of the unit).
3. Initiating conversation with an acquaintance during visiting hours.
4. Dealing with a particularly difficult female patient in the unit who constantly harassed Mr. S.
5. The mention of family-related material (e.g., wife's name, children's names).

Deep muscle relaxation is routinely taught to all patients in the unit. Mr. S learned to relax during this routine and continued practicing throughout his stay at the hospital. Anxiety hierarchies were derived from each of the anxiety-provoking situations mentioned above. Items from the hierarchies were presented twice a week during individual sessions. In addition, Mr. S was taught self-desensitization to enable him to use desensitization when the therapist was absent. All hierarchies were completed during a three-month period. The following items (beginning with the least disturbing) made up the hierarchy on the topic of initiating a conversation with a visitor:

1. A person you recognize appears in the unit.
2. The acquaintance is having a conversation with a staff member.
3. The acquaintance looks in your direction.

figure 2

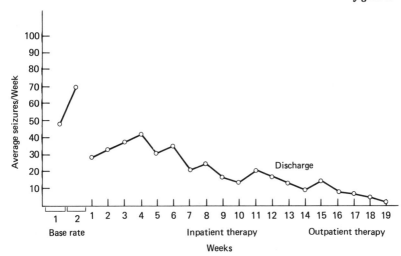

Weekly seizure activity (average).

4. The acquaintance and you make eye contact.
5. The acquaintance smiles at you from across the room.
6. The acquaintance starts walking towards you.
7. The acquaintance is getting very close to you.
8. The acquaintance extends his hand to you.
9. You shake hands with the acquaintance.
10. You engage in conversation with the acquaintance.

Figure 2 represents the seizure data collected during desensitization therapy. It indicates a great deal of improvement in Mr. S's condition during the 15 weeks of therapy. During this time, the seizure count dropped from a high point of 43 per day (4th week) to 10 per day in the 14th week. Mr. S was discharged to outpatient status in the 15th week (September, 1970). The figure shows an increase in seizure activity during Mr. S's first week back to full-time employment (15th week) and a reduction to 9, 6 and 3 daily seizures in the following weeks. Self-desensitization hierarchies which focused on the work situation were completed during outpatient treatment and accompanied by a gradual reduction of the seizures to zero.

The form of the seizures also changed significantly during therapy—from gross motor movements at the beginning to tic-like mannerisms at the termination of inpatient treatment. The response was then minimal and restricted to the facial region. The few seizures that did then occur usually went unnoticed by the casual observer.

Marital and vocational stresses had apparently precipitated Mr. S's illness. He had been relieved of certain responsibilities at work, which he had perceived as a demotion. Also, he had become painfully aware of difficulties developing with his wife whom he had suspected of having an affair with one of his best friends. As the stresses surrounding these situations were alleviated (by divorce and termination of employment), Mr. S's general disposition had improved; but, seizure activity had continued to be elicited by conditioned stimuli in the environment.

At the present time, Mr. S is continuing with outpatient treatment and is doing very well in adjusting to life outside the hospital. He is engaged to be married and has returned to full-time employment at the job he held before hospitalization. All medication has been withdrawn and he has remained seizure-free for approximately five months.

ETHICAL AND LEGAL CONSIDERATIONS

In the case of a psychologist who is referred a patient with seizure disorders, the major ethical consideration to keep in mind is the necessity for establishing a good working arrangement with the patient's medical caretaker. If the patient has not been examined by a neurologist, it would be wise to make the appropriate referral.

Among the behavioral treatment suggestions which the therapist may wish to consider for his patient, the one which carries the most potential for ethicolegal problems, perhaps, is the use of aversive stimuli for response suppression. Obviously this potential is greater when the patient is a child. When considering suppressive treatments particularly, the therapist should be certain to inform the patient and/or the patient's parents of the intent of the procedure and safety precautions being employed (such as having the therapist experience the shock level at the beginning of every training session). Treatment should not begin until informed consent is granted.

FUTURE EXPERIMENTAL AND
CLINICAL DESIGNS

The application of behavioral principles to the control or management of seizure disorders has a short history. As can be seen in Table 2, for example, most of the reports emerged after the mid-1960s. Since the field is in its infancy, it may not be surprising to note that almost all of the behavioral literature in this field consists of case reports, although some have included the single-subject research technique of reversal or removal of treatment conditions. Systematic experimentation remains

Table 2. Summary of reports of behavioral treatments

Author(s)	Date	Type of Report	Number of Samples	Age	Treatment	Outcome	Follow-up	Special Comments
Forster DQR = 4 (poor)	1969	Case study	1	Adult	Fading	+	–	Complex; expensive; EEG required
Parrino DQR = 4 (poor)	1971	Case study	1	Adult	Relaxation and systematic desensitization	+	6 mo	
Fabisch & Darbyshire DQR = 1 (poor)	1965	Case study	1	Child	Punishment	+	6 mo	Unprogrammed contingencies
Wright DQR = 5 (poor)	1973	Case study	1	Child	Punishment	+	7 mo	Electric shock used
Scholander DQR = 5 (poor)	1972	Case study	1	Child	Punishment	+	6 mo	Results confused by + response to medication
Johnson & Meyer DQR = 5 (poor)	1974	Case study	1	Adolescent	Relaxation & biofeedback	+	3 mo	46% reduction but patient unable to suppress

165

Table 2. (Continued)

Author(s)	Date	Type of Report	Number of Samples	Age	Treatment	Outcome	Follow-up	Special Comments
Kuhlman DQR = 6 (poor)	1975	Case study with reversal	5	Adult	Biofeedback	+	+	Reversal to random biofeedback did not increase response
Sterman et al. DQR = 9 (poor)	1974	Exploratory comparison	4 patients 4 normals	Child-adult	Biofeedback	+, 3:5	−	Comparisons between groups not clinically relevant
Zlutnick et al. DQR = 10 (poor)	1975	Case study with reversals	5	Child and adolescent	Interrupting chains	+, 4:5	6–12 mo	Inexpensive; useful when seizure predictable
Forster et al. DQR = 3 (poor)	1969	Case study	1	Adult	Competing response	+	−	
Efron DQR = 3 (poor)	1956	Case study	1	Adult	External inhibition	+	+	Must identify external inhibitor
Gardner DQR = 2 (poor)	1973	Case study	1	Child	Contingency management	+	−	

166

Table 2. *(Continued)*

Author(s)	Date	Type of Report	Number of Samples	Age	Treatment	Outcome	Follow-up	Special Comments
Gardner DQR = 4 (poor)	1967	Case study with reversal	1	Child	Contingency management	+	+	
Iwata & Lorentzson DQR = 6 (poor)	1976	Case study with reversal	1	Adult	Contingency management	+	+	
Fowler et al. DQR = 6 (poor)	1971	Case study	1	Adult	Contingency management & shaping	+	1 yr	
Pinto DQR = 4 (poor)	1972	Case study	1	Adult	Flooding	+	16 wk	
Ince DQR = 3 (poor)	1976	Case study	1	Child	Relaxation and systematic desensitization	+		
Anthony & Edelstein DQR = 3 (poor)	1975	Case study	1	Adult	Thought-stopping	+	6 mo	

to be done to determine (a) which interventions are most effective, (b) in which situations, and (c) with which patients. Although I have tried to suggest clinical cues which may help a therapist select a treatment modality, these suggestions must be empirically put to the test in future research. The goal of prescriptive psychotherapy, it seems, still eludes us.

Some problems with which future research will have to deal are those common to all behavior problems with organic involvement: namely, evaluating the contributions and interactions of both pharmacologic and behavioral interventions. In many of the case reports currently available, patients were referred for behavior therapy only after they had been declared to be "intractable," at which time their medication histories were often quite complex. In addition, it is often unclear in the available literature how the patient's medications are managed during and after behavioral interventions, which makes clear interpretations of effects more difficult.

For those treatments which seem to offer promise, but which, like biofeedback or Forster's fading program, are expensive and require elaborate electronic hardware, we may hope for future simplification. The cost of a treatment, both in terms of time and money, may be an important factor in evaluating its accessibility and ultimately its worth to the patient.

Some of the treatments reported herein were remarkably successful, some less so, and some worked for only a proportion of the patients treated. Post-hoc guesses about why treatment X worked for four out of five patients is a first step, but it will be important for future research to help us understand our limits and adapt our therapies to our clients more precisely.

An important factor, too often underplayed in behavioral therapy reports, is adequate detailed information about the seizures themselves and their effects on the patient and his interpersonal environment. In a recent review of the literature on seizures, Mostofsky and Balaschak (1977) state:

> It is often difficult to learn from the published reports whether baseline measurements were taken prior to the initiation of the program. If taken, how were they taken (self-report of the subject alone, trained observer, or several observers), and for what period of time (baseline charted daily or only estimated)? . . . Also, rarely is the subject himself queried sufficiently about certain aspects of his seizures. The conventional intake interview fails to probe the subject's subjective reactions to seizures or ability to control them. Such information may provide the therapist with insight into the relative reinforcement values that the respective contingencies of seizure states may offer. It is therefore essential to derive an appreciation of the subject's personality style, inter-

active abilities, and parent-child relationships (particularly as they relate to the subject's dependency, overprotectiveness, and manipulativeness) prior to undertaking a program of treatment.

Thus, careful review of the patient's self-report, untrained observer report (e.g., mother's report of a child's seizure), and trained observer report may reveal suggestions for treatment plans or the need for further information gathering.

In summary, although behavior therapy is a relative newcomer to the field of seizure disorders, it seems to have an open and promising future. To date, behavioral treatments of seizures have focused on helping the patient to (a) control the stimulus antecedents to the seizure, (b) reduce or eliminate the seizure episode itself, (c) change the consequences of the seizure so that sick behavior is not reinforced, and (d) control his anxieties about seizures. The therapist may discover, in fact, that the last step is actually best programmed first, since anxiety is itself a common precipitant to seizures. No matter what the focus of treatment, however, helping the patient to accept himself and "de-awfulize" his seizure problem may be the therapist's most useful overall intervention.

SUMMARY

Seizures are recorded as abnormal bursts of electrical activity in the brain, and are observed as sudden involuntary shifts in motor activity, either an abrupt increase or cessation of muscular movement. Most seizures are idiopathic (i.e., not traceable to clear organic conditions); the general label for recurrent idiopathic seizures is epilepsy.

Commonly, epilepsy is classified into four major types: grand mal seizures, petit mal seizures, Jacksonian seizures, and psychomotor epilepsy. On the whole, convulsive disorders affect 1–2 percent of the population, are more common in women than men, and most often have their onset before the age of 20. Direct evidence for inheritability of seizures is lacking, although many authorities suggest that a convulsive predisposition may be transmitted and expressed under physiologic or emotional stress.

Medical treatment of seizure disorders may include dietary restrictions (potentially useful only with very young children), surgery (when the seizures are a symptom of a tumor, abcess, or hematoma), and anticonvulsant medications. Although high success rates for pharmacologic treatments are often reported, the side effects of the medication may be troublesome.

Behaviorally, the relationship between convulsive behavior and environmental stimuli is well known. Some attacks are reliably predicted, and some patients report that they have some degree of control over their seizures. Therein lies the key to some of the new behavioral interventions. These interventions focus at one or more of the following sites: (a) antecedent stimuli, (b) the seizure behavior itself, (c) consequences of the seizure, and (d) cognitions of the patient, particularly as these in turn become seizure antecedents.

Some seizures are reliably predicted by triggering stimuli or stimulus complexes; these include sensory-evoked seizures, stress-evoked seizures, and self-induced seizures. For these seizure types, treatment may focus on control of the antecedent stimuli.

Sensory-evoked seizures are triggered by specific external stimuli, most commonly by a visual stimulus such as flashing light, a striking visual pattern, or even by repeated closings of the eyelid. A useful technique for such cases employs the procedure of fading to increase stimulus tolerance. Briefly, the offending stimulus is presented to the patient in a manner which will not elicit seizures. Gradually the intensity and/or duration of the stimulus is increased as long as seizures do not occur.

Stress-evoked seizures are elicited by feelings of anxiety in the patient, and procedures which have been used to render these antecedents less potent include relaxation and systematic desensitization. Relaxation training by itself may be particularly useful, since lack of sleep has been shown to be an important stress factor in these patients. Relaxation training has been well demonstrated to be useful with sleep difficulties.

Self-induced seizures are often of the petit mal type and are often induced by intermittent light stimulation or hyperventilation. Such seizures may be intrinsically reinforcing as well as being a manipulative social device. Such seizures have most often been treated by punishment or aversion techniques designed to suppress the pre-seizure eliciting behaviors.

Control of seizure activity itself may be possible in some cases in which the patient experiences the clear warning signals of a discrete seizure aura. For such patients, EEG biofeedback training may help them learn to control the attack by lowering cortical arousal.

Interference with seizure activity may also be possible for those patients whose seizures are preceded by clear motoric preliminaries. The seizure is thus viewed as the end of a longer behavioral chain, and treatment consists of consistent interruptions of this behavioral chain. Similarly, patients may be helped to develop competing responses to inhibit seizures. More rarely, a seizure patient may be able to identify an external stimulus which inhibits his seizures; principles of classical conditioning may be employed to transfer this inhibiting control to functionally useful and easily available stimuli.

The importance of seizure consequences should not be overlooked, the most significant being social attention and solicitude the patient receives from his family and friends. Principles of contingency management have been usefully applied to ensure plentiful positive reinforcement for nonseizure behavior, and to encourage the patient to give up his sick role.

The patient with convulsive disorders may not only suffer physical distress, but also social stigmatization and practical problems such as job discrimination. The emotional concomitants of the seizure may therefore be more severe than the convulsive disorder itself. A vicious cycle may thus be perpetuated in which the seizure itself produces stress, and thereby increases the probability of further seizures or other behavior problems. To help the patient deal with his fear, embarrassment, guilt, and so on of his seizure problem, a number of cognitive therapies have been successfully employed, including flooding, systematic desensitization, thought-stopping, and rational-emotive therapy. Thus, although the patient may not always be able to alter or control his seizures, he can certainly alter the degree of awfulness with which he invests them.

Behavioral treatments for seizure disorders are best conceived as a broad-spectrum set of treatment interventions which focus not only on the seizure itself, but also on the internal and external factors with which it interacts. The focus, therefore, is not merely on a symptom, but on the total patient as he interacts with his social environment.

The history of behavioral approaches to the treatment of convulsive disorders is a short one, less than ten years long, and as such consists mainly of clinical reports of successful treatment. A great deal of future research is needed to clarify the effective treatment ingredients, to increase our prescriptive abilities as therapists, and to help us understand our treatment failures. For the moment, however, it appears that behavioral treatments have a good clinical track record and a promising future.

NOTE

1. The case report of Mr. S on pages 160–164 is reprinted with permission from "Reduction of Seizures by Desensitization" by J. J. Parrino, *Journal of Behavior Therapy and Experimental Psychology,* 1971, *2,* 287–288. Copyright 1971 by Pergamon Press Ltd.

REFERENCES

Adams, K. M. Behavioral treatment of reflex or sensory-evoked seizures. *Journal of Behavior Therapy and Experimental Psychiatry*, 1976, *7*, 123–127.

Anthony, J. and Edelstein, B. A. Thought stopping treatment of anxiety attacks due to seizure-related obsessive ruminations. *Journal of Behavior Therapy and Experimental Psychiatry*, 1975, *6*, 343–344.

Bagley, C. *The social psychology of the epileptic child.* Coral Gables, Florida: Univ. of Miami Press, 1971.

Baird, H. W. *The child with convulsions.* New York: Grune & Stratton, 1972.

Birk, L., ed. *Biofeedback: behavioral medicine,* New York: Grune & Stratton, 1973.

Booker, H. E., Forster, F. M. and Klove, H. Extinction factors in startle acoustic motor seizures. *Neurology*, 1965, *15*, 1095–1103.

Brown, B. *Stress and the art of biofeedback.* New York: Harper & Row, 1977.

Carter, S. and Gold, A. Convulsions in children. *New England Journal of Medicine*, 1968, *278*, 315–317.

Cautela, J. R. and Flannery, R. B. Seizures: controlling the uncontrollable. *Journal of Rehabilitation*, 1973, June, 34–36.

Daube, J. R. Sensory precipitated seizures: a review. *Journal of Nervous and Mental Disorders*, 1965, *141*, 524.

Efron, R. The conditioned inhibition of uncinate fits. *Brain*, 1957, *8*, 251–262.

Ellis, A. *Humanistic psychotherapy: the rational-emotive approach.* New York: Julian Press, 1973.

Fabisch, W. and Darbyshire, R. Report on an unusual case of self-induced epilepsy with comments on some psychological and therapeutic aspects. *Epilepsia*, 1965, *6*, 335–340.

Forster, F. M. Conditioning in sensory evoked seizures. *Conditioned Reflex*, 1966, *1*, no. 4.

Forster, F. M. Conditioning of cerebral dysrhythmia induced by pattern presentation and eye closure. *Conditioned Reflex*, 1967, *2*, 236.

Forster, F. M. Clinical therapeutic conditioning in epilepsy. *Wisconsin Medical Journal*, 1969, *68*, 289–291.

Forster, F. M., Paulsen, W. and Baughman, F. Clinical therapeutic conditioning in reading epilepsy. *Neurology*, 1969, *19*, 71–77.

Fowler, R. S., Niranjan, S. C., Lehmann, J. F. and Tindall, V. L. An application of behavior therapy to a program of debilitating vertigo. *Behavioral Therapy*, 1971, *2*, 589–591.

Friis, M. L. and Lund, M. Stress convulsions. *Archives of Neurology*, 1974, *31*, 155–159.

Gaito, J. The kindling effect as a model of epilepsy. *Psychology Bulletin*, 1976, *83*, 1097–1109.

Gardner, G. G. Use of hypnosis for psychogenic epilepsy in a child. *American Journal of Clinical Hypnosis*, 1973, *15*, 166–169.

Gardner, J. Behavior therapy treatment approach to a psychogenic seizure case. *Journal of Consulting Psychology,* 1967, *31,* 209–212.

Gottschalk, L. A. Effects of intensive psychotherapy on epileptic children: report on three children with idiopathic epilepsy. *AMA Archives of Neurology & Psychiatry,* 1953, *70,* 361–384.

Ince, L. P. The use of relaxation training and a conditioned stimulus in the elimination of epileptic seizures in a child: a case study. *Journal of Behavioral Therapy and Experimental Psychiatry,* 1976, *7,* 39–42.

Iwata, B. A. and Lorentzson, A. M. Operant conditioning of seizure-like behavior in an institutionalized retarded adult. *Behavior Therapy,* 1976, *7,* 247–251.

Jacobson, E. *Progressive relaxation.* Chicago: Univ. Chicago Press, 1938.

Johnson, R. K. and Meyer, R. G. Phased biofeedback approach for epileptic seizure control. *Journal of Behavior Therapy and Experimental Psychiatry,* 1974, *5,* 185–187.

Katz, R. and Zlutnik, S., (eds.) *Behavior therapy and health care: principles and applications.* New York: Pergamon Press, 1974.

Livingston, S. *Comprehensive management of epilepsy in infancy, childhood, and adolescence.* Springfield, Il.: C. C. Thomas, 1972.

Miller, N. Learning of visceral and glandular responses. *Science,* 1969, *163,* 434–445.

Mostofsky, D. I. Behavior modification and the psychosomatic aspects of epilepsy. *Behavior modification with the individual patient.* Nutley, N.J.: Roche Laboratories, 1972.

Mostofsky, D. I. and Balaschak, B. A. Psychobiological control of seizures. *Psychology Bulletin,* 1977, *84,* 723–750.

Parrino, J. J. Reduction of seizures by desensitization. *Journal of Behavior Therapy and Experimental Psychiatry,* 1971, *2,* 215–218.

Pinto, R. A case of movement epilepsy with agoraphobia treated successfully by flooding. *British Journal of Psychiatry,* 1972, *121,* 287–288.

Puletti, F. Surgical treatment of epilepsy. *Wisconsin Medical Journal,* 1969, *68,* 285–288.

Reynolds, E. H. and Travers, R. D. Serum anticonvulsant concentration in epileptic patients with mental symptoms. *British Journal of Psychiatry,* 1974, *124,* 440–445.

Rimm, D. C. and Masters, J. C. *Behavior therapy: techniques and empirical findings.* New York: Academic Press, 1974.

Robb, J. P. Clinical diagnosis in epilepsy. *Wisconsin Medical Journal,* 1969, *68,* 292–296.

Rose, S. W., Penry, J. K., Markush, R. E. et al. Prevalence of epilepsy in children. *Epilepsia,* 1973, *14,* 133–152.

Schmidt, R. and Wilder, B. *Epilepsy.* Philadelphia, Pa.: F. A. Davis, 1968.

Scholander, T. Treatment of an unusual case of compulsive behavior by aversive stimulation. *Behavioral Therapy,* 1972, *3,* 290–293.

Small, L. *Neuropsychodiagnosis in psychotherapy.* New York: Bruner/Mazel, 1973.

Sterman, M. and Friar, L. Suppression of seizures in an epileptic following sensorimotor EEG feedback. *EEG & Clinical Neurophysiology,* 1972, *33,* 89–95.

Sterman, M., MacDonald, L. R. and Stone, R. K. Biofeedback training of the sensorimotor electroencephalogram rhythm in man: effects on epilepsy. *Epilepsia,* 1974, *15,* 395–416.

Walen, S. R., Hauserman, N. and Lavin, P. *Clinical guide to behavior therapy.* Baltimore: Williams & Wilkins, 1977.

Wright, L. Aversive conditioning of self-induced seizures. *Behavioral Therapy,* 1973, *4,* 712–713.

Wyler, A. R., Fetz, E. and Ward, A. A. Effects of operantly conditioning epileptic unit activity on seizure frequency and electrophysiology of neocortical experimental foci. *Experimental Neurology,* 1974, *44,* 113–125.

Zlutnik, S., Mayville, W. J. and Moffat, S. Behavioral control of seizure disorders: the interruption of chained behavior. *Journal of Applied Behavioral Analysis,* 1975, *8,* 1–12.

5
Drug Abuse

Edward J. Callahan
Kimberly Price
JoAnn Dahlkoetter

Man has used chemicals to alter his behavior and his perception of his environment throughout recorded history. Ironically, the evolution of society has brought with it increased use and abuse of chemical substances, creating problems primitive societies did not appear to suffer. The current paper will review the literature on behavioral attempts to deal with the problem of substance abuse (excluding alcohol) on individual and social levels. Before reviewing that specific literature, we will discuss how substance use and abuse is defined by the culture—the societal environment— how drug abuse in an individual might be acquired and maintained, and how the problem might be more exactly assessed and treated. Following the review of specific behavioral attempts to treat substance abuse, the needs for future definitive clinical interventions and studies on treatment and prevention of drug abuse will be covered, and ethical issues will be discussed.

SUBSTANCE USE AND CULTURE

Substances chosen for a society's use vary as broadly as do the norms for abuse. The appearance of the raw material in the natural physical environment appears to control drug selection, however. Sulkunen (1976) reports that the type of alcohol used by a society appears to be under environmental control historically. Those nations with the best soil for growing wine grapes have long histories of wine use; these histories have evolved traditions of wine drinking with ritual aspects which provide some social control of drinking (witness the Hebrew culture). Similarly, liquor consumption historically seems to occur most where grains are available for its production. For beer, however, consumption does not appear to be correlated with grain products. Ironically, Sulkunen points out that most alcohol is consumed in developed countries: 13 percent of the world's people live in Europe, yet half of the world's alcohol is consumed there. As the standard of living has risen in the post-World War II era, so has the consumption of alcohol. This may reflect increased stress as well as increased affluence. More primitive cultures tend to use naturally growing drugs in their environment rather than alcohol: psilocybin mushrooms were used by native North Americans in the Southeast and the Northwest, peyote was used by tribes in desert areas, and coca leaves are still used by natives in South America. In these "primitive" cultures, the use of these substances is usually governed by religious ritual passed on from generation to generation similar to Jewish traditions around alcohol. Thus, very little socially defined "abuse" is encountered. Abuse appears to become an issue only when a new substance is introduced to a culture, when an old substance becomes available for consumption in a new way, or when stress increases in a society. Let us review one example of each type of drug abuse.

Coffee was introduced to Europe in the Middle Ages. Overnight, secret societies sprang up in which members gathered late at night to drink large amounts of coffee, often resulting in hallucinations. This new substance—caffeine—was abused until the culture became more familiar with it. Its current use is covered by tradition and it is not ordinarily seen as a drug of abuse. Like nicotine, the most commonly used drug in the United States, coffee is rarely seen as a serious problem, yet excessive caffeine intake has medical effects (contributing to ulcers, high blood pressure, and possibly to heart attacks), and appears to be addicting. Caffeine is not ordinarily seen as an abusable substance, possibly because it increases rather than decreases productivity, a result which agrees with socially accepted values. However a long acceptable and available substance can become a societal problem with the introduction of a new way of using the substance.

Such a phenomenon occurred with opium when smoking tobacco was introduced to China in the early 18th century (Merry, 1975). Opium had long been used with no problem in the Chinese society. With the introduction of tobacco, however, opium was mixed with the tobacco to improve the enjoyment of smoking. Gradually, people began to smoke the opium alone without tobacco and addiction to opium became a serious problem for the first time in the Chinese culture.

An inverse variant of the cultural familiarity problem occurred during the Vietnam war. Here individuals entered a new culture and abused its drugs. Robins (1973) reports that 44 percent of the U.S. servicemen used heroin while in Vietnam, and that about half that number became addicted. Few continued use upon their return to the United States, however, further supporting the environment's impact on drug usage. Another example of environmental control of drug use is found when addictive behavior is considered as schedule-induced behavior (Callahan and Rawson, in press; Falk, 1972; Falk and Samson, 1976).

Falk and Samson (1976) point out that alcohol dependence has only been produced in laboratory rodents under conditions of schedule-induced behavior—a set of circumstances which is highly stressful to the animal. Ironically, under these circumstances alcohol is not used as a reward, it is merely available. This no doubt points to the importance of environmental stresses in substance abuse. This model has been applied to substance abuse in man (Callahan and Rawson, in press; Falk and Samson, 1976) and the interested reader is referred to these sources for a more complete discussion of this laboratory model. For now, let us turn our attention to a social issue: how man differentiates substance use from substance abuse.

Substance Use versus Abuse

There are two basic ways in which substance use can be differentiated from substance abuse. The first is de jure—by law, the substance can be defined as a substance of abuse: consumption of any amount of the drug will be considered substance abuse (e.g., heroin), consumption of excess amounts can be considered abuse (e.g., alcohol), or consumption not prescribed by a physician can be considered abuse (e.g., valium). The second means of defining substance abuse involves a functional analysis of the effect of the substance on the behavior of the individual. Substance abuse would be seen then as any behavior which leads to significantly impaired performance in a defined area of functioning. This definition is also somewhat confusing since some substances result in physical or psychological dependence (e.g., heroin), but do not hamper functioning when made freely available.

Our own society has various lists of chemicals which are not available to the general public legally. These lists include substances such as heroin and marijuana; these lists also include substances which are not addicting nor even pleasurable to take, such as naltrexone, a narcotic antagonist which blocks the euphoric effects of heroin. These lists do not include drugs prescribed by physicians. De jure marijuana is always a substance of abuse; de jure other substances such as valium are never substances of abuse when prescribed by a physician, yet that medication may show all the signs of being an addictive substance and may impair a person's day by day functioning (Maletzky and Klotter, 1976).

The alternative to de jure definition of drugs of abuse is an analysis of how a drug affects a person's behavior. Of special interest here is the behavior of a person who is physically dependent or psychologically dependent upon a substance. The term *dependence* is used here since the World Health Organization has recommended the substitution of physical and psychological dependence for the term addiction (Ng and Bunney, 1975). Ng and Bunney define physical dependence as the occurrence of physical symptoms of withdrawal when the person no longer has the substance available. Psychological dependence, however, is defined as the occurrence of urges or cravings for taking the substance when the individual tries to stop. Thus, tobacco-smoking and coffee-drinking could be defined as substance abuse if the individual experiences withdrawal upon ceasing consumption of the substance, either in physical symptoms (e.g., headaches, tremors) or psychological cravings. This broader definition of substance abuse may prove more useful for the behavioral practitioner, though de jure definitions of abuse will strongly influence the likelihood of a person seeking help to "kick" a habit. In order to understand the literature regarding the behavioral treatment of substance abuse, it will be useful to first review traditional and behavioral formulations of how people come to use a substance and how they become dependent.

Why Do People Become Substance Abusers?

Ironically, the low success rate in treating substance abusers has given rise to mountains of literature on why people abuse substances. These reasons range from genetic (Goodwin, 1971) to psychodynamic theory (Ausubel, 1961) to learning theory (Cahoon and Crosby, 1972; Crowley, 1972; and Wikler, 1973) to a laboratory model of addictive behavior (Falk, 1972).

Evidence for a genetic involvement in alcoholism appears strong in the 1974 review by Goodwin. He points out that nonadopted sons of alcoholics drink more than adopted sons. In addition, most alcoholics have one or more alcoholic parents, or else both parents abstain from alcohol. These facts might be interpreted to argue that children need models to demonstrate nonabusive drinking (e.g., Bandura, 1969) rather than that there is a genetic basis for alcoholism.

There is other evidence arguing for a genetic basis of alcoholism, however. One's physiological response to alcohol will probably influence consumption of alcohol. It has been found that Orientals flush quite readily when drinking alcohol; in addition, Orientals have a much lower rate of alcoholism than Caucasians (Ewing, Rouse, and Pellizari, 1974). This latter finding may be due to cultural influences, but here physiology may have helped shape the cultures involved as well. Little evidence exists in the study of the use of other substances to shed much light on genetic theories. In the United States, most heroin addicts are blacks or browns (Maurer and Vogel, 1974), but this can be more easily explained as a poverty problem. Thus genetics and culture may be too strongly interwoven to allow understanding of genetic contributions to substance abuse.

A second explanation used for the occurrence of substance abuse is personality characteristics. Because of the ease of generating data using paper and pencil tests, especially when studying an imprisoned or detained population, there exists a vast quantity of literature on the personality of the substance abuser. Unfortunately, many reports clash diametrically with other reports (see Glasscote et al., 1972).

The main area of agreement has focused on the contention that addicts are socially deficient (cf. Ausubel, 1961; Cameron, 1961; Kraft, 1969, 1970; Rason, 1958; and Seeyers, 1962). However, Platt, Hoffman, and Ebert (1976) have recently pointed out that young addicts show more social skills than similarly aged nonaddicts who are also in prison. Thus, the one consistently discovered personality trait of heroin addicts has not proven consistent over time.

Another set of explanations for why people abuse drugs comes from behavioral therapy. A variety of fairly consistent theories have been advanced to explain drug-taking from a behavioral perspective. Cahoon and Crosby (1972), and Crowley (1972) point out that particular drugs provide predictable patterns of reinforcement as might be expected in an operant conditioning paradigm. Wikler (1965) similarly describes the process of addiction to heroin in terms of both classical conditioning and operant conditioning. O'Brien (1974) shows interesting evidence that the physiological responses elicited by heroin administration generalize to cues associated with heroin-taking. These cues later elicit subjective craving for heroin; such cravings often result in relapse of long abstinent men when they are returned from prison to their old environment, according to O'Brien's formulation. Because of the mounting evidence for behavioral explanations of drug-taking and dependence, it will be worthwhile to present a detailed behavioral model of drug-sampling and dependence here.

A BEHAVIORAL MODEL OF DRUG ABUSE AND ADDICTION

There are several models which can be called upon to explain the etiology of drug abuse and addiction. In this section, we shall present a behavioral model for this phenomenon, though the concepts presented are hardly new. Crosby and Cahoon (1972), Crowley (1972), and Wikler (1965) all present theories fairly compatible with the one which follows. This section presumes some knowledge of operant conditioning; for anyone wishing a basic introduction to the area, Reynolds (1968) provides an excellent primer.

Becker (1953) observed that marijuana smokers *learn* to become "stoned" or intoxicated by watching others, imitating, experiencing social approval and finally, feeling the pharmacological effects of the drug itself. This is a sequence of events quite compatible with a learning model for the onset of drug abuse. Modeling, imitation, and social and pharmacological reinforcement are also factors critical to continuation of drug use, addiction, and relapse.

The first critical step in becoming a drug abuser is the process of first sampling the drug. While stories exist of innocents being slipped a drug without their knowledge, most drug initiates probably try a drug at the social urging of friends. The friend serves as a model; as a model he or she shows that the drug can be taken safely and gives instructions on what drug effects can be expected. For example, a novice marijuana smoker might be told "you're really going to get into this music" and a first-time heroin user might be told "you'll probably puke right away, but the rush will really be worth it." In addition to the specific modeling and instructing which occurs, our society provides modeling in the advertising media. Here some drug (or alcohol or cigarette) is romantically pictured as appropriate, necessary and "cool" for every difficult situation or relaxing moment. This general modeling phenomenon may facilitate the first drug contact even before specific peer modeling begins.

Once the initiate has taken the drug, the direct pharmacological effects of the drug can occur against the background of the instructions the taker has heard and read about the drug's effects. Feeling the rush of heroin or the relaxation and good feelings of marijuana, users receive a positive pharmacological reinforcement for drug-taking. These reinforcing effects often include somatic and psychological aspects. A bad acid trip, paranoia from marijuana, vomiting from heroin, and discomfort from amphetamines are all results likely to punish drug initiates and make it less likely for them to continue their drug use. However, other drug users may encourage further experimentation in pursuit of positive effects and this will be enough to continue the drug careers of many. In those later attempts, the chances of finding good experiences increase and the user may then be maintained by the positive reinforcement of drug effects. In addition to these positive physiological and psychological effects, many drugs offer an escape from noxious psychological states such as depression, fatigue, boredom, or feelings of inadequacy. Thus, drugs offer negative reinforcement by terminating noxious mood states or by facilitating escape or avoidance of an aversive environment. In this double-edged way, pharmacological and psychological drug effects can reinforce drug-taking.

Continued drug-taking further increases the likelihood of acceptance into the subculture of persons who regularly take the drug. This acceptance can be reinforcing by providing the person with a peer group, friendships, and the opportunity to feel superior to "straights" who fail to lead as exciting a life. (An excellent analysis of drug abuse reinforcement patterns or life scripts is provided by Steiner, 1971). All of this would be seen as secondary reinforcement in an operant paradigm. Lifestyle and identity can be affected by classical conditioning as well.

When a powerful drug is taken, the positive effects of the drug are paired with the people present so that they and people who look, dress, act, and speak similarly become secondary positive reinforcers in a classical conditioning sense. In this way the subculture is strengthened just as it strengthens the drug-taking of individuals. Obviously this process is no different from the way that associations are built up by church memberships, friendships, or professional conventions with the exception that the drugs might be more powerful physiologically and psychologically, and thus create stronger secondary reinforcement. Some fundamentalist religions may offer similarly strong physiological arousal. Other factors (such as needs for funds, pressures to give information to police to avoid prosecution, and so on) serve to create some mistrust and to weaken the conditioning effects. Still, the strength of this secondary reinforcement of the drug culture becomes a major problem in rehabilitation. Rehabilitation often requires radical changes in friendship patterns, self-identification, and living patterns as well as changing the actual ingestion of the drug. Classical conditioning is also a problem for heroin users who can stop using heroin, but who continue to get "high" from injecting saline or tap water. The persistence of shooting up among "needle freaks" (O'Brien, 1974) points to the strength of classical conditioning in the maintenance of drug-taking behavior.

Physiologically, the development of tolerance and dependence are critical factors in determining the maintenance level of drug usage. Tolerance simply means that in drugs such as heroin, the individual must increase drug dosage in order to get the usual pharmacological effect (reinforcement). Dependence means that the user experiences either psychological craving or physiological disturbance when drug use is discontinued. Since withdrawal symptoms are quite unpleasant (e.g., from heroin) and sometimes fatal (e.g., from barbiturates), they serve as a powerful negative reinforcer: continued drug use prevents or terminates aversive somatic feelings. This negative reinforcement (avoiding withdrawal) is probably a main reason for a heroin addict to continue using after tolerance increases deny him or her a significant positive high from the amount of the drug he or she can afford.

After proceeding through withdrawal, the addict in the abstinent state faces many problems associated with history of drug usage during the battle to avoid relapse. One of these problems may be continued physiological disturbance after abrupt discontinuation of heroin. For example, it has been noted that these physiological disturbances can occur for up to six months after withdrawal from heroin (Himmelsbach, 1942; Wikler, 1973). O'Brien (1974) has shown that the powerful physiological effects which heroin users evidence when presented with stimuli associated with shooting up and psychological cravings for drugs, are commonly not elicited in drug-free environments such as jail. However, these cravings do not extinguish; they are triggered again even years later as the person returns to the drug-taking environment. In fact, the same phenomenon has been observed in rats: rats who have been trained to self-administer morphine can be removed from the experimental situation for a year, yet will again respond to self-administer the drug when next returned to the drug-taking situation (Wikler and Pescor, 1970). Indeed Leitenberg, Rawson, and Bath (1970) have shown the critical importance of nonrewarded occurrence of a behavior for that behavior to be unlearned or extinguished. This underlines the tremendous impact of classical conditioning in causing a heroin addict to relapse. It also implies a powerful treatment role for narcotic antagonists, nonaddictive drugs which can block the euphoric effects of heroin while the addict returns to the natural environment. Narcotic antagonists will be discussed in a later section.

All of these conditioning factors may also have important implications for reconditioning the addict in a new stimulus situation. For example, it should be easier for returning Vietnam veterans to kick heroin addiction after leaving Vietnam than it has been for people who remain in the same physical and cultural environment. In fact, Robins (1973) reports that 91 percent of those addicted in Vietnam do not use heroin again on their return to the United States. Thus, one way to assist a drug user to change might be relocation to new environments. This might suggest that various clinics hundreds of miles apart trade off clients. On a more feasible level, an individual client could move from one drug-taking area to a less likely drug-taking area in a clinic's range. Such a simple manipulation points out the necessity of life management in controlling stimuli that an addict encounters. Another interesting application of learning theory to treatment involves using extinction trials: the addict might be asked to inject saline rather than heroin and thus overcome the arousal value of a needle.

This has been done in imagination by Götestam and Melin (1974), and in the real world by O'Brien (1974) while the addict had an antagonist blockade. So while conditioning theory leads to models which can help explain the etiology and maintenance of drug abuse, these models may in turn be used directly and imaginatively to help create treatments for drug abuse. Let us now turn our attention to social attempts to control the use of substance, first through laws, and secondly through behavioral interventions.

Legal Attempts to Control Substance Abuse

Behavior modification and therapy for substance abuse often serve as an adjunctive agent of the law. Before reviewing the specific therapeutic attempts to work with substance abusers, it will be informative to briefly review legal attempts to control substance abuse on a societal scale, an attempt with an extremely varied success rate.

Early encouragement for those seeking legal control of substance abuse can be found in the history of China (Merry, 1975). Following an Imperial edict in the early 1700s, severe penalties for opium use in China were instituted. As a result, the problem decreased until the British government forced repeal of the edict which was hurting British controlled opium smuggling into China. A later Chinese penalty for opium was proved quite successful: beheading became the penalty for use and no external forces changed Chinese law. Most later attempts to control substance abuse by legal means have been neither so punitive nor so effective.

As Azrin and Holz (1966) point out, the efficacy of a punishing agent depends upon its intensity. Less intense punishers were used in the United States following the Harrison Act of 1914 prohibiting opium sales, and after the 18th Amendment prohibiting alcohol production and consumption. These laws failed to suppress narcotic sales (Phares, 1975) and alcohol sales (Brecher et al., 1972), respectively. Instead, black-market sales became profitable. If substance abuse problems do not end with the passage of controlling legislation, is there any reason to maintain such legislation?

Stachnick (1972) maintains that there are four possible reasons for U.S. drug laws: (1) to discourage initial use, (2) to lower the probability of repeat offenses by those who are caught, (3) to provide a mandated entry into a treatment system, and (4) for societal retribution against those who violate society's customs. His analysis of the effects of legislation suggests that the first two purposes are not accomplished: initial drug sampling is not prevented by current U.S. laws; in fact, some feel these laws ironically increase sampling because they turn simple drugs into "forbidden fruit." The fantastically high relapse rate of drug offenders indicates that laws do not lower probabilities of repeated use. The third purpose is, however, fulfilled: offenders do enter mandated treatment, even though Stachnik reports that legally required treatment universally fails. Strong contrary evidence has recently been reported, however. Boudin, Valentine, Ingraham et al. (1977) report that those heroin addicts legally mandated into treatment are treated more successfully than those who report voluntarily, while Rawson, Callahan, Arias et al. (in press) find no difference in success rate for addicts with and without court pressure. Writing before the publication of these results, Stachnik concluded that the only purpose drug laws served was as retribution for society. That, he concluded, was not adequate justification for the laws.

Are there, then, other reasons or other data to support the continuation of drug laws? On a predictive basis, Hoffman (1975) argues the need for such laws: their removal, he feels, would result in vast increases in the numbers of those experimenting with particular substances, and thus also result in an increase in the number of those who become physically dependent upon substances. Interestingly, there is some data to support Hoffman's contention.

In recent years there have been significant changes in laws on alcohol use in Canada. These changes have been evaluated by Smart and his co-workers (Smart and Cutler, 1976; Smart and Schmidt, 1975). In the earlier study, Smart and Schmidt (1975) found that decreasing the legal age for drinking in Toronto increased the number of young people engaging in drinking. They also found that there was no increase in the amount drunk at any one time, however, and that more young people were beginning to drink at home with their parents. While the increase in numbers of young people drinking sounds discouraging, the other effects seem encouraging. When one considers that drinking rate appears to be under the influence of the rate modeled by one's drinking companions (Garlington and deRicco, 1977), it may be very useful for young people to have competent adult drinking models.

Another law change reflects an appreciation of the impact of modeling on behavior. Here, the government of British Columbia banned all advertising of alcoholic beverages for a short time. Smart and Cutler (1976) evaluated the impact of this law and found that it did not reduce the consumption of any alcoholic beverages, save wine. Wine consumption failed to increase again after the ban was lifted, however, leading the evaluators to speculate that the decrease in its consumption was not controlled by the legislation. Thus, the study of recently enacted legislation adds both further light and further confusion to the question of the effects of law on behavior. Another way to examine this interaction would be to look at other societies with different laws.

Hoffman (1975) did just this in a comparison of British and U.S. laws on heroin and in an examination of the impact of the Swedish experiment in legal prescription of all drugs. While Hoffman admits that Britain's system of legal heroin prescription has proven more successful than the U.S. policy of criminalization of heroin use, he also points out that this difference largely disappeared in the 1960s as the English system broke down. Careless prescription of heroin occurred during this period, and the English system had to be legislatively tightened to restrict the prescription of heroin to specialized heroin clinics in 1968. Further, Sessions (1976) points out that only about 15 percent of the British addicts maintained on heroin are working steadily. Finally, Hoffman (1975) points out that a Swedish adaptation of the legal prescription system failed because (1) it allowed maintenance prescription of amphetamines (amphetamine maintenance causes destructive physical effects in contrast to heroin maintenance which would not); and (2) a single physician was able to facilitate a nationwide increase in drug use and abuse by his unethical prescription of massive quantities of drugs to his patients. These prescriptions flooded the black market and resulted in an increase in the number of people addicted to amphetamines and heroin. Hoffman concluded that changing U.S. law would result in similar substantial increases in the number of drug users and abusers in the United States. Before leaving this topic, though, it may prove worthwhile to examine the arguments of Phares on drug legalization.

Pointing to the creation of black-market sales of narcotics due to the Harrison Act, Phares (1975) notes that the heroin addict is the ideal consumer. First, his addiction forces him to continue buying the drug regardless of other life constraints; and second, as his tolerance for narcotics increases, so does his demand. Phares argues that this set of circumstances means that the heroin problem has to approached in terms of economic supply and demand. Two "economic" solutions have been tried to date. Decreasing demand through the provision of therapy services has fallen woefully short, while attempts to decrease the supply of heroin have only resulted in higher prices on the street. Phares argues for a third solution: increasing availability of the drug. This would mean a return to the pre-Harrison Act status of heroin as an extremely cheap, freely available medication. He argues that heroin's effects are detrimental mainly in terms of the crime committed to pay the cost of using heroin (about $12 billion per year). Legalization would hypothetically eliminate the need for this crime. He further argues that the legalization of alcohol in the United States did not result in an increase in alcoholism, but that legalization of alcohol did result in fewer health hazards for the drinker. Stachnik (1972) similarly argues that eliminating the criminal status of drugs would result in fewer health risks to users.

It should also be pointed out that while society's laws will influence the behavior of the individual, the behavior (and attitudes) of the population will influence the content of the laws. Recent decriminalization of marijuana in California and Oregon may be seen as a result of this phenomenon; Hasleton and Simmonds (1975) foresee similar changes in the laws of Australia as a result of a shift in behavior among younger members of that society.

Bearing in mind that laws will influence the definition of drugs of abuse and may be part of the motivation of a person to seek treatment, let us now turn to a review of the behavioral treatment of various substances of abuse. This paper will severely restrict the attention given to alcohol abuse. For extensive reviews of this area see Bridell and Nathan (1976); Miller (1976); and Sobell and Sobell (1976). This section will be followed by a case example which will illustrate application of some of the more effective of the treatment strategies reviewed, and will be followed by a discussion of the ethical issues involved in these treatment procedures and their interface with the legal system.

BEHAVIORAL ASSESSMENT AND
TREATMENT OF SUBSTANCE ABUSERS

Assessment and treatment strategies for substance abuse have evolved considerably over the past 15 years. These strategies have evolved in parallel with conceptualizations of the subject matter of behavioral psychology. Eysenck and Rachman (1965) present an early theoretical formulation of behavioral disorders. In this formulation they separate behavioral disorders into two types: Type I, in which excessive "emotional" learning occurs due to an overactive autonomic nervous system (neurosis, phobias, obsessions and compulsions, and so on), and Type II, in which insufficient "emotional" learning occurs due to an underactive autonomic nervous system (psychopathy, drug addiction, sexual deviation, and so on). In Type II disorders, it was assumed that behavior was not suppressed because the autonomic nervous system did not respond to punishment. This early model stands in contrast to the later formulation of behavioral pathology advanced by Kanfer and Saslow (1969). In this later model, no attention is paid to the etiology of behavior. Instead, a catalogue of client excesses and deficits is developed. Treatment then targets a complex of specific behavioral problems with a variety of techniques, rather than aiming to cure a single specific syndrome with a single specific treatment. The reader will see that most early behavioral interventions conceptualized (or at least presented) drug use or addiction simplistically. The taking of the drug often seems to be the entire problem behavior, while later interventions take a more comprehensive approach to both assessment and treatment. In addition, the locus for treatment moves over the same period of time from a laboratory base into the natural environment, mimicking a move pioneered by Tharp and Wetzel (1969) through their in vivo treatment of delinquent teenagers, using behavioral engineering. Finally, the clients treated change from middle-class whites to more impoverished, less skilled clientele of different races. Let us now briefly review the assessment of substance abuse and then move to a review of the treatment studies.

Behavioral Assessment of Substance Abuse

Several fine reviews exist to point the practitioner to assessment strategies now available for the treatment of substance abuse. Sobell and Sobell (1976) and Bridell and Nathan (1976) present comprehensive reviews of the behavioral assessment of addiction, although they base their reviews substantially on assessment of alcohol problems. These reviews cover a variety of inpatient and outpatient assessment strategies. The present section of this chapter will emphasize strategies for outpatient assessment of drug abuse, especially as might be used in the behavioral treatment of the problem. Let us turn to inpatient assessment first.

Direct Observation in the Assessment Process

Surprisingly little work has been done in the direct observation of the effects of drugs on human beings, especially in the natural setting. Perhaps the earliest direct observation studies done with heroin addiction was a case report by Wikler (1952). In this study, a young inmate at the Lexington, Kentucky, federal treatment facility was allowed to use morphine while staff observed his behavior. Observations were done through a psychoanalytic perspective. Interestingly, over time the client became withdrawn and alienated from the staff. When warned that the study was about to end, he made fervent promises to begin cutting back on his daily dosage of morphine but in fact continued to use all of the morphine available.

Later studies by Meyer and his colleagues (Babor, Meyer, Mirin et al., 1976; McNamee, Mirin, Kuhnie, and Meyer, 1976; Mirin, Meyer, and McNamee, 1976) indicate that there are some common patterns of response to readdiction to heroin. These experimenters used paper and pencil measures as well as direct observations of an addict population who underwent experimental inpatient addiction. They noted an increase in withdrawal and suspiciousness with the administration of the drug in increasing doses. Their reports indicate that users soon lose the euphoria which appears to reinforce early use of the drug, only to continue administration in order to avoid painful withdrawal symptoms. Further research from direct observation studies may well indicate other general changes in mood and behavior characteristic of an addict as he/she undergoes readdiction. It seems likely, though, that individual differences will be quite great, and that it is very difficult to distinguish the occurrence of chipping (infrequent, nonaddictive use of heroin) except by frequent urinalysis. Direct observation has been used in other ways in the laboratory analysis of substance abuse, however.

Similar to the "taste tests" used with alcoholics (Miller, 1976), and laboratory bar observations (Schaefer, Sobell, and Mills, 1971), attempts have been made to measure drug consumption in the laboratory. While such work has been fairly extensive recently in the area of alcoholism, much less work has been done in the observation of drug abuse. Two interesting observation procedures were employed in recent studies at the University of Mississippi Medical Center. In one instance, a client was allowed free access to various substances in a "smell discrimination" task (Blanchard, Libet, and Young, 1973). The time that the client sniffed the paint made available was the dependent measure. In another elegant measurement procedure, clients were videotaped while shooting up (Elkin, Williams, Barlow, and Stewart, Note 5). These tapes were then replayed to the client in order to measure their physiological effects. It was assumed that the greater the physiological arousal generated, the greater the likelihood of drug abuse by the individual. However, there has been no validation of either measure. The validity of these measures as indices of the probability of substance abuse remains to be demonstrated. Laboratory measures of substance abuse are still at a rather primitive stage overall, and much further work must be done to establish the reliability and validity of measures that are employed.

Some of that work is being done in the psychophysiology laboratories of Charles P. O'Brien at the University of Pennsylvania. Recently, O'Brien, Testa, O'Brien et al. (1977) have demonstrated that addicts show conditioned physiological withdrawal symptoms to stimuli associated with heroin. These physiological changes may well be the cues that trigger heroin use after a person has been free from heroin use for years. This work has had only theoretical impact to date; its therapeutic impact has been limited. One short treatment excursion will be noted later in the review of the treatment literature. Other areas of psychophysiological assessment are even more speculative at this point.

For example, Quinton (1976) has found that six polydrug users show denser alpha wave than six nonuser controls in their electro-encephalograms (EEGs). Although there was no difference between the groups in their ability to increase alpha wave responses during conditioning trials, the author feels that alpha wave density may somehow be a determinant of drug usage. Goldberg, Greenwood, and Taintor (1976) similarly feel that such alpha wave conditioning will be important in the rehabilitation of substance abusing or "thrill-seeking" clientele. However, existing evidence is not solid enough to suggest alpha waves have any relationship to the likelihood of drug use. If alpha conditioning does produce treatment results with drug abusers, placebo factors may well be at work.

Urine Sampling

Since the addict is often under a variety of pressures to misrepresent drug usage (see Callahan and Rawson, in press), it is critical to have a direct assessment of the presence or absence of the target substance in the client's system. For alcohol abuse, the "Mobat" (Mobile Breath Analysis Test) will provide inexpensive breathalyzer tests (see Sobell and Sobell, 1975). For most drugs other than alcohol, however, it is necessary to send urine samples to a local laboratory for analysis. For less than five dollars per sample, most drug screening laboratories can provide feedback on the presence or absence of several drugs within a two- to three-day period with substantial accuracy (deAngelis, 1976). Goldstein and Brown (1970) recommend testing urine at a rate of once every three days for narcotic use; for barbiturates, results are only accurate for two days, while other drugs vary in their rate of metabolism and excretion. Random sampling of urines can be used to reduce cost, but true randomicity is critical: otherwise drug users can easily detect a pattern in urine sampling days and manage to escape detection of drug usage. If at all possible then, urine screens ought to be employed to validate the self-report of the drug abuser. This ought not be taken to imply that the verbal report of the user is without value.

Self-monitoring

Perhaps the most creative use of verbal report measures documented in the literature to date is that employed by Henry Boudin and his colleagues (Boudin, 1972; Boudin, Valentine, Ingraham et al. 1977) at the Gainesville, Florida, Drug Project and adapted by others (e.g., Callahan, Rawson, Glazer et al. 1976; Callahan, Rawson, McCleave et al., in press; Rawson et al., in press).

In these applications of verbal report procedures, the client is required to make between one and six telephone calls to the project each day. In each of these calls the client is asked to report each of several responses or "pinpoints" he is responsible for monitoring. These pinpoints might include such things as current anxiety level, frequency and intensity of drug urges, tokes of marijuana, ounces of alcohol, arguments with employer, and so on. A different set of pinpoints is derived for each client based upon the client's initial interviews; these pinpoints are then maintained or altered depending upon the experience of the client during treatment. The rationale behind this assessment is simply that of a functional analysis of behavior: every behavior is seen as a part of a chain of events which serves to cue or maintain the behavior (Nurnberger and Zimmerman, 1970).

Since a functional analysis of behavior assumes a set of stimuli which can reliably set the stage for a given behavior, monitoring that entire set of antecedent stimuli is the necessary prelude to the effective treatment of the problem behavior. For example, if a drug user reliably uses heroin following a demeaning interaction with an employer, treatment can then focus on teaching the user coping strategies or assertion techniques for handling the interaction better, or it might focus on placing the user in a less stressful job. However, if heroin use reliably follows interacting with one particular friend, treatment must focus on finding means of ending that relationship and forming new friendships. Such a strategy is also apparent in treatment of alcoholism (see Nathan and O'Brien, 1971).

In the process of monitoring both external and internal events which precede the unwanted behavior, a form of behaviorally induced "insight" into what controls one's own behavior is possible. While addiction will probably make the role of the drug in the person's stress and problem solving processes unclear, urges to use drugs when the client is abstinent will highlight the process quite well. Similar processes can be used in the treatment of any self-defined excessive behavior (see Callahan, 1976, for a discussion of how this has been applied to homosexuality).

For now, let us move from the behavioral assessment of substance use to a review of the behavioral treatment of substance abuse.

BEHAVIORAL TREATMENT OF SUBSTANCE ABUSE

The history of behavioral interventions in the treatment of substance abuse has been marked by a gradual evolution away from an over-simplistic model, both in assessment and intervention strategies. This evolution in the behavioral approach involves the realization that the problems of a drug abuser do not begin and end with drug-taking. Instead, the drug user is seen as a unique individual with a variety of behavioral assets and deficits. Concurrent with the evolution of this model of who the drug abuser is, treatment has moved gradually into the natural environment from the controlled inpatient setting, though a great deal of work still continues in such settings. This review will move somewhat historically from early single case studies into more recent applications in community-based programs with and without pharmaceutical supports.

Chemical Aversion Therapies

With the conception of drug abuse as a single problem (drug-taking) several early reports emphasized punishment or classical conditioning of drug-taking. The earliest of these used chemical aversion techniques to suppress drug-taking. For example, Raymond (1964) used apomorphine to treat a female physeptone addict. Treatment was temporarily discontinued as the patient became suicidal, but was resumed after ECT. This course of inpatient treatment was supplemented by follow-up booster sessions and family therapy to relieve marital distress. This case demonstrates that it is possible to conceptualize drug usage too simplistically. In addition, it fails to provide experimental demonstration of the effects that were reported.

Experimental control was provided in two single cases treated by Liberman (1968). In these cases a series of apomorphine aversion conditioning trials were followed by a saline placebo in a single blind test for classically conditioned aversion effects. If an aversion was indeed conditioned to the injection process by all of the prior trials, the saline injection ought to have conditioned aversive properties somewhat less than apomorphine, per se. This indeed proved to be the case, but one of the two clients dropped from treatment upon realizing the deception involved in the single blind trial. The other patient remained in the treatment and was reported to be functioning successfully at one-year follow-up. These are the only reported case studies using classical conditioning with chemicals reported, beyond Burroughs' (1953) autobiographical description of his self-treatment of heroin addiction. Other drugs have been used to suppress addiction as well.

Scoline is a drug which produces apnea or respiratory paralysis. Thomson and Rathod (1968) report on the treatment of heroin addicts using classical conditioning of heroin injection and scoline administration. They reasoned that the respiratory paralysis caused by scoline mimics the effects of heroin, thus making an ideal aversive event for classical conditioning. In the Thomson and Rathod study, statements reminding the client of the negative effects of drugs were repeated in the patients' ears during the time they were not breathing. While Thomson and Rathod's report of nine of ten clients clean at an average of eight months' follow-up is encouraging, the use of such a powerful conditioned stimulus has great potential for abuse. In fact it has been used questionably in later unpublished studies. At least one study using chemical aversion had a clear justification for the use of aversion therapy: in this case the client was a young paint sniffer who had undergone a series of other treatments unsuccessfully before being treated with aversion therapy.

In this study, Blanchard, Libet, and Young (1973) compared the effects of apneic aversion with covert sensitization, a verbal aversion therapy technique which paired the verbal description of unwanted behavior (sniffing glue) with verbal descriptions of aversive events (brain rotting, sniffing feces, and so on). The client was observed throughout the study on a "sniff test" in which the client had access to paint to sniff. In this study, 16 half-hour sessions of covert sensitization were initially unsuccessful in reducing drug usage in the sniff tests, while apneic aversion produced fairly substantial suppression in sniffing, which was continued by further covert sensitization. It seems unlikely that the small and transient amount of suppression of paint-sniffing produced initially by covert sensitization would have been sufficient treatment over time. It appears then that covert sensitization became more potent, or, in other terminology, the client became sensitized to the aversive accounts (the events became more aversive) in covert sensitization after experiencing apneic aversion. In the animal literature, sensitization occurs when an initially ineffective aversive event (one which does not suppress behavior) becomes an effective suppressant after the organism experiences a highly intensive presentation of the aversive event. Thus, an initially ineffective shock of .5 ma would become effective in suppressing behavior after the animal had received a single 5 ma shock. The analogy to the human event is not 100 percent clear in this case because the covert sensitization and apneic aversion are not merely two intensities of the same aversive event (such as shock), but instead are separate though possibly related aversive events. Whether this study indicates a generalization of aversive properties across two similar but not identical aversive events is not clear. It is quite possible that all of the suppression seen was solely an effect of the apneic aversion, and not at all of the covert sensitization.

Further apneic aversion has not been reported recently. With its great potential for misuse the drug may well be too dangerous to use in treatment. It will probably join emetic drugs as a therapeutic intervention shelved, not because of lack of effect, but for ethical and clinical considerations. Their use appears to raise too much conflict on the part of staff members using them, and thus to raise questions of their social utility.

Rachman and Teasdale (1969) dismissed emetic drugs for two reasons: (1) staff found their use quite distasteful, and (2) their effects could not be effectively controlled and predicted. Their hope for aversion therapy lay in electrical aversion, since its intensity and duration and time of onset could be so well controlled, and in covert sensitization. Let us move then to a consideration of these two strategies in the treatment of drug abuse.

Electrical Aversion Therapy

Electrical aversion has a fairly short history in the behavioral treatment of drug abuse. Wolpe (1965) presents the first case of electrical aversion for drug dependence in the behavioral literature. He worked with a physician addicted to demerol. After several office sessions, he gave the physician a portable shocker in order to extend punishment of drug urges to the community. Since the client moved to another city, treatment was not completed in this case study. The client was referred to another therapist in his new town and no follow-up is presented. Interestingly, the case is presented as one in which the whole problem consisted of drug dependence—no other clinical issues were mentioned. Since the client was a physician, it is possible that he had no social or employment difficulties. While it is easy to see that there might not be any employment problems, it seems less likely that the addiction could exist in the absence of either causal or resultant social problems. Other reports on the effects of electrical aversion similarly ignore possible complications.

Lubetkin and Fishman (1974) report a single case study in which they used electrical aversion for a graduate student with a history of "chipping," or using heroin without becoming addicted. They gave him 20 sessions of electric shock and reported good results. In another series of studies John O'Brien and his colleagues (O'Brien and Raynes, 1970; O'Brien, Raynes, and Patch, 1971) used both covert sensitization and electrical aversion therapy in the successful treatment of five cases of heroin addiction. They report follow-up of up to 14 months in this study. There have been no long-term follow-up studies on the effects of electrical aversion, and the procedure appears to be gradually fading from the behavioral treatment repertoire, being replaced with verbal aversion therapy and treatments oriented towards dealing with other problems in the user's life.

Covert Sensitization

While there has been a gradual movement away from the use of aversion therapy using physical aversive events, there is mixed data on the use of the verbal aversion therapy procedure, covert sensitization. Covert sensitization is a procedure derived from classical conditioning theory by Joseph Cautela (1966). In this procedure, the client relaxes and then listens to verbal descriptions of engaging in the undesired behavior. A chain of actions is then described which culminates in noxious events occurring to the client as he or she begins to engage in the unwanted behavior. The aversive events used can range from nausea and vomiting (Cautela, 1966) to wasp stings (Wisocki, 1973) to socially aversive events (Callahan, 1976). Imaginal covert sensitization has been supplemented with electrical aversion therapy (O'Brien et al., 1971) and with noxious odors (Maletzky, 1974) as "assisted covert sensitization."

Covert sensitization has been reported to be highly successful in the treatment of alcoholism (Anant, 1967), gasoline sniffing (Kolvin, 1967), and sexual deviation (Barlow, Agras, and Leitenberg, 1969; Callahan and Leitenberg, 1973). It is rarely used as the only treatment technique, however, often being supplemented with assertion training and other strategies. Evidence for the effectiveness of covert sensitization is still sketchy (see Curran and Little, 1978, for a recent review) as will be seen in the following review, since there is little follow-up available and treatment is never limited to only one procedure. However, this is a major problem in all clinical research: in order to fully evaluate the effects of a treatment process, that intervention should be applied alone while careful measurements of dependent variables are undertaken; similarly, follow-up should cover a substantial length of time during which no other therapeutic intervention is undertaken by the subject-client. Realistically, good clinical treatment usually demands more than one treatment being applied during the "experimental" application of intervention techniques, and also demands the availability of any necessary ancillary treatment during the follow-up period. Thus, clinical research as a term carries within it an ironic conflict between two standards of excellence in procedures. We will return to this point in the final discussion of this chapter. For now, let us turn to the issue of how well covert sensitization has worked in the treatment of substance abuse.

Duehn and Shannon (1973) report the use of covert sensitization in the treatment of LSD users. They had the clients imagine having "bad trips," vomiting, and so on, after using LSD. Two clients reported that they subsequently had bad trips when using LSD, and two others reported experiencing stomach cramps when offered LSD. Since it seems likely that these clients were seeking treatment under duress, it is questionable whether the use of covert sensitization was ethical. An LSD trip is a time when a person is extremely vulnerable to his or her own cognitions. Using covert sensitization almost guaranteed that their future experiences with LSD would bring on conditioned aversive thoughts and feelings—all this to an experience that has been described as mystical and religious by some researchers (e.g., Pahnke, Kurland, Unger et al., 1970). The authors seem more influenced by what the law says is an illegal substance, rather than by an examination of what the good and possible bad effects of the drug were for each individual. It is possible that treatment caused as many negative effects as positive effects, but that is not known. At 18 months' follow-up, 6 clients reported not using the drug again while a 7th client could not be located. Another instance of treatment would also seem to involve outside pressure: this is in the work of George Steinfeld at the Danbury State prison with narcotic addicts.

Steinfeld and his colleagues (Steinfeld, Rautio, Rice, and Egan, 1974) report the use of covert sensitization with addicts in a federal prison. They institute treatment to precede the client's release from prison. Each client treated volunteered and no one was offered any time off or early release in return for volunteering. Treatment was applied in the context of a therapeutic community. Results indicated that 6 of 8 clients were clean at 18-month follow-up. Interestingly, however, Steinfeld (personal communication, 1976) now indicates that covert sensitization is becoming a less critical part of the treatment procedure offered addicts in his program, with heavier emphasis being placed on other elective psychotherapies and the overall therapeutic milieu as well. It will be interesting to note how these program changes affect program efficacy. Steinfeld also indicates that the treatments offered are more readily accepted by those with white, middle-class backgrounds than by those who come from poor, minority back-grounds. Making more psychologically oriented treatments available to minorities may be missing the boat: as Maslow (1962) has pointed out, self-actualization cannot occur until a person's more basic needs are taken care of. Sometimes, however, covert sensitization or even more sophisticated techniques may be appropriate if the rest of a person's life is well integrated.

In a multiple baseline study, Epstein, Parker, and Jenkins (1976) showed that covert sensitization was responsible for decreasing the frequency of drug urges in a young addict client. In addition, it showed effects on actual number of dirty urines, and surprisingly, in assertiveness as measured on the ability of the client to say no to a pusher. The client's financial management skills, however, did not respond to covert sensitization but did respond to a contingency intervention.

Wisocki (1973) and Boudin (1972) both present single case studies in which they applied covert sensitization to reduce the frequency of drug urges. Their clients were well educated and treatment with covert sensitization was not the only treatment applied. A variety of other psychological interventions were administered to increase social behavior with "straight" persons in both instances. However, Wisocki does report that she found it more difficult to reduce the client's drug urges than to facilitate pro-social behavior, thus pointing out the need to reduce drug urges as a valid treatment goal as well. Drug urges have been attacked in a somewhat different manner by Maletzky (1974).

In this application of covert sensitization, Maletzky added punishment of drug urges by valeric acid, a noxious-smelling substance. In his study he compared the effects of this "assisted" covert sensitization to one-to-one drug counseling of approximately the same length. He found that the covert sensitization was significantly more effective in reducing self- and other-reported instances of substance abuse. While some of the substances abused would be difficult to test for (such as marijuana), others (such as cigarette smoking) did not carry legal sanction, so that self-report might have been reliable. Still other drugs (such as barbiturates and heroin) could be tested for using urine screening. Maletzky's work represents one of the few controlled outcome studies available in his area. Its focus on covert sensitization as a punishing agent stands in contrast to another means used to reduce the frequency of a behavior: extinction.

Extinction

One of the earliest principles discovered or described by psychology has been the law of effect. Presented simply by Thorndike (1913), the law of effect states that a behavior will be more likely to occur if it produces pleasant consequences, and less likely to occur if it produces noxious consequences. This principle has been gradually refined to the state it has reached with Skinner (1938) who states that the frequency of a behavior will increase when followed by a positive or negative reinforcer, and decrease when followed by an aversive event (punishment), or by no consequence (extinction). This latter principle of extinction has been applied imaginatively in the field of substance abuse.

Rubenstein (1931) gradually replaced morphine with saline for a group of tuberculoid addicts. The injections that they received gradually became 100 percent saline and thus, an extinction process was applied. He reported his treatment to be successful, even though he had follow-up for only one client and that follow-up consisted only of a three-month period. Thus, while the application of the extinction principle is evident in this study, it is not clear what kind of impact the treatment had on the clients.

A more recent attempt to use extinction provides better data, however. Götestam and Melin (1974) report their results with four amphetamine addicts. In this case they used imagined extinction rather than overt extinction. They followed the course of their clients' physiological responses to imagined scenes of self-injection. They reported that conditioned pulse, respiration, and galvanic skin response (GSR) changes all declined with the extinction trials. Three out of four of their clients reported no drug use in a four-month follow-up. It is not known how these clients did over a longer period of time, however. While Götestam and Melin reported on the effects of covert extinction, other investigators are beginning to report the effects of overt extinction trials.

O'Brien (1974) reports the effects of extinction trials on 20 heroin addicts. These people were blockaded from the effects of heroin by a narcotic antagonist, naloxone, in this instance. The effect of narcotic antagonist drugs is to prevent a person from feeling any of the euphoric effects of heroin injection, or ingestion of any narcotic in any form. It has been hypothesized that this occurs because the narcotic antagonist occupies those receptor sites in the brain which the narcotic must occupy in order to produce euphoria. Since the antagonist has greater binding potential for those sites, it will cause any narcotic in the person's system to be flushed immediately, causing severe withdrawal symptoms. However, if a person has the narcotic antagonist in his system before ingesting a narcotic, the narcotic simply has no effect. Thus, therapeutic application of narcotic antagonists requires that the person be free of narcotics at the time of taking the first antagonist, and requires that the antagonist be in the person's system before any narcotic is ingested. In this way, Wikler (1973) has hypothesized that heroin cravings can be unlearned by experiencing cravings which cannot be rewarded.

In one of the first laboratory tests of Wikler's hypothesis, O'Brien (1974) reported laboratory data on the results of self-injection for clients blockaded with a narcotic antagonist. Six patients completed a total of 50 self-injection trials while blockaded with the antagonist naloxone. Their self-report indicated that over the course of about 15 trials, the clients' feelings about injection gradually moved from very positive valence, with reports of conditioned feelings of euphoria upon injection, to very negative valence, during which trials the client began to find self-injection aversive. Thus, O'Brien was able to demonstrate the potential utility of a narcotic antagonist as a therapeutic tool in the laboratory at least. Four of the six clients treated in this way reported that they were drug-free at an eight-month follow-up. In many other treatments using narcotic antagonists, results have been much less hopeful. Often after using narcotic antagonists, clients still find they must return to methadone in traditional drug treatment settings (e.g., Hurzeler, Gewirtz, and Kleber, 1976). Some more encouraging results with the use of narcotic antagonists will be reported in the context of dealing with antagonists as a part of a comprehensive treatment procedure. First, however, let us complete the review of single interventions in the treatment of drug abuse. One other single intervention of possibly great importance is that of contingency management.

Contingency Management

Contingency management is the systematic application of principles of reinforcement, punishment, and extinction to a particular problem behavior or behaviors. In its simplest form, it involves the application of a single intervention, such as reinforcement, to a single behavior in order to increase the frequency of that behavior, or the application of an aversive consequence in order to decrease the frequency of a particular problem behavior. We have seen instances of such applications already in this review. There are examples of more complex applications of these principles, however.

O'Brien, Raynes, and Patch (1971) report the use of these principles in a systematic fashion on a ward-wide basis. They were able to increase therapy attendance and rule compliance on a treatment unit for substance abusers by implementing a contingency management procedure. Access to the recreation hall, television, and weekend passes were made contingent upon the occurrence of therapy attendance and other therapeutic behaviors. The results of this effort showed that these behaviors could be increased through the systematic application of these principles.

Similar results were found by Götestam and his colleagues (Melin and Götestam, 1973; Erikson, Götestam, Melin, and Öst, 1974). They devised a token economy which was successful in controlling the behavior of inpatient drug dependent clients. Unfortunately, controlling inpatient behaviors may still not have any impact on behavior in the outside world.

In fact, that finding was reported by Ottomanelli (1976). In this report he supplied follow-up on the results of an earlier intervention in which a token economy system had shown substantial control of the behavior of inpatients. The ultimate reinforcer in this original intervention was early release from the program. Immediate evaluation revealed that this system helped people earn their way through the program at a significantly more rapid rate than a control group achieved (Glicksman et al., 1971). Follow-up, unfortunately, indicated that those going through the program had no better long-term success than those who were in the control condition. This may imply that the key target behaviors for long-term adjustment are not those required to function well within an institution.

Contingency management has now been used in the natural environment by a number of investigators. One of the first reports of such contracting was presented by Boudin (1972). In this study, he used covert sensitization to decrease the frequency of drug urges for a client whose primary treatment was contingency contract. Later, Polakow and Doctor (1973) used contingency contracting with a married couple on probation for their use of barbiturates and marijuana. The contingency in this case was time off probation. By targeting therapeutic behaviors such as counseling sessions and clean urines, the authors (a probation officer and a psychologist) successfully treated the couple. Only short-term follow-up was provided, however, so the long-term impact of the treatment is unknown at this time.

Further encouraging results from the probation system are apparent in an unpublished report by Wiggenhorn (1974). In this effort, all treatment was done by probation officers who worked with each of the four clients individually in targeting small goals, such as increasing job-seeking efforts, increasing social contacts with straight friends, increasing self-esteem, and so on. The focus was on building pro-social behaviors. Three of the four clients provided clean urines one year after treatment, while the fourth client was not available for follow-up. This review will now move to a brief discussion of the demonstration of contingency management in other programs, and finally discuss the effects of behavioral programming in large scale program efforts. This section of the paper will then be followed by an illustrative case study.

Contingency Management in Other Drug Programs

Addicts who undertake methadone become addicted to this substance in place of heroin. While this treatment can increase adjustment and decrease crime (Dole and Nyswander, 1965), severe problems with dirty urines, behavior problems in the clinic, poor therapy attendance, and selling take-home methadone doses on the streets are also encountered (Bowden and Maddux, 1972). The earliest behavioral incursions into methadone programs have dealt with some of these problems.

Nightingale, Michaux, and Platt (1972) conducted a time-series analysis of the impact of contingencies on dirty urines in a methadone program. Merely stating contingencies ("A certain number of dirty urines will lead to your expulsion from the program"), led to a decrease in dirty urines. This initial decrease was followed by a much more substantial decrease in dirty urines when the contingencies were actually implemented. Some of the decrease in dirty urines occurred as the worst offenders were thrown out of the program, but there was also a marked decrease in the frequency of dirty urines given by those remaining in the program. Thus, contingency management appears to be a very appropriate tool for dealing with problems in a methadone maintenance program. This study did not experimentally demonstrate the impact of the contingencies in any controlled way. It remained for Stitzer, Bigelow, Lawrence et al., (1977) to do that.

In the Stitzer et al. study, take-home dosages of methadone were made contingent upon following program rules, attending therapy sessions, and providing heroin-free urines. In an A-B-A-B design, the authors contrasted phases in which clients received their methadone take-home doses noncontingently, and phases in which the clients had to earn their take-home doses by providing clean urines. Implementing contingencies reliably decreased dirty urines for each individual, providing experimental demonstration of the utility of combining behavioral treatment with methadone. This merger of contingency management (psychological treatment) and methadone maintenance involves some contradiction, however. Methadone programs rest on the assumption that heroin addiction must be treated medically because it involves an alteration in a person's physiology. Stitzer et al. suggest that alteration does not control the person's behavior as much as contingencies do. There is also some irony in the adaptation of behavioral principles to the Synanon model.

Synanon is a residential program based on a strategy of totally rebuilding a personality through total decimation and restructuring (Yablonsky, 1965). Much of the treatment takes place in both real and symbolic "haircuts" in which the person's destructive behaviors are pinpointed and attacked in group. In a behavioral adaptation of Synanon, MacDonough (1976) reports the evolution of a system called Feedback which is modeled on Synanon's haircut system. In this system, residents regularly give one another feedback on their therapeutic progress and compliance with program rules. From MacDonough's report, this feedback is given more positively and more systematically than in Synanon. In fact, cards are used which list desirable and undesirable behavior. In this study, MacDonough compared the effects of the Feedback program with a medically oriented program administered by the same hospital personnel. Drug-abusing residents responded slightly better under the Feedback program than under the medically oriented system. Alcoholic clients responded equally well to both programs. However, it should be pointed out that confrontation programs can lead to higher dropout rates than more constructively oriented programs, as discovered by Pomerleau, Pertschuk, Adkins, and Brady (in press) in their recent comparison of traditional and behavioral group treatments for alcoholics. While both group treatment approaches were equally successful with those who remained in the programs, confrontive therapy led significantly more individuals to drop out of treatment. Thus, a more supportive behavioral intervention may reach a higher percentage of those who sample treatment than confrontive programs. Such programs have traditionally severe problems with dropouts (Vaillant, 1974), and often reach only a white, middle-class population (Aron and Daily, 1976). These considerations will prove important when mounting community-based programs designed to deal with large numbers of drug abusers, especially employment training for minority addicts.

Since employment history has been shown to be a critical factor in determining probability of success in and following drug abuse treatment, employment training programs will no doubt be important in the establishment of successful treatment programs. Hall, Loeb, Norton, and Yang (1977) report on a comparison of two groups of methadone maintenance clients who went through a two-week experimental job-training workshop or a control condition. The experimental workshop included information on vocational resources, videotaped role plays of job interviews, feedback by the therapist, instructions on how to fill out applications, and relaxation training. Control subjects received the same vocational information but none of the other treatment procedures. Blind ratings of videotaped interviews and written job applications showed the experimental group to have improved job interviewing skills significantly more than the control group. More importantly, 50 percent of the treated group had jobs at three months' follow-up, while only 14 percent of the control group was employed. Even though these results are short term, they reflect a program that will be critical to the successful treatment of any substance abuser. They also imply the need for comprehensive community-based treatment for chronic drug abusers, an area we will turn to next.

Community-based Behavioral Treatment Program

Perhaps the single most important program dealing with behavioral intervention with chronic drug abusers has been the Drug Project. The Drug Project was located at the University of Florida and was directed by Henry Boudin. The program was based upon the concept of gradually shaping the user into learning a drug-free lifestyle. The major therapeutic tool was the contingency contract, often written to deploy major punishers (loss of a motorcycle or time in jail) to keep the client oriented towards therapeutic goals. The therapeutic program was described by Boudin and Valentine (1972), and some anecdotal evidence of its efficacy was provided covering three cases treated. More recently, Boudin et al. (1977) have described some of their long-term results. They found that a majority of the cases they treated had a positive outcome, a highly unusual finding in the treatment of heroin addiction. More precisely, Boudin et al. (in press) report that 14 of 18 clients showed clean urines in follow-ups ranging from 1–3 years. The one major flaw with the Boudin effort was that it reached only white clients in a community where the most severe heroin problem existed in the black community. Thus, its clients tended to be younger, better educated, and to have better job histories than their black colleagues who stayed away from the program. But the racial barrier has been crossed in another behavioral program.

Using the contracting model presented by Boudin et al., a behaviorally based treatment program was opened in Ventura County, California, and provided treatment for browns, blacks, and whites. Initial analysis of the population indicated that even though a smaller percentage of minority applicants successfully gained full client status by completing their initial contingency contract, race of the client was not a factor in how long the client stayed in treatment (Callahan et al. 1976).

In this program, the HALT Project (Heroin Antagonist and Learning Therapy Project), a comparison was made of the relative effects of behavioral treatments alone, a narcotic antagonist (naltrexone) alone, and the effects of the two treatments in combination. For all groups, contingency contracting was the basis for entry into the program:

everyone had to earn initial client status by fulfilling a contingency contract. Once in the program, however, clients were treated differentially according to random assignments to groups.

An initial analysis of the effects of the naltrexone alone and the combination group showed that combined clients stayed significantly longer periods in the program and took the drug longer as well (Callahan et al., 1976). These significant differences gradually faded as the performance of both groups of clients improved through the first three years of the program (Callahan et al., in press). Ironically, the behavior therapy group did well initially—until the Project's supply of naltrexone arrived from Washington. At this point, interest in the drug-free treatment waned and the effectiveness of the behavior therapy group decreased significantly. Over the three-year period the behavior therapy alone treatment became virtually completely ineffective except with female clients (Rawson et al., in press)—the only clients not cleared to take naltrexone. Thus, it seems that the availability of naltrexone as a treatment agent decreased the possible efficacy of behavior therapy alone, especially as compared to the results in the Boudin et al. (in press) research, and even as compared to the initial HALT Project results. Specific treatment procedures at the HALT Project will become clearer through a case example illustrating what the present authors feel are some of the more effective treatment procedures for critical target behaviors encountered in substance abuse clients.

Evidence from the existing literature appears to indicate that a particular set of behaviors are critical treatment targets for the substance abuser, and that there exists a set of intervention procedures which appear most promising for the remediation of those targets. The target behaviors are: (1) substance use, (2) therapy attendance, (3) drug urges, (4) work behavior, and (5) a nonabuser lifestyle. The following treatment modalities seem most promising to modifying these behaviors in the opinion of the present authors: (1) substance use—detoxification in an inpatient facility and continued use of urine tests (Goldstein and Brown, 1970); (2) therapy attendance—contingency contracting (Boudin et al., 1977); the use of threat of jail is a powerful contingency (the ethics of this will be discussed in a later area of this paper); (3) drug urges—extinction procedures (O'Brien et al., 1977) including a blocking agent such as naltrexone, if possible, and covert sensitization (e.g., Wisocki, 1973) seem most promising here; (4) work behavior—contingency contracting for work behavior and role playing of employment interviews (Hall et al., in press; Rawson et al., in press); and (5) lifestyle-life management training and contingency contracting

(Callahan et al., in press). In order to understand these clinical interventions more fully let us review their application to a single case of heroin addiction.

A CASE STUDY

The following case is derived mainly from one person's history and treatment, but some aspects of two other cases are woven in to allow the reader a full explanation of how each treatment might be applied. Treatment assumes the presence of a full project staff, but methods can be extrapolated to the one-to-one therapy situation with a motivated client. Client: The client is a 28-year-old Chicano with a 12-year history of addiction to heroin. He is the father of two children; his common-law wife is extremely supportive of his seeking treatment, yet is worried about whether his kicking heroin will destroy their relationship. His best friend is also an addict (a 52-year-old Chicano with a 35-year history of heroin addiction). Val has never held an officially recognized job and has supported his common-law wife through petty thievery and her use of welfare. He presents for treatment voluntarily but also knowing that he will have to face a charge of being under the influence in court in two months; this time he fears a long sentence as a multiple repeater. He reports to treatment with an $80-per-day habit.

Treatment

1. Detoxification Entrance Contract: After explaining the treatment procedures to be used should Val decide to become a client, the therapist writes a contingency contract to cover the period of time that the client is to be in detoxification (two weeks). The client has to earn the right to become a client by remaining the full two weeks for detoxification even though methadone is no longer provided after day eight.[1] In return for staying the full time and keeping a log of feelings and thoughts, the client earns the right to a treatment contract, the right to start taking naltrexone, and a ride home from detoxification. Because Val cannot read or write, a friend reads the contract to him and a staff member at the detoxification center agrees to write out his log for him.

    Val agrees to engage in all of these behaviors, signs his contract, and receives his own copy, knowing that the sanction for leaving detoxification is that he cannot reapply for treatment for at least three months. He enters detoxification, stays the full

14 days, keeps a fairly sketchy and not very targeted log, and returns to receive naltrexone and begin the next phase of treatment.

2. Probationary Contract: Completion of the detoxification contract allows Val to become a client. It does not guarantee the continuation of the therapeutic interaction, however. A new contract is written upon his release which details his responsibilities if he is to remain a client. These include daily taking of the narcotic antagonist drug, naltrexone, provision of a urine sample at least every three days (more often upon demand), attendance at three therapy appointments per week, two daily phone calls per day with data on drug urges, alcohol consumption, with whom he has spent time, and significant interactions with wife. Each of of these reports was included in the phone calls because the interview revealed that the client felt they might be associated with drug use. In return for fulfilling these obligations, the client earned the right to begin job interview training and to have his probation officer notified that he had successfully earned client status in the project.

3. Ongoing Contracts. The contract-writing procedure itself becomes a form of therapy as the client moves gradually from a managerial contract written by staff members, to a negotiated contract, and finally to a self-control contract. This process allows a gradual fading of therapeutic controls. In fact, as the client moves gradually through these contracts, he often becomes more reasonable in requests of the counselor and more self-reliant.

Over the phases of treatment, the client is required to give fewer urine samples, although these always remain on a random basis and can always be asked for spontaneously if a counselor suspects drug use. As the client builds a record of reliable naltrexone-taking for a full month, he is allowed to decrease the schedule of naltrexone taken from seven 50 mg doses per week to 5 mg doses, and one 100 mg dose on Saturday. After successful compliance with this drug-taking schedule for one month, he moves to a schedule of 100 mg doses on Monday and Wednesday, and a dose of 150 mg on Friday. Throughout the drug-taking period, the client takes the same overall quantity of medication: 350 mg per week, enough to block the occurrence of euphoria due to heroin-taking.

In fact, however, Val does test the naltrexone blockade within the first few days of treatment—possibly a response which would occur regardless of whether or not he was taking the drug. His immediate reaction to not getting high is a mixture of relief that he did not get high and anger that he was frustrated in the attempt. Val gets into a car accident on the day that this happens and his friend reports that he acted crazy. Later though, Val's progess on the medication leads one of his friends to become a client in the Project as well. Since his friend later drops out of treatment, a painful choice arises: whether to cut off the friendship or continue it at the risk of slipping back into heroin use.

Val elects to continue in treatment and is cautioned that continuing ties with his friend can have potentially damaging consequences to the progress he has made to date. Solidifying the apparent gains made with naltrexone becomes the focus of the treatment process. It takes place in several forms: employment training, life-management training; covert sensitization is reserved for application late in the treatment program. However, true to results found in the laboratory (Leitenberg, Rawson, and Bath, 1970), the response must occur in order for extinction to take place. Since urges do not occur during the taking of naltrexone, the immediate effect of removing the medication is an increase in urges to approximately the same level at which they existed before drug-taking. Thus, progress made in adjusting a person's life during their drug-craving free period is extremely critical. Several authors have pointed to the critical involvement of work in keeping clients free of drug abuse (Boudin et al., 1977; Hall et al., in press; Vaillant, 1974). Because of this relationship, one of the key goals in any rehabilitation program must be the acquisition and maintenance of meaningful employment.

Employment Counseling and Training

Participation in the employment rehabilitation aspects of the program has been a reinforcer in Val's therapeutic contract. In order to earn his first employment counseling session, he has to take naltrexone for three weeks with no missed doses; he also cannot show any dirty urines during this period. Continuation in the program is contingent upon fulfillment of 80 percent of the stated responsibilities in the client's contract. By complying well with the outlined responsibilities, Val moves through the initial background information interviews into role playing for initial interviews with County Manpower Development Programs. Because he has no recorded work history, Val will be quite difficult to place in a job. However, another privilege to be earned in his contract is being accompanied by the job counselor on the trip to the county employment training interview. In addition, Val will go through a series of videotaped rehearsals of that first County interview. The therapist will role-play the behavior of the County personnel from past observations, so that role-playing sessions are likely to be fairly accurate.

Over the six sessions of employment counseling, Val learns how to fill out a job application and how to present his past history and further job desires during an employment interview. With the support of the job counselor, his history of successful naltrexone-taking, and a letter of recommendation from his therapist, Val is likely to become one of the few recent addicts to be accepted for the vocational rehabilitation program. However, Val has a court date before going into an interview for the vocational rehabilitation program.

Court

By fulfilling his responsibilities with the Project, Val has earned a letter to the court which describes his status in the program. As a bonus for excellent performance, Val has earned the right to have his counselor accompany him to court. The counselor sits with Val and will confer with the judge or testify, depending upon the desires of the judge. His representation of Val's progress is descriptive of past and current performance rather than predictive, since most courts have heard many unfulfilled promises of future performance. By describing Val's progress in the program to date and suggesting that the court review his further performance in the program on a periodic basis, the letter is effective in preventing a jail sentence at this time for Val. This is not always true, however, and the therapist often has to deal with the client's reaction to punishment meted out several months after an offense. Ironically, this sometimes means punishment is temporally tied to the client's most successful life adjustment to date. The suspended sentence placed upon Val requires involvement in a treatment program, but does not specify that treatment must be from the current program. This specification was made at the insistence of the counselor. It guarantees that Val will always have the option of seeking another program more to his liking rather than having to choose between involvement in the current program or jail. He is to be reviewed by the court once again in three months; a letter describing his performance in the program will be provided regardless of his performance, while the therapist will again appear in court if a stated level of excellent performance occurs.

If he chooses, Val can sign a waiver releasing his urine results to his probation officer. While this will be more convenient for him, he is cautioned that it may result in a court sentence if even one slip occurs later. That one slip may not be destructive to his therapeutic progress in the long run, but its mandatory release could result in a return to jail. Despite this danger, Val decides to sign over his urine reports in order to minimize contact with a probation officer he dislikes. By signing over his urine results, he can avoid interacting with the officer on a three-time per week basis, settling into a once-per-month routine instead.

Employment Counseling—Continued

With his court date finally in the past, Val is now free to become involved in the local manpower training program. He elects to do so immediately. With his record of two months of clean urines and the job counselors' recommendation behind him, he is able to become a client of a local manpower training program within three weeks. He enrolls in a landscape maintenance program which begins two weeks later and continues for six months at the local community college. He refuses the counselor's suggestion of involvement in an evening class in reading, apparently out of embarrassment at not having this basic skill. This suggestion is then shelved while other life issues are dealt with in the program.

Life-Management Training

A key issue for treatment success for Val is a recording of his activities on a day-to-day basis. These measures are taken in order to begin to decrease involvement with other addicts, to learn new recreational outlets for himself and his wife and, it turns out, to handle an increasingly serious problem with drinking.

Early sessions of life-management training are held during individual treatment sessions, although Val is targeted to later join ongoing weekly group sessions. Val has some severe interpersonal deficits with nondrug users. He makes little eye contact and speaks quite softly when forced to engage in such contact, but will avoid these contacts if at all possible. Therefore, his daily phone calls to the project contain information about how frequently he has interacted with drug users and how frequently he has interacted with nonusers since his last phone call. Val initially reports that he has no interactions with nonusers and that he has frequent interactions with users. In fact, he has become quite impressed with the fact that he can watch users fix without feeling any desire to join them. While he sees this as evidence that the drug has "cured" his addiction, the counselor is well aware of the likely results of this behavior when fading from naltrexone begins. Through a series of questions about how Val would feel in this situation without naltrexone, the counselor points out the danger in this activity. Changing from this group of friends means breaking ties with his sister's husband and friends who are also strung out.

Gentle questioning and confrontation appear successful. Val reports dropping these friends over time, and this is fairly well supported by his wife. Unfortunately, until he begins vocational training, Val sits at home drinking beer all day long. The goals of life-management training then become to increase involvement with nonaddicts and to increase the frequency of "straight" and nondrinking activities.

Role-plays of interactions with "straights" occur in the context of individual treatment sessions. In addition, there is discussion of who in the client's circle seems to be both straight and "all right." As Val joins the ongoing life-management group, he role-plays these interactions with other clients and hears what they are doing within their own lives to increase nondrug activities. One of the reinforcers earned on a contract now is a pair of tickets to a dance in the Chicano community center. One of the activities Val targets is helping with his son's basketball team, since the coach is one of the few straights with whom Val now feels comfortable. The coach in turn introduces Val to other friends over time. Thus, over a three-month period the number of activities and contacts with new "straight" friends is gradually acquired. Over time, Val reports increasingly liking his new friends. Some of these friends are clients in the clinic while others are community residents he has met through the basketball activities and the rehabilitation training in landscape. His alcohol problem has not ceased, however.

A rationale for controlled drinking (Sobell and Sobell, 1976) is presented to Val: that is, Val is told that he has acquired some bad habits in his drinking to date. It is pointed out that he has learned to drink fast and in many situations. The therapist points out that the way in which he drinks is the problem, rather than the fact that he is drinking. The therapist goes into Val's home on two nights and talks about pacing the act of drinking. On these occasions he has a beer with the client with the stipulation that the client is to model his rate of consumption on the therapist, and then practice that exaggerated slow rate in his other drinking. Self-monitoring drinking pace is established as a pinpoint that Val will now phone in to the Project, in addition to amount drunk. Surprisingly, this fairly simple intervention appears to work for Val. His report and his wife's report indicate a decreased rate of becoming drunk. While these results are encouraging, they are also cause for further monitoring of the client's drinking activities. As time passes in the program, Val is approaching six months on naltrexone. Since he is also approaching the point at which he will be eligible for help in setting up a small landscaping business, it is extremely critical that the fading from naltrexone be as successful as possible. In order to maximize the likelihood of this success, Val is introduced to a series of treatment sessions involving covert sensitization.

Covert Sensitization

The rationale for treatment with covert sensitization was presented to Val early in the program, but by the time it is to be introduced (after five months on naltrexone), Val is reluctant to undertake the therapy. He feels quite exuberant about his ability to resist heroin at this point, and covert sensitization seems unnecessary. Pointing out that everyone who has taken naltrexone for six months loses track of what it is like facing heroin without it, the therapist strongly urges the start of covert sensitization. Since contracts have come increasingly under Val's control, the therapist has to negotiate with Val for the start of treatment. In return for an acceleration in the start date of the naltrexone fading process, Val agrees to begin covert sensitization.

The scenes used in covert sensitization now depict Val as a landscaper who suddenly runs into old street friends unexpectedly: their suggestion to score together or to share a "taste" results in an initial desire to comply, but the scenes develop into aversive consequences of vomiting on himself, of watching an old street friend die with a needle stuck into his vein, of his wife's discovery of him, and of the court trial after being caught by the police. The most effective aversive contingencies turn out to be imagining leaving his children in the courtroom as he is taken to prison in handcuffs.

Therapy begins with the client experiencing no drug urges at all. It continues after he returns with a dirty urine from his first three-day holiday. The effects of slipping during this episode are shattering to Val; it reduces his belief that he can make it without the naltrexone but it also has the effect of increasing his motivation to participate in covert sensitization. Covert sensitization continues for a total of 12 sessions and increasingly involves scenes of successful avoidance of heroin offers. In addition, Val is given frequent assignments to use the covert sensitization imagery to deal with spontaneous drug urges. With Val's increased motivation, covert sensitization becomes an effective tool in his treatment.

Naltrexone Fading

Since clients appear to establish a clear discrimination between naltrexone and nonnaltrexone periods, they unfortunately experience little or no drug craving while taking the medication. This obviates any opportunity for extinction of drug cravings. As a result, fading is a very critical period for the success of naltrexone treatment programs, and timing the start of covert sensitization with the fading schedule of naltrexone is probably important.

For Val, his first three-day holiday from naltrexone was unsuccessful. It meant that he would take the drug once again for a full month before attempting another fading period. He was assured that slipping with heroin use was a learning experience, one which was probably necessary to insure complete success in the program. He reports ironically that the heroin use was not as pleasurable as he had expected. Further fading from naltrexone takes place on the following schedule: one month clean—three-day holiday clean; one week naltrexone—four-day holiday clean; one week naltrexone—five-day holiday; one week naltrexone—one-week holiday. After one more week on naltrexone, Val is removed from the active roster of naltrexone participants, almost nine months after starting treatment. He begins to fade his involvement with the project over this period as well. At six months' follow-up he provides a clean urine and reports that he is doing well, although drinking still occurs at a higher than desired rate. He reports successful job performance, corroborated by his employer. He also reports that he used heroin once again during this six-month period. It was enjoyable but he feels comfortable now refusing it. Only long-term follow-up will reveal whether Val has really been successful in his attempt to kick heroin, although the immediate measures seem promising. Nothing has been done on marriage counseling in line with Val's wishes and Val continues to live near users. His long-term follow-up remains unknown, but short-term results are encouraging.

Future Research Needs

This review of behavioral excursions into the problem of substance abuse, excluding alcoholism, leads to the discouraging acknowledgement that very little controlled research has been done to date. There are encouraging signs, however, with two large scale treatment outcome projects recently completed (Boudin et al., in press; Callahan et al., in press; Rawson et al., in press). At the point of this writing, however, neither of those research programs is funded. One is definitely no longer in existence while the second has been denied further funding twice and is seeking funds a third time. Since the treatment results of both of these intervention projects has been quite good, the problem involved indicates that the National Institute of Drug Abuse must make a long-term commitment to allow good quality research on heroin addiction. Vaillant (1974) points out that programs need a minimum of five years' follow-up data to assess their effects; as it stands, research grants are ordinarily allotted for three years, which is really only a warm-up phase for a large scale drug abuse program (see

Callahan et al., in press). Only with long-term funding can behavioral substance abuse research move from the uncontrolled case-study phase in which it has been mired through most of its relatively brief history.

It is still necessary to test the long-term outcome of behavioral techniques in unselected populations. While Boudin et al.'s (in press) results have been extremely impressive, they are obtained from an almost exclusively white population in an area whose most significant heroin addiction problem lies in the black community. It will be necessary to know what populations will seek out and respond to particular programs. It will also be necessary to follow the progress of those who do not elect treatment. Does "maturing out" occur (Winick, 1962)? Does "maturing out" eliminate drug problems as effectively as structured therapy? What side effects in adjustment take place? Are those clients treated subject to subtle increases in dependency such as witnessed in the 30-year follow-up of men treated in the Cambridge-Somerville project (McCord, 1978)?

Perhaps most importantly, there is need for further evaluation of behavioral interventions, when administered alone and when administered in the confines of a combined behavior modification-narcotic antagonist program. (See Tables 1–5 in the Appendix of this chapter for evaluations of various drug treatment programs for each behavioral strategy.) These results ought to be contrasted to results found in traditional therapeutic communities, and other forms of intervention. Dropout rates must be examined as well as successes with those completing treatment. Finally, there is a need to document the cost-efficacy of such programs, especially considering crime and other social costs.

Thus, the literature on the behavioral treatment of substance abuse is at a very primitive stage; in fact, it is probably more primitive in drug abuse than alcohol abuse. Crawford and Chalupsky (1977), however, remind us that the quality of research in treatment of alcoholism is making rudimentary but significant gains with the first controlled outcome studies appearing only in the last few years. Hopefully, increased efforts to research behavioral interventions into substance abuse will show a growth spurt parallel to that occurring in alcohol treatment. Indeed, there is also a need for integrative research on projects treating both sets of problems: many people, like Val, experience both problems. Some elegant explorations of treatment effects can no longer be considered because they would infringe upon the clients' ethical rights to choose their own treatment. This ethical requirement obviates true random assignments. The next section in this paper will now turn to consideration of this and related ethical issues.

ETHICAL ISSUES

Two levels of ethical issues are apparent in the area of behavioral intervention for substance abuse. The first is the global issue of whether society has the right to determine what substances an individual can put into his or her own body. The second set of issues is more immediate. Seeing that society has claimed the right to shape behavior in this area, new ethical issues arises within the parameters of how this shaping is to be done. Clinicians must wrestle with the former issue in their consciences and the latter issue in their practice.

Szasz (1974) is an eloquent spokesperson for the notion that society has no right to interfere in the individual's process of self-medication. He points out that the World Health Organization defines drug dependence in terms of the physical and psychological harm done by the drug to the individual. Szasz argues that society ought to adopt the position of John Stuart Mill that society does not have the right to prevent an individual from harming himself, only the right to prevent the individual from harming others. Interestingly, this review has shown that some of the cures undertaken also represent great potential harm to the client. Perhaps this intensive response to the problem is elicited by the frustration that relapsing clients evoke in the clinicians assigned to help them.

Phares (1975) examines this point of harm by pointing out that the financial cost to society in heroin addiction is a function of its illegality: before passage of the Harrison Act in 1914, a person could maintain an addiction to heroin for pennies a day. Only the high price of illegally distributed heroin creates a societal crisis or social harm. But what of the harm to the individual?

Risks from drugs to the individual appear to be a function of the unsanitary administration conditions (hypodermics cannot be legally sold), poor health care due to hustling, and overdose due to unpredictable quality of street drugs. Stacknik (1972) contends that each of these sources of harm to the individual could be removed by clearing the books of anti-drug legislation. Indeed, approaching the problem of drug dependence from this perspective leads to many of these conclusions. However, other factors need to be considered first.

Hoffman (1975) notes that the highest addiction rate in this country occurred in the years 1900–1914. He feels that legalization of even marijuana will produce a further bout of drug experimentation and dependence in this country. In addition, arguments on the safety of freely available drugs are based mainly on the medical effects of prolonged heroin maintenance. These effects, with freely available heroin, are fairly minimal. Drugs, such as amphetamines, do have extremely toxic effects mentally and physically if taken for prolonged periods. Thus, Hoffman argues that society has the obligation to protect its members from these dangers to themselves and the potential danger drug-dependent persons imply to their neighbors.

Examining the issue of alcohol use on similar lines, Brecher (1972) points out that more people in this country are addicted to alcohol than to any drug, other than nicotine. There are 5–9 million alcoholics in this country, many of whom become dangerous to themselves or others, and many of whom are committed from time to time to state hospitals. The damage done in car accidents and violence by people who have been drinking are equally impressive. Thus, Brecher feels that alcohol has the most impressive record of danger to the citizens of this country, and that to fail to ban its use while banning heroin and marijuana is illogical, if not ridiculous. However, he does not recommend such a ban because pragmatically, such a ban failed miserably during Prohibition. Instead he argues for legalization of other substances. That legalization does not now exist, however. The clinician is thus presented with a more immediate set of ethical issues with which to deal.

These other issues center on how control and treatment of drug usage is established and maintained. For example, the National Institute of Drug Abuse bans the use of federal funds for treatment of anyone who is coerced into treatment. This translates into a requirement that a client must not be offered treatment as the sole alternative to incarceration. Treatment versus jail is not seen as providing the client a real alternative. If at least one other treatment alternative can be provided, a program can treat a client under threat of jail. Ironically, this could result in a program being unable to offer treatment to a client because no other viable treatment alternative existed, a problem for some rural programs. Another difficult ethical issue involves the use of urine records for probation and court use.

Here again, the federal government offers guidelines to protect the rights of the client. The client's treatment records are guaranteed confidential; they need not be turned over to courts or probation offices. However, urine records provide potentially valuable feedback to the court and probation systems that a client is in treatment and doing well. Clients can voluntarily sign over access to those records. The contingency of jail for too many dirty urines would pragmatically provide one of the most effective contingencies to maintain drug-free behavior, but ethically what is the clinician's behavior to be?

It is perhaps possible for the clinician to solve this issue through keeping confidential urine records which can be used to determine program status at a given point in time. The program could then determine how many dirty urines would result in the expulsion of a given client, and return that client to the court-treatment system for further adjudication, if any. Despite fears of an over-effective court system, most probation offices and court systems are quite slow in acting on those who drop out of or are expelled from treatment. Those individuals are not sent to jail immediately upon leaving treatment, and in fact jail is often not related to current behavior. These and other ethical issues will continue to arise in our examination of the treatment of substance abusers as our attention is directed to the problem more intensely.

CONCLUSION

Behavior modification for substance abuse is gradually moving beyond its single case infancy into an adolescence marked by more thorough assessment, more empathetic and comprehensive treatment, as well as more rigorous experimental design. Because of problems with regional population differences, behavioral treatment strategies will never be uniformly applied nor are uniform results likely to ensue. In light of these considerations, pursuit of experimental excellence is probably premature in a treatment area where the only hopeful long-term follow-up of heroin treatment results are recent. Boudin et al. (in press) report that 77 percent of their white population was still clean over three years, while Rawson et al. (in press) report that 48 percent of their racially mixed population was clean at one year follow-up. Treatment in this latter case involved both narcotic antagonist and behavior therapy. While these results offer encouragement for behavioral efforts, they do not suggest that the field's most urgent need is to develop more sophisticated experimental research. They do imply the need to develop more programs which effectively demonstrate control of the most recalcitrant substance abuse problems (e.g., heroin addiction), especially in the most disadvantaged populations (minorities). Indeed, they imply the need for primary prevention efforts to insure education and job opportunities for these populations (Callahan and Rawson, in press). Otherwise, the pursuit of effective secondary treatment procedures becomes a technology devoted to building better tools to shovel sand against the tide. Indeed, the tide must be stemmed earlier, first by clear and consistent definition of social values (i.e., what is drug abuse), and secondly, by social structuring to prevent its occurrence. Only when prevention and treatment efforts are made in synchrony is the problem very likely to be altered.

SUMMARY

Clinicians are currently caught in a constrictive web as they attempt to deal with clients who are labelled substance abusers. This chapter attempts to explore the make-up of social and interpersonal aspects of that web, and to suggest viable treatment strategies to the clinician as well.

It is important to realize that the use of chemical substances has been a part of every known society through recorded history. The particular substance(s) chosen for use appears to be influenced mainly by what substances grow naturally in a given area. Over time, societies usually develop rituals around substances' use which prevent abuse. There are particular times when a society is most susceptible to abuse of a substance, however: when a new substance is introduced to a society, when a familiar substance is used in a new way, and when members of society live temporarily in another society, abusing its known substances. Increased stress found in industrialized societies appears to bring increased problems with substances as well.

On an individual basis, substance abuse can be defined by law (de jure), or by an analysis of the effects of use of the substance on an individual's behavior. De jure, some substances are always substances of abuse (marijuana, heroin); others are substances which can be abused when not prescribed by a physician (valium, quaaludes); still others can never be abused de jure (nicotine, caffeine). By examining the effects of a substance on an individual's behavior, conflicting definitions of substance abuse can result. The clinician is affected by this discrepancy because the law will influence who seeks treatment.

Theories on how an individual becomes an abuser are reviewed, ranging from genetic to intrapsychic to learning. Learning theories are then presented fairly extensively covering modeling, classical conditioning, and operant conditioning. From these theories of etiology, basic strategies for intervention result.

Treatment procedures for substance abuse are reviewed historically by strategy. Early behavioral treatments portray substance abuse as a single behavior—ingestion of a substance. Consequently, early treatment focuses primarily on suppressing substance intake by various means: systematic desensitization to reduce anxiety thought to precede drug-taking; classical conditioning using emetic drugs, apneic drugs, or electric shock; operant punishment procedures; and operant reward procedures.

Later behavioral treatment efforts differ in two significant ways: (1) the locus of treatment moves increasingly into the natural environment; and (2) the target behaviors broaden to include interpersonal skills, employment skills, and individualized ancillary treatments as needed. Specialized behavioral drug treatment clinics come into existence and long-term controlled outcome studies are undertaken in the area of heroin addiction.

Two long-term studies are highlighted: The Drug Project of Gainesville, Florida (a contingency contracting program), and the HALT (Heroin Antagonist and Learning Therapy) Project of Oxnard, California (providing behavioral and psychopharmaceutical treatments). Treatment methodologies of both programs are described and a case example details their application.

Treatments include: the use of contingency contracts to systematically reward behaviors incompatible with drug use and punish drug use; urinalysis to monitor substance use; self-monitoring of behaviors related to substance abuse; employment interviewing skills training; taking of a narcotic antagonist (naltrexone) to prevent the euphoric high from taking opiates; life-management training to change from a substance abuse lifestyle; and verbal aversion therapy to decrease the desire to seek and use heroin. The case of Val, a young unemployed Chicano, is used to illustrate the treatment procedures.

Ethical issues are discussed as they impinge on the behavior of the clinician treating substance abuse. Needs for further clinical and research development are reviewed, and the issue of prevention as alternative strategy is raised.

NOTE

1. Many detoxification programs lose a large proportion of the clients as soon as methadone is withdrawn. These clients often return to their homes with high levels of physiological disturbance and psychological cravings due to their recent methadone withdrawal.

REFERENCES

Anant, S. A note on the treatment of alcoholics by a verbal aversion technique. *Canadian Psychologist,* 1967, *80,* 19–22.

Aron, W. S. and Daily, D. W. Graduates and splittees from therapeutic drug treatment programs: A comparison. *International Journal of Addictions,* 1976, *11,* 1–18.

Ausubel, D. P. Causes and types of narcotic addiction: A psychosocial view. *Psychiatric Quarterly,* 1961, *35,* 523–31.

Azrin, H. H. and Holz, W. C. Punishment. In W. K. Honig, ed. *Operant Behavior.* New York: Appleton-Century-Crofts, 1966.

Babor, T. F., Meyer, R. E., Mirin, S. M. et al. Behavioral and social effects of heroin self-administration and withdrawal. *Archives of General Psychiatry,* 1976, *33,* 363–367.

Bandura, A. *Principles of behavior modification.* New York: Holt, Rinehart and Winston, 1969.

Barlow, D. H., Agras, W. S. and Leitenberg, H. Experimental control of sexual deviation through manipulation of the noxious scene in covert sensitization. *Journal of Abnormal Psychology,* 1969, *74,* 597–601.

Becker, H. On becoming a marijuana user. *American Journal of Sociology,* 1953, *59,* 238–243.

Blachly, P. H. An electric needle for aversive conditioning of the needle ritual, 1971, *6,* 327–328.

Blanchard, E. B., Libet, J. M. and Young, L. D. Apneic aversion and covert sensitization in the treatment of hydrocarbon inhalation addiction: A case study. *Journal of Behavior Therapy and Experimental Psychiatry.* 1973, *4,* 383–387.

Boudin, H. M. Contingency contracting as a therapeutic tool in the deceleration of amphetamine use. *Behavior Therapy,* 1972, *3,* 604–605.

Boudin, H. M. and Valentine, V. E. Contingency contracting: A major treatment modality for drug abuse. Paper presented at Sixth Annual Meeting of the Association for Advancement of Behavior Therapy, New York, 1972.

Boudin, H. M., Valentine, V. E., Ingraham, R. D. et al. Contingency contracting with drug abusers in the natural environment. *The International Journal of the Addictions,* 1977, *12,* 1–16.

Boudin, H. M., Valentine, V. E., Ruiz, M. R., and Regan, E. J. Contingency contracting for drug addiction: An outcome evaluation. In L. Sobell and M. C. Sobell (Eds.), *Treatment outcome evaluation in alcohol and drug abuse.* New York: Pergamon Press, in press.

Bowden, C. L., and Maddux, J. F. Methadone maintenance: Myth and reality. *Scientific Proceedings of the 125th Annual Meeting of the American Psychiatric Association,* 1972, 243–44.

Brecher, E. M. et al., eds. *Licit and illicit drugs,* Toronto: Little, Brown and Company, 1972.

Bridell, D. W. and Nathan, P. E. Behavioral assessment and modification with alcoholics: Current status and future trends. In M. Hersen, P. Miller and R. Eisler, eds., *Progress in behavior modification,* vol. 2, New York: Academic Press, 1976.

Burroughs, W. *Junkie,* New York: Ace Publishing, 1953.

Cahoon, P. and Crosby, C. A learning approach to chronic drug use: Sources of reinforcement. *Behavior Therapy,* 1972, *3,* 64–71.

Callahan, E. J. Covert sensitization for homosexuality. In I. Krumbholtz and C. E. Thoreson. *Behavioral counseling techniques,* New York: Holt, Rinehart & Winston, 1976, 234–45.

Callahan, E. J. and Leitenberg, H. Aversion therapy for sexual deviation: Covert sensitization and contingent shock. *Journal of Abnormal Psychology,* 1973, *81,* 60–73.

Callahan, E. J. and Rawson, R. A. Behavioral assessment of narcotic addiction and treatment outcome. In L. C. Sobell and M. B. Sobell, eds.,

Treatment outcome evaluation in alcohol and drug abuse. New York: Pergamon Press, in press.

Callahan, E. J., Rawson, R. A., Glazer, M. et al. Comparison of two naltrexone treatment programs: Naltrexone alone versus naltrexone plus behavior therapy. In D. Julius and P. Renault, eds., *Narcotic antagonists: Naltrexone*, Washington, D.C.: NIDA Research Monograph, 1976, 150–157.

Callahan, E. J., Rawson, R. A., Arias, R. J. et al. Treatment of heroin addiction: Naltrexone alone and with behavior therapy. *International Journal of the Addictions*, in press.

Cameron, D. C. Addiction—current issues. *American Journal of Psychiatry* 1961, *35*, 523–31.

Cautela, J. R. Treatment of compulsive behavior by covert sensitization. *Psychological Record*, 1966, *16*, 33–41.

Crawford, J. J. and Chalupsky, A. B. The reported evaluation of alcoholism treatments, 1968–1971: A methodological review. *Addictive Behaviors*, 1977, *2*, 63–74.

Crowley, T. J. The reinforcers for drug abuse: Why people take drugs. *Comprehensive Psychiatry*, 1972, *13*, 51–62.

de Angelis, G. G. *Testing and screening for drugs of abuse.* New York: Dekker, 1976.

Dole, V. P. and Nyswander, M. A. Medical treatment for diaretyl morphine (heroin) addiction. *Journal of the American Medical Association*, 1965, *193*, 645–56.

Duehn, W. D. and Shannon, C. Covert sensitization in the public high school: Short term treatment of male adolescent drug abusers. Paper presented at the 100th Annual Forum of the National Conference on Social Welfare. Atlantic City, 1973.

Elkin, T. E., Williams, J. G., Barlow, P. H. and Stewart, W. R. Measurement and modification of intravenous drug abuse: A preliminary study using succinyl choline. Unpublished manuscript, University of Mississippi Medical School, 1974.

Epstein, L., Parker, and Jenkins, C. A multiple baseline analysis of treatment for heroin addiction. *Addictive Behaviors*, 1976, *1*, 327–30.

Eriksson, J. H., Götestam, K. G., Melin, L. and Ost, L. A token economy treatment of drug addiction. *Behaviour Research and Therapy*, 1975, *13*, 113–126.

Ewing, J. A., Rouse, B. A. and Pellizari, E. D. Alcohol sensitivity and ethnic background. *American Journal of Psychiatry*, 1974, *131*, 206–10.

Eysenck, H. and Rachman, S. *The causes and cures of neurosis.* London: Routledge and Kegan Paul, 1965.

Falk, S. L. The nature and determinants of adjunctive behavior. In R. M. Gilbert and J. D. Keehn, eds. *Schedule effects: Drugs, drinking and aggression.* Toronto: University of Toronto Press, 1972.

Falk, S. L. and Samson, H. H. Schedule-induced physical dependence on ethanol. *Psychopharmacological Reviews*, 1976, *27*, 449–64.

Garlington, W. K. and DeRicco, D. A. The effect of modelling on drinking rate. *Journal of Applied Behavior Analysis,* 1977, *10,* 207–11.

Glasscote, R. M. et al. *The treatment of drug abuse: Programs, problems, prospects.* Washington: Joint Information Services of the American Psychiatric Association and the National Association for Mental Health, 1972.

Glicksman, M., Ottomanelli, G. and Cutler, R. The earn-your-way credit system: Use of a token economy in narcotic rehabilitation. *International Journal of the Addictions,* 1971, *6,* 525–531.

Goldberg, R. J., Greenwood, I. C. and Taintor, A. Alpha conditioning as adjunct for drug dependence: Part I. *International Journal of the Addictions,* 1976, *11,* 1085–89.

Goldstein, A. and Brown, B. W. Urine testing schedules in methadone maintenance treatment of heroin addiction. *Journal of the American Medical Association,* 1970, *214,* 311–15.

Goodwin, D. W. Is alcoholism hereditary? A review and critique. *Archives of General Psychiatry,* 1971, *23,* 545–49.

Götestam, K. G. and Melin, L. Covert extinction of amphetamine addiction. *Behavior Therapy,* 1974, *5,* 90–92.

Götestam, K. G., Melin, L. and Ost, L. Behavior modification techniques in the treatment of drug addiction. Paper presented at 3rd European Congress on Behavior Modification, Amsterdam: 1973.

Hall, S., Loeb, P., Norton, J. and Yang, R. Improving vocational placement in drug treatment clients: A pilot study. *Addictive Behaviors,* 1977, *2,* 227–234.

Himmelsbach, C. K. Clinical studies of drug addiction: Physical dependence, withdrawal and recovery. *Archives of Internal Medicine,* 1942, *69,* 766–772.

Hoffman, F. G. Drug abuse and the law. In F. G. Hoffman, ed. *A handbook on drug and alcohol abuse.* New York: Oxford University Press, 1975, 294–316.

Hurzeler, M., Gerwirtz, D. and Kleber, H. Varying clinical contexts for administering naltrexone. In D. Julius and P. Renault, eds. *Narcotic antagonists: Naltrexone.* Research Monograph, Washington, D.C. N.I.D.A., 1976, 48–66.

Kanfer, F. H. and Saslow, G. Behavioral diagnosis. In C. Frank, ed. *Assessment and status of the behavior therapies.* New York: McGraw-Hill, 1969.

Kolvin, I. "Aversive imagery" treatment in adolescence. *Behaviour Research and Therapy,* 1967, *5,* 245–248.

Kraft, T. Successful treatment of a case of Drinamyl addiction. *The British Journal of Psychiatry,* 1968, *114,* no. 516.

Kraft, T. Treatment of Drinamyl addiction. *The International Journal of the Addictions,* March, 1969, *4,* 59–64.

Kraft, T. Successful treatment of a case of chronic barbiturate addiction. *British Journal of Addictions,* 1969, vol. *64,* 115–120.

Kraft, T. Successful treatment of 'Drinamyl' addicts and associated personality changes. *Canadian Psychiatric Association Journal,* 1970, vol. 15.

Kraft, T. Treatment of Drinamyl addiction. *The Journal of Nervous and Mental Disease,* 1970, *150,* (2).

Kram, L. A clinical tool with heroin addicts: The urine stall. *International Journal of the Addictions,* 1975, *10,* 633–641.

Leitenberg, H., Rawson, R. A. and Bath, K. Reinforcement of competing behavior during extinction. *Science,* 1970, *169,* 301–303.

Liberman, R. P. Aversive conditioning of a drug addict: A pilot study. *Behaviour Research and Therapy,* 1968, *6,* 229–31.

Little, L. M. and Curran, J. P. Covert sensitization: A clinical procedure in need of some explanations. *Psychological Bulletin,* 1978, *85,* 513–531.

Lubetkin, B. and Fishman, S. Electrical aversion therapy with a chronic heroin user. *Journal of Behavior Therapy and Experimental Psychiatry,* 1974, *5,* 193–197.

MacDonough, T. S. The relative effectiveness of a medical hospitalization program *vs* a feedback behavior modification program in treating alcohol and drug abusers. *International Journal of the Addictions,* 1976, *11,* 269–82.

Maletzky, B. M. "Assisted" covert sensitization for drug abuse. *International Journal of the Addictions,* 1974, *9,* 411–429.

Maletzky, B. M. and Klotter, J. Addiction to diazepam. *International Journal of the Addictions,* 1976, *11,* 95–116.

Maslow, A. H. *Toward a psychology of being.* New York: Van Nostrand, 1962.

Maurer, D. W. and Vogel, V. H. *Narcotics and narcotic addiction.* Springfield, Il.: C. C. Thomas, 1974.

McCord, J. A thirty year follow-up of treatment effects. *American Psychologist,* 1978, *33,* 284–9.

McNamee, H. B., Mirin, S. M., Kuhnle, J. C., and Meyer, R. E. Affective changes in chronic opiate users. *British Journal of Addiction,* 1976, *71,* 275–280.

Melin, G. L. and Götestam, K. G. A contingency management program on a drug-free unit for intravenous amphetamine addicts. *Journal of Behavior Therapy and Experimental Psychiatry,* 1973, *4,* 331–337.

Merry, J. A social history of heroin addiction. *British Journal of Addiction,* 1975, *70,* 307–10.

Meyer, S. M., Mirin, R. E., Altman, J. L., McNamee, B. A behavioral paradigm for the evaluation of narcotic antagonists. *Archives of General Psychiatry,* 1976, *33,* 371–77.

Miller, P. M. *Behavioral treatment of alcoholism,* New York: Pergamon, 1976.

Mirin, S. M., Meyer, R. E. and McNamee, B. Psychopathology and mood during heroin use: Acute *vs* chronic effects. *Archives of General Psychiatry,* 1976, *33,* 1503–80.

Nathan, P. E. and O'Brien, J. S. An experimental analysis of the behavior of alcoholics and non-alcoholics during prolonged experimental drinking: A necessary precursor of behavior therapy? *Behavior Therapy,* 1971, *2,* 455–476.

Nightingale, S., Michaux, W. W. and Platt, P. C. Clinical implications of urine surveillance in a methadone maintenance program. *International Journal of the Addictions,* 1972, *7,* 403–14.

Ng., L.K.Y. and Bunney, W. E. On understanding and treating narcotic dependence: A neuropharmacological perspective. *British Journal of the Addictions,* 1975, *70,* 311–24.

Nurnberger, J. I. and Zimmerman, J. Applied analysis of human behavior: An alternative to conventional motivational inferences and unconscious determination in therapeutic programming. *Behavior Therapy,* 1970, *1,* 59–69.

O'Brien, C. P. "Needle Freaks"—psychological dependence on shooting up. *Medical World News Review,* 1974, *1,* 35–6.

O'Brien, C. P., Testa, T., O'Brien, T. J. et al. Conditioned narcotic withdrawal in humans. *Science,* 1977, *195,* 1000–1002.

O'Brien, C. P., Testa, T., O'Brien, T. J., and Greenstein, R. Conditioning in human opiate addicts. *Pavlovian Journal of Biological Sciences,* 1976, *11,* 195–202.

O'Brien, J., Raynes, A. and Patch, V. D. An operant reinforcement system to improve ward behavior in inpatient drug addicts. *Journal of Behavior Therapy and Experimental Psychiatry,* 1971, *2,* 239–42.

Ottomanelli, G. A. Follow-up of a token economy applied to civilly committed narcotic addicts. *International Journal of Addictions,* 1976, *11,* 793–806.

Pahnke, W. N., Kurland, A. A., Unger, S. et al. The experimental use of Psychedelic (LSD) Therapy. *Journal of the American Medical Association,* 1970, *212,* 1856–63.

Phares, P. Between a rock and a hard place: What t'do about smack. *Journal of Psychedelic Drugs,* 1975, *7,* 59–71.

Platt, J. J., Hoffman, A. R., and Ebert, R. K. Recent trends in the demography of heroin addiction among youthful offenders. *International Journal of the Addictions,* 1976, *11,* 221–36.

Polakow, R. L. and Doctor, R. M. Treatment of marijuana and barbiturate dependency by contingency contracting. *Journal of Behavioral Therapy and Experimental Psychiatry,* 1973, *4,* 375–77.

Pomerleau, O. F., Pertschuk, M., Adkins, D. and Brady, J. P. Comparison of behavioral and traditional treatment for problem drinking. In M. B. Sobell and L. C. Sobell, *Outcome evaluation of alcohol and drug abuse programs.* New York: Plenum, in press.

Quinton, E. Correlation between polydrug abuse and alpha density. *Addictive Behaviors,* 1976, *1,* 133–38.

Rachman, S. and Teasdale, J. *Aversion therapy and behavior disorders: An analysis.* Coral Gables: University of Miami Press, 1969.

Rason, R. W. Narcotic addicts: Personality characteristics and hospital treatment. In P. Hoch and J. Zubin, eds., *Psychopathology of communication.* New York: Grune & Stratton, 1958.

Rawson, R. A., Callahan, E. J., Glazer, M. A., and Liberman, R. P. Behavior therapy *versus* naltrexone for heroin addiction. In N. Krasnegor, ed., *Behavioral treatment of the addictions.* Washington, D.C.: N.I.D.A., Research Monograph, in press.

Raymond, M. J. The treatment of addiction by aversion conditioning with apomorphine. *Behavior Research and Therapy,* 1964, *1,* 287–691.

Reynolds, G. S. *A primer of operant conditioning.* Glenview, Ill.: Scott, Foresman, 1968.

Robins, L. N. A follow-up of Vietnam drug users. Washington: Special Action Office for Drug Abuse Prevention, 1973.

Robins, L. N., and Murphey, G. E. Drug use in a normal population of young Negro men. *American Journal of Public Health,* 1967, *57,* 1580–96.

Rubenstein, C. Treatment of morphine addiction in turberculosis by Pavlov's conditioning method. *American Review of Turberculosis,* 1931, *24,* 682–5.

Schaefer, H., Sobell, M. B. and Mills, K. C. Baseline drinking behavior: Kinds of sips and sip magnitude. *Behavior Research and Therapy,* 1971, *9,* 23–27.

Seeyers, M. H. Medical perspectives on habituation and addiction. *Journal of the American Medical Association,* 1962, *181,* 92–98.

Sessions, K. B. Maintenance or suppression? A comparative look at the heroin addiction policies of Great Britain and the United States. *British Journal of Addiction,* 1976, *71,* 385–9.

Skinner, B. F. *The behavior of organisms.* New York: Appleton-Century-Crofts, 1938.

Smart, R. G. and Cutler, R. E. The alcohol advertising ban in British Columbia. *British Journal of the Addictions,* 1976, *71,* 12–21.

Smart, R. G. and Schmidt, W. Drinking and problems from drinking after a reduction in the minimum drinking age. *British Journal of Addiction,* 1975, *70,* 347–58.

Sobell, M. B. and Sobell, L. C. A brief technical report on the MOBAT: An inexpensive portable test for determining blood alcohol concentration. *Journal of Applied Behavior Analysis,* 1975, *8,* 117–120.

Sobell, M. B. and Sobell, L. C. Assessment of addictive behavior. In M. Hersen and A. Bellack, eds., *Behavioral Assessment—A practical handbook.* New York: Pergamon Press, 1976.

Stachnik, T. J. The case against criminal penalties for illicit drug use. *American Psychologist,* 1972, *27,* 637–42.

Stein, C. *Games alcoholics play.* New York: Ballantine Books, 1971.

Steinfeld, G. The use of covert sensitization with institutionalized narcotic addicts. *International Journal of the Addictions,* 1970, *5,* 225–32.

Steinfeld, G., Ratiou, E. A., Rice, A. H. and Egan, M. J. Group covert sensitization with narcotic addicts (further comments). *The International Journal of the Addictions,* 1974, *9,* 427–43.

Stitzer, M., Bigelow, G., Lawrence, L. et al. Medication take home as a reinforcer. *Addictive Behaviors,* 1977, *2,* 9–14.

Sulkunen, P. Production, consumption and recent changes of consumption of alcoholic beverages. *British Journal of the Addictions,* 1976, *71,* 3–11.

Szasz, T. The ethics of addiction. In W. White and R. F. Albano, eds., *North American Symposium on Drug Abuse.* Philadelphia: North American Publishing, 1974, 105–111.

Tharp, R. and Wetzel, J. *Behavior modification in the natural environment.* New York: Academic Press, 1969.

Thomson, I. G. and Rathod, N. H. Aversion therapy for heroin dependence. *The Lancet,* 1968, *2,* 382–84.

Thorndike, E. L. *The psychology of learning.* New York: Teachers College. Columbia University, 1913.

Vaillant, G. E. Outcome research in narcotic addiction: Problems and perspectives. *American Journal of Drug and Alcohol Abuse,* 1974, *1,* 25–36.

Wiggenhorn, A., McEveny, S., Benjamin, A. and Buese, E. Walden II—A multidimensional drug treatment project. Unpublished manuscript. Hollywood, Ca., 1974.

Wikler, A. A psychodynamic study of a patient during experimental self-regulated readdiction to morphine. *Psychiatric Quarterly,* 1952, *26,* 270–293.

Wikler, A. Conditioning factors in opiate addiction and relapse. In D. Wilner and G. Kassenbaum, eds., *Narcotics.* New York: McGraw-Hill, 1965.

Wikler, A. Dynamics of drug dependence: Implications of a conditioning theory for research and treatment. In S. Fischer and A. M. Freedman, eds., *Opiate addiction: Origins and treatment.* New York: Wiley, 1973, 7–22.

Wikler, A. and Pescor, F. T. Persistence of "relapse-tendencies" of rats previously made physically dependent on morphine. *Psychopharmacologia,* 1970, *16,* 375–48.

Winick, C. Maturing out of narcotic addiction. *U.N. Bulletin of Narcotics,* 1962, *14,* 1–7.

Wisocki, P. The successful treatment of heroin addict by covert conditioning techniques. *Journal of Behavior Therapy and Experimental Psychiatry,* 1973, *4,* 55–61.

Wolpe, J. Conditioned inhibition of craving in drug addiction. *Behaviour Research and Therapy,* 1965, *2,* 285–7.

Yablonsky, J. *The tunnel back: Synanon.* New York: Macmillan, 1965.

APPENDIX

Evaluation of Drug Treatment Programs

Table 1. *Systematic desensitization*

Treatment Author	Subjects	Drug Use	Procedures		Design and Control
T. Kraft, 1968	5	Varied	Systematic desensitization to social anxiety preceding drug use		Uncontrolled case reports
T. Kraft, 1969(b)	2	Drinamyl	Systematic desensitization to social anxiety preceding drug use		Uncontrolled case reports
T. Kraft, 1970	1	Drinamyl	Systematic desensitization to social anxiety preceding drug use		Uncontrolled case reports
T. Kraft, 1969(a)	1	Barbiturates	Systematic desensitization to social anxiety preceding drug use		Uncontrolled case reports

Results Author	Assessment Method	Results	
T. Kraft, 1968	Self-report	Hard data:	None
T. Kraft, 1969(b)	Self-report	Hard data:	No data given
		Soft data:	Nine-month follow-up with no reported drug use
T. Kraft, 1970	Self-report	Hard data:	None
		Soft data:	Self-report of ability to cope with social situations
T. Kraft, 1969(a)	Self-report	Hard data:	Clinical Response—Patient no longer required medication during the day, but required 3 grains tuinal at night.

Table 2. Chemical aversion therapy

Author	Subjects	Drug Use	Procedures	Concurrent Treatment	Design and Control
M. J. Raymond, 1964	1	Physeptone (addicted)	Classical conditioning Aversive pairing of apomorphine-induced nausea with self-injection of physeptone	6 months of outpatient care after aversive conditioning treatment	Case report
R. P. Liberman, 1968	2	Paregoric and heroin addiction	Classical conditioning Aversive pairing of apomorphine-induced nausea with self-injection of morphine	Supportive psychotherapy: residential treatment, milieu setting	Case reports with placebo challenge to test the presence of cr
I. G. Thompson, 1968 N. H. Rathod	19	Heroin dependence	Self-injection of heroin paired with respiratory paralysis produced by sunamethonium chloride (scoline)		Group outcome study with a "control group" which went through the same without drug (N = 6) and Ss who dropped out of aversion (N = 3)

Table 2. *(Continued)*

Treatment				
Author	Subjects	Drug Use	Procedures	Concurrent Treatment	Design and Control

Author	Subjects	Drug Use	Procedures	Concurrent Treatment	Design and Control
E. J. Blanchard, 1973 J. M. Libet L. D. Young	1	Hydrocarbon inhalation addiction (paint-sniffing)	Apneic aversion and covert sensitization	Follow-up treatment given weekly 4 months after covert sensitization and apneic aversion treatment consisting of (1) psychological support, (2) counseling on current life problem, (3) role-playing.	Single Case Report
T. E. Elkin, unpublished J. G. Williams D. H. Barlow W. R. Stewart	2	Intravenous drug abuse (heroin and amphetamines)	Chemical treatment (succinyl choline)	Videotapes	2 placebo control in one case; A-B design

Table 2. *(Continued)*

Results

		Immediate Results		Follow-up Results	
Author	Assessment Method	Drug-related Behavior	Other Behavior	Drug-related Behavior	Other Behavior
M. J. Raymond, 1964	Self-report	No further drug use reported		Abstinent	
R. P. Liberman, 1968	Self-report	One patient relapsed shortly after treatment ended		One patient drug-free by self-report at 1-year follow-up	
I. G. Thompson, 1968 N. H. Rathod	Urinalysis; self-report	Patient reports no longer needing drug (craving of drug but afraid to use it)		8 of 10 released Ss free of drugs on urinalysis at 8-month follow-ups (only one or two instances of dirty urines in other two); one S arrested with cannabis and amphetamines; control group all relapsed	Employment record of experimental group good

Table 2. *(Continued)*

Results

| Author | Assessment Method | Immediate Results | | Follow-up Results | |
		Drug-related Behavior	Other Behavior	Drug-related Behavior	Other Behavior
E. J. Blanchard, 1973 J. M. Libet L. D. Young	Counselor report; self-report; use of smell test and free access test	Elimination of paint-sniffing	Improved social relations	At 1 year follow-up, counselor reported S to be free from paint-sniffing; self-report of "occasional" lighter fluid inhalation	Improved social relations and steady full-time job
T. E. Elkin, unpublished J. G. Williams D. H. Barlow W. R. Stewart	Physiological response to videotape of shooting up; self-report; card sort	Decreased physiological response; S_1 left treatment after two sessions		S_1 at 12-month follow-up reported no IV drug use; for S_2, 6-month follow-up anecdotal data suggested no longer using heroin (S_1 reports continuing to fix others, but not self)	

Table 3. *Electrical aversion therapy*

Treatment

Author	Subjects	Drug Use	Procedures	Concurrent Treatment	Design and Control
J. Wolpe, 1965	1	Demerol addiction	Therapist- and self-administered shock for demerol stimuli craving	None	Case report anecdotal
J. S. O'Brien, 1970 A. E. Raynes	3	Heroin ingestion	Added late in treatment after evidence of relapse; fantasies–shock, covert sensitization, relaxation with instructor to generalize s.d.	Help with jobs, living problems	Multiple reports
J. S. O'Brien, 1972 A. E. Raynes V. D. Patch	2	Heroin addiction	Shock for fantasy, covert sensitization, relaxation training, and systematic desensitization	No data given	Multiple case reports

Table 3. *(Continued)*

Results

| Author | Assessment Method | Immediate Results | | Follow-up Results | |
		Drug-related Behavior	Other Behavior	Drug-related Behavior	Other Behavior
J. Wolpe, 1965	Self-report	Electric shock suppressed real world urges until shocker broke down		Patient was transferred to another therapist during treatment	No follow-up provided
J. S. O'Brien, 1970 A. E. Raynes	Self-report	One dropout (later returned); other two Ss drug-free		One drug-free for 6 months; 1 drug-free for 9 months	
J. S. O'Brien, 1972 A. E. Raynes V. D. Patch	Family reports; self-reports			No further needle tracks; family reports and self-reports indicate no further drug use	

Table 4. *Covert sensitization*

Treatment

Author	Subjects	Drug Use	Procedures	Concurrent Treatment	Design and Control
Kolvin, 1967	1	Gasoline (inhalation)	Covert sensitization	None	Single case study
S. S. Anant, 1968	1 drug addict; 25 alcoholics	Alcoholism and/or drug addiction	Relaxation and verbal aversion therapy	No data given	Group outcome study
S. O'Brien, 1970 E. Raynes	3	Heroin	Fantasies-shock; covert sensitization relaxation with instruction to generalize s.d.	Help with jobs and living problems	Multiple anecdotal case study
S. O'Brien, 1972 E. Raynes V. D. Patch	2	Heroin	Shock for fantasy, covert sensitization, relaxation training, and systematic desensitization	No data given	Case reports
W. D. Duehn, 1973 C. Shannon	7	LSD	Group covert sensitization	None	Group outcome study
E. J. Blanchard, 1973 J. M. Libet L. D. Young	1	Hydrocarbon inhalation addiction (paint-sniffing)	Apneic aversion and covert sensitization	Follow-up treatment given weekly 4 months after covert sensitization and apneic aversion treatment consist-	Single case report

Table 4. *(Continued)*

Treatment

Author	Subjects	Drug Use	Procedures	Concurrent Treatment	Design and Control
				ing of (1) psychological support, (2) counseling on "current life problems," (3) role playing	
P. A. Wisocki, 1973	1	Heroin	Covert sensitization, covert reinforcement, assertive training, relaxation, and systematic desensitization	None	Single case report
B. S. Lubetkin, 1974 S. T. Fishman	1	Heroin	Imagery plus electrical aversion	No data given	Anecdotal case report
G. J. Steinfield, 1974 E. A. Rautio A. H. Rice M. B. Egan	8	Narcotic addiction	Patients were trained in relaxation therapy with covert sensitization in group session	Therapeutic community counseling	Single group outcome study
B. M. Maletzky, 1975	10 exp. 10 con.	Variety of drugs abused from cigarettes to heroin	Treatment group received assisted covert sensitization plus individual counseling	Antabus used with all alcohol patients in both groups	Controlled group outcome study

Table 4. *(Continued)*

Treatment

Author	Subjects	Drug Use	Procedures	Concurrent Treatment	Design and Control
Epstein, Parker, Jenkins, 1976	1 24-year-old black male	Heroin	*Covert sensitization:* drug use and urges (a) aversive component—scene presentation subject became nauseous when he approached drug-taking; (b) relaxation component—subject felt good after turning away from drug-taking *Contingency contracting:* financial management and clean urines	None specified	Single subject multiple baseline design across behaviors

Table 4. *(Continued)*

Results

		Immediate Results		Follow-up Results	
Author	Assessment Method	Drug-related Behavior	Other Behavior	Drug-related Behavior	Other Behavior
I. Kolvin, 1967	Self-reports	Cessation of gasoline inhalation		13 months follow-up no further gas-sniffing	
S. S. Anant, 1968	Self-reports	Abstention from drugs and alcoholic beverages		9 months follow-up all clean	
S. O'Brien, 1970 E. Raynes	Family reports	Ceased heroin use			
S. O'Brien, 1972 E. Raynes V. D. Patch	Family reports Self-reports	No further needle tracks; No further drug use			
E. F. Duehn, 1973 C. Shannon	Self-reports	No further drug use		At 6-month and 18-month follow-up, all reported LSD free; two reported free of all drugs	
E. J. Blanchard, 1973 J. M. Libet L. D. Young	Counselor report; self-report; smell test; free access to paint test	Elimination of paint-sniffing in response to smell test and free access test		At 1 year follow-up, counselor reported S to be free from paint-sniffing but in-	Improved social relations and steady full-time employment

Results

		Immediate Results		Follow-up Results	
Author	Assessment Method	Drug-related Behavior	Other Behavior	Drug-related Behavior	Other Behavior
				volved in "occasional" lighter fluid vapor inhalation	
P. A. Wisocki, 1973	Self-report	Cessation of heroin use		At 12-month follow-up indicated drug-free	Improved school and work performance
B. S. Lubetkin, 1974 S. T. Fishman	Self-reports; wife's reports	Cessation of heroin use			
G. J. Steinfield, 1974 E. A. Rautio A. H. Rice M. G. Egan	Urinalysis; after-care service reports	Cessation of drug abuse		At follow-up, 7 of 8 Ss were providing clean urines	7 of 8 subjects reported to still be in or involved in school or working and not involved in criminal activities
B. M. Maletzky, 1975	Urine and blood test for alcohol; self-reported drug abuse (weekly incidents); observer reports	Suppression of drug abuse; significantly lower report of suspicions and incidents by observers		Continued suppression of drug incidents for covert sensitization group; controls increased drug incidents toward baseline levels	

Table 5. **Token economy**

Author	Subjects	Drug Use	Procedures	Concurrent Treatment	Design and Control
J. S. O'Brien, 1971 A. E. Raynes V. D. Patch	150	Heroin addiction (failure to follow unit rules)	Access to reinforcers (radio, TV, recreation room, visitors, passes) made contingent on following ward rules and attending therapy	Ward groups and individual counseling	A-B intervention
G. Lennart Melin, 1973 K. Gunnar Götestam	16	Intravenous amphetamine addiction	Detoxification of patients drug-free behavior management and rehabilitation based on token economy system	Only in exceptional cases were sleeping pills allowed	Group outcome with A-B-A design
K. G. Götestam, 1973 G. L. Melin	23	Intravenous amphetamine addiction	Modified token economy (built on operant principles)	Methadone maintenance	No comparison group
K. G. Götestam, G. L. Melin W. S. Dockens III	16	Intravenous amphetamine addiction	Behavioral management and covert extinction of amphetamine injection	Occasional sleeping pills	Single group study for token economy
J. H. Erickson, 1975 K. G. Götestam G. L. Melin L. G. Ost	52	Variety of drugs including amphetamine and hallucinogens	Contingency management using point system for access to privileges	No data given	Group study with A-B-A-B-E design
G. L. Melin, P. E. Andersson	25	Heroin addiction	Contingency management using point system for	Methadone maintenance	A-B-A-B¹-B design

Table 5. *(Continued)*

Results

		Immediate Results		Follow-up Results	
Author	*Assessment Method*	*Drug-related Behavior*	*Other Behavior*	*Drug-related Behavior*	*Other Behavior*
J. S. O'Brien, 1971 A. E. Raynes V. D. Patch	Pre- and post-measurement of target behaviors with contingencies and without contingencies	Increased therapy attendance and following of unit rules; raised percentage of rule compliance from 20% to 80%	Public decisions of different content became more frequent		Talks about drug use decreased and follow-up interviews on drug status, family relatives, work or school performance with confirmation by other person in client's surrounding
G. Lennart Melin, 1973 K. G. Götestam	Self-report; direct observation	Participation of the patients in the therapeutic activities, and physical exercise increased when tokens were contingently dispensed		None reported	
K. G. Götestam, 1973 G. L. Melin	Data comparison; recording of activity report before and following token economy	Activity points generally increased during modified token economy		None reported	

239

Table 5. *(Continued)*

Results

Author	Assessment Method	Immediate Results		Follow-up Results	
		Drug-related Behavior	*Other Behavior*	*Drug-related Behavior*	*Other Behavior*
K. G. Götestam, (in press) G. L. Melin W. S. Dockens III	Various activity measures; physiological self-report	Various activity measures showed effects of token economy; physiological and self-reports showed effects of covert extinction			
J. H. Erickson, 1975 K. G. Götestam G. L. Melin L. G. Ost	Recording performance; measurement of target behavior with contingencies (TE) and without contingencies; comparison of target behavior with contingencies and without contingencies	Recorded performance of target behavior	Self-care skills, physical exercise, and participation in therapeutic activities all increased with contingencies		
G. L. Melin, B. E. Anderson K. G. Götestam	Comparison measurement of target behaviors before and after introduction of token economy	% of performed behaviors increased with presence of contingencies decreased in their absence		None reported	

Table 6. *Contingency contracting*

Treatment Author	Subjects	Drug Use	Procedures	Concurrent Treatment	Design and Control
H. M. Boudin, 1972	1	Amphetamine use	Contingency contract using $10–$50: checks sent to KKK as contingency	None	Single case reports; variable baselines by history; no control group, no systematic data
L. Weathers, 1972 R. P. Liberman	6	Soft-drug abuse, but not addiction (delinquency)	Contingency contracting behavioral rehearsal with prompting, modeling, and videotape feedback	Probation	Multiple baseline across subjects
R. L. Polakow, 1973 R. H. Doctor	2	Marijuana and/or barbiturate abuse	Contingency contracts drawn up between therapist and clients including behavioral rehearsal	None	Multiple case report
H. M. Boudin, 1974 V. E. Valentine	Hard data for 2 cases presented	Heroin addiction and soft-drug abuse	Contingency contracting relaxation training behavior rehearsal aversive therapy, marriage counseling, other drugs (Quaaludes)	None	Uncontrolled case reports
G. Bigelow, 1974 C. Lawrence A. Harris	$N = 80$ with 2 years of drug abuse	Drug-taking	I. Contingency contracting II. Behavior therapy III. Contingency con-	Methadone maintenance; supportive counseling	2×2 randomized block design

241

Table 6. *(Continued)*

Author	Subjects	Drug Use	Procedures	Concurrent Treatment	Design and Control
B. D'Lugoff	8 white, 80% male		tracting and behavior therapy		
A. Wiggenhorn (unpublished) S. McEveny A. Benjamin E. Buese	4	Readdiction to heroin	Social retraining (1) motive growth counseling, (2) contingency, self-management of pre-social behavior analysis of drug relapse episodes		Multiple case study using A-B design; No control Ss
Stitzer, 1977 Bigelow Lawrence Cohen D'Lugaff Hawthorne	16 methadone maintenance clients, 13 males, 3 females, 22–42 years old	Heroin	(B-phase) contingency contracting: weekend medication, take-home privileges given for attending weekly counseling sessions; (A-phase) noncontingent take-home medication privileges	None specified	Within-subject design A_1-B-A_2-B-A_3
Boudin et al., 1977	47 began program; data analysis on 33 program graduates	Heroin, opiate, hallucinogens, barbiturates, sedatives, methaqualone, cocaine	Contingency contracting of drug dependence with work/school appropriate personal/social behaviors, meeting program requirements	None listed	Single subject A-B replications

Treatment

Table 6. *(Continued)*

Results

| Author | Assessment Method | Immediate Results | | Follow-up Results | |
		Drug-related Behavior	Other Behavior	Drug-related Behavior	Other Behavior
H. M. Boudin, 1972	Urinalysis; self-monitoring	Deceleration of amphetamine use during contingency contracting and availability of therapist		2-year follow-up indicates no return to amphetamine use	
L. Weathers, 1972 R. P. Liberman	Self-report; parent-report		No clear evidence that interventions improved school grades or attendance, curfew compliance, or recidivism		
R. L. Polakow, 1973 R. M. Doctor	Urinalysis	Success by treatment of marijuana and/or barbiturate abuse	Increase in social activities	At 12-month follow-up no drug usage was reported or found by urinalysis	Steady employment was being maintained

Table 6. *(Continued)*

Results

| Author | Assessment Method | Immediate Results | | Follow-up Results | |
		Drug-related Behavior	Other Behavior	Drug-related Behavior	Other Behavior
H. M. Boudin, 1974 V. E. Valentine	Urinalysis; several subjective measures; self-recording of drug-related behaviors, as drug urges drug thought, and daily journals		Very preliminary; percent of time spent at work or school		
G. Bigelow, 1974 C. Lawrence A. Harris B. D. Lugoff	Urinalysis; arrest records; work or school performance; percent of time spent at work/or school	Drug-taking reduced; arrest reduced	Work improved	Drug-taking reduced	Work improved
A. Wiggenhorn (unpublished) S. McEveny A. Benjamin E. Buese	Behavior recording	Patients completed 84–100% of requisite recording	Group average of 2.06 new behaviors recorded/day	20% drug relapsed over 364-day period	Subjects A, B, and D showed 33%, 89%, and 83% increases in days employed

Table 7. Multiple techniques

Treatment

Author	Subjects	Drug Use	Procedures	Concurrent Treatment	Design and Control
E. Lesser, 1967	1	Anxiety and excessive use of narcotic morphine	Relaxation training and self-assertion training; aversive conditioning (electrical shock)	Home practice of relaxation and self-assertiveness	Single case report
P. A. Wisocki, 1973	1	Heroin addiction	Covert sensitization, covert reinforcement, assertion training, and desensitization	None	Single case report
F. E. Cheek, 1973 T. Tomarchio J. Standen R. S. Altahary	29 males 14 females	Heroin dependency (low self-image, inappropriate assertiveness)	Patients were trained in relaxation systematic desensitization, self-image, self-assertiveness, rewarding of others, behavioral rehearsal, self-modification of undesirable behaviors	Methadone maintenance	Multiple case study use of A–B design Procedures: variable baseline, no control group or follow-up; large S population including women needed for comprehensive study
Hall, 1977 Loeb, Yang, Norton	49 methadone clients	Heroin	*Vocational workshop* (1) vocational information and resources; (2) videotaped feedback of inter-	Methadone maintenance program at drug clinic	2 group comparison, one experimental, one control pre-test, only one

Table 7. *(Continued)*

Author	Subjects	Drug Use	Procedures	Concurrent Treatment	Design and Control
			view practice; (3) relaxation training; (4) supervision in job placement; *control group:* only vocational information		treatment
MacDonough, 1976	260 hospitalization program; 232 behavioral feedback program	Multiple drug abusers	*Hospitalization program—* medically oriented four phases: (a) detoxification medically treated for withdrawal, (b) psychiatric counseling, (c) individually tailored treatment (e.g., marital counseling, group therapy), (d) follow-up treatment and progress reports *feedback behavior mod. program—*(a) contracting for desirable and undesirable behaviors, (b) individual feedback sessions (c) therapeutic group activities	None specified	Single-group A-B design, 2 treatment phases, no baseline, no control group

Table 7. *(Continued)*

Results

		Immediate Results		Follow-up Results	
Author	Assessment Method	Drug-related Behavior	Other Behavior	Drug-related Behavior	Other Behavior
E. Lesser, 1967	Self-report			No self-report of return to hard drug; 10-month follow-up report continued use of marijuana; 10-year follow-up self-report never again used narcotics	10-month follow-up revealed domination in self-reported anxiety and success in job. Happily married; employed steadily for several years
P. A. Wisocki, 1973	Self-report			12-month follow-up drug-free	
F. E. Cheek, 1973 T. Tomarchio J. Standew R. S. Alfahary	Standardized test, questionnaire evaluation, ISI measures, Taylor Manifest Anxiety Scale, Rotter I-E Scale, pre- and post-program measures of anxiety level, kind of reinforcement to which addicts susceptible, nature of	17 out of 20 level of anxiety fell (Taylor Manifest Anxiety Scale)—this is significant beyond 0.01 level; ISI measure 15 rose, 1 remained same, and 3 fell—significant at 0.01 level; assertiveness for those low in assertive-		6-month follow-up 48% of BM clients were reported to have been much improved while 45% of control group reported much improved in adjusting in community; performance of addicts with BM program	

247

Table 7. *(Continued)*

Results

Author	Assessment Method	Immediate Results		Follow-up Results	
		Drug-related Behavior	Other Behavior	Drug-related Behavior	Other Behavior
	help image & degree of assertiveness Assessment of social worker's reports	ness (7 out of 10) rose for those high on assertiveness dropped (8 out of 10); Rotter I-E scale showed that 6 males of 13 fell (became less susceptible to external control), 3 remained same, 4 rose, 2 female rose, 6 fell; the pre-program vs. post-program difference is significant to 0.02 level improved self-image lower anxiety level, more appropriate assertiveness, increased control		and those without it not statistically different counselor rating At 3-month follow-up 2 females and 1 male reported drug use: 3 had been stopped for questioning, 1 arrested for an old charge, Rest no contact with the law; 7 completely self-supporting, 2 partially so, 4 with some help from families, 1 completely supported by family, 6 on welfare, 1 disability pension; 13 reported they were better able to get along with families since BMP; 1 no difference	

6
Alcoholism

Mark S. Goldman

Alcoholism remains an enormous problem in the United States and abroad, both in terms of the number of persons affected, and the cost to business and the community. While it is impossible to specify the number of "alcoholics" in the United States due to definitional problems discussed below, Keller (1974, Chapter 1) reports "those under active treatment for alcoholism by public or private agencies are probably in the upper hundreds of thousands, but there may be as many as 10 million people whose drinking has created some problem . . . within the last year." The economic loss in this country due to alcohol-related problems was estimated to be over $25 billion in 1971 (Berry, Boland, Laxson et al., 1974), and one would have to assume it has risen since then.

Despite the unfortunate familiarity that our society has with this disorder, an operational definition has yet to be agreed upon. One source of this lack of definitional consensus is the great variability in drinking patterns associated with physical and/or behavioral dysfunction. How to select those patterns which are to be categorized "alcoholism" has not been clear. A second source of definitional debate centers around hypothesized etiological mechanisms which some investigators include as part of the definition. The most contentious of these debates concerns the appropriateness of viewing alcoholism as a "disease." These issues will be reviewed in subsequent sections, but at this point, suffice it to say that there may not even be a circumscribed entity that can be usefully characterized as alcoholism. The term alcoholism is best understood as a summary label which subsumes a variety of drinking and associated behaviors which provide a problem

Portions of this work were supported by Grants numbered AA 02898 and AA 07200 from the National Institute on Alcohol Abuse and Alcoholism to the author.

for the individual. Additional meaning accorded the term by any research or clinical group derives from theoretical, not empirical, considerations.

Clinicians recognize that certain social, psychological, and/or biological consequences can commonly result from long-term, excessive alcohol consumption. Although some authors attempt to define alcoholism by one or more of these consequences, such a definition is probably too restrictive because clinicians in treatment facilities tend to see only a selected population of alcoholics (Cahalan and Cisin, 1976a) who are typically at the latter stages of their drinking history. However, since practicing clinicians are likely to encounter such individuals, some of the most frequent consequences will be briefly discussed.

The social and psychological consequences of chronic alcohol misuse are so multifold as to be difficult to describe in a limited space. Loss of jobs, friends, and family may occur as well as problems with the police. The alcoholic may have a variety of psychological complaints including nervousness, depression, despair, guilt, and so on.

At the time of admission to treatment, many alcoholics are biologically addicted to alcohol. Addiction consists of tolerance to, and physical dependence upon, alcohol (Mendelson, 1971). With tolerance, an individual requires increasing doses to maintain the effects produced by the original dose. Physical dependence refers to the occurrence of withdrawal symptoms once drinking ceases. Withdrawal symptoms may occur even while subjects' Blood Alcohol Levels (BALs) remain as high as 100 mg percent (100 mg per 100 ml of blood—roughly 5 ounces of whiskey) (Isbell, Fraser, Wikler et al., 1955), and after as little as 4 consecutive days of drinking (Mello and Mendelson, 1969).

"Blackouts" or episodes of amnesia (anterograde) for events occurring during a drinking episode are frequently reported by alcoholics. While Jellinek (1952) believed them to signal the early stages of alcoholism, Goodwin, Crane, and Guze (1969) found that they may occur at any point in the drinking history and are not a special sign of impending alcoholism.

Chronic alcohol ingestion can have a pathological effect on just about all of the body's organ systems (Kissen and Begleiter, 1974, Chapters 7–14). These effects result either directly from alcohol toxicity, or indirectly, from various dietary deficiencies that often accompany excessive drinking. Gastritis and pancreatitis commonly occur, with the attendant pain being one of the most effective controls on extended drinking. Fatty liver, alcoholic hepatitis, and cirrhosis are all seen after prolonged drinking. Fatty liver is the least serious and most reversible of the liver conditions (Korsten and Lieber, 1976), while Lieber (1975) reports that cirrhosis ranks as the third or fourth leading cause of death in urban areas, such as New York City, in men between 25 and 45 years of age. The other most serious effect associated with prolonged alcohol consumption is on the Central Nervous System (CNS). However, two conditions commonly attributed to toxic alcohol effects, peripheral neuropathy and Wernicke's Syndrome, appear instead to result from B vitamin deficiencies (Victor and Adams, 1953), particularly thiamine in the case of Wernicke's Syndrome (Victor, Adams, and Collins, 1971). Korsakoff's psychosis, characterized by short-term memory loss, is commonly associated with Wernicke's Syndrome (to the point that the syndrome has been called the Wernicke-Korsakoff Syndrome), although a case can be made for a different etiology (Freund, 1976). A variety of other degenerative conditions of the CNS are also seen (Dreyfus, 1974).

Theoretical Analysis and Empirical Findings: Biological Physiological Findings. A variety of physiological aberrations have been theorized to predispose an individual to alcoholism. Notable among these have been an inherited metabolic defect leading to a nutritional insufficiency (Williams, 1959), and nutritional sensitivies leading to an addiction to certain food substances that can be satisfied by alcohol consumption (Randolph, 1956). However, these are older theories and little supporting evidence for them has accrued in recent years (Vitale and Coffey, 1971). More recently, Mendelson (1968) has reported that even chronic alcoholics show no identifiable differences in alcohol metabolic rates in as short a time as three weeks subsequent to heavy drinking.

The possible etiologic role of abnormalities of biogenic amine production and metabolism has been recently indicated. For example, Myers and Melchior (1977) found that rats can be induced to consume fairly high doses of ethanol by infusing tetrahydropapaveroline (THP), an abnormal metabolite of a naturally occurring brain neurotransmitter (dopamine) directly into the ventricles of the brain. However, considerable work remains to be done in accounting for the great variations in human patterns of alcohol abuse before these findings can be considered more than suggestive. More immediately applicable is the work of Wolff (1972) and Ewing, Rouse, and Pellizzari (1974), showing that Orientals, who have low rates of alcoholism, respond with more skin flushing, a higher heart rate, a greater blood pressure drop, and more discomfort to acute administration of alcohol, than do Occidentals. These findings suggest that particular physiological characterstics may eliminate some individuals from the pool of potential alcoholics, rather than selectively predisposing other individuals to alcoholism.

Genetic Findings.   Study of the behavioral genetics of both animals and humans has provided another means of establishing the presence of a physical predisposition to alcoholism. By inbreeding consecutive generations of mice, strains have been developed that prefer alcohol-water solutions to plain water (McClearn, 1973). However, despite the utility of these inbred strains for the study of the interaction between alcohol, physiology, and behavior, they do not provide a readily acceptable analog for human alcoholism. As Rogers (1972) indicates, most animals avoid solutions exceeding 15 percent alcohol to water, while humans commonly consume alcohol in 50 percent concentrations; animal research has been done mainly with unflavored alcohol solutions at room temperature, a generally unpalatable beverage to humans; the work that even inbred strains will do for alcohol is relatively small; food reduction by mice offered alcohol is small compared with humans who may reduce food intake 50–90 percent; and, finally, the mice may merely be inheriting an alcohol taste preference, an inherited characteristic that would not explain the magnitude and patterns of human alcohol abuse.

In humans, studies of concordance rates for alcoholism in relatives of alcoholics (Amark, 1951), half-siblings (Schuckit, Goodwin, and Winokur, 1972), monozygotic versus dizygotic twins (Kaij, 1960; Partanen, Bruun, and Markkanen, 1966), and male adoptees raised apart from alcoholic biological parents (Goodwin, Schulsinger, Hermansen et al., 1973) have been supportive of a genetic hypothesis. However, the findings of an early study by Roe (Roe, 1944; Roe and Burks, 1945) using male and female adoptees of alcoholic parents were contrary to such a hypothesis. The considerable methodological difficulties encountered by all such studies in separating the effects of heredity and environment, and in diagnosing alcoholism, have, to date, rendered their findings inconclusive. For example, in the highly regarded study by Goodwin et al. (1973), subjects were classified based on drinking frequencies, patterns, and the presence or absence of four categories of alcohol-related problems, including social disapproval or marital difficulties; job or police trouble; blackouts, tremors, or withdrawal symptoms; and loss of control drinking. The heavy drinker, problem drinker, and alcoholic classifications did not differ as to drinking behavior, but were instead distinguished by the appearance of alcohol-related problems. All were daily drinkers with frequent episodes of six or more drinks; heavy drinkers were those who had no problems; alcoholics had problems in at least three of the preceding groupings; problem drinkers had problems in less than three of the four groupings. Goodwin et al. (1973), favored a genetic interpretation based on the concordance rates between adoptees in the "alcoholic" group and their alcoholic parents. Tolor and Tamerin (1973), however, pointed out that this conclusion was based entirely on the somewhat arbitrary distinctions between the groups. Had the problem drinkers been included with the "alcoholics " (many researchers would support this inclusion), no such conclusion would have been possible. Had the heavy drinkers been included, the results would have in fact favored an environmental hypothesis.

Disease Concept. Whether or not to define alcoholism as a disease is a question that has been routinely connected with the search for a biological etiology. Despite much recent debate that has taken place between those favoring the disease definition (Keller, 1976; Seixas, Blume, Cloud et al., 1976) and those opposed (Davies, 1976; Pomerleau, Pertschuck, and Stinnett, 1976), the propriety of the term "disease" appears to depend largely upon what is meant by disease. Three aspects must be considered: the scientific implications, the sociological implications, and the implications for treatment.

First, to consider the scientific implications: If used broadly to refer to the deleterious effects that accrue to excessive drinkers, the term disease provides few scientific problems, since it is not incompatible with a wide variety of etiologic formulations, including behavioral. If used narrowly to refer to a unitary biological process that causes alcoholism and is most particularly characterized by a predictable progression, constitutionally based craving for alcohol (physical dependency), loss of control over drinking, and the inviolable requirement of abstention for successful treatment, then the term is misleading. The evidence for a unitary biological causation (as previously mentioned) remains scanty. Even Jellinek (1960), who described the progression of alcoholism that is most widely held today, recognized that other courses and outcomes were possible. More recent research has confirmed this observation (Clark and Cahalan, 1976). The interrelated notions of a constitutionally based craving, and "loss of control" over drinking, have been extensively investigated lately, but have also not held up. Mello (1972), after a review of a number of studies of alcoholics who were allowed to drink in laboratory settings, indicated that no subject allowed to freely program drinking showed a tendency to "drink to oblivion"; no subject consumed all alcohol available at one time; during prolonged drinking, subjects initiated and terminated several drinking episodes; abstinence could be "bought" from the subjects and drinking delays could be enhanced by single "priming" doses of alcohol; subjects sometimes stopped drinking for reasons other than physical illness even when alcohol was available; and some subjects "tapered" their drinking to avoid abrupt withdrawal. Unmitigated loss of control is also argued against by the fact that various environmental factors influence alcoholics' consumption, such as the work required to obtain alcohol (Mello and Mendelson, 1965), and the presence of interpersonal influences (Goldman, 1974). More direct tests have also failed to document the presence of craving and loss of control. Merry (1966) showed that alcoholics did not experience greater subjective craving when receiving small amounts of alcohol than when they received placebo. Engle and Williams (1972), going a step further, showed that the critical variable which influenced subjective craving was knowledge of the presence of alcohol in a drink, rather than the actual presence of alcohol. The most sophisticated methodology in this group of studies was used by Marlatt, Demming, and Reid (1973) who first primed alcoholics with a single dose of beverage and then, under the guise of a "taste-testing" experiment, allowed subjects to regulate their own beverage consumption for 15 minutes. The experimental design orthogonally manipulated the actual beverage consumed (alcohol or tonic-placebo) with what subjects were told (i.e., that they were given alcohol or that they were given plain tonic). Their finding was clear; actual consumption was determined by subjects' expectations, rather than by actual alcohol content. The only study that has recently supported the craving notion (Ludwig, Wikler, and Stark, 1974) argues for a classical conditioning explanation, rather than a physical explanation. Finally, the belief that successful treatment requires total abstention from alcohol has been countered by a number of studies (reviewed by Lloyd and Salzberg, 1975), the most recent of which is the now infamous Rand Report (Armor, Polich, and Stanbul, 1976). These studies have all found that a percentage of diagnosed "alcoholics" return to moderate drinking patterns after treatment. Armor et al. (1976, p. vi) in fact conclude that, even for definite "alcoholics," relapse rates for normal drinkers are no higher than those for long-term "abstainers." While methodologic shortcomings, such as potentially unreliable assessment of drinking during follow-up, limit the conclusiveness of these reports, their frequency in the literature cannot be ignored.

Next, to consider the sociologic aspects of the disease conceptualization: On the positive side, labelling alcoholism a disease removed a considerable moral stigma that had been attached to alcoholic individuals. It also allowed them to seek treatment for illness, rather than having to acknowledge some fault of character within themselves. On a less positive note, the use of the term disease set up professional rivalries regarding who was most appropriate to treat the "disease" (Keller, 1976).

Lastly, to consider some treatment implications of the disease conceptualization: While having the benefit previously noted of encouraging alcoholics to seek treatment, some negative consequences can also be envisioned. Until the individual is willing to self-identify as an alcoholic, usually under extreme circumstances, he may reject treatment. Secondly, acceptance of the disease view often means acceptance of the need for lifelong abstention. Consequently, certain potentially useful approaches to treatment that aim toward controlled drinking are precluded and a self-fulfilling prophecy may be set up; that is, that once the alcoholic takes even one drink, he might as well "go all the way."

In sum, it is best that the researchers not use the disease view as an heuristic. Those treating the alcoholic must take account of both the positive and negative implications of calling alcoholism a disease.

Biological Approach—Conclusion. Biological factors are obviously implicated in alcoholism. The extent to which they predispose an individual to the disorder remains unknown at this time.

THEORETICAL ANALYSIS AND EMPIRICAL FINDINGS: SOCIOCULTURAL

Sociocultural and epidemiological research has particularly highlighted the etiological importance of factors external to the individual. Extensive research in the United States has shown that rates and patterns of alcohol use and abuse are highly related to ethno-religious background, sex, age, socioeconomic status, education, and occupation (see recent reports of this research by Cahalan and Cisin, 1976a, b; and in Chapters I and II of Keller, 1974). It is improbable that these relationships are explainable solely by biological factors. They suggest, instead, the potency of interpersonal influences and acculturation on alcohol use. For example, it has become common knowledge that certain ethno-religious groups (Italians and Jews) use alcohol extensively, but show low rates of drinking problems. Blum (1967) summarizes such findings by pointing out that when drinking is part of family ritual, it is less prone to lead to problems than when it is used to fill leisure time. Recent epidemiological research has shown that the highest rates of problem drinking occur in men in their 20s, although most alcoholics in treatment are men in their 40s. Apparently, much of the research on alcoholism (which has been carried out largely on alcoholics in treatment) has not studied the major segment of the problem drinking population. When such groups are included (Clark, 1976; Clark and

Cahalan, 1976), our picture of the typical alcoholic changes. For example, these studies have not found typical alcohol-related problems, such as loss of control, belligerence, problems with spouse, police, jobs, and so on, to be well correlated with each other. Nor were problems found at one time in an individual necessarily present at subsequent evaluation. Furthermore, no common progression of alcoholism was noted, nor was loss of control more predictive of subsequent problems than was any other problem area.

Cross-cultural research has also suggested that the extent of alcohol use and behavioral reaction to alcohol can be regulated by the mores of culture, and that heavy drinking can sometimes occur without severe loss of control over behavior (Pittman and Snyder, 1962). Based on evidence of this sort, MacAndrew and Edgerton (1969) concluded that drunken behavior was socially controlled.

Sociocultural Approach—Conclusion. The recognition that there are no "instant alcoholics" (Cahalan and Cisin, 1976a) and that attitudes favorable to alcohol usually precede heavy drinking (Cahalan, 1970) clearly implicates learning and experience in the etiology of alcoholism. What is not provided by this approach is the specification of the precise mechanisms by which alcohol-related behaviors are acquired by an individual.

THEORETICAL ANALYSIS AND EMPIRICAL FINDINGS: PERSONALITY

Early psychological efforts to understand the etiology of alcoholism were predominantly derived from psychodynamic formulations and consequently emphasized personality traits and types. Reviewers of this early work were, however, forced to conclude that the mass of data accumulated was often conflicting, and overall, no particular personality trait or type was clearly a predictor of alcoholism (Armstrong, 1958; Sutherland, Schroeder, and Tordella, 1950; Syme, 1957). More recently, some researchers (Cahalan and Room, 1972) have reached similar negative conclusions, while others have continued to emphasize the role of personality traits. For example, McClelland (McClelland, Davis, Kalin, and Warner, 1972) has tried to show that individuals with power needs are particularly vulnerable to alcohol excess because alcohol can provide temporary satisfaction of such needs. Methodological deficiencies (primarily the use of projective personality tests which have been shown to have limited reliability and validity) weaken these claims, however. Perhaps more promising are recent studies (Nerviano, 1976; Skinner, Jackson, and Hoffmann, 1974), which have used factor analytic techniques to identify a number of personality types associated with alcoholism.

In any case, the scientific utility of personality terms remains limited due to their imprecision and their failure to delineate specific controlling variables or targets for intervention. Furthermore, they encouraged reification of intervening variables, and de-emphasized the potency of situational factors shown to be highly predictive of a variety of behaviors (Mischel, 1968, 1973).

THEORETICAL ANALYSIS AND EMPIRICAL FINDINGS: BEHAVIORAL

Tension-reduction Hypothesis.   The most frequently cited behavioral explanation of the etiology of alcoholism has been some variation of a "tension-reduction" hypothesis. This hypothesis presumes that alcohol pharmacologically reduces conditioned anxiety. It is, therefore, believed to serve as a negative reinforcer of drinking (increases the probability of drinking by terminating an aversive anxiety-tension state) in alcoholics who are presumed to have high prevailing levels of anxiety. Support for the hypothesis derived from early studies of experimentally induced conflict in animals (Conger, 1951, 1956; Masserman and Yum, 1946) and more recent work by Freed (1967) and Smart (1965) . The tension-reduction hypothesis has not been universally supported, however. Cappell and Herman (1972), extensively reviewed a variety of experimental interpretations of the tension-reduction hypothesis, including avoidance and escape learning, conflict and experimental neurosis, conditioned suppression, extinction and partial reinforcement, stress and behavioral disruption, psychophysiological studies, and human self-report and risk-taking studies. They concluded that the only studies providing consistent empirical support were those on conflict. Brown and Crowell (1974), in a further analysis, suggested that even these studies do not support a tension-reduction hypothesis, since closer approach to a bivalent goal after alcohol administration may actually increase conflict (due to the increased strength of both approach and avoidance tendencies closer to the goal). Additional reviews of exclusively human research have also indicated the inadequacy of a simple tension-reduction view of alcohol effects (Cappell, 1974; Marlatt, 1975; Mello, 1972). In addition, as Cappell and Herman (1972) observed, even if tension reduction was one possible reinforcing consequence of consuming alcohol, it is not necessarily the major motivation for drinking.

Apparently, no single behavioral mechanism will suffice to explain the development and maintenance of excessive drinking. Both the pharmacological effects of alcohol itself and numerous intero- and exteroceptive cues and reinforcers that are not directly a function of pharmacological effects must be considered to be operative. The task that remains is the explication of these operative mechanisms. Although we are just beginning this task, some of the relevant factors are beginning to be understood.

Expectancy and the Pharmacological Effects of Alcohol.   Only recently have the effects of alcohol been assessed independently of alcohol expectancy (placebo) effects in a methodologically sophisticated fashion. Marlatt, Demming, and Reid (1973), building on the work of Engle and Williams (1972), showed the potency of alcohol expectancy effects with their demonstration that alcoholics' drinking was determined by their belief that they were drinking alcohol, rather than by their actually consuming alcohol. Ludwig, Wikler, and Stark's (1974) finding that craving in alcoholics may be stimulated by alcohol-related cues, rather than by alcohol consumption itself, is readily interpreted as an expectancy effect.

A variety of emotional reactions commonly attributed to alcohol may also be multiply determined. For example, the capacity of alcohol to serve as a euphoriant has been shown (Pliner and Cappell, 1974) to be partly a reaction to situational cues, in this case, drinking alone or in a group. Grouped subjects reported more positive affect with alcohol, solitary subjects did not. Similar complex interactions in relation to alcohol and anxiety have been found. Using a variant of Marlatt's design, Polivy and her associates (Polivy and Herman, 1976; Polivy, Schueneman, and Carlson, 1976) concluded that independent of the influence of expectancy effects, alcohol acts as a sedative; but with expectancy effects operating, alcohol may actually induce dysphoria in certain situations, such as a laboratory setting. This conclusion is consistent with the findings of Steffen, Nathan, and Taylor (1974) who found that over 12 days of laboratory drinking, muscle activity decreased as blood alcohol levels (BAL) increased, while subjective distress increased as BAL increased. Thus, even though alcohol itself may act as physiological tension-reducer, subjective and behavioral effects may actually reflect tension-*increase.*

Despite the long-standing popular belief that alcohol increases aggressivity, Lang, Goeckner, Adesso, and Marlatt (1975), again using a variant of Marlatt's original design (Marlatt, Demming, and Reid, 1973), found that aggressive behavior was solely a function of expectancy, rather than the 100 mg percent BAL induced in this study. Similarly, although Wilson and Lawson (1976a, b) found that both men and women reported higher levels of sexual arousal when they believed they consumed alcohol (whether or not they actually did), Wilson and Lawson (1976b, 1978) and Briddell and Wilson (1976) in fact showed that alcohol actually decreases both penile and vaginal responses to erotic stimuli.

An inkling of the complexity of the interaction of factors that influence alcohol's behavioral effects is provided by recent work on alcohol and pain. In the first of these studies, Cutter, Maloof, Kurtz, and Jones (1976) found that alcoholics experienced a subjective decrease in pain that increased with dosage, while normals reported no pain decrease. Since no differential physiological response was found in the two groups, the subjective pain reduction was attributed to expectancy factors interacting with the interoceptive cues of the increased dosage. In a second investigation, Brown and Cutter (1977) reported that alcohol's effect on pain reduction in nonalcoholics was strongly influenced by prior drinking habits. For example, a higher alcohol dose reduced pain in solitary drinkers, but *increased* pain in subjects who usually drank at home with family or friends.

In sum, the behavioral effects of alcohol result from a complex interaction of factors. Although alcohol expectancies appear to influence behavioral effects, some studies have indicated that expectancies only produce effects while interacting with alcohol (e.g., Pliner and Cappell, 1974), while others suggest expectancies alone can produce certain effects (e.g., Lang, Goeckner, Adesso, and Marlatt, 1975). Expectancy itself is complex; it derives from belief systems, prior drinking experience, and the immediate physical and social setting of drinking. Such complexity suggests that the reinforcing capabilities of alcohol may be manifold.

Yet to be resolved is how the expectancy effect interacts with alcohol dosage and the rise and fall of the BAL. For example, Williams, Goldman, and Williams (1978) report that alcohol dose may, in fact, modify subjects' expectancies. In this study, when subjects' expectancies coincided with the beverage actually administered, performance on a variety of psychomotor tasks was significantly better than when expectancy and actual beverage differed. Remarkably, subjects showed no performance decrement even at a BAL of 60 mg percent, as long as they knew they were receiving alcohol. Furthermore, Jones (1973), and Jones and Vega (1972), have shown that some behavioral effects commonly attributed to alcohol occur only on the ascending limb and not the descending limb of the BAL curve. Whether this relationship interacts with the potency of the expectancy effect remains to be seen.

Social Learning Factors. There is also considerable evidence that alcohol use is both cued and reinforced by factors other than the effects of alcohol itself. Jessor, Collins, and Jessor (1972), and Jessor and Jessor (1975), have shown that introduction to alcohol use is an integral part of adolescent peer-group interactions. O'Leary, O'Leary, and Donovan (1976) have further suggested that pre-alcoholics can be identified by their social skills deficits in adolescence. A number of laboratory studies of drinking by alcoholics have also implicated social stimuli as both cues and reinforcers for drinking (e.g., Griffiths, Bigelow, and Liebson, 1975). Miller, Hersen, Eisler, and Hilsman (1974) have further shown that when alcoholics are subjected to the interpersonal stress of making assertive responses, they are more likely to turn to alcohol than are social drinkers. Imitation of a role model has also been shown to increase drinking in male social drinkers (Caudill and Marlatt, 1975).

Randall and Lester (1975) have even found that peer influences can modify the drinking behavior of animals. Mice that were either inbred for drinking or nondrinking were raised with mice of the same or opposite strain. Although strain-specific phenotypes were not reversed (drinker mice continued to consume more alcohol than nondrinkers), the drinker mice raised with nondrinkers drank one-half as much as when raised with their own strain. Similarly, nondrinkers raised with drinkers consumed twice as much as when raised with their own strain.

Other Drinking Cues. Emotional states such as anger (Kosturn and Marlatt, 1974), anxiety in anticipation of electric shock (Higgins and Marlatt, 1973), fear of interpersonal evaluation (Higgins and Marlatt, in press), and depression induced by learned helplessness (Noel and Lisman, 1977) have all been shown to cue alcohol consumption. Certain dry food reinforcement schedules have also been shown to induce consumption of liquids in animals, and Falk and Samson (1976) have recently argued for their possible role in excessive alcohol consumption in humans.

Behavioral Approach—Conclusion

The behavioral contingencies that control alcohol consumption are only just beginning to be elucidated but knowledge of such contingencies has clearly become a critical factor for the behavioral clinician. Until and unless some special biological mechanism is discovered which clearly separates "true alcoholics" from other portions of the social drinking and problem drinking populations, the investigation of alcoholism as a learned behavior is a potentially fruitful endeavor.

ASSESSMENT

Excellent reviews of general (Miller, 1976a) and behavioral (Briddell and Nathan, 1975) assessment methods have recently been completed and should be consulted for further information. Assessment in the alcoholism field has traditionally been of two types: (1) techniques for distinguishing "alcoholics" from the general and psychiatric populations, and (2) techniques for delineating individual differences and general characteristics of previously identified alcoholics. It is only recently that assessment methods have been developed that have direct utility for treatment planning.

Projective. Examination of the mass of studies using projective techniques for differential diagnosis of alcoholism reveals no projective indicator that has been clearly established by methodologically sound and replicable research. Likewise, reviews which include projective test studies of personality patterns of alcoholics have discovered that just about every personality trait and type has been linked with alcoholism, many, in fact, which are contradictory (Armstrong, 1958; Miller, 1976a; Sutherland et al., 1950; Syme, 1957).

Objective. The majority of the objective assessment devices in this area have been designed to discriminate alcoholics from nonalcoholics in settings in which alcoholics may not readily self-identify. These devices are designed either to (1) directly query the subject about alcohol use and related behaviors, or to (2) distinguish alcoholics by use of empirically derived scales.

Of the first variety, the Alcadd Test (Manson, 1949) consists of 60 alcohol-related items which were selected from a larger item pool by quantitative item analysis. The 60 items are scored into 5 factors which were subjectively derived by Manson. The Iowa Scale of Preoccupation with Alcohol (ISPA) (Mulford and Miller, 1960) contains 12 items of a type commonly used by clinicians for querying chronic alcoholics about their symptoms. The Michigan Alcoholism Screening Test (MAST) (Selzer, 1971) uses 25 items to question the respondee about customary drinking habits. Miller (1976a) reports only finding one study directly validating the Alcadd for diagnosis in clinical settings, and none validating the ISPA. According to Miller (1976a), the MAST has received some cross-validational support for use as method of distinguishing alcoholics from a general psychiatric population, but further validational work is necessary before the MAST can be fully accepted as a screening instrument.

The second variety of scales is derived empirically by administering items which are not necessarily related to the question at hand,

and then selecting for future use those items to which the criterion group, i.e., alcoholics, and a control group respond differentially. Of this type, the Manson (1948) and a number of MMPI-derived scales have received some cross-validational support. The Manson Evaluation (1948) consists of 72 items which were selected from an original 470-item pool. Like Manson's (1949) Alcadd, this test can be scored on several subscales which were subjectively derived by the author. The Manson Evaluation has not received a great deal of cross-validation, and especially lacking is cross-validation in a typical clinical sample. Three early scales, Am, Al, and Ah constructed from the item pool of the MMPI (Button, 1956; Hampton, 1953; Hoyt and Sedlacek, 1958) also failed in cross-validational attempts in other than normal populations (MacAndrew and Geerstma, 1964). The MacAndrew scale, AMac (MacAndrew, 1965), was constructed by comparing alcoholics with psychiatric outpatients, but cross-validational attempts have met with mixed results (Miller, 1976a). Recent studies have found that alcoholics, heroin addicts, and polydrug users obtain similar scores on the AMac (Lachar, Berman, Grisell, and Schooff, 1976), indicating that this scale taps characteristics associated with substance abuse (Kranitz, 1972) rather than those specific to alcoholism. A further scale, ARos, consisting of items common to the AMac, Ah and Am was constructed by Rosenberg (1972) and seems to have had some limited cross-validational success (Hoffman, Loper, and Kammeier, 1974).

In fairness to these scales, the difficulty of constructing an adequate scale for a criterion group as ill-defined as alcoholism must be noted. From a treatment standpoint, however, a test to identify alcoholics who wish to hide their problem has questionable utility.

Behavioral. Behavioral assessment methods were used originally to study the general topology of drinking behavior and are gradually evolving into a methodology for studying individual drinking patterns for the purpose of treatment planning. All direct methods of behavioral assessment employ observation of freely emitted drinking and related behavior. Automated equipment is frequently used to dispense and/or monitor drinks. Early studies (see Mello, 1972; Nathan and O'Brien, 1971) employed a method still used, that of having a live-in environment where subjects typically performed some operant response (button-pushing, simulated driving apparatus, and so on) to earn points which could be exchanged for alcohol or other reinforcers. This method permitted assessment of frequency, rate, and reinforcement value of drinking. To enhance the realism of an otherwise sterile laboratory environment, a simulated bar was often incorporated, with bar stools, soft lights, a bartender, and so on. The bar setting was later used independently by Schaefer, Sobell, and Mills (1971) to study alcohol consummatory behavior: alcoholics were found to gulp straight drinks rather than sipping mixed drinks, as did nonalcoholics. These investigators then attempted to modify drinking style to help control excessive drinking. To reduce the reactivity of these measures (deriving from the drinker's knowledge of being observed) more recent studies have employed a "taste-rating" task (Marlatt, Demming, and Reid, 1973) which ostensibly requires subjects to assign descriptive labels (i.e., sour, sweet, salty, and so on) to various beverages. Actually, the amount of alcohol consumption in a limited time period is the measure of interest.

Despite the reduction in reactivity afforded by the taste-rating task, the question of how drinking behavior assessed by any of these methods compares with "real-world" behavior is yet unanswered. Their utility for treatment planning therefore remains to be determined. Some predictive utility has, however, already been demonstrated by Miller, Hersen, Eisler, and Elkin (1974) who found that pre-treatment operant rate for earning alcohol was predictive of alcoholics' response to treatment by an eight-week behavioral program. Real-world drinking may, of course, be directly assessed by unobtrusive observation in a naturalistic setting (Kessler and Gomberg, 1974) or by having an investigator appear at unpredictable times to take BAL readings (Miller, 1975).

Indirect behavioral devices (based on alcoholics' self-report) have recently been developed in close association with treatment implementation. Marlatt's Drinking Profile (1975) is a 19-page questionnaire which is completed by an interviewer. It consists of closed and open-ended questions on drinking preferences, rates, patterns, settings, and motivations for drinking. This thorough behavioral analysis is designed to provide a comprehensive basis for treatment planning. The obvious limitation of such a procedure is that it depends on the alcoholics' accurate self-report of prior behavior. Such accuracy cannot be automatically assumed (Summers, 1970), although recent work indicates alcoholics' self-reports are sometimes quite accurate (Sobell, Sobell, and Samuels, 1974). A possible way to overcome the limitations of memory during an interview is to have drinkers monitor and record their own behavior as it occurs. Such a procedure has been elaborated by Miller and Munoz (1976) who use daily record cards on which is recorded time, type, and amount of drink and the drinking situation. Of course, self-monitoring relies on accurate recording, which may not occur when individuals are drinking excessively. Reliability of both of the preceding assessments may be improved by using other individuals in the drinkers' environment for corroboration.

BEHAVIORAL TREATMENT PROCEDURES

Detailed reviews of behavioral treatment studies have proliferated in recent years (Franks, 1970; Hamburg, 1975; Marlatt and Nathan, in press; W. Miller, 1976b; Nathan, 1976; Nathan and Briddell, 1977; Nathan and Goldman, in press; Nathan and Lipscomb, 1978). Rather than bear upon the already overburdened literature with another such review, let me use the benefit of hindsight to provide a sensible clinical perspective on the current behavioral treatment literature (Appendix, p. 296).

A few points should be covered prior to the literature review: First, there are no miracle "cures" for alcoholism, behavioral or otherwise. As the earlier review of the theoretical and empirical literature hopefully indicated, alcoholism is an extremely complex behavioral manifestation which is far from completely understood. Each alcoholic presents a different response constellation and has a different drinking history prior to presenting for treatment. It is remotely conceivable, but yet farfetched, that a unitary treatment technique will satisfactorily handle this nonunitary behavior disorder. When we consider the manifold behavioral problems that alcoholics reaching treatment commonly manifest in addition to excessive drinking, this recognition becomes especially crucial. The more sophisticated treatment studies recently completed recognize the need for multiple treatment approaches. These studies will be emphasized in the following review by elaboration of their procedures and assignment of Design Quality Ratings. As an aside, it might be noted that the most promising intervention is probably prevention at a societal level. By the time many alcoholics actually enter treatment, the drinking response is so overlearned, so many cues and reinforcers have become associated with it, and so many alternative reinforcers (jobs, family interactions, and so on) have been sacrificed, that it is impressive when an intervention does show promise.

Second, certain experimental design considerations, which are especially critical for alcoholism treatment studies, have often received less than their share of attention. Since some studies are thereby rendered inconclusive, these considerations will be emphasized above and beyond the Design Quality Rating Criteria. Foremost among these is subject selection. As Vogler and colleagues (Vogler, Compton, and Weissbach, 1975) have pointed out, based on their own work and the work of others (Ruggels, Armor, Polich et al., 1975), pretreatment subject characteristics may account for as much as 70 percent of the variance in outcome. In fact, Baekeland (1977) goes so far as to suggest that behavioral treatments give no better results than other treatments if the highly selected nature of the treatment volunteers is taken into account. However, since behavioral treatment is only just beginning to acquire sophistication, this observation is premature, although sobering to overzealous behavior modifiers.

It is also necessary to preface the discussion of alcoholism treatment studies with a consideration of treatment goals. The research findings cited earlier, which suggested that alcoholics do not have biologically induced craving, or loss of control, and may not always require lifelong abstention for successful treatment, produced considerable contention in the field. The obvious implication of these findings, that beneficial treatment may consist of training alcoholics to control but not to cease drinking, produced nothing short of acrimony. However, while the debate continues to simmer, behavior modifiers, whose own views are not only consistent with this position but even fuel the debate, continue to develop controlled drinking treatments.

There are points to be made for both sides of this issue (Miller and Caddy, 1977; Nathan and Goldman, in press) even without polemicizing over the disease concept. Against controlled drinking: (1) Alcoholics who are currently, or who have very recently been, addicted should refrain from drinking lest they quickly re-addict. (2) People with serious alcohol-related medical problems, e.g., liver disorders, CNS disorders, and so on, obviously should not drink. (3) Our knowledge of the etiology of alcoholism is far from perfect; many alcoholics may, in fact, be unable to satisfactorily maintain drinking control. (4) It will never hurt one physically to cease drinking. (5) It is easier to know if one has had zero drinks than it is to accurately monitor the number of drinks already consumed; therefore, excessive drinking is more likely once drinking begins.

In favor of controlled drinking: (1) It is difficult to remain abstinent in our society; numerous social situations demand drinking, and drinking cues, i.e., bars, advertisements, constantly surround us. (2) Some alcoholics experience more subjective disturbance and more behavior dysfunction when sober for prolonged periods than when drinking moderately. (3) Some alcoholics who have repeatedly failed in abstinence-oriented treatment may be more successful at achieving control. (4) Some problem drinkers may be more willing to accept treatment if they are not required to self-identify as an alcoholic.

At present, controlled drinking therapies must be considered experimental, not just because their effectiveness remains unproven, but also because the criteria for including a particular drinker in such a program is yet unspecified. To fill this gap, Miller and Caddy (1977) have developed a selection procedure based on contraindications to either controlled drinking or abstention-oriented programs. However, a contraindications approach only begins to address the problem and much further research is necessary.

Despite these cautions, however, the argument for pursuing the development of controlled-drinking therapies is compelling. First of all, the success of abstention-oriented programs has not been over-whelming (Baekeland, 1977), leaving considerable room for further treatment development. The most potent argument is that the early successes of controlled drinking therapies have been instrumental in forcing the sort of reconceptualization that this chapter represents. Their ultimate utility may be with individuals first developing drinking problems, and with those at "high-risk" for alcoholism (based on ethnic group, family history, and so on). Even earlier in the drinking sequence, these techniques may be incorporated into school programs for people first learning to drink. At this point in our knowledge, it is clear that novel approaches to the persistent problem of alcohol misuse must be encouraged, rather than inhibited. In any case, from a be-havioral perspective (without the constraints imposed by the disease view), this entire debate may be a pseudo-issue, since the only treat-ment differences between the two approaches may be what the patient is told about his goals. In other words, abstinence may be viewed as just the end point of drinking reduction.

Making Drinking Noxious

The earliest behavioral techniques for treating alcoholism were based on the idea that alcoholics drank because alcohol was immediately reinforcing for the drinker. Therefore, to eliminate drinking, it would be necessary to make drinking aversive via counterconditioning pro-cedures. It is obvious from recent research that such an approach, which ignores numerous antecedent cues and reinforcing consequences of drinking, would be doomed to failure. However, these techniques must still be seriously considered as potential components of more comprehensive approaches.

Electrical Aversion.   Presentation of electric shock in some form of contingent relationship with alcohol and/or alcohol-related cues was both the earliest and most superficially advantageous procedure for making alcohol noxious. It was the earliest because Kantorovich (1930) used a Pavlovian CS-UCS procedure for pairing shock and alcohol 50 years ago in Russia. It appeared advantageous because shock is easily controlled with regard to intensity, duration, and presentation schedule (Franks, 1970; Rachman and Teasdale, 1969). Shock aversion has been tried in one of three formats. McGuire and Vallance (1964) used *classical aversion conditioning* by pairing shock and alcohol in a manner similar to Kantorovich. Blake (1965, 1967) combined aversion and *escape conditioning* by initiating shock when a sip of alcohol was taken into the mouth and terminating shock when it was expectorated. Blake also antedated current multimodal approaches by showing that aversion training plus progressive relaxation to decrease tension (Blake, 1965) was superior to aversion training alone (Blake, 1967). MacCulloch, Feldman, Orford, and MacCulloch (1966) shocked subjects shortly after presentation of photographic slides of alcoholic beverages, unless the subject terminated the slide prior to shock onset. This was viewed as an *anticipatory avoidance conditioning* procedure. A number of other aversion conditioning studies have been completed, with varying levels of experimental design sophistication, and with varying levels of success (Hallam, Rachman, and Falkowski, 1972; Hsu, 1965; Sandler, 1969). Without discussing the design merits and demerits specific to each of the above studies, in sum, their findings must be viewed as inconclusive due to various design faults. These include inadequate follow-up and failure to compare the experimental treatment with other forms of treatment.

Using somewhat better experimental methodology, Miller, Hersen, Eisler, and Hemphill (1973) found no support for the comparative efficacy of Blake's (1965) aversion-escape procedure. They employed this procedure with the added advantage of having ensured that the electric shock was indeed aversive by predetermining a shock level that produced pain and forearm flexion. This treatment was compared with a similar treatment that used subpainful shock (to control for "expectancy") and more traditional group therapy. Miller and Hersen's (1972) taste-rating task, similar to that used by Marlatt, Demming and Reid (1973), was used as a pre- and post-treatment analog measure of drinking. Despite the fact that the expectancy control may have been transparent as not an actual treatment, there were no significant differences between groups in amount consumed post-treatment. Hedberg and Campbell (1974), in a study comparing four behavioral outpatient treatments, reported a similar lack of support for the efficacy of the anticipatory avoidance technique used originally by MacCulloch et al. (1966). Although some success was noted for the systematic desensitization, covert sensitization, and behavioral family counseling treatments, the failure of this study to provide data on base-rate improvement for this patient population in traditional treatment makes the results unconvincing. Note that in both the Miller et al. (1973), and Hedberg and Campbell (1974) studies, treatments were still of a unitary nature.

A series of studies by Vogler and his colleagues highlights the changes in treatment approach and research strategy that have occurred since the early 1970s. In the original study, reported in 1970, Vogler, Lunde, Johnson, and Martin compared five treatment conditions: (1) shock aversion plus escape conditioning combined in a manner identical to Blake's (1965), administered in 20 inpatient sessions and three outpatient "booster" sessions; (2) same as Treatment 1 minus the "booster" sessions; (3) same as Treatment 1 but substituting random for contingent shock (pseudoconditioning); (4) same as Treatment 1 but without any shock administration; and (5) "routine hospital treatment." Vogler et al. reported in 1970 that Treatment 1 subjects maintained abstinence significantly longer at an 8-month follow-up, but after a 12-month follow-up, Vogler, Lunde, and Martin reported in 1971 that the conditioning treatment subjects were as likely to be rehospitalized as were the pseudoconditioning subjects. Furthermore, regarding the 1970 study, Briddell and Nathan (1976) point out that the failure to record patient dropouts in the conditioning groups as treatment failures artifactually inflated the apparent success of the conditioning procedures. Baekeland (1977) additionally suggests that the two conditioning control treatments were transparent as nontreatments.

Thus, in 1975 (Vogler, Compton, and Weissbach) and in 1977 (Vogler, Weissbach, Compton, and Martin), Vogler's group altered their strategy in three important ways. Treatment was targeted at controlled drinking rather than abstinence. The electric shock procedure was coupled to blood alcohol discrimination training, and was designed to punish violation of prescribed BAL limits. Finally, treatment conditions were multimodal and all groups received actual rather than pseudo treatment. Further, the 1977 study was carried out on "problem drinkers" rather than "chronic alcoholics." These studies will be elaborated upon in subsequent sections.

In sum, electrical aversion has not received much support as a useful alcoholism treatment. Some writers (Wilson, 1978) have, therefore, advocated discontinuing its use, especially since Wilson, Leaf, and Nathan (1975) reported that it does not even produce a conditioned aversion (negative reaction to alcohol). Others have observed that most negative studies have employed an escape paradigm. A punishment paradigm, in contrast, may be efficacious in decreasing rather than terminating drinking due to decreased motivation to drink, instead of true conditioned aversion (Miller, 1976b). However, as in most treatment areas, the research literature is not of such quality as to make for final conclusions, and electrical aversion has not yet been tested as part of a multimodal package which has been tailored to each drinker's own drinking history. At this point, however, there is little to recommend it.

Chemical Aversion. Chemically induced aversion superficially appears more promising for alcoholism treatment, perhaps because it has yet to receive thorough empirical testing. One appealing aspect of chemical aversion is that its impact is on the gastrointestinal tract, and it, therefore, conforms to the topography of the drinking response itself (Wilson and Davison, 1969). Chemical aversion treatment typically employs a nauseating agent such as emetine or apomorphine, which is administered (usually prior to drinking) so that nausea is produced immediately following presentation of alcohol. Apnea-inducing agents such as succinylcholine chloride have also been used. The intended consequences of these techniques is a classically conditioned aversion.

Only single subject and single group studies have been reported for emetine conditioning, making conclusions impossible. The preponderance of data on this technique has been reported from the Shadel Sanitarium in Seattle, Washington, by Voegtlin, Lemere, and associates (e.g., Lemere and Voegtlin, 1950). Their procedure included five conditioning treatments spaced over five to ten days of inpatient hospitalization. Booster treatments following discharge were also used. For each session, a patient was put in a room with a variety of alcoholic beverages. The patient was administered the emetic agent and when nausea first began, he was given a drink to smell and taste. The session lasted from 30 minutes to one hour with additional drinks. A survey of 4,096 of 4,468 patients treated by this program over 13 years revealed abstinence in 44 percent overall. However, these patients were individuals of almost exclusively higher socioeconomic status (SES) who agreed to participate in a rather unpleasant treatment. As Baekeland (1977, p. 410) points out, "when the trials . . . are corrected for retreatment of relapsed patients, they give long-term abstinence rates that range from 30 to 40 percent, certainly not even as good as those obtained with other treatment methods in similar patients." Other reports on similar procedures have reported higher success rates (e.g., 63 percent, Wiens, Montague, Manaugh, and English, 1976), but over shorter time spans. Again, patients were screened, upper SES individuals. Note that all these studies included traditional aspects of treatment in addition to aversion conditioning (counseling, AA, and a supportive inpatient milieu). Note also that Lemere and Voegtlin (1950) were forced to conclude, based on attempts to treat 100 charity cases, that aversive conditioning was useful only with the higher SES patients.

Apnea-inducing agents (succinylcholine chloride) have been introduced for aversion conditioning (1) to increase the severity of the UCR (to extreme limits because the effect of this drug must feel like terminal asphyxiation; in fact, without considerable care, such might indeed be the case), and (2) to avoid using a central nervous system depressant, e.g., apomorphine, which might interfere with conditioning. Despite this impressive rationale, the results of such treatment have not been impressive (Clancy, VanderHoof, and Campbell, 1967; Madill, Campbell, Laverty et al., 1966). Considering the actual risks of this procedure, the results from both case studies and controlled investigation hardly merit even continued experimental use.

Limited testing of *covert sensitization* (aversion) as developed by Joseph Cautela (1967) has also occurred. In this procedure, the by now well-known nausea-vomiting scene is verbally conjured up for the patient to image, following presentation of imagery of the patient's typical drinking situation. The appeal of this technique is its ability to handle the patient's own personal drinking cues without apparatus. The patient might also employ it as a self-control procedure while in an actual drinking situation. Once again, however, experimental support is of the case study (Cautela, 1970) or single-group (Anant, 1967) variety. The single-control group study (Ashem and Donner, 1968) reported marginal effects in the context of a weak and inconclusive experimental design.

In sum, the clinician is left with far from convincing empirical support for any of the aversion procedures. However, as Rachman and Teasdale (1969) pointed out, and Davidson (1974) reiterated, "The surprising thing about aversion therapy is not that its effects are uncertain, but that it works at all" given the less than sophisticated application of the procedures. The procedural details of these treatments hardly conforms to those of the conditioning methods originally developed in experimental psychology laboratories. Furthermore, mere removal of an unwanted behavior is insufficient as therapy; efforts must be made to build in desired alternative responses (Bandura, 1969). The ultimate dilemma for the clinician is whether to reject potential treatments for an extremely difficult behavioral problem, because of weak evidence from largely poorly designed studies which have employed procedures in an unsophisticated fashion. This dilemma is not easily resolvable, but, hopefully, a solution will ultimately come from a better understanding of the parameters of alcoholism itself.

Reducing Underlying Anxiety

The clinician is largely in a similar bind with regard to employing *systematic desensitization* (SD) with alcoholics. This procedure has been used to reduce the anxiety that presumably motivates alcohol consumption. Kraft and Al-Issa (1967), and Kraft (1969), found no significant changes in drinking from SD, and did not compare it with traditional treatment effectiveness in their treatment population. SD has been incorporated into some multimodal approaches in recent studies, however, and will be mentioned again in that context.

Blood Alcohol Level (BAL) Discrimination Training

BAL discrimination training was the first technique specifically developed for achieving controlled drinking rather than abstention in alcoholics. Since Lovibond and Caddy's (1970) report, a few studies of the efficacy of BAL discrimination training as part of an actual treatment package have been undertaken. The majority of studies in this area have, however, been laboratory analyses of the BAL discrimination process itself.

In the first phase of Lovibond and Caddy's (1970) original procedure, alcoholic patients were to attend to subjective cues associated with varying BALs (up to 80 mg percent). They were to use these cues to make repeated BAL estimates, which were followed by accurate feedback on actual BAL as measured by a Breathalyzer. Alcoholics' BAL estimates were inaccurate at the outset, but improved during training. In the second study phase, this procedure was repeated, except that painful electric shock was administered via throat electrodes whenever BALs exceeded 65 mg percent. Between five and ten shock sessions were used, with patients receiving a mean of seven shocks/session. A matched group of alcoholics receiving noncontingent shocks constituted the experimental control. Twelve and 24-month follow-up improvement rates were claimed to be 85 percent and 59 percent, respectively. In 1976, Caddy and Lovibond reported a three-group study. Group 1 received BAL discrimination training, discriminated aversive conditioning, and training in "self-regulation" (self-implemented stimulus control analysis). In Group 2, shock was eliminated and in Group 3, self-regulation training was excluded. Immediately after treatment and at a six-month follow-up, Group 1 subjects showed significantly more improvement than the other group.

As with other treatments, encouraging results have been rendered inconclusive by design limitations. First, we do not know base-rate of improvement in this "alcoholic" population because no traditional treatment control is provided. Second, in both studies, the primary treatment group gets more treatment than the other groups. Third, as Nathan and Goldman (in press) indicated, no check was ever made as to whether patients could reliably discriminate BAL once feedback was discontinued.

A series of laboratory studies designed to answer just this question found that alcoholics trained to attend to interoceptive cues were not able to maintain BAL discrimination accuracy in the absence of feedback (Lansky, Nathan, and Lawson, 1978; Silverstein, Nathan, and Taylor, 1974) perhaps due to functional tolerance to alcohol that develops from frequent alcohol usage (Nathan and Lipscomb, 1978). Nonalcoholics with similar training were able to transfer BAL discrimination accuracy (Huber, Karlin, and Nathan, 1976) from a feedback to nonfeedback condition, although research by Maisto and Adesso (1977) has recently suggested that such ability may be due to expectancy factors plus the subjects' use of external cues. These theoretical issues are less important from a clinical perspective, however, since both alcoholics (Lansky et al., 1977) and social drinkers (Huber et al., 1976) are able to accurately estimate BAL from calculations involving alcohol dose, time since drinking, and metabolic rate. For example, the average individual's BAL increases by 20 mg percent with every one-ounce shot of whisky consumed, and decreases by 20 mg percent with every hour that passes. More precise calculations can be made from tables giving BAL-dose relationships based on body weight (a slide-rule device for BAL estimation is available from the Rutgers Center of Alcohol Studies, New Brunswick, NJ, 08903).

In sum, evidence does not now exist to support the exclusive use of BAL discrimination training for attaining controlled drinking. However, the exclusive use of such training does not make much sense from a clinical perspective anyway. BAL discrimination training has recently been employed in multimodal programs (e.g., Miller, 1978; Vogler et al., 1977), and will be reviewed in this context shortly.

Altering Antecedents and Consequences of Drinking— "Operant Methods"

To this point, methods for directly suppressing the drinking response have been emphasized. In recent years, an intervention strategy has evolved which has instead emphasized altering the environmental reinforcement contingencies and their associated antecedent cues which may serve as discriminative stimuli for drinking. This strategy has been referred to by many behavior modifiers as "operant methods." (This is technically an inappropriate distinction because many of the afore-mentioned techniques also fit into an operant paradigm. Hence, the quotation marks around "operant methods.")

Naturally occurring environmental contingencies have a tremen-dous impact on drinking. As these have become recognized (see p. 260), the advantage (even necessity) of altering these contingencies as part of treatment has become obvious. A variety of laboratory studies, in which the experimenter can exert considerable control over environ-mental contingencies, have confirmed that altering contingencies can decrease drinking. For example, when an enriched ward environment is made contingent on moderate drinking by alcoholics, they will indeed moderate their drinking (Cohen, Liebson, Faillace, and Allen, 1971). Similarly, contingent administration of isolation (Bigelow, Liebson, and Griffiths, 1974), and alcohol on a subsequent drinking day (Bigelow et al., 1973), has effectively decreased drinking by alco-holics.

Modification of drinking by manipulation of consequences has been instituted on a limited basis outside the laboratory in the form of contingency contracting. In contingency contracting, the desired re-sponse is specified to the subject *prior to* the institution of the rein-forcement procedure. Sometimes response and reinforcement con-tigencies are written down in the form of a contract. Miller, Hersen, Eisler, and Watts (1974) lowered a single outpatient alcoholic's drinking by administering VA Hospital commissary coupons if his BAL was zero (on a Breathalyzer test) whenever a research assistant made a visit to the patient's natural living environment. The timing of these visits was unpredictable by the patient. Bigelow, Strickler, Liebson, and Griffiths (1976) aided alcoholics to maintain abstinence by returning a small portion of funds they had deposited with the experimenters if they appeared regularly at a clinic to receive Antabuse.

Other programs have made far more extensive use of contingency contracting. These will be reviewed subsequently as part of the cover-age of multimodal procedures. They are not reviewed here because the "reinforcers" employed affect the patient's entire lifestyle. In these cases, it is difficult to know if drinking decreases solely because of the contingency instituted, or because the patient's overall living condi-tions are so improved.

Comprehensive and Multimodal Procedures

The following group of studies most closely approximates the current "state of the art" in behavioral treatment of alcoholism, at least that portion of the art that has been experimentally scrutinized. The treatments used in these studies derive from an explicit or implicit recognition of the complex nature of alcoholism.

Lazarus (1965) was the first to recommend a comprehensive treatment package aimed at multiple components of the problem as he saw it at the time. Among other techniques, he advised aversive conditioning for reduction of drinking, assertive training to improve social functioning, and desensitization for decreasing the anxiety thought to be the major motivation for drinking. Although his package did not receive thorough empirical testing, it does anticipate some of the comprehensive programs used recently.

"Individualized Behavior Therapy for Alcoholics" (IBTA) (Sobell and Sobell, 1973a) is among the earliest programs to tailor treatment to the drinking history of each patient. Treatment was multifaceted. (Treatment in all these studies is too complex to present thoroughly herein. Interested readers should consult original sources.) It included: specifying prior cues for heavy drinking, and training subjects to generate and perform alternative responses in the presence of these cues; stimulus control training including electric shock punishment of inappropriate drinking (at a bar set up on the treatment premises); videotape replay of drunken behavior for increasing treatment motivation; exposure of subjects to an actual failure experience (impossible tests) for the analysis of subject's response to failure. With slight modifications, the program could be directed toward either controlled drinking or abstinence. The controlled drinking aspect used the procedure reported originally by Mills, Sobell, and Schaefer (1971), in which alcoholics were shocked when they drank in a manner dissimilar to social drinkers. Shock was, therefore, administered when alcoholics ordered straight drinks, ordered too many or too frequent drinks, or gulped, rather than sipped drinks. These procedures did produce decreased drinking while the shock contingencies were in effect, but during probe sessions (nonshock) during the course of treatment, subjects returned to excessive drinking. At six-week follow-up, controlled drinker experimental subjects (behavior modification program) were functioning better and drank less than their controls (conventional treatment). At six-month and one-year (Sobell and Sobell, 1973b) follow-ups, both the controlled drinker and nondrinker experimentals performed better than their respective controls, but did not differ from each other. At the two-year follow-up (Sobell and Sobell, 1976), only the controlled drinking experimentals maintained superiority over their respective controls.

These results have been used to support the efficacy of IBTA over conventional treatment, especially when aimed toward controlled drinking. While impressive in scope and extent of follow-up, methodological problems once again necessitate cautious interpretation of results. Two of the most serious problems were: (1) Subjects were selected for the controlled drinking treatment because they had social support systems outside the hospital. They, therefore, had a better prognosis even before treatment began. (2) Experimental subjects received 17 behavioral sessions, *in addition to* the conventional therapy received by the controls. Other criticisms have been detailed by Emrick (1975), Baekeland (1977), and Nathan and Goldman (in press).

A very similar treatment program, differing primarily in that BAL discrimination training was substituted for the Mills et al. (1971) social drinking procedure, has been developed by Vogler and his colleagues. The BAL discrimination training used in this program incorporated shock administration for BALs exceeding 50 mg percent. The program was tested with outpatient alcoholics (Vogler, Compton, and Weissbach, 1975) and outpatient problem drinkers (Vogler, Weissbach, Compton, and Martin, 1977), and used preplanned "booster sessions" to follow up the initial treatment. In the 1975 study design, the treatment package was compared with conventional treatment. In the 1977 study, a four-group design was used to test the entire package against subsets of its components.

One-year follow-up of both studies showed that *all* groups improved significantly, with roughly 62 percent of patients becoming abstinent or controlled drinkers following treatment. The only noteworthy difference between the two was that in the 1975 study, experimental subjects did consume significantly less alcohol than controls, while in the 1977 study, no differences between groups were observed. Two additional observations have considerable interpretive significance. First, the best predictor of outcome in both studies was pretreatment alcohol intake with lower amounts predictive of better outcomes. Second, in the 1977 study, the group that received only alcohol education did as well as the other more complex and longer treatments. Apparently, even for current behavioral programs, treatment technique is less important than patient characteristics. This conclusion is inescapable since these studies are reasonably well designed, keeping to a minimum the possibility that selection or treatment bias could produce artifactual differences between groups. In fact, Vogler et al. (1977) indicated that 70 percent of outcome variance was due to pre-treatment subject characteristics, thus leaving very little room for the demonstration of significant between-treatment effects. In fairness to the behavioral procedures, however, it must also be noted that the more "traditional" control treatments used in these studies were, in fact, quite behaviorally oriented, and perhaps superior to standard treatments.

Similar results have very recently been reported by W. Miller (1978) in a study that emphasized comprehensive self-control training for self- and court-referred problem drinkers. Three treatments were compared: aversive counterconditioning, behavioral self-control training, and a "controlled drinking composite." All treatments included self-monitoring on record cards. The aversion procedure used a classical conditioning temporal sequence except that shock was self-administered, and was delivered only 70 percent of the time. The behavioral self-control training included stimulus analysis of and practice in alternative behaviors. The composite procedure was similar to the program offered by Vogler et al. (1975). A traditional treatment control group was indirectly included by randomly referring some acceptable candidates back to the original referring source (a traffic safety clinic) for standard treatment. At the 12-month follow-up, no differences between treatments were found, despite considerable differences in the amount of therapist time required by the four treatments. All groups had improved, including the traditional treatment "control." The aversive counterconditioning procedure was judged less effective, however, because fewer gains were found for this technique after three months, and because improvement after one year may have been due to a self-control treatment manual issued to some subjects at the three-month follow-up. Miller (1978) concluded that adding components to multimodal approaches may not always be cost-effective.

An alternative strategy for comprehensive treatment is to change the living environment so as to alter the patient's behavior, rather than to directly change the patient. As explained earlier, this method reflects an extension of laboratory-derived operant learning technology. Studies utilizing this method are included as comprehensive treatments because the magnitude of the intervention goes far beyond administration of simple reinforcers.

Hunt and Azrin's (1973) "community-reinforcement" program actually organized the patient's environment so that family interactions, job, and social interactions were made contingent on sobriety. Sixteen alcoholic inpatients were divided into two matched groups. One group received the standard hospital therapy. The experimental group was first exposed to a variety of behavioral techniques, including behavioral rehearsal and cognitive restructuring, designed to improve their social functioning. Following this portion of the program, experimental patients were helped to find employment, and improve their family and social contacts. Once discharged, these natural reinforcers were made contingent on sobriety; that is, if drinking was detected, people in the patient's environment were instructed to make themselves unavailable to the patient. Not surprisingly, experimental subjects' functioning was considerably better than that of the control group. After all, their entire life circumstance had been improved for them, while no such effort had been made for control subjects. Whether the reinforcement contingency was instrumental in their improvement remains impossible to say. In a recent modification of the community-reinforcement program, Azrin (1976) added the use of Antabuse, a network of community individuals to give early warning of drinking, a "buddy" system for social support, and group rather than individual counseling. These changes were made to improve the program while reducing costs. Results again supported the program's efficacy. While the limitations in experimental design and methodology preclude definitive conclusions, the approach used in these studies should not be underrated. For alcoholics without many social supports (typically having poor prognosis) successful treatment may require such an approach.

Another example of a contingency contracting approach is Miller's (1975) program for chronic public drunkenness offenders. Twenty such individuals were divided into experimental and control groups. For the experimental group, a variety of important goods and services supplied by local community agencies was made contingent upon sobriety. These included housing, employment, medical care, clothing, meals, cigarettes, and counseling. Alcohol consumption was measured by assessment of gross intoxication and by spot checks using breath analysis. If intoxication was observed, or if BAL exceeded 10 mg percent, access to these goods and services was denied for five days. Control subjects had access to all the same goods and services, but access was not made contingent on drinking behavior. After two months of this program, experimental subjects showed fewer arrests, lower BALs (measured at BAL "probe" times), and better employment records than did controls. Longer follow-up is necessary for definite conclusions, but such results offer promise.

(EQUIVOCAL) CONCLUSIONS AND (LOOSELY STATED) CLINICAL PRESCRIPTION

To quickly sum up: Aversion procedures have received little empirical support from well-designed studies, and so, given their intrinsic unpleasantness, there remain few arguments for their continued use. Systematic desensitization and BAL discrimination training have not been well supported for use by themselves, and their contribution to multimodal programs is yet uncertain. If used, BAL discrimination training should be based on external, rather than interoceptive, cues. The alteration of naturally occurring reinforcement systems as in contingency contracting offers promise, but requires more and better empirical validation. On theoretical grounds, multimodal procedures make a great deal of sense. As yet, however, proof of their superiority over standard treatments is lacking.

Since the emphasis of this book is on empirically validated treatment, there is an obvious temptation to say at this point, "No treatment is ready for clinical use as yet. Come back in a few years for an update." However, to repeat the old cliché, clinicians cannot work that way; patients need treatment now. Further, a number of factors mitigate the negative conclusions that superficially derive from the treatment research.

First, recent treatment programs have been tailored to individual patients by making use of individual antecedents and reinforcers for drinking. The working clinician is much more likely to select treatment techniques based on individual needs, rather than employing a fixed program. Controlled research has yet to test this truly personalized approach, possibly because well-designed research is difficult when so many sources of variation exist.

Second, it is obvious by now that experimental investigation of a new treatment is reactive with treatment outcome. In the preceding studies, a variety of factors could conceivably have worked either for or against the demonstration of treatment success. For example, participants in "experimental" treatments have high expectations, are perhaps more motivated, may be more subject to demands for improvement, and so on. If control subjects (blind in their actual assessment) should happen to view the "control" treatment as authentic "experimental" treatment, then the outcome of the control treatment may be artificially raised to the level of the real treatment. However, if control subjects should recognize (and be disappointed by) the nature of their treatment, outcome in the experimental groups may look overly good by contrast.

Third, and possibly most important, when abstention was the sole aim of treatment, successful treatment was difficult to achieve. Recently, however, decreased drinking and improved functioning in other life areas have become acceptable goals. Consequently, achieving a positive treatment outcome is now much easier, thus allowing pretreatment patient characteristics to become a significant predictor of treatment success. Put another way, a continuous distribution of treatment outcomes (from poor, through moderate, to excellent) allows for a high correlation with heterogeneous pre-treatment patient characteristics. With pre-treatment patient characteristics accounting for much of the variance in treatment outcome, it becomes difficult to demonstrate the power of a treatment (Vogler et al., 1977). Future research must, therefore, evaluate the success of treatment for more homogeneous patient groupings; particularly, those typically having a poor or guarded prognosis. With such patient groups, the approaches that make clinical and theoretical sense will have more of an opportunity to compare favorably with other treatments.

As far as clinical prescription, the best that can now be done is to recommend those approaches that do make clinical and theoretical sense, and have some limited empirical validation. Thorough analysis of the drinker's history, emphasizing drinking settings, and antecedent cues and reinforcers for drinking appear fundamental. Self-monitoring can augment this analysis. Using such an analysis, the patient must learn to at least attend to, if not avoid, these stimuli. The therapist must be alert to circumstances triggering prior relapses, since they may occur again. Alternative behaviors must be practiced. The patient should be given the sort of broad knowledge that the therapist possesses. This includes the short- and long-term physical and behavioral effects of alcohol, the implications of choosing controlled drinking or abstinence (if such a choice remains medically or psychologically possible), and how to monitor BAL and drink in the fashion of a social drinker. (These last two may be taught even when the goal of treatment is abstinence because they could be useful if a relapse should occur. There is some limited evidence that these behaviors can be placed under instructional control [Miller, Becker, Foy, and Wooten, 1976], and thereby not require elaborate apparatus or technique.) A comprehensive behavioral treatment going beyond the specifics of excessive drinking seems advisable. This may include cognitive restructuring, anxiety-reduction techniques, social skills, and assertive training, and so on. The patient's social environment should be involved, e.g., wife, family, friends, co-workers, perhaps with contingency contracts. Since patients with more favorable prognoses appear to be those who, at earlier points in their drinking history, still maintain environmental supports, treatment for such patients should be encouraged without requiring that they self-identify as "alcoholics." For poor prognosis patients, attempts should be made to set up environmental supports that improve the patient's circumstances and may be used for contingency contracting.

Last, but not least, medical complications play a large role in the treatment of the excessive drinker. Referrals for physical exams are mandatory, as is medical supervision of detoxification if addiction is present. The patient's physical condition obviously must influence treatment setting (inpatient or outpatient), treatment choice, and treatment goal. Likewise, the patient's ability to adhere to a treatment program if he is not being continually monitored determines whether hospitalization is required.

ETHICAL AND LEGAL ISSUES

Alcoholism shares some ethicolegal considerations with other behavioral disorders, while a few are fairly particular to this disorder.

1. Individuals who drink excessively may have a variety of resultant medical problems by the time they reach treatment. Medical evaluation and, if necessary, treatment, is of critical importance.
2. Since treatment techniques are yet unproven, the therapist is always in the dilemma of having to refrain from "overselling" his approach without undermining treatment. Obviously, a middle-of-the-road attitude is advisable.
3. Because referrals are often necessary, and because the patient may at some future point reach another treatment source when encountering problems, no treatment approach should ever be derogated to the patient. This rule applies to organizations such as Alcoholics Anonymous, whose philosophy runs strongly counter to beliefs shared by behavior therapists.
4. The use of unproven aversive procedures, especially the more severe forms, runs into by now obvious ethical problems.
5. Since many patients will be referred under some sort of coercion, e.g., courts, wife, employers, the therapist must guard against being oversolicitous to the coercive agent at the expense of the patient. Coercion may not be all bad, however, and is sometimes the only way of getting certain patients into treatment. Coercion to treatment is obviously a complex ethical issue and must be re-examined each time it occurs. A particularly difficult aspect of this problem occurs when a therapist is called upon to help a patient avoid serious legal or job-related consequences by notifying a court or employer that the patient is in treatment. The therapist must be careful not to imply that treatment will be successful.
6. Frequently, there are victims of alcoholism in addition to the drinker, e.g., the alcoholic's wife and children. Treatment must be offered to these people as well.
7. Individuals with a history of problem drinking, who are successfully maintaining abstinence, should not be encouraged by a therapist to attempt controlled drinking.

SUGGESTIONS FOR CLINICAL AND EXPERIMENTAL RESEARCH

While the need for various types of behavioral research has been indicated throughout this chapter, a number of questions may be posed to briefly delineate potentially fruitful avenues of investigation.

In the experimental/theoretical realm:

1. Why do humans initiate drinking? All available evidence indicates that without some experimental manipulation, alcohol is not preferentially selected for consumption by animals. How is the "human animal" different?
2. How is drinking maintained past the initial contact?
3. Why does drinking accelerate in some individuals? Answering these first three questions requires specification of the reinforcing properties of alcohol itself (as a pharmacological agent) and alcohol use (as an operant response).
4. What leads certain individuals toward physical and social deterioration in connection with alcohol consumption? Since heavy alcohol use does not by itself lead inevitably to deterioration (Clark and Cahalan, 1976), the controlling mechanisms must yet be identified.

In the clinical realm:

1. Which patients are most successful with which treatments, and which patients should be directed toward abstinence versus controlled drinking?
2. How well will a truly personalized multimodal treatment work with different homogeneous patient groups?

CASE STUDY

It would be contrary to the empirical emphasis of this chapter to present an elaborate case study as a model instance of treatment, since no such model has been validated. Instead, a brief vignette is presented to challenge biases that tend to exist in the field (the case description is, of course, disguised).

Mr. A, age 42, seeks treatment because his second wife threatens to leave him if his drunken episodes continue. He returns home reeling drunk three to four nights per week. History-taking reveals that he had been a moderate drinker since his late teens, but, roughly six years ago, one year prior to a divorce, he began his drunken episodes. They increased in frequency when he lived alone between marriages, and persisted at a steady rate after marrying his second wife, whom he met in a bar. He had sought treatment before, but had always rejected it when he was forced to admit he was an alcoholic. He had retained his job as a semiskilled factory worker throughout his drinking, and rarely missed work.

Although Mr. A appeared to have a very serious drinking problem requiring extensive intervention, behavioral analysis revealed that he always drank to excess in bars, and never drank excessively in other settings. Between marriages, he frequented bars, and maintaining social relations with co-workers was difficult without going to the bar after work. Treatment consisted of alerting Mr. A to the stimulus control characteristics of bars, and to developing social relationships in settings other than bars. Assertion training turned out to be unnecessary, since he had no trouble refusing invitations to go to bars, or to forming new relationships in civic organizations. At a two-year follow-up, Mr. A continued to stay away from bars and had had no drunken episodes. He did drink some alcohol at some social occasions, but never to excess.

Of course, anyone with experience in the alcoholism field could contrast this case with thousands for whom extensive behavioral and/ or other intervention, family counseling, vocational counseling, and so on, did no good whatsoever. This case is only presented to indicate how clinicians' biases can thwart treatment. This man refused to acknowledge that he was an alcoholic and only by not requiring this acknowledgment was treatment accomplished. Even then, treatment was much simpler than anyone could have expected, considering the extent of his drinking. Only by *not* fitting all "alcoholics" into a common category can important individual characteristics be used to facilitate treatment.

SUMMARY

Despite the enormous effect that alcoholism continues to have on our society, an operational definition has yet to be agreed upon. This lack of consensus is in part due to the behavioral variability of the disorder, as well as theoretical considerations about etiology. At this point, "alcoholism" is best understood as a summary label which subsumes a variety of problematic drinking and associated behaviors.

Efforts to understand the etiology of alcoholism have been pursued from biological, sociological, and psychological perspectives. Although many leads have been developed, the etiology remains unclear.

In the biological realm, alcohol has been shown to have deleterious effects on just about every organ system, but since these effects are consequent, rather than antecedent to excessive alcohol use, they cannot be considered central to etiologic formulations. No physiological or genetic study has yet conclusively established an etiological factor, although some findings are suggestive and need to be pursued. Correspondingly, the often prevailing "disease" concept of alcoholism is probably not a useful scientific heuristic.

Sociocultural research has clearly established the etiological influence of acculturation and socialization patterns on eventual alcohol use. Generally, when alcohol is used in a circumscribed manner as part of family ritual, it is less likely to be abused. More recent findings have shown that the population of alcoholics reaching treatment facilities may not be at all representative of the entire population of problem drinkers in the community.

Personality approaches to alcoholism have largely resulted in conflicting, inconclusive findings that have not been useful from an etiologic standpoint. There may be more merit to recent factor analytic studies which have attempted to group alcoholics into personality subtypes.

The prevailing behavioral formulation, labelled the "tension-reduction" hypothesis, has not received consistent empirical support. Recent work has shown that the reinforcing capacity of alcohol use may result from a complex interaction of biochemical, cognitive, effective, and social-learning factors which have yet to be thoroughly delineated.

Assessment techniques for alcoholism have traditionally been directed toward discriminating alcoholics from populations of normals or other psychiatric patients. It is not surprising, considering the heterogeneity of the alcoholic population, that such assessment devices have had only limited success. A variety of behavioral techniques for monitoring freely emitted drinking and related behaviors has been used effectively for studying alcoholism. Some techniques have also had some limited applicability to treatment planning, such as those which have identified social drinking—as opposed to problem drinking—patterns with subsequent training of alcoholics in social drinking styles. More directly applicable to treatment have been a number of self-report and self-monitoring procedures for specifying the relevant cues and reinforcers for a particular individual's drinking.

When planning behavioral treatment of alcoholism, the clinician must recognize the complexity of the cue-reinforcement contingencies for each individual and the consequent need for a multimodal approach. The merits of controlled drinking as an alternative to abstinence have been recently debated in the literature. Clinicians should approach controlled-drinking programs with caution for a variety of reasons, but they should still be encouraged to consider them, if only on an experimental basis.

The history of the behavioral research has shown a progression from early treatments employing one or two techniques, to more recent multimodal approaches. Among the earliest behavioral interventions were those designed to make alcohol noxious to the drinker by aversively counterconditioning with electric shock or noxious chemicals. The considerable body of research on these procedures may be summed up as equivocal at best, negative at worst. Similarly, the reduction of underlying anxiety via the sole use of systematic desensitization has not been supported. Although a number of researchers have attempted to train alcoholics to discriminate their own blood alcohol levels as an aide to self-control of drinking, the clinical use of these procedures requires more convincing demonstration of their effectiveness. In any case, such training should rely on external, rather than interoceptive cues. The control of drinking by manipulation of external reinforcement contingencies has shown promise in laboratory studies, and, to date, has received limited support in actual clinical trials.

A variety of multimodal programs, tailored to the specific drinking history of the individual drinker, have been tested recently. Although they make theoretical sense, convincing empirical validation is still lacking.

However, since recent studies have shown that up to 70 percent of outcome variance may be due to pre-treatment subject characteristics, it will be necessary to compare treatments on selected subsets of alcoholics before effective procedures can be clearly identified. The working clinician is, therefore, wise to treat alcoholism as an extremely complex behavior by tailoring treatment to the individual, and by using ingenuity in the selection of techniques. To date, truly individualized treatment that does not rely on treatment "packages" has yet to be thoroughly tested, and may offer the most promise.

REFERENCES

Amark, C. A study in alcoholism. Clinical, social-psychiatric and genetic investigations. *Acta Psychiatrica et Neurologica Scandinavica,* 1951 Supplement 70, 1–284.

Anant, S. S. A note on the treatment of alcoholics by a verbal aversion technique. *Canadian Psychologist,* 1967, *1,* 19–22.

Armor, D. J., Polich, J. M., and Stanbul, H. B. *Alcoholism and treatment.* Prepared for the United States National Institute on Alcohol Abuse and Alcoholism. Santa Monica, CA.: Rand Corporation, 1976.

Armstrong, J. D. The search for the alcoholic personality. *Annals of the American Academy of Political and Social Science,* 1958, *315,* 40–47.

Ashem B., and Donner, L. Covert sensitization with alcoholics: A controlled replication. *Behaviour Research and Therapy,* 1968, *6,* 7–12.

Azrin, N. H. Improvements in the community reinforcement approach to alcoholism. *Behaviour Research and Therapy,* 1976, *14,* 339–348.

Baekeland, F. Evaluation of treatment methods in chronic alcoholism. In B. Kissen and H. Begleiter, eds., *The biology of alcoholism* (vol. 5), *Treatment and rehabilitation of the chronic alcoholic.* New York: Plenum Press, 1977.

Bandura, A. *Principles of behavior modification.* New York: Holt, Rinehart, and Winston, 1969.

Berry, R., Boland, J., Laxson, J. et al. The economic costs of alcohol abuse and alcoholism. In M. Keller, ed., *Alcohol and health, new knowledge.* United States Department of Health, Education, and Welfare; National Institute on Alcohol Abuse and Alcoholism. Second Special Report to the United States Congress. Washington, D.C.: United States Government Printing Office, 1974.

Bigelow, G., Liebson, I., and Griffiths, R. R. *Experimental analysis of alcoholic drinking.* Paper read at the American Psychological Association Convention, August, 1973.

Bigelow, G., Liebson, I., and Griffiths, R. R. Alcoholic drinking: Suppression by a behavioral time-out procedure. *Behaviour Research and Therapy,* 1974, *12,* 107–115.

Bigelow, G., Strickler, D., Liebson, I., and Griffiths, R. Maintaining disulfiram ingestion among outpatient alcoholics: A security deposit contingency contracting procedure. *Behaviour Research and Therapy,* 1976, *14,* 378–381.

Blake, B. G. The application of behaviour therapy to the treatment of alcoholism. *Behaviour Research and Therapy,* 1965, *3,* 75–85.

Blake, B. G. A follow-up of alcoholics treated by behaviour therapy. *Behaviour Research and Therapy,* 1967, *5,* 89–94.

Blum, H. Mind-altering drugs and dangerous behavior: Alcohol. In *Task-force report: Drunkenness* (Appendix B), President's Commission on Law Enforcement and Administration of Justice. Washington, D.C.: U.S. Government Printing Office, 1967.

Briddell, D. W., and Nathan, P. E. Behavior assessment and modification with alcoholics: Current status and future trends. In M. Hersen, R. M. Eisler, and P. M. Miller, eds., *Progress in behavior modification.* New York: Academic Press, 1976.

Briddell, D. W., and Wilson, G. T. The effects of alcohol and expectancy set on male sexual arousal. *Journal of Abnormal Psychology,* 1976, *85,* 225–234.

Brown, J. S., and Crowell, C. R. Alcohol and conflict resolution, a theoretical analysis. *Quarterly Journal of Studies on Alcohol,* 1974, *35,* 66–85.

Brown, R. A., and Cutter, H. G. Alcohol, customary drinking behavior, and pain. *Journal of Abnormal Psychology,* 1977, *86,* 179–188.

Button, A. D. A study of alcoholics with the Minnesota Multiphasic Personality Inventory. *Quarterly Journal of Studies on Alcohol,* 1956, *17,* 263–281.

Caddy, G., and Lovibond, S. H. Self regulation and discriminated aversive conditioning in the modification of alcoholics' drinking behavior. *Behavior Therapy,* 1976, *7,* 223–230.

Cahalan, D. *Problem drinkers.* San Francisco: Jossey-Bass, 1970.

Cahalan, D., and Cisin, I. H. Epidemiological and social factors associated with drinking problems. In R. E. Tarter, and A. A. Sugerman, eds., *Alcoholism, interdisciplinary approaches to an enduring problem.* Reading, Massachusetts: Addison-Wesley Publishing Company, Inc., 1976a.

Cahalan, D., and Cisin, I. H. Drinking behavior and drinking problems in the United States. In B. Kissen and H. Begleiter, eds., *Social aspects of alcoholism,* New York: Plenum Press, 1976b.

Cahalan, D. and Room, R. Problem drinking among American men aged 21–59. *American Journal of Public Health,* 1972, *62,* 1473–1482.

Cappell, H. An evaluation of tension models of alcohol consumption. In Y. Israel et al., ed., *Research advances in alcohol and drug problems.* New York: John Wiley and Sons, Inc., 1974.

Cappell, H. and Herman, C. P. Alcohol and tension reduction: A review. *Quarterly Journal of Studies on Alcohol,* 1972, *33,* 33–64.

Caudill, B. D. and Marlatt, G. A. Modelling influences in social drinking: An experimental analogue. *Journal of Consulting and Clinical Psychology,* 1975, *43,* 405–415.

Cautela, J. R. Covert sensitization. *Psychological Reports,* 1967, *20,* 459–468.

Cautela, J. R. The treatment of alcoholism by covert sensitization. *Psychotherapy: Theory, Research and Practice,* 1970, *7,* 86–90.

Clancy, J., VanderHoof, W., and Campbell, P. Evaluation of an aversive technique as a treatment for alcoholism; controlled trial with succinylcholine-induced apnea. *Quarterly Journal of Studies on Alcohol,* 1967, *28,* 476–485.

Clark, W. B. Loss of control, heavy drinking and drinking problems in a longitudinal study. *Journal of Studies on Alcohol,* 1976, *37,* 1256–1290.

Clark, W. B. and Cahalan, D. Changes in problem drinking over a four-year span. *Addictive Behavior,* 1976, *1,* 251–259.

Cohen, M., Liebson, I. A., Faillace, L. A., and Allen, R. P. Moderate drinking by chronic alcoholics. *Journal of Nervous and Mental Disease,* 1971, *153,* 434–444.

Conger, J. J. The effects of alcohol on conflict behavior in the albino rat. *Quarterly Journal of Studies on Alcohol,* 1951, *12,* 1–29.

Conger, J. J. Alcoholism: Theory, problem and challenge. II. Reinforcement theory and the dynamics of alcoholism. *Quarterly Journal of Studies on Alcohol,* 1956, *17,* 291–324.

Cutter, H.S.G., Maloof, B., Kurtz, N. R., and Jones, W. C. "Feeling no pain" differential responses to pain by alcoholics and non-alcoholics before and after drinking. *Journal of Studies on Alcohol,* 1976, *37,* 273–277.

Davidson, W. S. II Studies of aversive conditioning for alcoholics: A critical review of theory and research methodology. *Psychological Bulletin,* 1974, *81,* 571–581.

Davies, D. L. Definitional issues in alcoholism. In R. E. Tarter, and A. A. Sugerman, eds., *Alcoholism, interdisciplinary approaches to an enduring problem,* Reading, MA.: Addison-Wesley Publishing Company, 1976.

Dreyfus, P. M. Diseases of the nervous system in chronic alcoholics. In B. Kissen and H. Begleiter eds., *The biology of alcoholism,* vols. I–III. New York: Plenum Press, 1971–1974.

Emrick, C. D. A review of psychologically oriented treatment of alcoholism. *Journal of Studies on Alcohol,* 1975, *36,* 88–108.

Engle, K. B., and Williams, T. K. Effect of an ounce of vodka on alcoholics' desire for alcohol. *Quarterly Journal of Studies on Alcohol,* 1972, *33,* 1099–1105.

Ewing, J. A., Rouse, B. A., and Pellizzari, E. D. Alcohol sensitivity and ethnic background. *American Journal of Psychiatry,* 1974, *131,* 206–210.

Falk, J. L., and Samson, H. H. Schedule-induced physical dependence on ethanol. *Pharmacology Review,* 1976, *27,* 449–464.

Franks, C. M. Alcoholism. In C. G. Costello, ed., *Symptoms of psychopathology.* New York: Wiley, 1970.

Freed, E. The effect of alcohol upon approach-avoidance conflict in the white rat. *Quarterly Journal of Studies on Alcohol,* 1967, *28,* 236–254.

Freund, G. Diseases of the nervous system associated with alcoholism. In R. E. Tarter and A. A. Sugerman, eds., *Alcoholism, interdisciplinary approaches to an enduring problem.* Reading, Ma: Addison-Wesley, 1976.

Goldman, M. S. To drink or not to drink: An experimental analysis of group drinking decision by four alcoholics. *American Journal of Psychiatry,* 1974, *131,* 1123–1130.

Goodwin, D. W., Crane, J. B., and Guze, S. B. Alcoholic "blackouts": A review and clinical study of 100 alcoholics. *American Journal of Psychiatry,* 1969, *126,* 191–198.

Goodwin, D. W., Schulsinger, F., Hermansen, L. et al. Alcohol problems in adoptees raised apart from alcoholic biological parents. *Archives of General Psychiatry,* 1973, *28,* 238–243.

Griffiths, R. R., Bigelow, G. E., and Liebson, I. A. Effect of ethanol self-administration on choice behavior: Money versus socializing. *Pharmacology Biochemistry and Behavior,* 1975, *3,* 443–446.

Hallam, R., Rachman, S., and Falkowski, W. Subjective, attitudinal and physiological effects of electrical aversion therapy. *Behaviour Research and Therapy,* 1972, *10,* 1–13.

Hamburg, S. Behavior therapy in alcoholism: A critical review of broad-spectrum approaches. *Journal of Studies on Alcohol,* 1975, *36,* 69–87.

Hampton, P. J. The development of a personality questionnaire for drinkers. *Genetic Psychology Monographs,* 1953, *48,* 55–115.

Hedberg, A. G., and Campbell, L. A comparison of four behavioral treatments of alcoholism. *Journal of Behavior Therapy and Experimental Psychiatry,* 1974, *5,* 251–256.

Higgins, R. L. and Marlatt, G. A. Effects of anxiety arousal on the consumption of alcohol by alcoholics and social drinkers. *Journal of Consulting and Clinical Psychology,* 1973, *41,* 426–433.

Higgins, R. L. and Marlatt, G. A. Fear of interpersonal evaluation as a determinant of alcohol consumption in male social drinkers. *Journal of Abnormal Psychology,* in press.

Hoffmann, H., Loper, R. G., and Kammeier, M. L. Identifying future alcoholics with MMPI alcoholism scales. *Quarterly Journal of Studies on Alcohol,* 1974, *35,* 490–498.

Hoyt, D. P. and Sedlacek, G. M. Differentiating alcoholics from normals and abnormals with the MMPI. *Journal of Clinical Psychology,* 1958, *14,* 69–74.

Hsu, J. J. Electroconditioning therapy of alcoholics. A preliminary report. *Quarterly Journal of Studies on Alcohol,* 1965, *26,* 449–459.

Huber, H., Karlin, R., and Nathan, P. E. Blood alcohol level discrimination by non-alcoholics: The role of internal and external cues. *Journal of Studies on Alcohol,* 1976, *37,* 27–39.

Hunt, G. M. and Azrin, N. H. The community-reinforcement approach to alcoholism. *Behaviour Research and Therapy,* 1973, *11,* 91–104.

Isbell, H., Fraser, H., Wikler, A. et al. An experimental study of the etiology of "run fits" and delirium tremens. *Quarterly Journal of Studies on Alcohol,* 1955, *16,* 1–33.

Jellinek, E. M. Phases of alcohol addiction. *Quarterly Journal of Studies on Alcohol,* 1952, *13,* 673–684.

Jellinek, E. M. *The disease concept of alcoholism.* Highland Park, NJ: Hillhouse Press, 1960.

Jessor, R., Collins, M. I., and Jessor, S. L. On becoming a drinker: Social-psychological aspects of an adolescent transition. *Annals of the New York Academy of Sciences,* 1972, *197,* 199–213.

Jessor, R. and Jessor, S. L. Adolescent development and the onset of drinking; a longitudinal study. *Journal of Studies on Alcohol,* 1975, *36,* 27–51.

Jones, B. M. Memory impairment on the ascending and descending limbs of the blood alcohol curve. *Journal of Abnormal Psychology,* 1973, *82,* 24–32.

Jones, B. M. and Vega, A. Cognitive performance measured on the ascending and descending limbs of the blood alcohol curve. *Psychopharmacologia,* 1972, *23,* 99–114.

Kaij, L. *Alcoholism in twins: Studies on the etiology and sequels of abuse of alcohol.* Stockholm: Almquist and Wiksell, 1960.

Kantorovich, N. An attempt at associative-reflex therapy in alcoholism. *Psychological Abstracts,* 1930, *4,* 493. (Abstract)

Keller, M., ed., *Alcohol and health, new knowledge.* United States Department of Health, Education, and Welfare; National Institute on Alcohol Abuse and Alcoholism. Second Special Report to the United States

Congress. Washington, D.C.: United States Government Printing Office, 1974.

Keller, M. The disease concept of alcoholism revisited. *Journal of Studies on Alcohol,* 1976, *37,* 1694–1717.

Kessler, M. and Gomberg, C. Observations of barroom drinking: Methodology and preliminary results. *Quarterly Journal of Studies on Alcohol,* 1974, *35,* 1392–1396.

Kissen, B. and Begleiter, H., eds., *The biology of alcoholism.* vols. I–III. New York: Plenum Press, 1971–1974.

Korsten, M. A. and Lieber, C. S. Medical complications of alcoholism: Hepatic system. In R. E. Tarter and A. A. Sugerman, eds., *Alocholism, interdisciplinary approaches to an enduring problem.* Reading, Ma.: Addison-Wesley, 1976.

Kosturn, C. F. and Marlatt, G. A. *Elicitation of anger and opportunity for retaliation as determinants of alcohol consumption.* Paper presented at the annual meeting of the Western Psychological Association, San Francisco, 1974.

Kraft, T. Alcoholism treated by systematic desensitization: A follow-up of eight cases. *Journal of the Royal College of General Practice,* 1969, *18,* 336–340.

Kraft, T. and Al-Issa, I. Alcoholism treated by desensitization: A case study. *Behaviour Research and Therapy,* 1967, *5,* 69–70.

Kranitz, L. Alcoholics, heroin addicts and nonaddicts; comparisons on the MacAndrew Alcoholism Scale of the MMPI. *Quarterly Journal of Studies on Alcohol,* 1972, *33,* 807–809.

Lachar, D., Berman, W., Grissell, J. L., and Schooff, K. The MacAndrew Alcoholism Scale as a general measure of substance misuse. *Journal of Studies on Alcohol,* 1976, *37,* 1609–1615.

Lang, A. R., Goeckner, D. J., Adesso, V. T., and Marlatt, G. A. The effects of alcohol on aggression in male social drinkers. *Journal of Abnormal Psychology,* 1975, *84,* 508–518.

Lansky, D., Nathan, P. E., and Lawson, D. M. Blood alcohol level discrimination by alcoholics: The role of internal and external cues. *Journal of Consulting and Clinical Psychology,* 1978, *46,* 953–960.

Lazarus, A. A. Towards the understanding and effective treatment of alcoholism. *South African Medical Journal,* 1965, *39,* 736–741.

Lemere, F. and Voegtlin, W. L. An evaluation of the aversion treatment of alcoholism. *Quarterly Journal of Studies on Alcohol,* 1950, *11,* 199–204.

Lieber, C. S. Liver disease and alcohol: Fatty liver, alcoholic hepatitis, cirrhosis, and their interrelationships. *Annals of the New York Academy of Sciences,* 1975, *252,* 63–84.

Lipscomb, T. R. and Nathan, P. E. Effect of family history of alcoholism, drinking pattern, and tolerance on Blood Alcohol Level discrimination. *Archives of General Psychiatry,* in press.

Lloyd, R. W. and Salzberg, H. C. Controlled social drinking: An alternative to abstinence as a treatment goal for some alcohol abusers. *Psychological Bulletin,* 1975, *82,* 815–842.

Lovibond, S. H., and Caddy, G. R. Discriminated aversive control in the moderation of alcoholics' drinking behavior. *Behavior Therapy,* 1970, *1,* 437–444.

Ludwig, A. M., Wikler, A., and Stark, L. H. The first drink; psychobiological aspects of craving. *Archives of General Psychiatry,* 1974, *30,* 539–547.

MacAndrew, C. The differentiation of male alcoholic outpatients from non-alcoholic psychiatric outpatients by means of the MMPI. *Quarterly Journal of Studies on Alcohol,* 1965, *26,* 238–246.

MacAndrew, C. and Edgerton, R. B. *Drunken comportment: A social explanation.* Chicago: Aldine Publishing Company, 1969.

MacAndrew, C. and Geertsma, R. H. A critique of alcoholism scales derived from the MMPI. *Quarterly Journal of Studies on Alcohol,* 1964, *25,* 68–76.

MacCulloch, M. J., Feldman, M. P., Orford, J. F., and MacCulloch, M. L. Anticipatory avoidance learning in the treatment of alcoholism: A record of therapeutic failure. *Behaviour Research and Therapy,* 1966, *4,* 187.

Madill, M. F., Campbell, D., Laverty, S. G. et al. Aversion treatment of alcoholics by succinylcholine-induced apneic paralysis; an analysis of early changes in drinking behavior. *Quarterly Journal of Studies on Alcohol,* 1966, *27,* 483–509.

Maisto, S. A. and Adesso, V. J. Effect of instructions and feedback on blood alcohol discrimination training in nonalcoholic drinkers. *Journal of Consulting and Clinical Psychology,* 1977, *45,* 625–636.

Manson, M. P. *The manson evaluation.* Beverly Hills, Ca.: Western Psychological Service, 1948.

Manson, M. P. *The alcadd test.* Beverly Hills, Ca.: Western Psychological Service, 1949.

Marlatt, G. A. *Alcohol, stress, and cognitive control.* Paper read at NATO-sponsored International Conference on Dimensions of Stress and Anxiety, 1975(a).

Marlatt, G. A. The Drinking Profile: A questionnaire for the behavioral assessment of alcoholism. In E. J. Mash & L. G. Terdal, eds., *Behavior therapy assessment: Diagnosis, design and evaluation.* New York: Springer, 1975(b).

Marlatt, G. A., Demming, B., and Reid, J. B. Loss of control drinking in alcoholics: An experimental analogue. *Journal of Abnormal Psychology,* 1973, *81,* 233–241.

Marlatt, G. A. and Nathan, P. E., eds., *Behavioral assessment and treatment of alcoholism.* Rutgers Center of Alcohol Studies, New Brunswick, N.J., in press.

Masserman, J. H. and Yum, K.S. An analysis of the influence of alcohol on experimental neurosis in cats. *Psychosomatic Medicine,* 1946, *8,* 36–52.

McClearn, G. E. The genetic aspects of alcoholism. In P. G. Bourne and R. Fox, eds., *Alcoholism, progress in research and treatment.* New York: Academic Press, 1973.

McClelland, D. C., Davis, W. N., Kalin, R., and Warner, E. *The drinking man: Alcohol and human motivation.* New York: Free Press, 1972.

McGuire, R. J. and Vallance, M. Aversion therapy by electric shock, a simple technique. *British Medical Journal,* 1964, *1,* 151–152.

Mello, N. K. Behavioral studies of alcoholism. In B. Kissen and H. Begleiter, eds., *The biology of alcoholism* (vol. II, Physiology and Behavior) New York: Plenum Press, 1972.

Mello, N. K. and Mendelson, J. H. Experimentally induced intoxication in alcoholics: A comparison between programmed and spontaneous drinking. *Journal of Pharmacology and Experimental Therapeutics,* 1969, *173,* 101.

Mello, N. K. and Mendelson, J. H. Operant analysis of drinking patterns of chronic alcoholics. *Nature,* 1965, *206,* 43–46.

Mendelson, J. H. Ethanol – $1-C^{14}$ metabolism in alcoholics and nonalcoholics. *Science,* 1968, *159,* 319–320.

Mendelson, J. H. Biochemical mechanisms of alcohol addiction. In B. Kissen and H. Begleiter, eds., *The biology of alcoholism,* (vol. I, Biochemistry). New York: Plenum Press, 1971.

Merry, J. The "loss of control" myth. *Lancet,* 1966, 1, 1257–1258.

Miller, P. M. A behavioral intervention program for chronic public drunkenness offenders. *Archives of General Psychiatry,* 1975, *32,* 915–918.

Miller, P. M., Becker, J. V., Foy, D. W., and Wooten, L. S. Instructional control of the components of alcoholic drinking behavior. *Behavior Therapy,* 1976, *7,* 472–480.

Miller, P. M. and Hersen, M. Quantitative changes in alcohol consumption as a function of electrical aversive conditioning. *Journal of Clinical Psychology,* 1972, *28,* 590–593.

Miller, P. M., Hersen, M., Eisler, R. M., and Elkin, T. E. A retrospective analysis of alcohol consumption on laboratory tasks as related to therapeutic outcome. *Behaviour Research and Therapy,* 1974, *12,* 73–76.

Miller, P. M., Hersen, M., Eisler, R., and Hemphill, D. P. Electrical aversion therapy with alcoholics: An analogue study. *Behaviour Research and Therapy,* 1973, *11,* 491–497.

Miller, P. M., Hersen, M., Eisler, R. M., and Hilsman, G. Effects of social stress on operant drinking of alcoholics and social drinkers. *Behaviour Research and Therapy,* 1974, *12,* 67–72.

Miller, P. M., Hersen, M., Eisler, R., and Watts, J. G. Contingent reinforcement of lowered blood alcohol levels in an outpatient chronic alcoholic. *Behaviour Research and Therapy,* 1974, *12,* 261–263.

Miller, W. R. Alcoholism scales and objective assessment methods: A review. *Psychological Bulletin,* 1976, *83,* 649–674(a).

Miller, W. R. Controlled drinking therapies: A review. In W. R. Miller and R. F. Munoz, eds., *How to control your drinking.* Englewood Cliffs, NJ: Prentice-Hall, Inc., 1976(b).

Miller, W. R. Behavioral treatment of problem drinkers: A comparative outcome study of three controlled drinking therapies. *Journal of Consulting and Clinical Psychology,* 1978, *46,* 74–86.

Miller, W. R. and Caddy, G. R. Abstinence and controlled drinking in the treatment of problem drinkers. *Journal of Studies on Alcohol,* 1977, *38,* 986–1003.

Miller, W. R. and Munoz, R. F. *How to control your drinking.* Englewood Cliffs, N.J.: Prentice-Hall, Inc., 1976.

Mills, K. C., Sobell, M. B., and Schaefer, H. H. Training social drinking as an alternative to abstinence for alcoholics. *Behavior Therapy,* 1971, *2,* 18–27.

Mischel, W. *Personality and assessment.* New York: Wiley, 1968.

Mischel, W. Toward a cognitive social learning reconceptualization of personality. *Psychological Review,* 1973, *80,* 252–283.

Mulford, H. A. and Miller, D. E. Drinking in Iowa: IV. Preoccupation with alcohol and definitions of alcohol, heavy drinking and trouble due to drinking. *Quarterly Journal of Studies on Alcohol,* 1960, *21,* 279–291.

Myers, R. D. and Melchior, C. L. Alcohol drinking: Abnormal intake caused by tetrahydropapaveroline in brain. *Science,* 1977, *196,* 554–556.

Nathan, P. E. Alcoholism. In H. Leitenberg, ed., *Handbook of behavior modification.* New York: Appleton-Century-Crofts, 1976.

Nathan, P. E. and Briddell, D. W. Behavior assessment and treatment of alcoholism. In B. Kissen and H. Begleiter, eds., *The biology of alcoholism,* vol. 5. New York: Plenum Press, 1977.

Nathan, P. E. and Goldman, M. S. Problem drinking and alcoholism. In O. F. Pomerleau and J. P. Brady, eds., *Behavioral medicine: Theory and practice.* Baltimore: Williams & Wilkins, in press.

Nathan, P. E. and Lipscomb, T. R. Behavior therapy and behavior modification in the treatment of alcoholism. In J. H. Mendelson and N. K. Mello, eds., *Diagnosis and treatment of alcoholism.* New York: McGraw-Hill, 1978.

Nathan, P. E. and O'Brien, J. S. An experimental analysis of the behavior of alcoholics and nonalcoholics during prolonged experimental drinking. *Behavior Therapy,* 1971, *2,* 455–476.

Nerviano, V. J. Common personality patterns among alcoholic males: A multi-variate study. *Journal of Consulting and Clinical Psychology,* 1976, *44,* 104–110.

Noel, N. E. and Lisman, S. A. *Alcohol, depression and learned helplessness in females.* Paper presented at the Association for the Advancement of Behavior Therapy Convention, 1977.

O'Leary, D. E., O'Leary, M. R., and Donovan, D. M. Social skill acquisition and psychosocial development of alcoholics: A review. *Addictive Behavior,* 1976, *1,* 111–120.

Partanen, J., Bruun, K., and Markkanen, T. *Inheritance of drinking behavior. A study on intelligence, personality, and use of alcohol in adult twins.* Vol. 14, Helsinki: The Finnish Foundation for Alcohol Studies, 1966.

Pittman, D. and Snyder, C. (eds) *Social culture and drinking patterns.* New York: John Wiley and Sons, Inc., 1962.

Pliner, P. and Cappell, H. Modification of affective consequences of alcohol:

A comparison of social solitary drinking. *Journal of Abnormal Psychology*, 1974, *83*, 418–425.

Polivy, J. and Herman, C. P. Effects of alcohol on eating behavior: Influence of mood and perceived intoxication. *Journal of Abnormal Psychology*, 1976, *85*, 607–610.

Polivy, J., Schueneman, A. L. and Carlson, K. Alcohol and tension reduction: Cognitive and physiological effects. *Journal of Abnormal Psychology*, 1976, *85*, 595–606.

Pomerleau, O., Pertschuck, M., and Stinnett, J. A critical examination of some current assumptions in the treatment of alcoholism. *Journal of Studies on Alcohol*, 1976, *37*, 849–867.

Rachman, S. and Teasdale, J. *Aversion therapy and behavior disorders: An analysis*. Coral Gables, Fl.: University of Miami Press, 1969.

Randall, C. L. and Lester, D. Social modification of alcohol consumption in inbred mice. *Science*, 1975, *189*, 149–151.

Randolph, T. The descriptive features of food addiction: Addictive eating and drinking. *Quarterly Journal of Studies on Alcohol*, 1956, 17, 198–224.

Roe, A. The adult adjustment of children of alcoholic parentage raised in foster homes. *Quarterly Journal of Studies on Alcohol*, 1944, *5*, 378–393.

Roe, A. and Burks, B. *Adult adjustment of foster children of alcoholic and psychotic parentage and the influence of the foster home*. New Haven: Quarterly Journal of Studies on Alcohol, 1945.

Rogers, D. A. Factors underlying differences in alcohol preference of inbred strains of mice. In B. Kissen and H. Begleiter, eds., *The biology of alcoholism* (Vol. II, Physiology and Behavior). New York: Plenum Press, 1972.

Rosenberg, N. MMPI alcoholism scales. *Journal of Clinical Psychology*, 1972, *28*, 515–522.

Ruggels, W. L., Armor, D. J., Polich, J. M. et al. A follow-up study of clients at selected alcoholism treatment centers funded by NIAAA, Menlo Park, CA.: Stanford Research Institute, May, 1975 (NTIS No. PB-242204).

Sandler, J. *Three aversive control procedures with alcoholics: A preliminary report*. Paper read at Southeastern Psychological Association, April, 1969.

Schaefer, H. H., Sobell, M. B., and Mills, K. C. Baseline drinking behaviors in alcoholics and social drinkers: Kinds of drinks and sip magnitude. *Behaviour Research and Therapy*, 1971, *9*, 23–27.

Schuckit, M., Goodwin, D., and Winokur, G. A study of alcoholism in half siblings. *American Journal of Psychiatry*, 1972, *128*, 122–216.

Seixas, F. A., Blume, S., Cloud, L. A. et al., Definition of alcoholism. *Annals of Internal Medicine*, 1976, *85*, 764.

Selzer, M. L. The Michigan Alcoholism Screening Test: The quest for a new diagnosis instrument. *American Journal of Psychiatry*, 1971, *127*, 1653–1658.

Silverstein, S. J., Nathan, P. E., and Taylor, H. A. Blood alcohol level estimation and controlled drinking by chronic alcoholics. *Behavior Therapy*, 1974, *5*, 1–15.

Skinner, H. A., Jackson, D. N., and Hoffmann, H. Alcoholic personality types: Identification and correlates. *Journal of Abnormal Psychology,* 1974, *83,* 658–666.

Smart, R. G. Effects of alcohol on conflict and avoidance behavior. *Quarterly Journal of Studies on Alcohol,* 1965, *26,* 187–205.

Sobell, M. B. and Sobell, L. C. Individualized behavior therapy for alcoholics. *Behavior Therapy,* 1973a, *4,* 49–72.

Sobell, M. B., and Sobell, L. C. Alcoholics treated by individualized behavior therapy: One year treatment outcome. *Behaviour Research and Therapy,* 1973b, *11,* 599–618.

Sobell, M. B., and Sobell, L. C. Second-year treatment outcome of alcoholics treated by individualized behavior therapy: Results. *Behaviour Research and Therapy,* 1976, *14,* 195–215.

Sobell, M. B., Sobell, L. C., and Samuels, F. H. Validity of self-reports of alcohol-related arrests by alcoholics. *Quarterly Journal of Studies on Alcohol,* 1974, *35,* 276–280.

Steffen, J. J., Nathan, P. E., and Taylor, H. A. Tension-reducing effects of alcohol: Further evidence and some methodological considerations. *Journal of Abnormal Psychology,* 1974, *83,* 542–747.

Summers, T. Validity of alcoholics' self-reported drinking history. *Quarterly Journal of Studies on Alcohol,* 1970, *31,* 972–974.

Sutherland, E. H., Schroeder, H. G., and Tordella, C. L. Personality traits and the alcoholic. *Quarterly Journal of Studies on Alcohol,* 1950, *11,* 547–561.

Syme, L. Personality characteristics of the alcoholic. *Quarterly Journal of Studies on Alcohol,* 1957, *18,* 288–301.

Tolor, A., and Tamerin, J. S. The question of a genetic basis for alcoholism; comment on the study by Goodwin, et al. *Quarterly Journal of Studies on Alcohol,* 1973, *34,* 1341–1345.

Victor, M., and Adams, R. D. The effect of alcohol on the nervous system. *Research Publication of the Association for Research in Nervous and Mental Diseases,* 1953, *32,* 526–573.

Victor, M., Adams, R. D., and Collins, G. H. The Wernicke-Korsakoff syndrome. In F. Plum and F. H. McDowell, eds., *Contemporary Neurology Series,* vol. 7. Philadelphia: F. A. Davis, 1971.

Vitale, J. J., and Coffey, J. Alcohol and vitamin metabolism. In B. Kissen and H. Begleiter, eds., *The biology of alcoholism,* vol. I, Biochemistry. New York: Plenum Press, 1971.

Vogler, R. E., Compton, J. V., and Weissbach, T. A. Integrated behavior change technique for alcoholics. *Journal of Consulting and Clinical Psychology,* 1975, *43,* 233–243.

Vogler, R. E., Lunde, S. E., Johnson, G. R., and Martin, P. L. Electrical aversion conditioning with chronic alcoholics. *Journal of Consulting and Clinical Psychology,* 1970, *34,* 302–307.

Vogler, R. E., Lunde, S. E., and Martin, P. L. Electrical aversion conditioning with chronic alcoholics: Follow-up and suggestions for research. *Journal of Consulting and Clinical Psychology,* 1971, *36,* 450.

Vogler, R. E., Weissbach, T. A., Compton, J. V., and Martin, G. T. Integrated behavior change techniques for problem drinkers in the community. *Journal of Consulting and Clinical Psychology,* 1977, *45,* 467–479.

Wiens, A. N., Montague, J. R., Manaugh, T. S., and English, C. J. Pharmacological aversive conditioning to alcohol in a private hospital: One year follow-up. *Journal of Studies on Alcohol,* 1976, *37,* 1320–1324.

Williams, R. *Alcoholism: The nutritional approach.* Austin: The University of Texas Press, 1959.

Williams, R. M., Goldman, M. S., and Williams, D. L. *Alcohol dose and expectancy effects on cognitive and motor performance.* Paper presented at the American Psychological Association Convention, Toronto, August, 1978.

Wilson, G. T. Alcoholism and aversion therapy: Issues, ethics and evidence. In G. A. Marlatt and P. E. Nathan, eds., *Behavioral assessment and treatment of alcoholism.* Rutgers Center of Alcohol Studies, New Brunswick, NJ, 1978.

Wilson, G. T., and Davison, G. C. Aversion techniques in behavior therapy: Some theoretical and metatheoretical considerations. *Journal of Consulting and Clinical Psychology,* 1969, *33,* 327–329.

Wilson, G. T., and Lawson, D. M. Expectancies, alcohol, and sexual arousal in male social drinkers. *Journal of Abnormal Psychology,* 1976a, *85,* 587–594.

Wilson, G. T., and Lawson, D. M. Effects of alcohol on sexual arousal in women. *Journal of Abnormal Psychology,* 1976b, *85,* 489–497.

Wilson, G. T., and Lawson, D. M. Expectancies, alcohol and sexual arousal in women. *Journal of Abnormal Psychology,* 1978, *87,* 358–367.

Wilson, G. T., Leaf, R., and Nathan, P. E. The aversive control of excessive drinking by chronic alcoholics in the laboratory setting. *Journal of Applied Behavior Analysis,* 1975, *8,* 13–26.

Wolff, P. H. Ethnic differences in alcohol sensitivity. *Science,* 1972, *175,* 449–450.

APPENDIX: *Summary of behavioral treatment reports*[a]

Author(s)	No. Ss	Type of S	Treatment Goal	Outcome	Follow-up	Design Quality Rating
Electrical Aversion						
Blake, 1965 (includes Relaxation Training)	37	Inpatient	Abstinence	+	6 & 12 mo	4
Blake, 1967	25	Inpatient	Abstinence	Not As + As 1965 Procedure	1967 report follows up 1965 subjects	Same as above
Hallam et al., 1972	18	Inpatient	Abstinence	−	4 mo	19.5
Hedberg & Campbell, 1974	49	Inpatient	Abstinence or controlled drinking	−	6 mo	7.5
Hsu, 1965	40 began 16 completed	Inpatient	Abstinence	+	2 mo	2
Kantorovich	20	Inpatient	Abstinence	+	to 20 mo	b
MacCulloch et al., 1966	4	Inpatient	Abstinence	−	Not applicable	4
McGuire & Vallance, 1964	7	Not Clear	Abstinence	−	1 mo	.5

APPENDIX: (Continued)

Author(s)	No. Ss	Type of S	Treatment Goal	Outcome	Follow-up	Design Quality Rating
Miller et al., 1973 (analog)	30	Inpatient	Abstinence	–	Not applicable	17.5
Vogler et al., 1970	73	Inpatient	Abstinence	– *(see text)*	1 yr	11.5
Chemical Aversion						
Clancy et al., 1967	42	Inpatient	Abstinence	–	12 mo	14.5
Lemere & Voegtlin, 1950	4,468	Inpatient	Abstinence	+	1–13 yr	6.5
Madill et al., 1966	45	Inpatient	Abstinence	–	3 mo	19
Wiens et al., 1976	261	Inpatient	Abstinence	+	12 mo	1.5
Covert Aversion						
Anant, 1967	26	Outpatient	Abstinence	+	8–15 mo	c
Ashem & Donner,	23	Inpatient	Abstinence	+	6 mo	12

[a]Only actual clinical treatment studies are included. See text for other studies testing theoretical issues bearing upon treatment. The reader is strongly encouraged to consult the text for study characteristics that cannot be accommodated above.
[b]The original article is published in Russian. The abstract does not provide enough detail for rating purposes.
[c]Not enough detail is presented to enable a rating.

APPENDIX: (Continued)

Author(s)	No. Ss	Type of S	Treatment Goal	Outcome	Follow-up	Design Quality Rating
Systematic Desensitization						
Kraft & Al-Issa, 1967	1	Inpatient	Abstinence	+	15 mo	4
BAL Discrimination						
Caddy & Lovibond, 1976	60	Outpatient	Controlled drinking	+ (No traditional control group included)	6 mo	26 *(but see text)*
Lovibond & Caddy, 1970	44	Outpatient	Controlled drinking	+ (No traditional control group included)	16–60 wk	23 *(but see text)*
"Operant" Techniques						
Bigelow et al., 1976	20	Outpatient	Abstinence	+	20 mo (maximum)	8.5
Miller et al., 1974	1	Outpatient	Controlled drinking	+	None	(not relevant— ABAB Design)

APPENDIX: *(Continued)*

Author(s)	No. Ss	Type of S	Treatment Goal	Outcome	Follow-up	Design Quality Rating
Comprehensive Treatments						
Azrin, 1976	20	In–Outpatient	Abstinence	+	2 yr	17
Hunt & Azrin, 1973	20	In–Outpatient	Abstinence	+	6 mo	7.5
P. Miller, 1975	20	Outpatient	Sobriety (below 10% BAL)	+	2 mo	23
W. Miller, 1978	46	Outpatient Problem Drinkers	Controlled drinking	−	12 mo	26
Sobell & Sobell, 1973	70	Inpatient	Controlled drinking	+	2 yr	19
Vogler et al., 1975	42	Outpatient Alcoholics	Controlled drinking	+ − *(see text)*	12 mo	25
Vogler et al., 1977	80	Outpatient Problem Drinkers	Controlled drinking	−	12 mo	24

[a]Only actual clinical treatment studies are included. See text for other studies testing theoretical issues bearing upon treatment. The reader is strongly encouraged to consult the text for study characteristics that cannot be accommodated above.
[b]The original article is published in Russian. The abstract does not provide enough detail for rating purposes.
[c]Not enough detail is presented to enable a rating.

7
Depression

Thomas L. Boyd
Donald J. Levis

What is depression? What causes this state and what factors are responsible for maintaining it over time? How can it be best treated? These and other questions concerning depression have occupied investigators' interest since this clinical syndrome was first identified by Hippocrates in the fourth century BC. Answers to these questions are of critical importance since depression, perhaps more than any other psychological reaction, has resulted in enormous amounts of human anguish, suffering, loss of productivity and life. Around 15 percent of American adults reputedly manifest significant depressive features with this syndrome, now rivaling schizophrenia as the nation's number one mental health problem (Secunda, 1973).

Thousands upon thousands of articles, case descriptions, research reports, and books have been devoted to the subject of depression. Numerous definitions of the syndrome exist as well as explanatory accounts. Akiskal and McKinney (1975), for example, described ten separate models of depression reflecting five schools of thought. Well over 100 different treatment approaches have been tried in hopes of alleviating this problem. In spite of these attempts and in spite of the stark personal and social realities of depression, concrete, verified answers to our introductory questions have not been forthcoming. The syndrome of depression is perhaps the most complex, diversified, and least understood psychological problem currently confronting researchers and clinicians.

Consider the issue of establishing a commonly accepted definitional structure for depression. Attempts to classify this syndrome vary extensively, depending upon whether depression is viewed as essentially a single entity or conceptualized as encompassing several dichotomies. Currently used categories have classified this syndrome according to whether the eliciting stimulus is internal or external (endogenous versus exogenous), the nature of the response pattern (autonomous versus reactive), the level of anxiety (agitated versus retarded), the occurrence of mood swings (unipolar versus bipolar), and the level of reality testing (psychotic versus neurotic). Subtypes of depression have also been classified along personality dimensions such as passive-dependent, obsessive, hysteroid, paranoid, schizoid, bipolar manic, and schizoaffective. (For a review of these classification schema see Beck, 1973 and Becker, 1977.)

Such attempts to produce a commonly accepted definitional structure for depression clearly have failed. Levitt and Lubin (1975) concluded that almost every symptom known to psychiatry has been included in the depressive syndrome by some investigator. These authors listed some 38 depressive symptoms obtained from 13 selected sources, in addition to 54 symptom classifications taken from 16 selected depression measurement inventories. Depressive behavior is also subsumed under any number of separate diagnostic labels or categories. Therefore, it is not surprising that such a fragmented approach has led investigators to conclude that the traditional classification of the depressive disorders ". . . confuses etiological and behavioral descriptions, gives inexact composite portraits of dubious reliability as a basis for diagnosis, and fails to offer exact classificatory decision rules" (Klein, 1976, p. 127).

As is the case with the definitional problem, controversy exists over issues related to etiology, maintenance, and treatment. A careful review of all these issues is prohibited by the complexity of the task at hand, abundance of literature, and space limitations imposed for this chapter. Therefore, the strategy adopted is to concentrate primarily on providing a review of the relatively new conceptual viewpoints of depression referred to as behavioral.

Prior to discussing the various behavioral models of depression, it may prove useful to provide a descriptive analysis of those symptoms and states usually associated with the depressive syndrome. Agreement exists that the effects of depression can be manifested at an emotional, cognitive, motivational, physical, and behavioral observation level. For example, according to an analysis provided by Beck (1973), emotional manifestations of depression are reflected in the occurrence of dejected mood states, negative feeling toward self, loss of hedonic gratification, loss of emotional attachment, crying spells, and the loss of a sense of humor. However, cognitive manifestations can be detected through the occurrence of low self-evaluation, negative expectations, self-blame and self-critical references, indecisiveness, and reported distortion of body image. Examples of motivational manifestations can be seen in a decreased drive for positive reinforcement, in avoidance and escape behavior, in an increase in withdrawal and suicidal wishes, and in a desire to increase dependency; while physical manifestations are reflected in reported loss of appetite, sleep disturbance, loss of sexual interest, and fatigability. Behaviorally, observed changes in the depressed person are commonly noted in appearance, psychomotor retardation, and manifest agitation. Issues of frequency, duration, intensity, and relative change must be considered before labelling these behaviors as depressive. Furthermore, it should be noted that each of these descriptive signs can be found associated with other disorders. Nevertheless, the preceding outline of depressive behaviors may prove to be useful in assessing the comprehensiveness and scope of the following conceptual and treatment approaches.

THEORETICAL ANALYSIS

In order to establish a degree of conceptual understanding, most theorists have constructed a model of depression by selecting one or more defining symptoms, often to the exclusion of others. For the most part such models are unidirectional in that causal primacy is given to a particular fraction of the depression syndrome. Attempts are then made to order the remaining response classes into an understandable sequence of events. Such a tier-building, ordering process includes under the same framework seemingly widely separated phenomena. Problematic here is the often mistaken assumption that such causal inferences are able to account for the assumed interdependence of the observed heterogeneous response classes of the depression syndrome. Considering the temporal or sequential ordering of events as an assumed natural consequence of the primary causal event, may provide one only with an illusion of explanation or understanding.

The preceding issue is important to consider, not only with respect to evaluating etiological models of depression, but also their corresponding treatment strategies. The search for the causes and conditions which tend to elicit and maintain depression will provide, of necessity, the foundation upon which effective treatment strategies can be built.

Nonbehavioral

Although the nonbehavioral models of depression are not the focal point of this chapter's concern, a cursory review of this area should prove useful in establishing a comparative basis for contrasting the behavioral approaches. This section is divided into biological and psychoanalytic theories.

Biological Theories. From the biological perspective, depression behavior is hypothesized to be a direct function of brain deficiencies in two groups of biogenic amines, norepinephrine and serotonin (Izard, 1972; Schildkraut, Davis, and Klerman, 1968). These biogenic amines have been identified as the chief neurochemical transmitters within the brain. Deficiencies in the availability of these neurotransmitters in storage at the presynaptic neuron is suggested to result in the failure of transmission of the neuronal impulses, from the presynaptic neuron to the postsynaptic receptor. Such a state of affairs is hypothesized to be the precursor of depressive behavior.

Other biological correlates have also been reported. Some studies of depressed patients have found an increased level of cortisol, a steroid hormone produced by the adrenal cortex (Rubin and Mandell, 1966). As a result, Mendels (1969) hypothesized that changes in the relative proportions of various sex hormones could lead to mood and behavioral changes associated with depression. To support his position, Mendels cites frequency of involutional depression and of depression reportedly caused by oral contraceptives which contain steroid hormones. A disturbance of sodium and potassium metabolism in depressed and manic patients has also been reported (Coppen, 1967; Shaw, 1977), as well as evidence for a genetic factor (see Perris, 1973). (For a more comprehensive analysis of the biological viewpoint, the reader is referred to Mendels' 1973 edited volume).

Psychoanalytic Viewpoints. In a major review of the psychoanalytic concepts of depression, Mendelson (1974) credited Abraham (1911) and Freud (1917) with developing the foundations for this viewpoint. Since these early writings, succeeding psychoanalytic theories of depression have been as diverse as the characteristic signs of depression. As Mendelson concluded:

> [The] relative multiplicity of depressed states—associated in some instances perhaps with private biases on the parts of the authors—has led to a variety of psychodynamic formulations and conceptualizations of the depressive reactions, each with partial validity but with only too many of them implicitly claiming general application. For different writers 'depression' has not only different components but also different purposes. For one author it is, in essence, emptiness and loneliness; for another it is rage and guilt. For one observer it is passive consequence of having sustained a loss of self-esteem; for another it is an active though distorted attempt to undo this loss (Mendelson, 1974, p. 292).

A recurring theme expressed in such different theoretical frameworks is that adult depressives recapitulate early infantile disappointments or frustrations. Depression is seen as beginning with loss of a love object, as thought to occur in the oral-cannibalistic stage of psychosexual development (see Izard, 1972), and to be perceived as oral frustration. With the frustration of hypothesized narcissistic needs at this stage of development, self-esteem diminishes. Such individuals presumably react to frustration with ambivalence as manifested through violence or hatred and love. For an object loss to result in depression, Freud believed it is necessary to have an identification of the ego with the abandoned or lost object, which is subsequently incorporated. Incorporation of the love object presumably can result in inner-directed hostility and guilt (Fenichel, 1945; Izard, 1972).

Comments. By reducing depressive symptoms to neurochemical imbalances, the biological approaches have a distinct advantage of providing formal specification of definitional terms. Unfortunately, such reductionistic precision is not matched by measurement capabilities. Existing technology does not permit direct measurement of neurochemical levels within the brains of depressed people. Peripheral measurement of decreases in serotonin and norepinephrine via urine, blood serum, and cerebrospinal fluid metabolites appear to be related to activity level, as well as to depression (Post, Kotin, Goodwin, and Gordon, 1973). Since depressives generally appear less active than normals (see Miller, 1975), noted biochemical deficiencies may be a result of depression rather than a cause. Although these issues are yet to be resolved, the biological approaches to depression have generated considerable theoretical and empirical research.

However, the psychoanalytic models demonstrate a lack of concern for formal specification of terms and criteria used for evaluation of propositions. While such a concern is not essential for generating a more valid or basic explanation of behavior, it is critical in producing more precise and reliable answers to propositions generated by the model. Constructs like the ego must be linked to antecedent conditions if predictable power is to be enhanced. Lacking this, such constructs only provide an illusion of explanation and lead to circular reasoning.

Behavioral

A renewed interest in the theoretical analysis of depression has recently been stimulated by theorists who primarily view the principles of learning or behavior as playing an essential role in development and maintenance of the depressive response. For organizational purposes behavioral models can be subdivided into four conceptual approaches: S-R nonmotivational; S-R motivational; S-S nonmotivational; and S-S motivational theories. The S-S approaches are frequently referred to as behavioral cognitive models.

S-R Nonmotivational Models.   The strategy involved in the present approach has been to focus on a functional analysis of the behavioral manifestations of the depression syndrome, while providing an explanatory model couched in more rigorous stimulus-response terminology. The writings of Ferster (1973, 1974), Lewinsohn (1974a, 1974b), Costello (1972), and Lazarus (1968) reflect this behavioral orientation, with Ferster and Lewinsohn being the major contributors.

For Ferster, the general concern of the behaviorists is to account for why and how individuals fail to approach and sustain positive aspects of their environment and avoid negative consequences. In other words, the depressed person manifests a reduced frequency of "adjustive behaviors" which, according to Ferster, is the main cause of depression. This reduction in frequency of adjusted behaviors is believed to lead to less reinforcement for appropriate approach behavior which in turn leads to greater reduction in such activity. From this analysis the topography of depressive behavior is viewed as similar to that of nondepressive behavior, except for the reduced frequency for depressives of positively reinforced behavior.

Ferster has outlined a variety of factors which may be responsible for the etiology and maintenance of depression. An important determinant or response frequency involves the type of schedule of reinforcement under which a person is operating. Individuals who engage in repetitive, routine jobs, like housewives, may be more susceptible to depression because of their exposure to a fixed reinforcement ratio. Such a schedule requires considerable activity to maintain reinforcement and is more vulnerable to extinction. Sudden and drastic environmental changes like loss of a loved one, loss of a job, divorce, physical injury or illness may also markedly alter the density of reinforced activity and negate the effectiveness of previously learned reinforced behavior.

To account for the observation that depressives emit a greater amount of nonreinforced behavior, Ferster suggested that depressives may have a distorted perception of their environment. Nonreinforced behaviors are sustained by low activity rates because of insufficient opportunity for discrimination learning to occur, via exposure to differential reinforcement contingencies. Such a state of affairs is believed to result in frequent encounters with aversive events. It is unclear, however, whether Ferster assigned perceptual distortions a causal role in the development of depression (see Becker, 1977).

Lewinsohn and his associates have been careful to avoid too much speculation, keeping much closer ties to their data. Depression is viewed as a learned maladaptive condition with deficient social skill as the common precursor. Lewinsohn defined depression operationally by analyzing score patterns on the self-rated Minnesota Multiphasic Personality Inventory (MMPI), and from interviewer ratings on scales developed by Grinker, Miller, Sabshim, Nunn, and Nunnally (1961). Although some depressed outpatients have been studied, Lewinsohn's subjects have mainly involved groups of mildly depressed college students. Lewinsohn also sees little utility in subtyping depressive and leaves open the possibility of a biological component underlying depression. But his central point stressed the importance of socioenvironmental factors in eliciting depression (Becker, 1977).

As a result of his empirical work, Lewinsohn (1974a) has formulated the following major assumptions:

1. A low rate of response-contingent positive reinforcement acts as an eliciting (unconditional) stimulus for some depressive behaviors, such as feeling of dysphoria, fatigue, and other somatic symptoms.
2. A low rate of response-contingent positive reinforcement constitutes a sufficient explanation for other parts of the depressive syndrome, such as the low rate of behavior. For the latter, the depressed response is considered to be on a prolonged extinction schedule.
3. The total amount of response-contingent positive reinforcement received by an individual is presumed to be a function of three sets of variables: (a) the number of events which are potentially reinforcing; (b) the number of potentially reinforcing events that can be provided by the environment; and (c) the instrumental behavior of the individual.

Thus, the main difference between depressives and nondepressives resides in the deficiency of instrumental skills needed to obtain and sustain reinforcement.

Costello (1972) noted that the apparent loss of reinforcer effectiveness per se in depressives such as are involved in sex, eating, and work has been a neglected issue, and he entertains the possibility that a biochemical and/or neurophysiological change may account for this change in endogenous depression. For reactive depression, Costello admittedly speculates that the reinforcer effectiveness of all the components of the chain of behavior is contingent upon the overt or covert completion of the chain. The loss of a significant reinforcer or discriminative stimulus (e.g., loss of a loved one) can in turn disrupt the chain with the negative effects generalizing to seemingly nonrelated events like eating, work, or sex. However, Lazarus (1972) argued that the depressive apparent decrease in responsivity following a significant personal loss does not simply reflect ineffectiveness of reinforcement, or a search for substitute reinforcers, but represents a desire or "yearning" for restoration of the loss. Such a state, in turn, mitigates previous reinforcer effectiveness.

S-R Motivational Models. In the foregoing section, an inductive, S-R analysis of depression was presented comprised of Skinnerian or operant derivatives. To the extent that lawful regularities between stimulus and responses are not observed, it then becomes necessary to break away from an inductive analysis to one that incorporates intervening variables or hypothetical constructs between S-R events (Spence, 1944). The models to be presented under the present heading and under the remaining categories adopt this strategy.

The S-R motivational viewpoint offered here is a derivative of a more general model of psychopathology developed by Stampfl (Stampfl and Levis, 1967; 1969) involving an extension of Mowrer's two-factor theory of avoidance learning (Mowrer, 1947, 1960) and Miller's (1959) conflict theory. Synonymous with Mowrer's approach, this theory identifies two response classes inherent in the development of psychopathology. The organism first learns to respond in a negative emotional manner to previously "neutral" stimuli following repeated exposure with an inherent aversive event-producing pain. The resulting conditioning effect is also viewed as a secondary source of drive, possessing motivational or energizing effects as well as reinforcing effects. The motivational properties of the conditioned aversive response leads to the learning of the second class of responses, referred to as avoidance behavior or symptoms. The latter behavior is reinforced because of the effect of this response class to terminate or reduce the presence of conditioned aversive stimuli. An important refinement of the model is the analysis of the nature of the CS complex, and the role which the serial ordering of conditioned cues plays in maintaining avoidance responses over time (Levis and Hare, 1977; Stampfl and Levis, 1973).

Extrapolating from the general theory of psychopathology, Stampfl and Levis (1969) have suggested two different conditioning models for outlining the etiology of the depressive symptom.

According to the first model, depression is seen as resulting from a complex combination of a loss of positive affect plus anxiety arousal. Corresponding to those principles of conditioning previously outlined for the development of aversive stimuli, stimuli systematically paired with a positive reinforcement acquire the capacity to elicit a positive emotional response (Mowrer, 1960). When a person is described as feeling good emotionally, as having a sense of well being and of security, certain environmental and internal cues conditioned to elicit such positive affect are hypothesized. The elimination or reduction of these cues is postulated to lead to a corresponding reduction in the degree of positive affect experienced. Such an experience is hypothesized to generate a negative emotional state, resulting in the aversive conditioning of those cues correlated with the reduction in stimulation of the positive affective cues. Depending upon the individual's previous conditioning history, such a sequence of events can elicit additional cues (thoughts/images/memories) representing similar conditioning sequences.

Thus, behavior may become inhibited because of the presence of stimuli previously conditioned which were associated with a reduction in the positive emotional state (e.g., rejection). The topography of the depressive response is reinforced as it serves to inhibit the impact of these anxiety-eliciting cues, and to reduce the aversiveness of further internal and external cues associated with prior withdrawal of love and subsequent exposure to stimuli eliciting further negative affect. The child may learn that by responding in a passive, depressive manner the negative behavior of the parents can be more quickly terminated. The subsequent reduction in guilt (cues associated with withdrawal of love and anticipated further punishment) becomes further associated with the previous externally induced and self-imposed punishment. The depressive reaction may be reactivated by renewed violations of the individual's or parental system of values. In the absence of any further primary aversive stimuli, each nonreinforced exposure to the conditioned, avoided cues leads to some extinction of the depressive reaction. With sufficient extinction, the depressed individual becomes more active, increasing the probability for the activity to be positively reinforced. This process provides an explanation for the noted time course observed for the depressive reaction. According to this model, the main cue areas partially avoided by the depressive reaction are those associated with loss of positive affect, feelings of rejection, and anticipation of punishment.

The second model to be described is based on a conflict, multiprocess approach-avoidance paradigm and is not inconsistent with Amsel's (1972) frustration-based theory of persistence (Levis, in press, a). The first stage consists of conditioned anxiety being associated to cues which precede punishment for the child's participation in some forbidden act. Repeated primary and secondary punishment for such behavior continues to heighten anxiety associated with the punished act. However, when the completion of the taboo behavior culminates in positive reinforcement as well (e.g., sexual behavior, eating candy), the punishment serves an additional purpose of thwarting the completion of behavior leading to primary positive reinforcement. This results in a frustration-effect which in turn may elicit the response of anger.

Anger is then associated with stimuli surrounding the omission of positive reinforcement, or the frustrating situation. The emotional response of anger can elicit aggressive behavior which becomes conditioned when it terminates the frustrating conditioned and/or unconditioned stimuli associated with the painful stimulation. If such aggressive behaviors are punished, they too become inhibited by anxiety arousal. Thus, the resulting depressive reaction involves not only a fear of rejection and loss of love, but also an inhibition of aggressive responses. The depressive reaction helps prevent full exposure to these aversive situations.

Other models have been developed by Stampfl and Levis which could relate to the depressive reaction. These include avoidance of fears of failure, loss of control, and avoidance of cues associated with responsibility. They will not be presented here, but the interested reader is referred to their source (Levis in press, b; Stampfl and Levis, 1969).

S-S Nonmotivational Model. The present and following section will deal with stimulus-stimulus connections or cognitive models of depression, most notably those proposed by Seligman and Beck. Under the present heading, Seligman's (1974, 1975) learned helplessness model will be considered. Seligman extended his infrahuman model (Maier and Seligman, 1976) to encompass clinical reactive depression primarily because of three symptom manifestations common to both settings: (1) behavior passivity—the failure or slowness of the organism to initiate responses; (2) negative expectations—the readiness with which the subjects construe their actions, even if they succeed, as having failed or being futile; and (3) the reported sense of helplessness or hopelessness which frequently occurs. These symptom manifestations are viewed as a reflection of three major behavioral deficits, respectively: motivational, cognitive, and emotional. Seligman (1974) maintains it is not trauma as such that produces interference with later adaptive responding, but rather the organism's lack of control cover trauma.

The theory advanced to explain the development of learned helplessness (Maier and Seligman, 1976) is described as involving three separate stages. The first stage consists of the organism receiving information that the probability of the outcome is independent of performing a given response class. The distinction between controllable and uncontrollable reinforcement is central to the theory. The concepts of controllability are operationally defined within a response-reinforced contingency space. If the conditional probability of that outcome (i.e., reinforcement), given a specific response, does not differ from the conditional probability of that outcome in the absence of that response, then the outcome is independent of responding and, by definition, uncontrollable. However, if the conditional probability of an outcome, given a specific response, is not equal to the conditional probability of the outcome in the absence of that response, then the outcome is controllable. A person or infrahuman is "helpless" with respect to some outcome when the outcome occurs independently of all voluntary responses.

The critical stage of the theory involves the organism registering and processing cognitively the information obtained from the contingency exposure in which responding was independent of outcome. This event can be subdivided into two processes for the helplessness organism: (a) learning that a contingency exists concerning the independence of responding and outcome, and (b) developing the expectation that responding and outcome will remain independent on future trials. Coinciding with the second stage is a reduction in the motivation (activity) to control the outcome and thus, the designation of nonmotivational theory once depression or helplessness is learned. The final stage includes the generalization and transference of the expectations developed that responding and outcome are independent of new learning situations. The behavioral outcome of this generalization is referred to as the learned helplessness effect, or depression.

Abramson, Seligman, and Teasdale (1978) have extended Seligman's earlier position to include attribution theory. They have added to the model the response class of self-esteem which is considered orthogonal to controllability, presumably being dependent upon attributional considerations. For these writers the expectation of response-outcome performance is regarded only as a sufficient condition for depression. Other factors like physiological and hormonal states, postpartum conditions, chemical depletions, and loss of interest in reinforcers may also produce depression in the absence of expectations of uncontrollability.

S-S Motivational Model. Under this section, the cognitive approach of Beck (1967, 1974) will be discussed. For Beck, the individual's negative perception and appraisal of environmental events, his cognitive set, provides the sustaining force for most depressive-responding, with the possible exclusion of some severe endogenous and bipolar disorders. The depressed patient manifests specific distorted perceptions known as the *cognitive triad:* a negative view of the self, the world, and the future. The nature of the cognitive disorder can be determined by analyzing the thematic content of the logical distortions. Five detected distortions involve (1) the use of arbitrary inference: reaching conclusions without or with contrary evidence; (2) selective abstraction: fixating on a detailed aspect of a situation while ignoring the context; (3) overgeneralization; (4) magnification and minimization of events or information; and (5) personalization: viewing impersonal events with excessive subjective significance. These cognitive distortions appear quite plausible to the depressed person and are elicited involuntarily and automatically (Becker, 1977).

The onset and development of depression is hypothesized to be causally related to experiences connoting loss to the patient. The individual begins to distort such experiences, regarding himself as ". . . deficient, inadequate, unworthy, and is prone to attribute unpleasant occurrences to a deficiency in himself . . . The patient's sadness is an inevitable consequence of his sense of deprivation, pessimism, and self-criticism" (Beck, 1976, p. 129).

Like Seligman's model, Beck noted that the depressed person experiences a marked change in motivation state involving not only an avoidance of formerly gratifying reinforcements, but a development of a tendency to remain passive. The various behavioral manifestations of depression such as inertia, fatigability, and agitation are expressions of the depressive's loss of spontaneous motivation. This tendency of a depressive to be fatigued results from their continuous expectations of negative outcomes. In the same vein, agitation is related to the thought content. However, unlike Seligman's learned helplessness individuals who appear to be passively resigned to their fate, Beck views the agitated depressives as individuals fighting desperately to find a solution to their predicament. The failure to find a solution results in frantic motor activity, such as pacing the floor or scratching various parts of their body. In a similar vein, the vegetative signs of depression (loss of appetite, libido, and sleep) are believed a result of a psychological arousal accompanying depression. The physiological signs of depression are seen as analogous to the autonomic nervous system manifestation of anxiety. It is this latter perspective that prompted the label *motivational*.

Comments.   Despite the general labelling of each position reviewed as behavioral, marked differences in conceptualizing the depressive state are apparent. The empirical finding that depression is correlated with reports of thought disturbance is generally accepted. Lewinsohn and Ferster tended to ignore this finding, and stressed the importance of a deficit in reinforcement. Ferster (1974), however, did address the issue of the depressive's incessant complaints. He suggested that such complaints probably had reinforcing consequences historically, and are used by the depressive as inappropriate "extended demands" reinforced in the manner of "superstitious" responding.

However, cognitive factors play a central theoretical role in the models offered by Seligman, Beck, and Stampfl. Seligman and Beck are in agreement that cognitive distortions are not only the central characteristic of depression, but they also manifest primary causal significance. The learned avoidance position of Stampfl also acknowledges the role of cognitive sets in affecting behavior, but they are not seen as causal. Rather, depression is viewed as a response class analogous to passive avoidance-responding which comprises both behavioral and cognitive components. Both components are designed to aid the individual in escaping or defending against the presence or elicitation of conditioned aversive stimulation. Such cognitive sets serve as motivators in maintaining the behavioral (passive-avoidance) component and in preventing memories involving previous conditioning events (Stampfl and Levis, 1969). The motivational objectives of such cognitive sets and their corresponding verbalizations and motoric behavior can be divided into four categories: (1) an attempt to reduce the full impact of aversive cues associated with new experiences by anticipating the negative consequences, thereby mitigating the reactions of others; (2) the emitting of secondary punishers with the objective of eliciting guilt cues in others or punishing them by the resulting passive-aggressive behavior; (3) the emitting of self-punitive behavior to avoid experiencing cues associated with anger or feeling of "wrong-doing"; and (4) the emitting of behavior designated to elicit from others sources of secondary gain or positive reinforcement (e.g., avoiding meeting one's responsibility or eliciting statements of sympathy).

Neither of the foregoing cognitive conceptualizations represents an inherently superior explanatory approach, but the verification of causality does demand an independent identification for the construct. Research concerned with cognitive sets has not been particularly successful in dealing with the preceding issue (see Miller, Seligman, and Kurlander, 1975). In a critical review of learned helplessness theory, Levis (1976) found the cognitive construct lacking in definitional precision because of the strategy to rely solely on dependent or outcome behavior. Without an independent method for identifying events, the relationship between cognitive sets and depression becomes circular and relegated only to a conceptual framework. Such a relationship precludes a causal analysis. Aware of this point, McReynolds (in press) has recently reinterpreted Seligman's position using S-R terminology as a particular case of a schedule-shift effect (see also Levis, in press, a).

Seligman (1975), Beck (1967), and Stampfl and Levis (1969) also address the issue of motivation. For Seligman, an aversive motivational state may be associated with the depressive reaction during the initial learning sequence, but such reactions are believed to extinguish quickly. From the viewpoint of theory, the intact depressive reaction involves a nonmotivated state. Beck and Stampfl view depression as a more affective state accompanied by considerable avoidance and escape behavior. Ferster (1974) also noted this latter point in his analysis of depression. However, unlike the others, Stampfl and Levis (1969) postulated a one-to-one correlation between the occurrence of the depressive reaction and the conditioned emotional response. Similar to Seligman and Beck, Stampfl's model postulates a decrease in negative affect over time, but not completely, and not because it extinguishes. Rather, a decrease in affect will occur as the defensive pattern becomes overlearned and effective in warding off aversive stimuli. Upon the reintroduction of the avoided cues, a marked increase in anxiety or other motivational states (frustration and anger) should occur.

Unfortunately, Stampfl's model has not been subjected to careful research scrutiny. However, some indirect support exists. Forrest and Hokanson (1975) found that depressives have a higher preference for self-punitive behavior than normals with accompanying rapid autonomic arousal reduction, and Atkinson and Polivy (1976) provide support for the notion that a relationship exists between anger and depression. Nevertheless, the causal components of the models offered have not been established empirically.

Seligman and Beck's theories have been much more successful in generating a substantial amount of research activity. Although research on Seligman's model has been successful in demonstrating at the analogue level important behavioral effects following exposure to uncontrollable events, it may be argued that such effects are not specific to depression, and have not provided an unambiguous causal account of depression (Blaney, 1977). While evidence exists in support of Beck's hypothesized cognitive distortions among depressed individuals (Beck, 1963; 1967; 1976; Loeb, Beck, and Diggory, 1971; Teasdale and Bancroft, 1977), such evidence is correlational in nature and not necessarily specific to a cognitive model (Blaney, 1977). Methodological issues have been raised elsewhere which have not allowed the preclusion of alternative explanations in supporting data (Blaney, 1977; Boyd, 1978; Wortman and Brehm, 1975).

While the operant approach of Lewinsohn has also generated considerable analogue research, Blaney (1977) has correctly noted the correlational nature of such findings. As such, Lewinsohn's data like that of Beck's, have not provided an unambiguous causal account of depression. Attempts to elucidate the proposed causal relations between response-contingent reinforcement deficits and subsequent behavioral changes have been contradictory (see Lewinsohn and Graf, 1973; Lewinsohn and Libet, 1972). However, Lewinsohn's data do point to a correspondence between an individual's participation in pleasant activities (or lack of), and the presence of depression. Nevertheless, as Blaney (1977) suggested: ". . . perhaps the theory should be treated as a characterization of the depressed person's interaction with his environment rather than as a hypothesis concerning the causal antecedents of the depressive episodes. Indeed, Lewinsohn has given relatively little attention to the circumstances resulting in a drop in the rate of response-contingent positive reinforcement (p. 210)."

ASSESSMENT

Issues of assessment, like issues of definitional precision and theory, become problematic because of the diverse range of symptoms often associated with the label "depression." This state of affairs exists not only with respect to etiological questions, but also relates to the problem of providing directives to the therapist regarding the most effective target modality. Attempts have been made to establish a degree of order within the assessment area by the classification of depression symptomatology into various subcategories. As noted in our introduction, such efforts have focused on either a unitary or binary system of classification and are based on an assessment analysis of the presenting symptom clusters, rating scale data, and solicited self-report measures (see Levitt and Lubin, 1975). Considerable controversy exists within the literature in relation to the status of these classification efforts and in relation to the methods by which depression is assessed (for overviews of this research see Kendell, 1968; Levitt and Lubin, 1975).

This section of the chapter will be limited to providing an overview of the assessment area with emphasis on highlighting the various strategies adopted and discussing general methodological concerns. For organization purposes, three different approaches to investigating issues of assessment have been delineated: the factor analytic method, psychometric testing, and the functional assessment analysis.

Factor Analytic. The factor analytic method represents a statistical approach for interpreting scores and correlations of scores from such sources as tests and interview material. The strategy adopted is to search for a factor, or set of factors, which represent for the individuals under study an area or region of behavior within which responding can be obtained in a consistent manner independently of exposure to particular stimuli. Quantitatively, an attempt is made to search for factors which, under stated restrictions, can be multiplied to give all the correlation coefficients of each test with each other. Ideally, the factors should be as few as possible and still reproduce all the correlations.

Factor analytic methods have provided the major source of evidence pertaining to the binary theory of depression. Mendels and Cochrane (1968) and Levitt and Lubin (1975) together reviewed the findings of ten factor analytic studies. Of these studies, presumably nine have provided evidence for a bipolar factor. However, as Levitt and Lubin (1975) indicated, these results are not entirely convincing. A summary of their critique of this area of research includes the following points:

1. The factor analytic studies were carried out by investigators who believe in a two-factor theory. Kendell (1968) has manipulated this variable and has found that "unitarian" psychiatrists do rate patients on a single dimension, while "binarians" rate the *same* patients bimodally. The potential for the functioning of this source of error is particularly apparent in Kiloh and Garside's (1963) study. Here "non-pure" diagnosed depressed patients were discarded from the final analysis, in addition to the fact that those clinicians who adjudged the presence or absence of individual symptoms within each factor also assigned the patients to the diagnostic categories. Most of the remaining studies reviewed did note whether or not this potential source of error was controlled.

2. A problematic outcome of the factor analytic studies was their failure to achieve a consensus. Of some 27 factors that were found to be indicative of endogenous depression within 6 of the studies reviewed, only 1 factor, retardation, was common to all 6. In a replication of Hamilton and White (1959), Weckowicz, Muir, and Cropley (1967), using 52 depressed patients, found no evidence for the matching of the 4 factors reported by Hamilton and White (1959). In a series of studies by Weckowicz and his colleagues (Cropley and Weckowicz, 1966; Weckowicz, Muir, and Cropley, 1967; Weckowicz, Yonge, Cropley, and Muir, 1971), overlapping patient samples were examined. The 1966 study yielded 6 factors; the 1967 study only 3; while the 1971 study again yielded 6 with each year's combined factors accounting for differing percentages of the common variance.

3. The nature of the samples can exercise a marked influence on the findings obtained. Mahrer and Bornstein (1969) found identical factors from a sample of depressive and a sample of male inpatients with other diagnoses. Using a sample of depressives without restriction of diagnosis (in contrast to Kiloh and Garside's procedure), McConaghy, Jaffe, and Murphy (1967) failed to support a bipolar theory of depression.

At the present time the results for a bipolar theory of depression appear somewhat equivocal. Not only have investigators had difficulty in identifying consistently potential subcategories of depression, but a major problem has existed in differentiating depression from other major psychiatric disorders. As mentioned, the only common factor of endogenous depression in the major factor analytic studies reviewed was that of retardation (Levitt and Lubin, 1975). Payne and Hewlett (1960), however, failed to discriminate endogenous depressives from schizophrenics on Nufferno Speed Test, a reputed measure of intellectual speed. Korboot and Yates (1973) found similar results on a visual inspection task, although these investigators failed to control for potential age differences between depressed and schizophrenic patients.

The studies on psychomotor retardation clearly demonstrate that slowness of responding is not specific to depression. In a systematic review of the literature, Miller (1975) concluded that depressives have not been shown to be any more retarded than schizophrenics. Beck, Feshback, and Legg (1962), controlling for both age and vocabulary levels, found that "neurotic" depressives did not differ from nondepressed patients on a Digit Symbol scores. "Psychotic" depressives did exhibit decrements but were not significantly different from schizophrenics. In a well-controlled study, Friedman (1964) matched 55 depressives and 65 normals for age, sex, education, vocabulary score, and nativity. These subjects were tested on 33 cognitive, perceptual, and psychomotor tests, yielding some 82 test scores. While depressed subjects rated themselves more negatively on 82 percent of the items on a mood scale, they actually performed more poorly on only 4 percent of the test scores. Beck (1967) points out that these statistically significant performance scores could be due to chance alone, given the number of measures taken in Friedman's study. Granick (1963) also failed to find differences between depressed and normal subjects.

The issue of response deficits in depression also would appear to be an open question at this time. There is little evidence for deficits that are unique to depression (see Miller, 1975). While Miller (1975) reviews considerable confirming evidence for psychological deficits in depressed as compared to normal subjects, a few studies such as those reported here have failed to find these differences.

Studies designed to search for biological factors have also been confronted with similar measurement difficulties. For example, Mendels and Frazer (1974) have noted inconsistent and time-limited correlations between biogenic amine reduction and behavioral changes believed compatible with depression. Such behavioral changes do not appear persistent enough to be considered synonymous with clinical depression. As Mendels and Frazer (1974) concluded: "When one considers how much amine reduction is necessary to produce behavioral deficits in animals, it seems unlikely that such severe depletion could occur in depressed patients and not be more readily detectable."

Psychometric Testing. The psychometric strategy refers to any quantitative assessment of an individual's psychological attributes or traits. In attempting to provide a quantitative assessment of depression, most investigators have relied upon self-report inventories designed specifically for that purpose. General personality tests, like the MMPI, which contain a "depression" scale have mainly been used only for initial screening purposes. Lewinsohn (1974), for example, included the MMPI in the initial assessment procedure of his study to insure a population comparison between depressed patients and nondepressed psychiatric controls. The utility of the MMPI, depression scale, has been questioned on the basis of it being too gross a measure and, at times, its inability to differentiate between depressives and patients simply displaying high anxiety states (Pichot, 1972), or other behaviors (Comrey, 1957).

Projective indices like the Thematic Apperception Test (TAT) and the Rorschach Test have been used primarily only at a clinical level for evaluating depression. Their research usage in current literature has been limited by the failure of these tests to establish valid and reliable quantitative indices for separating depressed from nondepressed individuals.

Of the self-report inventories designed specifically to assess depression, the Beck Depression Inventory (BDI) is the most widely used scale in depression research. The 21 items in this inventory are individually ranked in order to reflect degree of severity. Beck, Ward, Mendelson et al., (1961) obtained high correlations between the BDI and ratings of depression level made by independent clinicians upon a heterogeneous sample of psychiatric patients (.65 and .67, replicated). Beck (1967) has shown that this questionnaire is sensitive to changes in depression over time. Further, Williams, Barlow, and Agras (1972) demonstrated that the BDI correlates well (.67) with certain behavioral ratings of depression (i.e., talking, smiling, and motor activity).

Another useful scale is Lubin's Depression Adjective Check List (Lubin, 1965). This inventory presents lists of adjectives from which the patient is required to select those that describe his or her present mood state. Significant correlations between the Depression Adjective Check List and the MMPI Depression scale and the BDI have been obtained (see Bellack and Hersen, 1977; Lubin, 1966).

A somewhat different strategy for assessing depression is reflected in the Pleasant Events Schedule (see Lewinsohn and Libet, 1972). This approach represents a rating scale for assessing potential activities and events for depressed patients. As Bellack and Hersen's (1977) summary indicates: (1) Responses on the Pleasant Events Schedule correlate positively with mood ratings (Lewinsohn and Libet, 1972); (2) there is a substantial relationship between reported number of pleasant activities engaged in and reported mood level for depressed, nondepressed psychiatric controls, and normal subjects (Lewinsohn and Graf, 1973); and (3) depressed subjects scored lower than others on scales derived from the Pleasant Events Schedule measuring pleasure, activity level, and reinforcer potential of varied activities (MacPhillamy and Lewinsohn, 1974). As Bellack and Hersen (1977) have noted, however, there exists a notable lack of independent validation of the Pleasant Events Schedule. Independent validation with in vivo activity level through naturalistic observation, and other overt behavioral monitoring, is desirable (i.e., Williams, Barlow, and Agras, 1972).

Representative of observer rating scales is the Hamilton Rating Scale for Depression (Hamilton, 1960; 1967). The scale contains 17 variables, some of which are defined in terms of a series of categories of increasing intensity. Test administration necessarily requires a trained interviewer. The Hamilton Rating Scale appears to be sensitive to changes in depression over time (Hamilton, 1960), and correlates well with the BDI (.82) and overt behavioral ratings of depression (.71) (Williams, Barlow, and Agras, 1972).

Although additional validation work needs to be conducted on each of the instruments previously discussed, they have proved useful in separating populations for research purposes. It should also be noted that the preceding scales represent only a fraction of those instruments designed solely for the measurement of depression. Levitt and Lubin (1975), for example, have compiled a list of 36 such tests. However, the scales reviewed in this section represent the most frequently used research instruments.

Functional Assessment. Because of the numerous problems associated with classifying depressives, a functional approach to the evaluation of depression behavior has received a major behavioral observational impetus. While some investigators have even gone so far as to deny the conceptualization of depression as a separate and distinct clinical entity or syndrome (see Mahrer and Bornstein, 1969), most would likely agree that there exists a certain intuitive appeal, if not a social mandate to continue attempts at investigation.

As Ferster (1965) noted, ". . . a functional analysis of behavior has the advantage that it specifies the causes of behavior in the form of explicit environmental events which can be objectively identified and which are potentially manipulable." Kanfer and Saslow (1965) are perhaps best known for their espousal of a functional approach to classifying abnormal behavior. As these authors noted, such an approach assumes that ". . . a description of the problematic behavior, its controlling factors, and the means by which it can be changed are the most appropriate 'explanations'." To the extent that the controlling factors of behavior are able to be identified and validated, treatment concerns regarding appropriate target modalities are necessarily solved.

As previously alluded to, Lewinsohn and his colleagues have generated considerable observational data as providing a basic framework from which to assess and evaluate the functional relationship between hypothesized important behavioral and environmental events. In a systematic review of these findings, Lewinsohn (1974b) noted a number of important correlational findings:

1. Depressed individuals elicit fewer behaviors from other people than do control subjects (Shaffer and Lewinsohn, 1971; Libet and Lewinsohn, 1973).
2. The total amount of reinforcement obtained is less in nondepressed persons (MacPhillamy and Lewinsohn, 1972).
3. Depressed individuals appear more "sensitive" to aversive stimuli (Lewinsohn, Lobitz, and Wilson, 1973). (These results are not consistent with earlier reports, however, e.g., Greenfield, Katz, Alexander, and Roessler, 1963; McCarron, 1973.)
4. Depressed individuals appear to have fewer "social skills" as operationalized by decreased emission of positive reactions toward others (Libet and Lewinsohn, 1973), and increased response delays by depressed subjects (Libet and Lewinsohn, 1973).

Lewinsohn's findings have obtained some support and elaboration from other investigators. Coyne (1976) observed significantly increased depression, hostility, and rejection in normal subjects who had interacted with depressed subjects, compared with those who had interacted with other normal or psychiatric controls. Hammen and Peters (1978) supported these findings in an analogue study of enacted roles of depression. Prakachin, Craig, Papegeorgis, and Reith (1977) observed deficits in nonverbal communication skills in depressed subjects relative to normal and psychiatric control subjects.

The ongoing functional analysis of the depressives' interactions with significant others has proved to be a potential discriminating instrument among depressives, normals, and nondepressed psychiatric controls. It is to be noted, however, that the explicit identification of environmental and behavioral events represents only an important initial step toward the process of systematically evaluating a theoretical approach. Inherent in the functional approach is the specification of hypothesized, causal factors of behavior. However, whether or not those factors specified by the boundary conditions of the theory are satisfied becomes strictly an empirical issue.

Initial efforts toward such validation, while only preliminary, have not been entirely successful. As noted, Lewinsohn and Libet (1972) and Lewinsohn and Graf (1973) were unable to verify a strong relationship between activities change and subsequent mood or affect change, a presumably critical interaction given Lewinsohn's causal account. Blaney (1977) reviewed other research which findings were either nonsupportive or inconclusive (see Hammen and Glass, 1975; Padfield, 1976; Werner and Rehm, 1975; see also Buchwald, 1977).

Despite these difficulties, the functional analysis of depression via behavioral observation continues to provide a basic framework from which to assess and evaluate the potential relationship between hypothesized important behavioral and environmental events. While it remains to be determined whether or not the operant model as presently specified will prove to be the most viable model, such an evaluative approach affords the potential to confirm or disconfirm.

A functional analysis can also be applied in different manners than that suggested by the operant model. It has already been indicated that a notable problem in conferring a behavioral explanation upon depression is the intrinsic historical nature of behavioral explanations. Such difficulty perhaps is reflected in the initial predicted interaction effects between engagement in pleasant activities and mood changes for individual subjects. Lewinsohn (1974b; 1975) reported this relationship to range between 0 and –.75. This lack of predictive utility for this model necessarily reflects a substantial amount of variance which is unaccounted for. Taken from a historical perspective, these findings could perhaps have been predicted.

Knowledge of previous individual conditioning histories could shed light on these findings. As hypothesized from the avoidance model of depression, the engagement in pleasant activities may elicit cues (thoughts/images) which were previously associated with the reduction of positive-affect experienced. The elicitation of such cues presumably would initially generate associated negative emotional affect as opposed to the hypothesized more positive mood changes. The course of this affect change necessarily would reflect the total amount of nonreinforced exposure (extinction to such cue), in addition to any resulting positive reinforcement subsequent to engagement in such activities.

This brief, hypothetical analysis raises an important issue with respect to the use of a functional analysis. A functional assessment is a continual evaluative process. With respect to the preceding example, engaging in self-reported "pleasant activities" does not imply that the subject will experience pleasure. This is an empirical issue which must be evaluated independently and over the process of activity involvement. Levis (in press, b) presented a brief outline of how such a validating process might proceed. As indicated, depression is viewed as an active avoidance reaction to ward off and escape the full impact of conditioned aversive stimulation. The S-R motivational models presented specify that those cues previously associated with loss of positive affect, punishment, and anger are highly correlated with the depressive reaction. As a validating procedure it is imperative first, to determine objectively if those hypothesized cues do in fact lead to an increase in anxiety upon their presentation. Second, if the anxiety response is functionally related to the depression reaction, affective reduction (extinction) must correlate positively with a decrease in symptomology. Less than confirmation of these points necessarily will invalidate the avoidance model. This kind of functional assessment can also be applied to other theoretical models and may prove useful in establishing relationships between environmental events, internal states, and depressive responding.

Comments.   Each of the strategies of assessment review has inherent advantages and disadvantages in the attempt to resolve the assessment controversy. The strict reliance on any method will most likely lead to imperfect conclusions but the functional approach appears to show the greatest potential. From an S-R behavioral viewpoint it is the method of choice. This decision does not preclude an acceptance of the role of other aspects of depression to which the nonbehavioral or S-S behavioral models have assigned causal primacy. In fact, it is being suggested that by broadening the use of a functional analysis to the areas of emotional responding as previously suggested (see Levis and Boyd, submitted) and to cognitive sets, advances in theoretical precision as well as assessment would be achieved.

TREATMENT

As it was stated at the onset, the search for the causes and conditions that tend to elicit and maintain depression should provide important guidelines for treatment. As this review indicates, considerably more work is needed on issues of theory and etiological validation before one can assess the strength of the foundation upon which various treatment approaches rest. In this section a treatment review will be provided but, as was the case with the foregoing issues, no concrete recommendations can be reached. It also should be noted that while therapeutic efficacy lends credence to a proposed model, such efficacy, if established, does not validate, in itself, the proposed etiological statements suggested by the theory and treatment technique.

Nonbehavioral

Biological Approaches. The biological approaches to depression have developed an extensive collection of research studies using clinically depressed patients. Although the review of this material is beyond the scope of this paper, Morris and Beck's (1974) survey is representative. They reviewed 146 double-blind studies involving antidepressant medication. Their analysis revealed that tricyclic antidepressant medication was found to be more effective than a placebo in 61 of 93 group comparisons (66 percent of all reports). Criteria for inclusion in this review were simply that the study used a control group, that patients be randomly assigned to treatment groups, and that a double-blind research design be used.

Interestingly, differences were observed by Morris and Beck (1974) with regard to patient characteristics, assessment of patient improvement, time elapsed between treatment and evaluation, nature of control or comparison treatment, schedule of drug administration, physiological variances within and among patients, and statistical analysis of the data. Yet, the authors praised the overall efficacy of antidepressant medication. Confronted with such a potpourri of potential confounding variables, one can only admire the optimism of these reviewers. (For additional reviews of antidepressive drugs see Bradley, 1963; Cole, 1964; Hordern, 1965; and Klein and Davis, 1969).

Not inconsistent with the biological model of depression and its treatment is the use of electroconvulsive shock therapy (ECT). While the specific therapeutic mechanisms are as of yet not elucidated, principal consideration has usually been given to possible underlying biological factors, particularly to cerebral protein synthesis or biogenic amine levels (Schuyler, 1974). While claims for the demonstrated efficacy of ECT for depressed patients are to be found in the literature, a cursory examination of a few representative studies indicates certain difficulties. Bruce, Come, Fitzpatrick et al., (1960) reportedly treated 50 depressed patients with either ECT or Tofranil. Of the 22 patients receiving ECT only, 21 were reported to be "very much better" at one month following treatment, while 16 of 19 patients receiving Tofranil only, were reported to be "greatly improved." No indication was given of the relevant measures used to ascertain improvement. Further, no comparison was made with no-treatment controls. As Seligman, Klein, and Miller (1976) noted, since depression is usually a relatively short-term disorder (see also Beck, 1967), this would appear to be a critical control comparison.

McDonald, Perkins, Merijerrison, and Podilsky (1966) compared ECT and Amitriptyline treatment with a drug placebo and "sham" ECT control group. Results for this well-controlled, double-blind study are not especially conclusive. ECT and Amitriptyline treatments were significantly improved over control groups on only approximately one-half of the assessment devices, with some evidence for regression to the mean from pre-testing to post-testing. As with Bruce et al. (1960), no follow-up evaluations were made.

Rose (1963) treated 49 endogenous and reactive depressives with ECT and assessed effects with the Hamilton Rating Scale at one and three months following treatment. The results suggested that diag-nosed endogenous depressives had a better outcome with ECT then did the reactive depressives. No comparison control groups were in-cluded in this study. Greenblatt, Grosser, and Wechsler (1964) com-pared ECT with drug and drug-placebo groups comprised of 281 severely depressed patients of various diagnostic categories. As deter-mined by clinical ratings, ECT-treated patients were significantly im-proved over drug and drug-placebo groups. As the authors noted, problematic with this study was the fact that while the drug-treated and placebo groups were handled in a double-blind fashion, no similar control attempt was made for the ECT group. This becomes particularly problematic in light of the high improvement rate for the drug-placebo group (ECT = 92 percent; imipramine = 74 percent; phenelzine = 79 percent; isocar boxazid = 56 percent; placebo = 69 percent).

While the efficacy for ECT has been long praised, a critical evaluation of this treatment technique yields inconclusive evidence. Nevertheless, some investigators claim treatment success with ECT administered to endogenous depressives as compared to reactive de-pressives (Rose, 1963; see also, Roth, 1959; Carney, Roth, and Gar-side, 1965; Mendels, 1965). Levitt and Lubin (1975) have argued effectively against this distinction on the basis of treatment outcome. Although it is beyond the scope of this chapter to detail further the effectiveness of ECT, it is to be noted that the overall intrusiveness (i.e., memory loss, confusion, physical concomitants) of this procedure necessarily dictates continued investigation within controlled experi-mental methods.

Psychotherapy. Suggestions for treating depression via psychother-apy have been extensive and have varied from recommending in-depth analysis to advocating supportive therapy. Contradictions in strategies are abundant. Kraines (1957), for example, argued that the depressed individual should engage in social activity, while Campbell (1953) recommended rest and relaxation. Resolution of these and other issues through controlled research has not been forthcoming. The failure of proponents of various approaches to even recognize the need for an objective, controlled analysis of their viewpoints is, in itself, an indictment of the current state of the art.

Behavioral

Unlike the nonbehavioral, psychotherapy approaches, the behavioral movement has been actively concerned with issues of treatment evaluation. The techniques offered also appear to be more closely tied to the underlying theoretical position advanced. Our initial hope was that a review of this area would produce some concrete, empirical-based suggestions for the practicing clinician. Unfortunately, any such recommendations would be premature. Our review uncovered very few evaluative studies that dealt with a clinically depressed population which sought treatment. Most of the work in this area involves case reports or experimental work with human-analogue, depressed populations involving mostly college students. Athough analogue studies are valuable in their own right (see Levis, 1970), the potential differences between a clinical and analogue population are so great that it would be inappropriate to cite them as providing direct evidence for or against a given treatment approach. They are suggestive, however, of how clinical population research might proceed.

A review of the treatment literature for each of the behavioral viewpoints is presented below. Table 1 is provided as an evaluative summary for the studies discussed.

S-R Nonmotivational Models. In discussing issues of assessment, it was noted that the extent to which the controlling factors of behavior are able to be identified and validated, treatment concerns regarding appropriate target modalities are solved. Within this context a model for the functional analysis of depressive behavior was reviewed and shown to have a degree of initial success. From an operant viewpoint this is the first step required for effective treatment. Once the target behavior has been identified, treatment primarily consists of systematic manipulation of those controlling environmental factors so as to increase reinforcement density for the reestablishment of nondepressive behaviors (for a review, see Lewinsohn, 1974a; 1974b).

The operant strategy has mainly supported its treatment evaluation process via case studies and single-group designs. Such a strategy is less than satisfactory if interest exists in determining causal relationships. Case reports by Lewinsohn and Atwood (1969) and Lewinsohn

Table 1. Behavioral studies of depression

Authors	Number of Subjects	Age of Subject	Type of Report	Treatments	Follow-up	Design Quality Rating
Hersen et al. (1973)	3	32–54	Case Study with Reversal	Operant-Token Economy	—	—
Kilpatrick-Tabak & Roth (1978)	56	College Students	Experimental	Cognitive-Solvable Anagrams	—	Very Good (22)
Klein & Seligman (1976)	66	College Students	Experimental	Cognitive-Solvable Discrimination Task	—	Good (18)
Lewinsohn & Atwood (1969)	1	38	Case Study	Operant-Conjoint, Interaction Patterns	—	—
Lewinsohn & Shaffer (1971)	3	20–28	Case Study	Operant-Conjoint, Interaction Patterns	—	—
Lewinsohn et al. (1970)	9	College Students	Single Group Design	Operant-Social Skills Training, Peer Pressure	—	Very Good (22.5)
Liberman (1970)	1	34	Case Study	Operant-Conjoint Interaction Pattern	8 months	—

Table 1. *(Continued)*

Authors	Number of Subjects	Age of Subject	Type of Report	Treatments	Follow-up	Design Quality Rating
McAuley & Quinn (1975)	1	50	Case Study	Operant-Satiation of Verbal Behavior	3 months	—
Novaco (1977)	1	38	Case Study	Operant-Cognitive: Stress-Innoculation	—	—
Robinson & Lewinsohn (1973a)	1	50	Case Study with Reversal	Operant: Contingency Management of Verbal Behavior	—	—
Robinson & Lewinsohn (1973b)	20	College Students	Experimental	Operant: Contingency Management of Verbal Behavior	—	Good (18.5)
Rush et al. (1977)	41	Adult	Experimental	Cognitive vs. Drug Therapy	3 & 6 months	Very Good (21)
Shaw (1977)	32	18–26	Experimental	Cognitive vs. Behavioral and Control	1 month	Very Good (21.5)

and Shaffer (1971) provide illustrative examples of this point. Lewinsohn and Atwood (1969) treated a depressed female patient (age 38) both individually and with her husband in a three-month, time-limited period. Although the patient's past test scores improved on the MMPI, Depression Adjective Checklist, and interviewer rating scale, and although a positive change was observed in the interaction pattern between the patient and her husband and children, the contributing factors responsible for change remain unknown. A follow-up of the treatment results also was not reported.

In a similar vein, Lewinsohn and Shaffer (1971) continued the home-observation method of assessment and treatment of a 28-year-old depressed housewife, a 20-year-old depressed male student and father. For two of the cases, post-therapy home observations indicated changed family interactions consistent with the operant model's expectations. For one case, no data were reported. As with the Lewinsohn and Atwood (1969) study, it is impossible to determine the responsible factors. Treatment involved individual and joint sessions, with primary focus upon communication patterns within the home setting. The lack of control over variables and multiple outcome measures is problematic. Nevertheless, it still may prove profitable in a heuristic sense to discuss additional case reports using an operant strategy.

Lewinsohn, Weinstein, and Alper (1970) treated nine depressed college students in a group setting. Sessions were again time-limited (three months) and involved a form of social skills training by therapists and group peers. Coding of various behavioral processes-interactions across sessions yielded comparable interaction changes concomitant with less depression. Treatment appeared to range from techniques of interpretation to direct behavioral training. No follow-up was reported.

Robinson and Lewinsohn (1973a) provided an interesting account of modifying the rate of verbal output of a 50-year-old depressed male. Using a rather haphazard reversal design, the authors did appear to be able to influence the rate of speech of this patient through the use of reinforcement. However, as Seligman, Klein, and Miller (1976) correctly noted, no report was made regarding the generalization of treatment effects to extra therapeutic situations, nor was any empirical relationship noted between verbal behavior change and depression. No follow-up was cited.

Robinson and Lewinsohn (1973b) examined four groups of mildly depressed college females (N = 20). Similar to Robinson and Lewinsohn (1973a), this study attempted to modify depressed verbal behavior (complaints, and so on) through the Premack principle. Here, "depressed talk" was allowed contingent only upon nondepressed verbal behavior. While the Premack group showed significantly increased nondepressed talk, a yoked control group (noncontingent allowance of "depressed talk" yoked to the Premack group) showed equivalent nondepressed verbal behavior increases. It would appear that increased nondepressed verbal behavior was a direct result of simply restricting depressed verbal behavior, and not a result of the contingencies imposed. Comments similar to those made regarding the Robinson and Lewinsohn (1973a) study would apply here.

Hersen, Eisler, Alford, and Agras (1973) treated three depressed, male inpatients on a token economy ward using an A-B-A design. Increased behavioral indices of depression (i.e., Williams, Barlow, and Agras, 1972). Clinical ratings were made by ward personnel. It was not reported whether or not they were blind to the experimental procedure and expected results. Each patient was also on drug therapy during the token program. No follow-up was reported.

Similar to Lewinsohn's conjoint interventions, Liberman (1970) reported successful behavioral intervention with a 34-year-old depressed mother and her husband. Treatment focused upon the husband's interactions with the patient. Liberman (1970) reported self-report mood elevation following five sessions and sustained over an eight-month follow-up. As with Lewinsohn's reports, the particular treatment factor involved is impossible to assess here.

In another case report, McAuley and Quinn (1975) reported a successful treatment of a 50-year-old female inpatient who displayed a persistent grief reaction two-and-one-half years after the death of her husband. A treatment strategy of satiation of verbal hostility and depressed talk required the patient to talk to nurses about her grief, write essays, and listen to herself over tapes approximately six hours per day for three weeks, These authors reported sustained improvement at three-month follow-up.

The last case report to be reviewed under this section may be mislabelled since the treatment approach adopted used a variety of behavioral techniques. Novaco (1977) introduced a procedure called "stress innovation" to treat a 38-year-old depressed male inpatient. While this technique has been labelled a cognitive therapy, many of its treatment components would be consistent with the behavioral model presented here. The stress inoculation approach involves three phases of treatment: (1) cognitive preparation—an educational approach to anger and its effect, identifying important situational determinants of anger; (2) skill acquisition and rehearsal—learning coping strategies through modeling and behavioral rehearsal, relaxation training, self-instruction training, and assertion training; (3) applied practice—proficiency testing through imaginal and role-playing instructions. Novaco (1977) thus stressed a multidimensional view that incorporates potential cognitive, affective, and behavioral components of the depressed patient. Novaco (1977) reported decreased behavioral ratings of anger, increased relaxation, and improved self-ratings of anger and anger management in this patient. This behavior appeared to generalize to the home upon discharge in his interactions with his children during treatment. No follow-up was reported. More research is needed on this technique to determine the effective treatment components involved.

S-R Motivational Models.   As previously stated, the models reviewed under this section essentially conceptualized depression as avoidance behavior designed to prevent the depressive person from confronting even stronger aversive reactions than those resulting from the avoidance or depressed posture. The critical conditioning sequences that are hypothesized to be avoided involve both environmental and related cues stored in memory that, upon exposure, are expected to elicit a strong negative emotional response. Avoidance or escape from stimuli associated with feelings of rejection, failure, hostility, guilt, and loss of love are believed to be motivating the depressive response.

Therapy is designed to discharge the emotional eliciting conditioned stimuli via the principle of Pavlovian extinction. Procedurally, extinction is attained through repeated nonreinforced presentations of those conditioned stimuli previously associated with the unconditioned stimulus. The objectives of therapy, then, are to represent, reinstate, or symbolically reproduce, in the absence of physical pain (the unconditioned stimulus), the cue patterns to which the avoidance response has been conditioned. To allow for a maximally encompassing extinction effect, the therapist's usual implosive strategy is to attempt to reproduce the hypothesized avoided CS cues through an imagery technique, rather than by simple verbal statement or a reliance upon in vivo stimulus presentation (see Levis, in press, b). Through verbal instructions to imagine, implosive scenes are presented to the client which include the various stimuli (visual, auditory, tactual) hypothesized to have been present in the original conditioning events. It is assumed that all cues presented in imagery which elicit negative affect do so because of previous learning, and are therefore extinguishable. Images per se are not considered inherently aversive.

As Levis (in press, b) noted, the therapist's task is to approximate for the client the presentation of the total avoided conditioned stimulus complex (e.g., S1, S2, S3, and so on) by presenting scenes. Such scene exposure should elicit a strong emotional reaction followed by an extinction effect, since the images presented are nonreinforced (no primary reinforcement). By repetitive presentations of the scene, the emotional response should extinguish. Once sufficient drive value of the aversive stimulus has been extinguished through repeated exposure and by varying cue presentation, symptomatic behavior should be markedly reduced or eliminated (see Levis, in press b; Stampfl and Levis, 1967, 1973)

Levis and Hare (1977) provide an extensive review of the human analogue and patient studies using the technique of implosive or flooding therapy. The results of their review suggest the technique shows considerable therapeutic promise, but studies dealing solely with depressed population have not been conducted. An illustrative case using this technique is provided later in the chapter.

Although not previously reviewed, Wolpe's (1958, 1971) technique of systematic desensitization would fall under the heading of an S-R motivated technique. Rather than using a direct extinction approach, he suggested a counterconditioning procedure in which the patient is taught to relax and then to visualize a sequence of stimuli that are associated with progressively increased amounts of anxiety. Systematic studies using depressed populations have not been conducted with this technique. However, a couple of successfully treated case reports using this approach have been reported with an acutely suicidal wrist slasher, and phobic depression (Elliot, Smith, and Weldman, 1972; Wanderer, 1972).

S-S Nonmotivational Model. According to Seligman's learned helplessness model, depression is stimulated by a cognitive perception of lack of control. According to the helplessness viewpoint, the central objective of successful therapy is to alter the patient's negative cognitive sets. This can be achieved by having the patient relearn that his response system can produce the gratifications desired (Seligman, 1974).

Following the preceding strategy, investigators have attempted to alleviate the effects of induced helplessness in normal subjects and measured response deficits in depressed college students by forcing exposure to solvable therapy problems. These results have not been conclusive. Klein and Seligman (1976) noted in their first experiment that a reversal in shuttlebox escape deficits occurred for helpless and depressed subjects following performing solvable therapy problems involving a discrimination task. In their second experiment, they obtained predicted reversals in expectancy changes on a skill task for depressed and helpless subjects. Noted methodological flaws included a potential confound between controllability and response feedback (correct versus incorrect), in addition to a failure to validate independently the "skill" and "chance" tasks utilized.

Negative evidence is also appearing which suggests that the solvable therapy-problems approach does not always lead to a removal of the performance deficits in depressed subjects (see Kilpatrick-Tabak

and Roth, 1978). Cognizant of this potential failure, Abramson, Seligman, and Teasdale (1978) have outlined a new treatment approach
couched within an attributional framework. Four treatment strategies
emerge from the reformulation. They are as follows:

1. Change the estimated probability of the relevant event's occur-
    rence: Reduce estimated likelihood for aversive outcomes and
    increase estimated likelihood for desired outcomes.
2. Make the highly preferred outcomes less preferred.
3. Change the expectation from uncontrollability to controllability.
4. Change unrealistic attributions for failure toward external, un-
    stable, specific; change unrealistic attributions for success toward
    internal, stable, global.

The effectiveness of the preceding suggestions have yet to be systematically evaluated.

S-S Motivational Model.   The particular therapeutic approach utilized by Beck was recently described in a new book (Beck, 1976). The
first task of the therapist is to formulate the problems of the depressed
patient in cognitive terms. Depression is viewed as resulting from an
underlying shift in the depressed patient's cognitive organization toward negative concepts. These negative concepts contribute to other
symptoms, such as sadness, passivity, self-blame, loss of pleasure
response, and suicidal wishes. Such negative thinking results in a
vicious cycle where unpleasant affects and self-defeating motivations
reinforce each other. The strategy of therapy is to use techniques that
help the patient reshape the negative cognitive concepts of being a
"loser," to positive concepts of viewing oneself as a "winner."

To achieve this objective, the therapist must separate the syndrome of depression into its specific components—emotional, motivational, cognitive, behavioral, or physiological. In principle, the therapist can start with any of the symptoms and concentrate on changing
the symptom cluster. Each symptom cluster should be conceptualized
as a problem and potential target for intervention. Changing one
cluster should effect changes in others.

The initial selection of a given target behavior and the technique
used depends upon many factors (see Beck, 1976). Beck's approach to
treatment mainly reflects a strategy rather than a carefully delineated
treatment technique. Some of the techniques found useful by him can
be labelled as follows: (1) scheduling activities with the patient; (2)
graded task assignment; (3) mastery and pleasure therapy; (4) cognitive

reappraised; (5) alternative therapy; (6) cognitive rehearsal; and (7) homework assignments. Detailed descriptions of these approaches can be found in Beck (1976).

Research on Beck's cognitive therapy is only beginning to emerge. Beck (1976) describes the results of a number of studies with clinical populations which suggest cognitive therapy may produce positive results. Unfortunately, the work cited was not as yet published precluding a careful critical review. In a recent study, Shaw (1977) reported greater reduction of self-report (Beck Depression Inventory and Hamilton Rating Scale) measures of depression relative to S-R behavioral, nondirective, or no-treatment control groups. These results were not particularly long-lasting, as initial differences between the cognitive and S-R behavioral groups collapsed at a one-month follow-up evaluation. This collapse was attributable to the relative partial loss of previous gains for the cognitive group, while the behavioral group remained stable with respect to its initial improvement. A nondirective treatment group was included in this design "to attempt to provide a procedure that was plausible and yet did not involve therapeutic techniques developed specifically for depressed clients." Following "treatments," the nondirective group did not reliably differ from the behavioral group on the dependent measures. No follow-up evaluation was done on this group.

In another study, Rush, Beck, Kovacs, and Hollon (1977) compared cognitive psychotherapy with drug therapy (imipramine). The cognitive therapy group showed faster initial improvement relative to drug therapy on BDI and Hamilton Anxiety scores up to three months' follow-up, and a nonsignificant trend at six months (see also Burns and Beck, 1978). A no-treatment control group was not included in this investigation. Additional work is needed before any statements concerning the efficacy of Beck's suggestions can be made. Given the interest in this approach, additional research should be forthcoming.

Comments

As the foregoing review suggests, issues of treatment effectiveness for depression have yet to be resolved. Considerably more work with better methodological controls is needed if the issues raised in this review are to be answered. For one thing, the operant approach must come to grips with the need to unravel treatment manipulations, to include control conditions, and to increase sample size. For another, the cognitive positions, like that proposed by Beck, must address the need for formal specification of such terms as "faulty pattern of thinking" and the measures by which this state is assessed. For example, even though independent raters in the Shaw (1977) study were able to identify reliably that the cognitive technique used was what a cognitive technique should entail, judgments of this type fall far short in validating the boundary conditions dictated by this theoretical approach. Such a state of affairs currently exists for each of the other positions reviewed. Hopefully, critical reviews of the type presented will stimulate the needed work in this area.

CLINICAL PRESCRIPTION

In cases where depression is a dominant factor, the initial interview should be concerned with issues of severity and suicidal risk. In addressing the severity issue, a careful evaluation is needed of the vegetative and physical manifestations of depression such as loss of appetite, sleep, sex, interest, and endurance. In addition, an analysis of the patient's posture, voice quality, dress, eye contact, sense of humor, and psychomotor retardation can be of help. As the number of depression indices increases with a moderate or severe rating (see Beck, 1973), so does the extent and seriousness of the problem.

Suicide fantasies and actual attempts should be ascertained and discussed with the patient in terms of potential risk. Furthermore, questions in this area should be phrased as if the assumption has been made that such behavior is ongoing. For example, say: "Tell me about your last suicide fantasy?" "How often do you have them?" "By what method do you consider killing yourself?" "When was the last time you tried?" Do not say: "Have you ever had suicidal fantasies or attempted suicide?" The latter type of questioning permits an easy "no" answer. If negative answers are given in this area and a long-latency response occurs between a question and answer, the possibility increases that the patient is holding back important material. Return to the area under discussion at a later point in time. Other questions of interest are as follows: If actual attempts have occurred do they involve violent (gun) or passive methods (pills)? Does the patient see his or her attempts as serious? Were others present at the time, and to what extent was secondary gain involved? Has the patient been seen by another professional for this problem? Has he or she been hospitalized? What medication is the individual currently taking?

If the depression is deemed severe and/or suicide risk is high, hospitalization should be considered, as well as removing as many environmental stress factors as possible. Chemotherapy should not be relied upon as the sole form of treatment since at least two or three weeks is required before the antidepressive medication can take effect. If the suicide attempts appear mainly manipulative and are not judged as serious, steps should still be taken to eliminate them. Many people kill themselves by accident in carrying out such attempts. For example, following the taking of a large number of pills, a patient expects the husband to rescue her when he returns from work, but he is late coming home resulting in her death.

If the patient is not in any immediate danger, then time exists for a complete work-up. Careful family, religious, childhood, sexual, and interpersonal histories should be obtained. Duration and extent of each depressive episode should be plotted and correlated with environmental factors. Attempts to determine the variables responsible for eliciting the initial onset should also be made, as well as assessing current stresses at work, home, and in interpersonal relationships. An assessment also should be made as to whether the individual is avoiding expressions of anger, guilt, fear of rejection, or loss of control. Are attempts being made to deny the presence of the depression, and to what extent has the subject removed himself or herself from positive social reinforcements? How are people around the patient affected by the depression, and has depression been a family problem? Is the patient also anxious or agitated, and to what extent is the patient motivated to accept treatment? Answers to these and other similar questions should provide an important source of valuable information.

Prior to treatment a thorough work-up by a physician should be obtained, and consideration should be given to administering psychometric tests. The Beck's depression scale, the Affective Adjective Checklist, and the MMPI have been found to be useful paper-pencil inventories in assessing depression. Projective tests like the TAT and Rorschach Test have also been used in this regard. Following such a careful assessment, strategy will then permit a more rationale formulation of a treatment plan.

CASE REPORT

The case to be reported here involved an individual who was diagnosed as having a severe, "psychotic" depressive reaction and who was treated by implosive therapy by the second author (This case is reported in Levis, in press, b.). Both authors have found implosive therapy to be quite effective in removing depression in a surprisingly short period of time (1–15 sessions), but controlled research with this population has yet to be forthcoming. It is our hope this case will stimulate more research interest.

The patient, a male, was 45 years old at the time of treatment. His pre-test, MMPI T-scores were as follows: L(46), F(56), K(49); Hs(72), D(101), Hy(77), Pd(72), MF(53), Pa(56), Pt(85), Sc(62), Ma(64), Si(32). These test results are consistent with the reported diagnosis of a severe depression. The patient refused to eat, spoke in a monotone voice, and reported that he was seriously considering committing suicide. In fact, the suicide ruminations had started some two years prior to the start of therapy. Recently he had been going down into his cellar daily where he would stare at a rafter that he was going to use to hang himself. He would then try to muster the "courage" to commit suicide. He expressed having difficulty with his boss and his wife, neither of whom he felt appreciated him. The patient seemed unable to assert himself appropriately or to express direct overt anger. He knew his wife was faithful to him, being a "good" Catholic, but he could not shake the "paranoid thought" that she was secretly having an affair with his brother-in-law. The patient's father was described as a strict disciplinarian that nobody would dare talk back to or contradict.

The therapist was given three days to treat the patient since he was scheduled to be hospitalized on the fourth day if the depression persisted. The patient was seen for a two-hour period on each of the three successive days. Because of the imposed time restriction, the therapist moved into the hypothesized cue areas more quickly than would normally be the case. It was hypothesized that the patient had internalized considerable hostility to his wife and boss, and that he was experiencing a great deal of guilt over this matter. He also was continually frustrated both at home and in the work situation because of his inability to take a stand on issues. The therapist treatment plan was to first extend the depression in order to confront the patient with the rejection cues he was avoiding. Once the patient was fully experiencing the rejection cues in imagery, the next task was to elicit the internalized anger by developing scenes in which the patient was asked to see himself expressing aggression. The attempt was to design a scene which the client could feel justified in his expression of aggression. Once the rejection cues were experienced, the anger in theory would be closer to the surface and more easily elicited. It was decided that if the aggressive material was introduced prematurely the patient's avoidance behavior might be too strong to produce much involvement. After the aggression was easily expressed, an attempt would be made to get the patient to accept responsibility for his negative emotions and behavior. The plan was to follow this scene with a punishment sequence and more rejection cues.

The first scene introduced described the patient walking down his basement stairs, walking over to the rafter he planned to use, throwing a rope around the rafter, and hanging himself. The rafter was described in great detail as was each aspect of the hanging scene. When the patient was asked to see himself standing on a chair with the rope around his neck, he was also given the opportunity to complete the hanging scene in imagery. He said: "I kicked the chair out from under me and I died." The therapist said: "No, you're not dead yet, feel the rope closing tightly around your neck, feel it burning against your skin, the breath is going out of you. You are struggling, you don't want to die but it is too late. Feel the pain, the loss of breath and see your body twitching and struggling for life." The death scene lasted about five minutes, the patient repeatedly tried to hurry the process, and the scene generated a high level of anxiety.

Once the patient visualized himself as dead hanging from the rafter, the therapist had the wife come down the basement stairs. At this point the therapist asked the patient to get a clear image of his wife's face. He was asked to continue the scene. The patient said: "She's crying. Now she will be sorry that I am dead. Now she will miss me and realize how important I was." At this point the therapist interrupted and said: "No, you're wrong! Look at her face again. See the smile as she looks at your body hanging from the rafter. She's glad you're dead." In fact, the wife was described as being so glad she immediately called up her friends and they threw a party in the basement around the patient's body. Each person verbalized why they were glad he was dead. The scene elicited considerable anxiety. As the scene developed, the friends left except for the patient's brother-in-law who was dancing with the patient's wife. An explicit sexual encounter between the patient's wife and brother-in-law was described. Emphasis was placed on the details of their kissing, touching of her breast, disrobing, and sexual intercourse, in order to "prime" the patient for the aggressive scenes which were planned to follow.

Following the sexual scene, the patient was told to imagine himself as not really being dead but that he was only testing his wife's loyalty. The patient's facial expression changed from one of anxiety to anger. He saw himself take the rope off his neck, pick up a sharp knife, and attack his wife and brother-in-law. An almost primary process aggressive scene followed with the patient castrating his brother-in-law and cutting his wife's breast. The anger "flooded" forth and the patient got so involved that he started swinging his fist and kicking the desk directly in front of him. The theme of aggression was repeated using different victims (e.g., the patient's father, mother, boss, until an extinction effect was obtained).

The final scene was an attempt to deal with the resulting guilt associated with the feeling of expressing anger. The scene involved the patient being placed in jail for killing his wife, and so on. A courtroom scene developed in which the patient was asked to confess his guilt and "sinful" actions to the judge and jury. The scene provided for additional replication of the aggressive scene material. The jury did not bother to go out and deliberate, the patient was found guilty and condemned to die in the electric chair. The electric chair was selected because of the stimulus similarity to pain and fire associated by the patient to his image of hell. (Using hindsight, it perhaps would have been better to have death occur by hanging.) The patient's "sins" were considered so horrible that after the confession of all his life's wrongdoings (those which actually occurred and those made up by the therapist) to a priest, the priest refused absolution. The death march to the electric chair was described in detail as was the placement in the chair. The warden threw the switch and left it on until the patient's body was burned to a crisp. The patient's soul went before God and another replication of the aggression and confession scenes occurred. God condemned him to eternal damnation in hell which really shook up the patient who thought God would even forgive him for committing suicide. The patient blurted out: "God, no, not hell, purgatory." In the scene God held fast and the patient's soul was described as tumbling to hell. The patient saw God as a brilliant light and as he fell, the light became smaller and smaller until it faded out. Somewhat surprisingly, this latter scene also produced a very high level of anxiety in the patient. The patient was held in hell for about 20 minutes, visualizing all his sins of omission (e.g., not giving to his wife) and commission. He was asked to experience the pain in hell which was designed to serve as punishment for his "evil" behavior.

The patient's depression lifted after the second session. His appetite returned, as did his voice inflection. He reported no more suicide ruminations. The Depression Scale T-score on his pre-test MMPI was over 100. On the post-test the Depression T-score was in the normal range, as was each of the other four scales (Hs, Hy, Pd, Pt) which were above 70 on the pre-test. The post-test T-scores were: L(40), F(53), K(55), Hs(53), D(63), Hy(53), Pd(60), MF(56), Pa(50), Pt(69), Sc(50), Ma(78), Si(41). A follow-up evaluation a year later indicated that treatment effects were holding. Although case studies are not to be used in scientific support of the technique, the preceding test data for this case are presented because they substantiated the clinical observation that the technique appears to produce fast results in reducing feelings of depression. Hopefully, these observations will stimulate more objective work on this topic.

From the foregoing case description, it might appear that the implosive procedure is a complex technique to utilize. It should be understood that this case presentation involves the use of the technique with rather severe psychopathology. In many cases the approach is straightforward, with the therapist mainly developing scenes around cues correlated with symptom onset. Experience also indicates that many of the background cues used for one patient can be used for others (e.g., courtroom scenes, hell scenes). Furthermore, the basic themes of rejection, punishment, loss of love, sex avoidance, expression of anger, and acceptance of responsibility are common to the problem areas of many patients. With experience, the technique becomes easy to administer. For additional case material, the reader is referred to Levis, in press, b; Stampfl and Levis, 1967, 1969, and 1973.

ETHICAL AND LEGAL ISSUES

The ethical and legal issues in treating a depressed patient are basically the same as involved in treating other cases. However, unlike other cases the depressive potentially can be a danger to his or her own physical well-being. Steps must be taken to avert the possibility of suicide. If such danger exists, hospitalization should be considered, as well as informing significant other persons. Suicide attempts can also involve a legal question. If a serious attempt has been made and if the patient is in danger of dying, authorities should be contacted if the therapist is unable to deal with the problem. Issues of confidentiality and under what situations it may be broken should be discussed with the patient. Therapists should be familiar with the contents of the ethical manual of their respective mental health profession, as well as being familiar with the existing laws pertaining to this matter. The use of drugs or ECT raises the additional question of potential side effects. The overdose of certain drugs can cause death. In depressive cases that may involve suicide attempts. Pills should be controlled by someone other than the patient. ECT is frequently recommended over drugs in cases where suicide is a danger, but the procedure is probably riskier than drugs. The most frequent complications from ECT are fractures and dislocations produced by the muscular contractions during the convulsions. ECT administered with pentobarbital-succinylcholine produces relaxation markedly, or completely reduces the complications (Holmberg, 1963). Cardiovascular accidents represent the most serious danger, but this can be reduced by administering certain drugs in conjunction with treatment (Beck, 1973). Back pain and loss of memory may persist for a couple of weeks.

Drugs, ECT, and psychotherapy take time to be effective. In severe depressive cases, the immediate removal of environmental stress factors should be considered.

SUGGESTIONS FOR CLINICAL AND
EXPERIMENTAL RESEARCH

Throughout this chapter an attempt has been made to focus the reader upon the important problems confronting the depression area. Difficulties associated with the topics of definitional precision, theory, assessment, and treatment already have been outlined. Increased methodological precision is needed with better focus on critical issues. Until the topic of definitional precision and assessment are better delineated, the term "depression" will not have much functional utility. Perhaps the best strategy at this point is to dispense with the term and describe the problem area in terms of descriptive correlates of depression. This latter objective could be achieved by developing a set of dependent measures which would separate the emotional, cognitive, motivational, physical, and behavioral effects attributed to the depressive syndrome. If such a constellation of dependent measures could be established, then the interrelationship among variables also could be assessed through experimental manipulation.

Concerning the issue of theory, it is unlikely that any one theoretical structure will encompass an explanatory guideline for all the behaviors labelled under the depression umbrella. But it is also believed that issues related to etiology and treatment will not be resolved until theoretical models are provided which generate contrasting differential predictions. What appears to be happening now is that each theorist assigns causal primacy to one piece of the pie while ignoring the rest. Differential predictions, however, can be made and research on them would help eliminate certain models and sharpen others. For example, it is important to determine whether the depressive state involves a motivational variable, and if so, does the manipulation of this variable affect the depressive state. Does depression reflect learned helplessness, active or passive avoidance, or simply a reinforcement deficit? Are specific stimulus categories like rejection, fear of failure, guilt, or aggressive cues correlated with the response output-side of depression? Are cognitive changes the result of depression, its cause, or simply a defense pattern designed to reduce aversive stimulation? Each of these and other such questions can be tested at an experimental level. The resulting forthcoming answers would not only stimulate new questions, but result in significant theoretical advances.

Research and clinical issues related to treatment effectiveness are also of paramount concern. Long-term developmental studies are needed. Attempts at standardizing treatment effectiveness should be made with attention being paid to analyzing changes in cognitive, emotional, and behavioral response patterns. Work with clinical populations is essential, with a careful eye on defending them in an operational manner so replication can be insured.

Comparative analysis across approaches is perhaps premature, at least for the behavioral techniques. What is needed at first are efficient, well-designed, two-group comparisons of a treatment package versus a nontreated control. If the treatment package shows repeated success then parametric analysis of the package would appear warranted to determine the critical change-agent(s). Once this has been established, the treatment approach can be modified to enhance the effectiveness of the therapeutic change-agent. At this point, comparative analysis should be encouraged, with additional studies being designed to determine the effects of therapist variables, subject characteristics, and so forth.

Clinical studies are difficult to execute, time-consuming, and costly. The preceding suggestion of first showing that a treatment package works before costly designs are used should not only save time in the long run, but should encourage more clinical work. Of course, providing a careful assessment of follow-up effectiveness is a critical component in such a research study.

Overall, what is needed is an abundance of careful, well-controlled, systematic research in each of the areas discussed. The pay-off of such research should greatly benefit society by reducing one of its major mental health problems—depression.

SUMMARY

What is depression? What causes this state and what factors are responsible for maintaining it over time? How can it be treated? These were introductory questions raised at the onset of our review. At the completion of our survey of the literature, these questions were still inadequately answered. Despite the volumes of material on this subject, depression remains as one of the most complex, diversified, and least understood psychological problems confronting researchers and clinicians.

The problem of defining depression is plagued by the tendency of investigators to take sides on the issue of whether depression should be conceptualized as a unitary or dichotomous syndrome. This issue is further complicated by the finding that almost every psychological symptom known has been included in the depressive syndrome by some investigator. Problematic also is the finding that depressive behavior is subsumed under any number of separate diagnostic labels or categories. Considerable agreement does exist, however, that depression can be manifested at an emotional, cognitive, motivational, physical, and behavioral level.

Issues of etiology are also plagued by the foregoing problems associated with definitional precision and utility. Most models of depression are unidirectional in that causal primacy is given to a particular fraction of the depressive syndrome. Problematic here is the often mistaken assumption that such causal inferences are able to account for the assumed interdependence of the observed heterogeneous response classes associated with depression.

In reviewing the various theories of depression, emphasis was given to the recently developed behavior models. However, a cursory review was provided for the nonbehavioral approaches represented in the biological and psychoanalytic viewpoints. By reducing depressive symptoms to neurochemical imbalances, the biological approaches have a distinct advantage of providing formal specification of definitional terms. Unfortunately, this reductionistic precision is not matched by measurement capabilities. Furthermore, the noted biochemical deficiencies may be a result of depression rather than a cause. However, the psychoanalytic models showed a lack of concern for formal specification of terms and criteria, reducing predictive and analytic power.

The behavioral viewpoints were divided into four distinct conceptual approaches: (1) *S-R nonmotivational;* (2) *S-R motivational;* (3) *S-S nonmotivational;* and (4) *S-S motivational.* The writings of Ferster and Lewinsohn reflect the behavioral orientation discussed under the first heading. Ferster has suggested that depression is caused and sustained by the loss of positive environmental reinforcers and the resulting extinction effort of approach behaviors. Similarly, Lewinsohn presented a model which views depression as resulting from the individual's low rate of response-contingent positive reinforcement. Approaches under this heading are frequently referred to as operant analysis.

The second conceptual S-R category is reflected in the writings of Stampfl and Levis. According to their viewpoint, depression symptoms are viewed as avoidance behavior designed to terminate or reduce conditioned aversive stimuli. Two separate etiological models were reviewed which involve the avoidance of cue areas associated with feelings of rejection, failure, guilt, anger, and frustration. Cognitive thought processes are believed to be associated with depression. However, they are viewed from this position as defense mechanisms designed to protect the individual, rather than as causal factors or processes reflecting the effects of depression.

The third and fourth categories included are the cognitive models of depression reflected in the writings of Seligman and Beck. Seligman proposed that reactive depression results from a state of learned helplessness stimulated by a cognitive perception of having lack of control over events. For Beck, the individual's negative perception and appraisal of environmental events, one's cognitive sets, provide the sustaining force for depressive responding. Supporting evidence for each of the above behavioral positions was reviewed and found lacking in demonstrating causal efficacy.

Issues of assessment were also discussed under the headings of factor analytic, psychometric testing, and approaches involving functional assessment. Although the assessment area is plagued with serious methodological problems, the functional assessment approach reflected in the work of Lewinsohn appears to be the most promising strategy.

Although numerous treatment techniques have been applied in the treatment of depression, controlled studies using patients as subjects were noticeably few in number. The only exception to this finding involved studies analyzing the effect of medication and ECT treatment. Some supporting evidence can be marshaled in favor of both treatment approaches, but issues of population samples, evaluation, and follow-up assessment preclude concrete judgments of efficacy. The behavioral technique varied from manipulation of reinforcement contingencies, cognitive restructuring, expectancy manipulations, and emotional extinction techniques. Adequate supporting data from clinical populations were also lacking for each of the techniques reviewed.

The chapter was rounded out by providing a clinical prescription for assessing depression, and by discussing a case report treated by implosive therapy. Ethical and legal issues pertaining to depression were also discussed, as well as suggestions for clinical and experimental research.

REFERENCES

Abraham, K. Notes on the psychoanalytic investigation and treatment of manic-depressive insanity and allied conditions. In *Selected papers on psychoanalysis.* New York: Basic Books, 1960, pp. 137–156.

Abramson, L. Y., Seligman, M.E.P., and Teasdale, J. D. Learned helplessness in humans: Critique and reformulation. *Journal of Abnormal Psychology,* 1978, *87,* 49–74.

Akiskal, H. S., and McKinney, W. T. Overview of recent research in depression. *Archives of General Psychiatry,* 1975, *32,* 285–305.

Amsel, A. Behavioral habituation, counter-conditioning, and a general theory of persistence. In A. H. Black and W. F. Prokasy, eds., *Classical conditioning II.* New York: Appleton-Century-Crofts, 1972.

Atkinson, C. and Polivy, J. Effects of delay, attack, and retaliation on state depression and hostility. *Journal of Abnormal Psychology,* 1976, *85,* 570–576.

Beck, A. T. Thinking and depression. *Archives of General Psychiatry,* 1963, *9,* 324–333.

Beck, A. T. *Depression: Clinical, experimental, and theoretical aspects.* New York: Hoeber, 1967.

Beck, A. T. *The diagnosis and management of depression.* Philadelphia: University of Pennsylvania Press, 1973.

Beck, A. T. The development of depression: A cognitive model. In R. J. Friedman and M. M. Katz (eds), *The psychology of depression: Contemporary theory and research.* New York: John Wiley & Sons, 1974.

Beck, A. T. *Cognitive therapy and the emotional disorders.* New York: International Universities Press, Inc., 1976.

Beck, A. T., Feshbach, S., and Legg, D. The clincial utility of the digit symbol test. *Journal of Consulting Psychology,* 1962, *26,* 263–268.

Beck, A. T., Ward, C. H., Mendelson, M. et al. An inventory for measuring depression. *Archives of General Psychiatry,* 1961, *4,* 561–569.

Becker, J. *Affective disorders.* New Jersey: General Learning Press, 1977.

Bellack, A. S. and Hersen, M. Self-report inventories in behavioral assessment. In J. D. Cone and R. P. Hawking, eds., *Behavioral assessment: New directions in clinical psychology.* New York: Brunner/Mazel, 1977.

Blaney, P. H. Contemporary theories of depression: Critique and comparison. *Journal of Abnormal Psychology,* 1977, *86,* 203–223.

Boyd, T. L. Learned helplessness: A critical investigation of the response-outcome contingency space. Dissertation, State University of New York, Binghamton, 1978.

Bradley, J. J. Severe localized pain associated with the depressive syndrome. *British Journal of Psychiatry,* 1963, *109,* 741–745.

Bruce, E. M., Crone, N., Fitzpatrick, G. et al. A comparative trial of ECT and Tofranil. *American Journal of Psychiatry,* 1960, *117,* 76.

Buchwald, A. M. Comments on "Depressive affect: A test of behavioral hypotheses" by Wener and Rehm. *Journal of Abnormal Psychology,* 1977, *86,* 553–554.

Burns, D. D. and Beck, A. T. Cognitive behavior modification of mood disorders. In J. P. Foreyt and D. P. Rathjen, Eds., *Cognitive behavior therapy: Research and application.* New York: Plenum Press, 1978.

Campbell, J. D. *Manic-depressive disease.* Philadelphia: Lippincott, 1953.

Carney, M.W.P., Roth, M., and Garside, R. F. The diagnosis of depressive syndromes and the prediction of ECT response. *British Journal of Psychiatry,* 1965, *111,* 665–674.

Cole, J. O. Therapeutic efficacy of antidepressant drugs. *Journal of American Medical Association,* 1964, *190,* 448–455.

Comrey, A. L. A factor analysis of items on the MMPI Depression Scale. *Educational Psychological Measurements,* 1957, *17,* 578–585.

Coppen, A. The biochemistry of affective disorders. *British Journal of Psychiatry,* 1967, *113,* 1237–1264.

Costello, C. G. Depression: Loss of reinforcers or loss of reinforcer effectiveness. *Behavior Therapy,* 1972, *3,* 246–247.

Coyne, J. C. Depression and the response of others. *Journal of Abnormal Psychology,* 1976, *85,* 186–193.

Cropley, A. J. and Weckowicz, T. E. The dimensionality of clinical depression. *Australian Journal of Psychology,* 1966, *18,* 18–25.

Elliot, T. N., Smith, R. D. and Weldman, R. W. Suicide and systematic desensitization: A case study. *Journal of Clinical Psychology,* 1972, *28,* 420–423.

Fenichel, O. *The psychoanalytic theory of neurosis.* New York: W. W. Norton & Co., Inc., 1945.

Ferster, C. B. Classification of behavior pathology. In L. Krasner and L. P. Ullman, eds., *Research in behavior modification.* New York: Holt, Rinehart and Winston, 1965.

Ferster, C. B. A functional analysis of depression. *American Psychologist,* 1973, *28,* 857–870.

Ferster, C. B. Behavioral approaches to depression. In R. J. Friedman and M. M. Katz, eds., *The psychology of depression: Contemporary theory and research.* Washington, D.C.: Winston-Wiley, 1974.

Forrest, M. S. and Hokanson, J. E. Depression and autonomic arousal reduction accompanying self-punitive behavior. *Journal of Abnormal Psychology,* 1975, *84,* 346–357.

Freud, S. Mourning and melancholia. (1911) In J. Strachey, ed., *Collected works of Sigmund Freud: The standard edition,* Vol. 14. London: Hogarth Press, 1957.

Friedman, A. S. Minimal effects of severe depression on cognitive functioning. *Journal of Abnormal and Social Psychology,* 1964, *69,* 237–243.

Granick, S. Comparative analysis of psychotic depressives with matched normals on some untimed verbal intelligence tests. *Journal of Consulting Psychology,* 1963, *27,* 439–443.

Greenblatt, M., Grosser, G. H. and Wechsler, H. Differential response of hospitalized depressed patients to somatic therapy. *American Journal of Psychiatry,* 1964, *120,* 935–943.

Greenfield, N. S., Katz, D., Alexander, A. A. and Roessler, R. The relationship between physiological and psychological responsivity: Depression and galvanic skin response. *Journal of Nervous and Mental Disease,* 1963, *136,* 535–539.

Grinker, R. R., Miller, J., Subshin, M. et al. *The phenomena of depression.* New York: Harper & Row, 1961.

Hamilton, M. A rating scale for depression. *Journal of Neurology, Neurosurgery, and Psychiatry,* 1960, *23,* 56–62.

Hamilton, M. Development of a rating scale for primary depressive illness. *British Journal of Social and Clinical Psychology,* 1967, *6,* 278–296.

Hamilton, M. and White, J. M. Clinical syndromes in the depressive states. *Journal of Mental Science,* 1959, *105,* 985–998.

Hammen, C. L. and Glass, D. R., Jr. Depression, activity, and evaluation of reinforcement. *Journal of Abnormal Psychology,* 1975, *84,* 718–721.

Hammen, C. L. and Peters, S. D. Interpersonal consequences of depression: Responses to men and women enacting a depressed role. *Journal of Abnormal Psychology,* 1978, *87,* 322–332.

Hersen, M., Eisler, R. M., Alford, G. S. and Agras, W. S. Effects of token economy on neurotic depression: An experimental analysis. *Behavior Therapy,* 1973, *4,* 392–397.

Holmberg, G. Biological aspects of electroconvulsive therapy. In C. Pfeiffer and J. Smythers, eds., *International review of neurobiology.* New York: Academic Press, 1963.

Hordren, A. The antidepressant drugs. *New England Journal of Medicine,* 1965, *272,* 1159–1169.

Izard, C. E. *Patterns of emotions: A new analysis of anxiety and depression.* New York: Academic Press, 1972.

Kanfer, F. H. and Saslow, G. Behavioral analysis: An alternative to diagnostic classification. *Archives of General Psychiatry,* 1965, *12,* 529–538.

Kendell, R. E. *The classification of depressive illness.* London: Oxford University Press, 1968.

Kiloh, L. G. and Garside, R. F. The independence of neurotic depression and endogenous depression. *British Journal of Psychiatry,* 1963, *109,* 451–463.

Kilpatrick-Tabak, B. and Roth, S. An attempt to reverse performance deficits associated with depression and experimentally induced helplessness. *Journal of Abnormal Psychology,* 1978, *87,* 141–154.

Klein, D. F. Differential diagnosis and treatment of the dysphorias. In D. M. Gallant and G. M. Simpson, eds., *Depression: Behavioral, biochemical, diagnostic and treatment concepts.* New York: Spectrum Publications, Inc., 1976.

Klein, D. F. and Davis, J. M. *Diagnosis and drug treatment of psychiatric disorders.* Baltimore: Williams and Wilkins, Co., 1969.

Klein, D. C. and Seligman, M.E.P. Reversal of performance deficits and perceptual deficits in learned helplessness and depression. *Journal of Abnormal Psychology,* 1976, *85,* 11–26.

Korboot, P. and Yates, A. J. Speed of perceptual functioning in chronic nonparanoid schizophrenics: Partial replication and extension. *Journal of Abnormal Psychology,* 1973, *81,* 296–298.

Kraines, S. H. *Mental depression and their treatment.* New York: Macmillan, 1957.

Lazarus, A. A. Learning theory and depression. *Behavioral Research and Therapy,* 1968, *6,* 83–89.

Lazarus, A. A. Some reactions to Costello's paper on depression. *Behavior Therapy,* 1972, *3,* 248–250.

Levis, D. J. The case for performing research on nonpatient populations with fears of small animals: A reply to Cooper, Furst, and Bridges. *Journal of Abnormal Psychology,* 1970, *76,* 36–38.

Levis, D. J. Learned helplessness: A reply and an alternative S-R interpretation. *Journal of Experimental Psychology: General,* 1976, *105,* 47–65.

Levis, D. J. The learned helplessness effect: An expectancy, discrimination deficit, or motivational induced persistence. *Journal of Research in Personality,* in press, a.

Levis, D. J. Implementing the technique of implosive therapy. In E. B. Foa and A. Goldstein, eds., *Handbook of behavioral interventions.* New York: Wiley, in press, b.

Levis, D. J. and Boyd T. L. Functional depression: Learned helplessness or learned avoidance? Submitted.

Levis, D. J. and Hare, N. A review of the theoretical rationale and empirical support for the extinction approach of implosive (flooding) therapy. In M. Hersen, R. M. Eisler and P. M. Miller, eds., *Progress in behavior modification.* New York: Academic Press, 1977.

Levitt, E. E. and Lubin, B. *Depression: Concepts, controversies, and some new facts.* New York: Springer Pub. Co., 1975.

Lewinsohn, P. M. A behavioral approach to depression. In R. J. Friedman and M. M. Katz, eds., *The psychology of depression: Contemporary theory and research.* Washington, D.C.: Winston-Wiley, 1974a.

Lewinsohn, P. M. Clinical and theoretical aspects of depression. In K. S. Calhoun, H. E. Adams, and K. M. Mitchell, eds., *Innovative treatment methods in psychopathology.* New York: Wiley, 1974b.

Lewinsohn, P. M. Engagement in pleasant activities and depression level. *Journal of Abnormal Psychology,* 1975, *84,* 729–731.

Lewinsohn, P. M. and Atwood, G. E. Depression: A clinical-research approach. *Psychotherapy: Research and Practice,* 1969, *6,* 166–171.

Lewinsohn, P. M. and Graf, M. Pleasant activities and depression. *Journal of Consulting and Clinical Psychology,* 1973, *41,* 261–268.

Lewinsohn, P. M. and Libet, J. Pleasant events, activity schedules, and depression. *Journal of Abnormal Psychology,* 1972, *79,* 291–295.

Lewinsohn, P. M. and Shaffer, M. Use of home observations as an integral part of the treatment of depression: Preliminary report and case studies. *Journal of Consulting and Clinical Psychology,* 1971, *37,* 87–94.

Lewinsohn, P. M., Lobitz, C., and Wilson, S. "Sensitivity" of depressed individuals to aversive stimuli. *Journal of Abnormal Psychology,* 1973, *81,* 259–263.

Lewinsohn, P. M., Weinstein, M. S., and Alper, T. A behavioral approach to the group treatment of depressed persons: A methodological contribution. *Journal of Clinical Psychology,* 1970, *26,* 525–532.

Liberman, R. P. Behavioral approaches to family and couple therapy. *American Journal of Orthopsychiatry,* 1970, *40,* 106–118.

Libet, J. and Lewinsohn, P. M. The concept of social skill with special reference to the behavior of depressed persons. *Journal of Consulting and Clinical Psychology,* 1973, *40,* 304–312.

Loeb, A., Beck, A. T., and Diggory, J. Differential effects of success and failure on depressed and nondepressed patients. *Journal of Nervous and Mental Disease,* 1971, *152,* 106–114.

Lubin, B. Adjective checklists for the measurement of depression. *Archives of General Psychiatry,* 1965, *12,* 57–62.

Lubin, C. Fourteen brief depression adjective checklists. *Archives of General Psychiatry,* 1966, *15,* 205–208.

MacPhillamy, P. J. and Lewinsohn, P. M. Relationship between positive reinforcement and depression. University of Oregon, 1972 (mimeo).

MacPhillamy, D. J. and Lewinsohn, P. M. Depression as a function of levels of desired and obtained pleasure. *Journal of Abnormal Psychology,* 1974, *83,* 651–657.

Mahrer, A. R. and Bornstein, R. Depression: Characteristic syndromes and a prefactory conceptualization. *Journal of General Psychology*, 1969, *81*, 217–229.

Maier, S. F. and Seligman, M.E.P. Learned helplessness: Theory and evidence. *Journal of Experimental Psychology: General*, 1976, *105*, 3–46.

McAuley, R. and Quinn, J. T. Models of depression, In J. T. Quinn, R. J. Graham, J.J.M. Harbison, and H. McAllister, eds., *Progress in behaviour therapy*. New York: Springer-Verlag, 1975.

McCanon, L. T. Psychophysiological discriminants of reaction depression. *Psychophysiology*, 1973, *10*, 223–230.

McConaghy, N., Jaffe, A. D., and Murphy, B. The independence of neurotic and endogenous depression. *British Journal of Psychiatry*, 1967, *113*, 479–484.

McDonald, I. M., Perkins, M., Merjerrison, G. and Podilsky, M. A controlled comparison of Amitriptyline and Electroconvulsive therapy in the treatment of depression. *American Journal of Psychiatry*, 1966, *122*, 1427–1429.

McReynolds, W. T. Learned helplessness as a schedule-shift effect. *Journal of Research in Personality*, in press.

Mendels, J. Electroconvulsive therapy and depression, III. A method for prognosis. *British Journal of Psychiatry*, 1965, *111*, 687–690.

Mendels, J. Urinary 17-Ketosteroid fractionation in depression: A preliminary report. *British Journal of Psychiatry*, 1969, *115*, 581–585.

Mendels, J., ed., *Biological psychiatry*. New York: John Wiley & Sons, 1973.

Mendels, J. and Cochrane, C. The nosology of depression: The endogenous-reactive concept. *American Journal of Psychiatry*, 1968, *124*, 1–11.

Mendels, J. and Frazer, A. Brain biogenic amine depletion and mood. *Archives of General Psychiatry*, 1974, *30*, 447–451.

Mendelson, M. *Psychoanalytic concepts of depression* (2nd ed). New York: Spectrum Publications, Inc., 1974.

Miller, W. E. Liberalization of basic S-R concepts: Extensions to conflict behavior, motivation and social learning. In S. Koch, ed., *Psychology: A study of a science*, II. New York: McGraw-Hill, 1959.

Miller, W. R. Psychological deficit in depression. *Psychological Bulletin*, 1975, *82*, 238–260.

Miller, W. R., Seligman, M.E.P., and Kurlander, H. M. Learned helplessness, depression, and anxiety. *Journal of Nervous and Mental Disease*, 1975, *161*, 347–357.

Morris, J. B. and Beck, A. T. The efficacy of antidepressant drugs. *Archives of General Psychiatry*, 1974, *30*, 667–674.

Mowrer, O. H. On the dual nature of learning—a reinterpretation of "conditioning" and "problem-solving." *Harvard Educational Review*, 1947, *17*, 102–148.

Mowrer, O. H. *Learning theory and behavior*. New York: John Wiley and Sons, Inc., 1960.

Novaco, R. W. Stress inoculation: A cognitive therapy for anger and its application to a case of depression. *Journal of Consulting and Clinical Psychology*, 1977, *45*, 600–608.

Padfield, M. The comparative effects of two counseling approaches on the intensity of depression among rural women of low socioeconomic status. *Journal of Counseling Psychology*, 1976, *23*, 209–214.

Payne, R. W. and Hewlett, J.H.G. Thought disorder in psychotic patients. In H. J. Eysenck, ed., *Experiments in personality* (vol. 2). London: Routledge and Kegan Paul, 1960.

Perris, C. The genetics of affective disorders. In J. Mendels, ed., *Biological psychiatry*. New York: John Wiley & Sons, 1973, pp. 385–416.

Pichot, P. The problem of quantifying the symptomatology of depression. In P. Kielholz, ed., *Depressive illness: Diagnosis, assessment, treatment*. Baltimore: Williams and Wilkins, Co., 1972.

Post, R. M., Kotin, J., Goodwin, F. K. and Gordon, E. K. Psychomotor activity and cerebrospinal fluid amine metabolites in affective illness. *The American Journal of Psychiatry*, 1973, *130*, 67–72.

Prakachin, K. M., Craig, K. D., Papegeorgis, D. and Reith, G. Nonverbal communication deficits and response to performance feedback in depression. *Journal of Abnormal Psychology*, 1977, *86*, 224–234.

Robinson, S. C. and Lewinsohn, P. M. Behavior modification of speech characteristics in a chronically depressed man. *Behavior Therapy*, 1973a, *4*, 150–152.

Robinson, J. C. and Lewinsohn, P. M. Experimental analysis of a technique based on the Premack principle changing verbal behavior of depressed individuals. *Psychological Reports*, 1973b, *32*, 199–210.

Rose, J. T. Reactive and endogenous depressions—response to E.C.T. *British Journal of Psychiatry*, 1963, *109*, 213–217.

Roth, M. The phenomenology of depressive states. *Canadian Journal of Psychiatry*, 1959, *4*, (Special Supplement), 532–553.

Rubin, R. T. and Mandell, A. J. Adrenal cortical activity in pathological emotional states: A review. *American Journal of Psychiatry*, 1966, *123*, 387–400.

Rush, A. J., Beck, A. T., Kovacs, M., and Hollon, S. Comparative efficacy of cognitive therapy and pharmaco therapy in the treatment of depressed outpatients. *Cognitive Therapy and Research*, 1977, *1*, 17–37.

Schildkraut, J. J., Davis, J. M., and Klerman, G. L. Biochemistry of depressions. In D. H. Efron, J. D. Cole, J. Levie, and J. R. Wittenborn, eds., *Psychopharmacology: A review of progress 1957–1967*. Washington, D.C.: Public Health Service Publication, 1968.

Schuyler, D. *The depressive spectrum*. New York: Jason Aronson, Inc., 1974.

Secunda, S. K. *Special report: 1973 the depressive disorders*. National Institute of Mental Health, 1973.

Seligman, M.E.P. Depression and learned helplessness. In R. J. Friedman and M. M. Katz, (eds), *The psychology of depression: Contemporary theory and research*. New York: John Wiley & Sons, 1974.

Seligman, M.E.P. *Helplessness: On depression, development, and death*. San Francisco: W. H. Freeman, 1975.

Seligman, M.E.P., Klein, D. C., and Miller, W. R. Depression. In H. Leitenberg, (ed.), *Handbook of behavior modification and behavior therapy*. Englewood Cliffs, N.J.: Prentice-Hall, Inc., 1976.

Shaffer, M. and Lewinsohn, P. M. Interpersonal behaviors in the home of depressed versus nondepressed psychiatric and normal controls: A test of several hypotheses. Paper presented at meeting of the Western Psychological Association, 1971. Mimeo, University of Oregon, 1971.

Shaw, B. F. Comparison of cognitive therapy and behavior therapy in the treatment of depression. *Journal of Consulting and Clinical Psychology,* 1977, *45,* 543–551.

Spence, K. W. Types of constructs in psychology. *Psychological Review,* 1944, *51,* 47–68.

Stampfl, T. G. and Levis, D. J. Essentials of implosive therapy: A learning based psychodynamic behavior therapy. *Journal of Abnormal Psychology,* 1967, *72,* 496–503.

Stampfl, T. G. and Levis, D. J. Learning theory: An aid to dynamic therapeutic practice. In L. D. Eron and R. Callahan, eds., *The relation of theory to practice in psychotherapy.* Chicago: Aldine Publishing Co., 1969.

Stampfl, T. G. and Levis, D. J. *Implosive therapy: Theory and technique.* New Jersey: General Learning Press, 1973.

Suarez, Y., Crowe, M. J., and Adams, H. E. Depression: Avoidance learning and physiological correlates in clinical and analogue populations. *Behaviour Research and Therapy,* 1978, *16,* 21–31.

Teasdale, J. D. and Bancroft, J. Manipulation of thought content as a determinant of mood and corrugator electromyographic activity in depressed patients. *Journal of Abnormal Psychology,* 1977, *86,* 235–241.

Wanderer, Z. W. Existential depression treated by desensitization of phobias: Strategy and transcript. *Journal of Behavior Therapy and Experimental Psychiatry,* 1972, *3,* 111–116.

Weckowicz, T. E., Muir, W., and Cropley, A. J. A factor analysis of the Beck Inventory of Depression. *Journal of Consulting Psychology,* 1967, *31,* 23–28.

Weckowicz, T. E., Yonge, K. A., Cropley, A. J., and Muir, W. Objective therapy predictors in depression: A multivariate approach. *Journal of Clinical Psychology,* 1971, Monograph Supplement No. 31.

Werner, A. E. and Rehm, L. P. Depressive affect: A test of behavioral hypotheses. *Journal of Abnormal Psychology,* 1975, *84,* 221–227.

Williams, J. C., Barlow, D. H. and Agras, W. S. Behavioral measurement of severe depression. *Archives of General Psychiatry,* 1972, *27,* 330–333.

Wolpe, J. *Psychotherapy by reciprocal inhibition.* Stanford, Ca.: Stanford University Press, 1958.

Wolpe, J. Neurotic depression: Experimental analog, clinical syndromes and treatment. *American Journal of Psychotherapy,* 1971, *25,* 362–368.

Wortman, C. B. and Brehm, J. W. Responses to uncontrollable outcomes: An integration of reactance theory and the learned helplessness model. In L. Berkowitz, ed., *Advances in experimental social psychology* (vol. 8). New York: Academic Press, 1975.

Author Index

Numbers in *italic* refer to reference lists at the end of chapters.

Subject Index